Presented to Purchase College
by
Gary Waller, PhD Cambridge

State University of New York
Distinguished Professor

Professor
of Literature & Cultural
Studies, and Theatre &
Performance, 1995-2019
Provost 1995-2004

Reading Relations
a dialectical text/book

Bernard Sharratt

Lecturer in English,
University of Kent at Canterbury

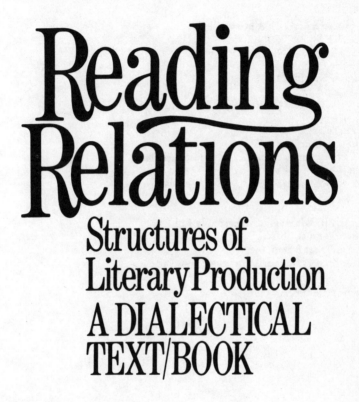

Reading Relations

Structures of Literary Production

A DIALECTICAL TEXT/BOOK

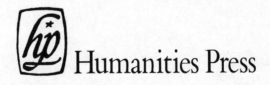
Humanities Press

First published in the USA in 1982 by
HUMANITIES PRESS INC
Atlantic Highlands, New Jersey 07716

Library of Congress Cataloging in Publication Data

Sharratt, Bernard.
Reading relations.
1. Reader-response criticism. 2. Reading. I. Title.
PN98.R38S5   1982   801'.95   81-20218
ISBN 0-391-02557-0   AACR2

Typeset by Rowland Phototypesetting Ltd
Bury St Edmunds, Suffolk
Printed in Great Britain by
Redwood Burn Limited, Trowbridge, Wiltshire

To my parents

———, my first fruits present themselves to thee;
Yet not mine neither: for from thee they came,
And must return.

HORS D'OEUVRE

Aperitifs: Epée-graphs

Hence it is always necessary to establish what *doxa* an author is opposing (this can sometimes be a very minority *doxa*, holding sway over a limited group). A teaching may equally be evaluated in terms of paradox, provided it is built on the following conviction: that a system calling for corrections, translations, openings, and negations is more useful than an unformulated absence of system . . .

Roland Barthes

I said, I was anxious of your Esteem; but my Thoughts are like Surinam Toads—as they crawl on, little Toads vegetate out from back & side, grow quickly, & draw off the attention from the mother Toad.—Now then straight forward.

S. T. Coleridge

You! *hypocrite lecteur!—mon semblable,—mon frère!*

T. S. Eliot

8.2.2.2. Secondly, in terms of the indexemes they cover and their functional level sequence generations, for if it is postulated in S.8.2.1. that any character is potentially the form of the assumption of a function, the sign-ification being read at the level of the decipherment of the economy of the system of distribution of the functions, that the text contains a further system of generation at the indexical level in the indexemes, a system, that is to say, functionally generative, paratactic with the other.

'Cleanth Peters', from an essay on *Joseph Andrews*, in *Signs of the Times: Introductory Readings in Textual Semiotics*, Cambridge, 1968.

If Lenin could explain dialectics starting from a glass of water, why the——can't you?

Kent Miner, 1974.

3

Brecht's work stressed the fact that an act of theatre is always an encounter between people and that the terms of this encounter are as important as the contents of the play . . . dramatic communication may be established not just between two people, as in normal conversation, but between three, since the spectator may perceive the entertainer's own personal attitudes as separate from the attitudes of whatever persona or mask he has adopted. For Brecht the work of staging was as important as the work of writing. Every prop, every gesture, every movement was a significant element in a stage language more comprehensive than that of the spoken word alone. Indeed, the action in a play by Brecht is frequently designed to contradict the words that are being spoken, to show that their meaning is just one element in a complex situation whose total significance is quite different.

David Bradby

Professors Thody (*THES* July 21st) and Flower (August 18th) do not go far enough. Their cogently argued defence of bad lecturing must be supported by a call for more bad books, completely unreadable and sprinkled with erroneous facts and judgements to discourage students from having recourse to them as a substitute for original thinking. They could be printed backwards, as a typographical equivalent to the inaudibility which is a recommended feature of the bad lecture.

Roy Lewis, from letter to *THES*, 25.8.78

Cultural traditions have their own, vulnerable, conditions of reproduction. They remain 'living' as long as they take shape in an unplanned, nature-like manner, or are shaped with hermeneutic consciousness. (Whereby hermeneutics, as the scholarly interpretation and application of tradition, has the peculiarity of breaking down the nature-like character of tradition as it is handed on and, nevertheless, of retaining it at a reflective level.) The critical appropriation of tradition destroys this nature-like character in discourse. (Whereby the peculiarity of critique consists in its double function: to dissolve analytically, or in a critique of ideology, validity claims that cannot be redeemed discursively; but, at the same time, to release the semantic potentials of the tradition.) To this extent, critique is no less a form of appropriating tradition than hermeneutics.

Jürgen Habermas

The minute I cook my own dinner or nail four boards together into a chair, I escape from the whole cycle of Marxian economics. . . . It costs no more to cook a dinner well than to cook it badly. . . . Over a decade ago, Major Douglas admitted that I had made a contribution to the subject when I pointed out that my grandfather had built a railroad probably less from a desire to make money or an illusion that he could make more that way than some other, than from inherent activity, artist's desire to MAKE something, the fun of constructing and the play of outwitting and overcoming obstruction. Very well, I am not proceeding according to Aristotelian logic but according to the ideogrammic method of first heaping together the necessary components of thought.

Ezra Pound

All this must be considered as if spoken by a character in a novel—or rather by several characters. For the image-repertoire, fatal substance of the novel, and the labyrinth of levels in which anyone who speaks about himself gets lost—the image-repertoire is taken over by several masks (*personae*), distributed according to the depth of the stage (and yet *no one*—*personne*, as we say in French—is behind them). The book does not choose, it functions by alternation, it proceeds by impulses of the image-system pure and simple and by critical approaches, but these very approaches are never anything but effects of resonance: nothing is more a matter of the image-system, of the imaginary, than (self-)criticism. The substance of this book, ultimately, is therefore totally fictive.

Roland Barthes par Roland Barthes

Did you stop this week's deliberate mistake?

Parish newsletter

The frontiers of a book are never clear-cut: beyond the title, the first line and the last full stop, beyond its internal configuration, its autonomous form, it is caught up in a system of references to other books, other texts, other sentences: it is a node within a network. And this network of references is not the same in the case of a mathematical treatise, a textual commentary, a historical account and an episode in a novel cycle; the unity of the book, even in the sense of a group of relations, cannot be regarded as identical in each case. The book is simply not the object that one holds in one's hands; and it cannot remain within the little parallelepiped that contains it: its unity is variable and relative. As soon as one questions that unity it loses its self-evidence; it indicates itself, constructs itself, only on the basis of a complex field of discourse.

Michel Foucault

Benjamin's ideal of producing a work consisting entirely of quotations, one that was mounted so masterfully that it could dispense with any accompanying text, may strike one as whimsical in the extreme and self-destructive to boot, but it was not, any more than were the contemporaneous surrealistic experiments which arose from similar impulses. . . . What mattered to him above all was to avoid anything that might be reminiscent of empathy, as though a given subject of investigation had a message in readiness which

5

easily communicated itself, or could be communicated, to the reader or spectator: 'No poem is intended for the reader, no picture for the beholder, no symphony for the listener' (*The Task of the Translator*).

Hannah Arendt

Crudités: False Notes

'Other thoughts fill me than the ones I am talking about—not thoughts, but images, memories.'

(Benjamin)

A memory of Latin America, the late 1960s:
   An anthropologist was invited to a meal in an Indian hut
     in a poor mountain village.
   The mother of the family handed round bowls of food,
     first to him, then to her four small children.
   The portions were very meagre indeed.
   The anthropologist began to eat.
   A fifth child, an infant, lying in a corner of the hut
     and unnoticed up to now, began to cry. Weak whimpers.
   The mother and the other children continued eating, ignoring
     the cries.
   After a while, the anthropologist asked, hesitantly, whether
     the child was ill.
   ——No, hungry, said the mother.
   ——Are you not going to feed it?
   ——I have stopped feeding her.
   The anthropologist was silent.
   The mother patiently explained.
   ——We can only get enough food for five. She is another
     mouth. If we all eat less, we all die slowly. It is better
     that one should die soon and the rest live. She is the youngest.
   I have stopped feeding her.
   The anthropologist was silent a long time.
   Thoughtfully, he continued eating.

A memory of an anecdote, an anecdote from a book. Third-hand. Now fourth-hand. The original details, whatever they were, have gone. I doubt if I ever knew them. The story was told to me, once, by someone who had read the book. I tell it now. Probably its life will continue.

*

Another memory of Latin America, the late 1970s:

Two days before Christmas, I arrive in a capital city. I am met at the airport by two old friends. They look puzzled, distracted, worried. After the greetings, I ask what is wrong. In the car, they mention a name. Yes, I am due to meet him that evening, a trade union organiser, a known opponent of the present military regime. They have just seen him at the airport, in the departure lounge. He does not keep the appointment. There is no message.

Ten days later, a phone call. He is back in the country. We arrange the meeting, during which he explains, apologetically: he had received yet another assassination threat. (He is in his early thirties; most trade union leaders here are dead by thirty-five; in the last ten years 20,000 people have 'disappeared'.) But this threat was different: 'If you are in the country on Christmas Day, we will kill you in front of your children.' 'I did not want to spoil the Christmas for the children,' he explains, apologetically.

A week later, I am back in England. The term has started and with it the flow of UCCA forms, the interviewing of candidates, the familiar details, the familiar questions:
'And why did you choose this university?'
'What have you been reading recently? . . . for A-level or in your own time . . . OK, what would you say about . . . ?'
'Why do you want to study English literature?'

*

Anyone who sets out to write a book about marxism and literature is likely to be faced with this kind of juxtaposition, in experience or in imagination. The sharp contrasts, the nagging sense of utter irrelevance, the awareness of privileged positions and of dis-connections within a single world so clearly divided and yet so bound together—these cannot be kept out of the work, they shadow it and question it.

**The Plebeians Rehearse
the Uprising**   (Grass)

It's easy enough to sketch the possible relationships, to hold the questions at a distance. Even easier to spell out, relentlessly, the implied irrelevance. To have accepted, in advance, the fatuity of the exercise would be to abandon it. But is writing any different, in that respect, from teaching? And is reading a book on marxism and literature (yet another book) any different, in that respect, from writing it? Yet I teach, and you are reading. So if we think first about the possible relationships between 'marxism' and 'literature', the thinking can, initially, be crude; its very crudity may be enough to enforce the irrelevance.

'Marxism'
—If you think of marxism primarily as a science the object of which is social formations, or, more specifically, how and why social formations change in (as) history, the study of literature will have as its task, within that science, the clarification of how literature 'fits' (into) a social formation. A marxist would

8

then approach literature with a number of related interests: to grasp, through an understanding of the literature of a period, how a particular social formation was constituted and maintained and how it changed or was open to change; the study of literature is then seen as hopefully providing evidence to support a particular historical account, and this kind of study thereby becomes part of, and subordinate to, a more general science of history.

—If you emphasise the role of marxism as a means of waging a political struggle in the immediate present, an interest in literature would basically involve seeing 'literature' as itself a means of struggle or an arena in which a political intervention is necessary or appropriate. A marxist might then seek to write literary works of a polemical or agitational kind, or to utilise already available works for such purposes; and, perhaps as a consequence of this activity or as an accompaniment to it, the practices and norms of literary criticism might become an arena of struggle—a marxist critic might want to justify some works and attack others, as a way of creating a critical space for agitational works; further, certain practices and norms of literary criticism might be regarded as themselves politically undesirable, as contributing to the maintenance of an undesirable society, and attempts made to dislodge or erode them on those grounds.

> in order to live in Parisian society today, at whatever level or on whatever plane, one is forced to prostitute oneself in one way or another   (Godard)

The second of these emphases indicates certain problems about practising 'literary criticism' as a marxist; obviously, an interest in literature thereby becomes part of, and subsidiary to, a more general political strategy, just as an interest in literature might be secondary to an interest in history. Such an interest would be a provisional one: if something 'better' than 'literature', as historical evidence or as political means, were available, 'literature' would cease to be of interest to the marxist, *qua* marxist. This happens, of course. But the second emphasis also suggests a problem about the practice of writing criticism: if it is appropriate to try to create agitational literature, is it also appropriate to write agitational criticism, and what kind of writing would that be? And if it is appropriate to regard criticism itself as an area of struggle, how can one combat undesirable practices in criticism without ceasing to practise 'criticism' altogether, how can one write a form of literary criticism that itself changes those practices, rather than reproduces them or merely accompanies them? Such a task seems one not only of replacing one mode of criticism by another which can merely take its place alongside the displaced modes on a library-shelf which records the history of critical practices; is it possible, rather, somehow to destroy existing works of criticism by an act of criticism which also, necessarily, destroys itself as criticism? Probably not. But if critical works continue to be written, can they perhaps be read differently?

9

> I have indeed found myself
> thinking of Leavis's critical work
> as a kind of novel in which the
> main events are certain novels and
> plays,
> and most of the characters
> are from fiction and drama, with a
> scattering
> of intensely representative figures
> from life; but in which the central
> consciousness and the central
> attention is on what he calls
> 'the lived question': an exploration,
> a dramatisation, an inward finding
> and realisation of values through this
> composed and apparently objective
> medium.   (Raymond Williams)

The first emphasis, on marxism as a mode of historiography, raises other problems, which feed back on these. Yesterday I read *Wuthering Heights*. Yesterday. If I treat *Wuthering Heights* as written in 1847, I can indeed connect it in a variety of ways to that date, that period. But, always, I am *reading* the novel *now*. My having read it yesterday, or ten years ago, means that *Wuthering Heights* is a memory for me. And 1847 can also be a kind of memory for me, at second- or third-hand; *Wuthering Heights* can become for me a kind of memory-trace of 1847. A peculiar, but familiar, process. But the act of reading *Wuthering Heights* is a process that occurs in a present, not as memory (though remembering is involved deep within that process) but as activity. That activity cannot occur, for me, in 1847. To treat *Wuthering Heights* 'as written in 1847' I have to distance myself from that activity of reading now, yet the novel can only exist for me as an act of reading now or as a memory of reading, of having-been-read. A novel can be assigned to its date of *writing* only by a peculiar attempt at objectifying it, treating it as a thing, an object distinct from the process whereby I know it as a novel.

What leads me on is the sense that a (marxist) historical placing of a novel leaves out of account, by a curious sleight-of-hand, that very act of reading which allows the novel to figure in the historical account at all—unless my account is to rest on someone else's reading, a second-hand knowledge about *Wuthering Heights* but not a knowledge of *Wuthering Heights*. This happens, of course. Increasingly, perhaps, we read the critic, not the tale. More importantly, a novel read *now* is only open to a historical account insofar as the now is already history—which it is, but not, yet, available to any historiography. Yet we read novels now, including novels written in 1847 or 1747 or 1977. What is at stake here is not only a general, and familiar, problem of hermeneutics or a problem about the ontological status of a work of art, or a metaphysics of presence—though all these hover in the wings. What nags is the question of reading 'literature' at all.

listening to the Archduke Trio is not
only a matter of hearing evidence
about the declining role of
Archdukes in the Hapsburg Empire

And since written literary criticism, like any book, is also read, a marxist
account of the practices and norms of literary critics which also simply places
those critics historically—or which holds back from the act of reading them,
treating them only as having-already-been-read—may be leaving inexplic-
able how it can be that some critics, like some novels, are 'worth reading' in
the first place.

'I have thought of these things.'
'That is why I tell you.'   (T. S. Eliot)

And if marxist literary criticism is worth writing, how should it be written, in
what style, in what mode, to what effect?

Bertolt Brecht proposed some possible answers to this question (which he did
not ask?):

Literalising entails punctuating 'representation' with 'formulation' . . .

Some exercise in complex seeing is needed—though it is perhaps more important to be able to
think above the stream than to think within the stream.

Quotation
Standing in a free and direct relationship to it, the actor allows his character to speak and move;
he presents a report. He does not have to make us forget that the text isn't spontaneous, but has
been memorised, is a fixed quantity . . . His attitude would be the same if he were simply speaking
from his own memory . . .

Dramatic	*Epic*
the human being is taken for granted	the human being is the object of inquiry
he is unalterable	he is alterable and able to alter
eyes on the finish	eyes on the course
one scene makes another	each scene for itself
growth	montage
linear development	in curves
evolutionary determinism	jumps
man as a fixed point	man as a process

The audience has got to make its own sense of the material I put before it.

The continuity of the ego is a myth. A man is an atom that perpetually breaks up and forms anew.

At least, enjoyment was meant to be the object of the inquiry even if the inquiry was intended to
be an object of enjoyment.

'I'm having a lot of trouble: I'm preparing my next mistake,' answered Mr K.

To write; to establish a fixed position; to write from a stable ego; not to make mistakes; to dominate; to master the material—and the reader?

To give answers; to provide suggestions; to present materials; to write from above the stream; to read from within the stream.

Reasons; arguments; proof? Tableaux, *gestus*, quotes.

*

Roland Barthes suggests, in a brief essay, some connections between Diderot, Brecht and Eisenstein. He develops Diderot's notion of the *tableau* and relates it to Brecht's practice of constructing a play as a pattern of individual scenes, cut as segments of meaning, arranged emphatically, as a series of limited demonstrations. The whole is not the locus of a fixed, overall meaning. Eisenstein's films are made up of contiguous episodes, juxtaposed shots, each an image of aesthetic perfection, a jubilant instant, a moment of cinematic pleasure.

Roland Barthes, in a provocative essay, considers the relationships between Writers, Intellectuals, Teachers. He pinpoints the problem of Authority and analyses the dilemmas of speaking, as a teacher; either one accepts the prepared position of Authority, the Lawgiver of meaning, or one seeks to subvert, disown, that position, by stumbling, wavering, fumbling, only to have the performance attributed to an Authority that yet remains human, all too human, a friendly policeman whose watch remains, despite everything, trustworthy. Writing, he thinks, is different.

*

'If I try to understand and overcome these dilemmas, it is on enjoyment and pleasure that I focus and on the act of reading that I fix. If criticism is a parasitic pleasure, it remains a pleasure contributory to the pleasure of literature, the enjoyment of reading. That enjoyment is persistent; as I write, even, I prefer to read. To add another book, for others to read, defeats my pleasure, postpones the enjoyment of reading another book; writing is an interruption, a deferment; reading constantly intrudes, as I consult another book, take up another essay, already written, awaiting. At the core of this preference is a magic: the other book appears, unwritten, a pleasure to read; this one is a labour, an imposition, it should be already written, awaiting my reading. I smuggle reading into writing, permit myself distraction, quote:

Writers are really people who write books not because they are poor but because they are dissatisfied with the books which they could buy but do not like.

Thus, Benjamin's essay 'Unpacking my Library'. But aren't all books to be dissatisfied with, each in turn *de trop*? Another book lurks on the stack, in the catalogue, among the reviews. Reading may be an asymptotic search for *the* Book (I re-read Borges's 'The Library of Babel', quickly). Writing could only be the vain hope of making the book to include all books, to render all other books superfluous simultaneously, to make otiose the deferment. All such writing is a defeat. But so is all such reading. For Benjamin's true collector does not read the books he borrows, retains, buys, retrieves, possesses. They are a fetish, an impossible promise that can never be revoked or finally put to the test, a divine covenant. And commentary, criticism, keeps alive that promise: the work of literature, read, remains suspended, a memory modified and made vivid by its repetition in another writing, a critic's reading for me to read. Criticism is a reverse asymptotes: the point of infinite intersection is already the starting line to be moved away from in an interminable curve. All writing, all reading, all literature, beckons to an impossible fusion, a simultaneity, a *tota simul*.'

*

It is precisely this sharp opposition between work and leisure, which is peculiar to the capitalist mode of production, that separates all intellectual activity into those activities which serve work and those activities which serve leisure. And those that serve leisure are organised into a system for the reproduction of the labour force. Distractions must not contain anything which is contained in work. Distractions, in the interest of production, are committed to non-production.

Bertolt Brecht

Brecht wanted a theatre for both pleasure and instruction, but there seems to be a tension in the way he formulated his distinction between dramatic theatre and epic theatre. Quoted earlier is the second half of his list of differences. The first half of that list makes the tension clearer.

On the 'dramatic' side, he lists, for example, 'experience', 'the spectator is involved in something', 'provides him with sensations', 'the spectator is in the thick of it, shares the experience'. What interests me here is that if these are characteristics of reactionary drama, are they also characteristics of reactionary literature? If I try to read, say, a love-poem by John Donne, or Hopkins's 'The Windhover', how *can* I *read* them without being 'involved in something', without at least attempting to 'share the experience'? If you try to apply Brecht's 'epic' list to the process of reading a love-poem, it would seem that most of the *pleasure* to be found (made) in *reading* would be excluded, made impossible; indeed, some of the phrases in that 'epic' list seem appropriate to precisely that kind of 'reading' which literary scholars and critical dissectors are often accused of: 'turns the spectator into an observer', 'the spectator stands outside, studies'. There is, perhaps, a kind of pleasure possible in the distanced, scholarly stance, but it is not the same as, and arguably should not be divorced from, the pleasure of reading a poem precisely in an involved way, reading 'with feeling', and that pleasure demands a certain loss of self, a subordination of the ego to the movement of the poem. It is here that the tension arises. For what the second half of the list of characteristics of epic drama seems to point to is something like a loosening of the fixed, unitary self: 'he is alterable and able to alter', 'man as a process'. To enact the movement of feeling in a poem, as one reads it fully and responsively, *is* to have one's 'eyes on the course' (epic), to dislodge oneself from the 'fixed point' (dramatic) of identity. It is almost as if the act of reading a poem (as distinct from the activity of studying it) cannot be brought under the heading of 'epic'; the epic attitude seems impossible when it is not a matter of looking at a stage but of performing a poem oneself.

Marxist approaches to literature, with a historical or political emphasis, tend not to take account of the peculiar process of actually reading a work of literature; and in today's circumstances that means, normally, a silent and solitary reading. Partly as a consequence of avoiding, or ignoring, discussion of that act of reading, marxist criticism tends to be silent about the pleasure of reading, the actual enjoyment of literature; and this goes with a tendency to regard literature as something to be studied, in an educational context only; marxist critics thereby see their own 'intervention' primarily in academic terms—to combat other critics, other academics, to displace one mode of professional practice by another, perhaps to replace one reading-list, of primary or secondary works, by another, more 'radical' reading-list. It's then not surprising that marxist literary critics tend to be uneasy with the problem of 'literary value'; at best, the question of the value of literature becomes a postscript, a final chapter, a loose end to be alluded to. For the notion of 'value' in literature is not only related to analysing previous evaluations of literary works (another period's, another critic's), and disclosing the ideological and political significance of those evaluations; as a reader of literary works, I have at least to ask the question why *I* 'value' literature, why I read it at all. And involved in that question is, basically, the question of why I continue to spend time reading poems and novels while, to put it brutally, comrades are being shot and Indian villagers are starving. There are various kinds of possible answer to that last question, but one line of inquiry seems to slide between a merely tactical response and mere special pleading. It is too easy to argue for a chain of connections linking one's academic or cultural 'interventions' in England to some putative global strategy of liberation, an alliance at a distance or a sectoral solidarity. And it is just as easy to probe the palimpsest of hypocrisy, self-deceit and bad faith, to reveal the guilty privilege and repressed self-interest that lies behind an armchair security, a soft option. That debate, with oneself and with others, continues; but in those terms it curiously bypasses the fact that, whatever its alleged political usefulness or otherwise, whatever its interest or serviceability as historical evidence, whether I am paid to do so or not, whether I 'teach literature' or not, I continue to read literature.

I am paid, more or less, to teach, to write, to review, to give papers, to lecture, to write this book—about literature. And that means that reading is part of my job. But unless I am finally to accept a division between 'work' and 'leisure', I do indeed read for pleasure while I read for money, and conversely I keep that job partly because it allows me to enjoy reading. That in itself is a paradoxical position within capitalism. The temptations of literature, the pleasures of reading, are what intrigue me here; by exploring them, I might begin to probe another kind of relationship between 'marxism' and 'literature', perhaps between politics and pleasure.

*

As we stood at the departure gateway, my hand-luggage littering the floor, some farewell gesture seemed demanded. An English embarrassment. Solidarity? Assistance? Support? What final offer? I left it open-ended, found some

14

off-hand formula inviting their suggestion; anything. They mentioned a familiar name. Yes, as they knew, I actually had a copy in my bag, ready to read on the plane . . .

Potage: conférence

I've been asked to talk, in a way that might interest an audience of philosophers, about the relations between marxism and literary criticism, and, more generally, about politics and art. It's a tall order, and as usual there is the problem of how to begin. I'm going to start from a very simple point and see where it leads me. Marx's critique of political economy and literary criticism have, on the face of it, one term at least in common, the term 'value'. In the discussion of literature, at some point or other, the notion of 'literary value' will come into play. And in the first couple of pages of *Capital* Marx sets up a distinction which underpins a great deal of his analysis: the distinction between 'use-value' and 'exchange-value'. If we begin from Marx's use of those terms and pursue them with an eye on 'literary value', it might be interesting to see whether we ever arrive at some connection between the two.

Let me summarise Marx's distinction between use-value and exchange-value by quoting two paragraphs from *Capital* which make the basic points clearly enough:

The usefulness of a thing makes it a use-value. But this usefulness does not dangle in mid-air. It is conditioned by the physical properties of the commodity, and has no existence apart from the latter. It is therefore the physical body of the commodity itself, for instance iron, corn, a diamond, which is the use-value or useful thing. This property of a commodity is independent of the amount of labour required to appropriate its useful qualities. . . . Use-values are only realised in use or in consumption. They constitute the material content of wealth, whatever its social form may be. In the form of society to be considered here they are also the material bearers of exchange-value.

Exchange-value appears first of all as the quantitative relation, the proportion, in which use-values of one kind exchange for use-values of another kind. This relation changes constantly with time and place. Hence exchange-value appears to be something accidental and purely relative, and consequently an intrinsic value, i.e. an exchange-value that is inseparably connected with the commodity, inherent in it, seems a contradiction in terms.

That distinction seems clear enough—at first. But there is an intriguing moment in his writings when Marx suddenly asks himself a basic question about those terms. In the notebooks of drafts for *Capital*—the *Grundrisse* —we find the following:

The use-value which the worker has to offer to the capitalist, which he has to offer to others in general, is not materialised in a product, does not exist apart from him at all, thus exists not really, but only in potentiality, as his capacity. It becomes a reality only when it has been solicited by capital, is set in motion, since activity without object is nothing, or, at the most, mental activity, which is not the question at issue here. As soon as it has obtained motion from capital, this use-value exists as the worker's specific, productive activity; it is his vitality itself, directed toward a specific purpose and hence expressing itself in a specific form.

In the relation of capital and labour, exchange-value and use-value are brought into relation; the one side (capital) initially stands opposite the other side as exchange-value,

Suddenly at this point, interrupting the flow, there is a long note by Marx, a side-thought or marginal jotting, which I want to quote the beginning of:

Is not *value* to be conceived of as the unity of use-value and exchange-value? In and for itself, is value as such the general form, in opposition to use-value and exchange-value as *particular* forms of it? Does this have significance in economics? Use-value presupposed even in simple exchange or barter. But here, where exchange takes place only for the reciprocal use of the commodity, the use-value, i.e. the content, the natural particularity of the commodity has as such no standing as an economic form. Its form, rather, is exchange-value. The content apart from this form is irrelevant; is not a content of the relation as a social relation. But does this content as such not develop into a system of needs and production? Does not use-value as such enter into the form itself, as a determinant of the form itself, e.g. in the relation of capital and labour? the different forms of labour?—agriculture, industry, etc.—ground rent?—effect of the seasons on raw product prices? etc. If *only* exchange-value as such plays a role in economics, then how could elements later enter which relate purely to use-value, such as, right away, in the case of capital as raw material etc.? How is it that the physical composition of the soil suddenly drops out of the sky in Ricardo?

Apart from its fascination as an example of Marx struggling with an apparent blockage in his own thinking, this tortuously probing passage has a particular interest if we think of 'literary value'. For if we try to apply the terms 'use-value' and 'exchange-value' to literature, one might suggest that exchange-value would refer to, if nothing else, the market-value of a book, a book as an object (a line of thought that might bring into play first-editions, and manuscripts, as well as the price of a new book), or perhaps the economic value of an established literary reputation (a Nobel Prize is worth a great deal to the recipient's publisher). But 'use-value' is a bit trickier, even at first glance, since, as Marx says himself, 'Every useful thing is a whole composed of many properties; it can therefore be useful in various ways'.

As a physical object, a book, Shakespeare's works can be useful in a variety of ways: as a paper-weight, a doorstop, a missile, etc. And even as that curious thing 'a play', *Hamlet* can be 'useful' as a way of passing an evening, as a means of employment for actors or profit for a theatre management, or as a mine of quotable lines. Somehow, one wants to say, its 'literary value' isn't to be equated with any of these. One might be tempted to push in the same direction as Marx's note and ask something like: 'is literary value as such the general form, in opposition to some of these use-values as particular forms of it?' Or one might even want to extend Marx's question and ask: 'is value as such the general form, in opposition to use-value, exchange-value and literary-value as particular forms of it?' I suspect that both these questions, and indeed Marx's own term 'value as such', would lead to dead-ends if explored further. But it's not, I think, an accident that this question—what *is* 'value'?—strikes Marx in connection with a passage that mentions, *en passant*, that 'activity without object is nothing, or, at the most, mental activity, which is not the question at issue here,' since Marx's notion of use-value seems to be tied to *physical objects*: 'It is therefore the physical body of the commodity itself, for instance iron, corn, a diamond, which is the use-value or useful thing.' Yet as soon as one thinks of the 'value' of Marx's own *thinking*, for example, it seems slightly odd to restrict that 'value' to the 'physical body of the commodity itself', even if we recognise that writing, or 'thinking', is a physical activity and the product of writing is a material thing. For it is not any particular material thing (this copy of *Hamlet*, this edition of *Capital*), as such, that we are interested in. More generally, we could put the problem in these terms: how is the term 'use-value' related to intellectual labour or imaginative creation?

In a curious way, the marginal note in the *Grundrisse* already looks forward to the context in which Marx himself toys further with this problem. The note begins to tussle with Ricardo at the point where I left off quoting it. Much of Marx's detailed analysis of Ricardo and other political economists is to be found in the papers known as *Theories of Surplus Value*. In a section of notes concerned with 'Theories of productive and unproductive labour', Marx makes some comments on Henri Storch's *Cours d'économie politique*, particularly about Storch's views on 'spiritual production', 'the elements of civilisation', 'immaterial values', or what he calls 'internal goods'—i.e. that area of activity we might now call 'culture'. Marx writes:

According to Storch, the physician 'produces' health (but also illness), professors and writers produce enlightenment (but also obscurantism), poets, painters, etc., produce morals, preachers religion, the sovereign's labour security, and so on. It can just as well be said that illness produces physicians, stupidity produces professors and writers, lack of taste poets and painters, immorality moralists, superstition preachers and general insecurity produces the sovereign. This way of saying in fact that all these activities, these services, produce a real or imaginary use-value is repeated by later writers in order to prove that they are productive workers in Adam Smith's sense, that is to say, that they directly produce not products *sui generis* but products of material labour and consequently immediate wealth.

It's fairly clear from this that Marx regards Storch, and others, as mistaken when they draw terms from the field of political economy and attempt to use them in the field of 'culture' as if those terms could simply mean the same in the two different regions. And one corollary of that misapplication is the tendency to justify cultural work in illegitimate ways. It would seem from this passage, at least, that Marx would look rather coldly on any attempt to link directly the use of the term 'value' in his critique of political economy and the use of the same word in literary criticism—just as he might well regard as slipshod and Storch-like the currently fashionable use of phrases such as 'intellectual production', 'theoretical production', 'literary production'.

Marx's own notion of productive labour is made clear enough in another passage from *Theories of Surplus Value*, which, interestingly, uses literary activities as an example:

The *same* kind of labour may be *productive* or *unproductive*. For example, Milton, who wrote *Paradise Lost* for five pounds, was an *unproductive labourer*. On the other hand, the writer who turns out stuff for his publisher in factory style, is a *productive labourer*. Milton produced *Paradise Lost* for the same reason that a silk worm produces silk. It was an activity of *his* nature. Later he sold the product for £5. But the literary proletarian of Leipzig, who fabricates books (for example, Compendia of Economics) under the direction of his publisher, is a *productive labourer*; for his product is from the outset subsumed under capital, and comes into being only for the purpose of increasing that capital. A singer who sells her song for her own account is an *unproductive labourer*. But the same singer commissioned by an entrepreneur to sing in order to make money for him is a *productive labourer*; for she produces capital.

The problem of the distinction between productive and unproductive labour is, for Marx, an aspect of the broader problem of the division of labour, and in *Capital*, I, chapter 14, he makes this general comment about historically distinct ways of thinking about the division of labour:

Political economy, which first emerged as an independent science during the period of manufacture, is only able to view the social division of labour in terms of the division found in manufacture, i.e. as a means of producing more commodities with a given quantity of labour, and consequently of cheapening commodities and accelerating the accumulation of capital. In most striking contrast with this accentuation of quantity and exchange-value is the attitude of the writers of classical antiquity, who are exclusively concerned with quality and use-value. As a result of the separation of the social branches of production, commodities are better made, men's various inclinations and talents select suitable fields of action, and without some restriction no important results can be obtained anywhere. Hence both product and producer are improved by the division of labour. If the growth of the quantity produced is occasionally mentioned, this is only done with reference to the greater abundance of use-values. There is not a word alluding to exchange-value, or to the cheapening of commodities. This standpoint, the standpoint of use-value, is adopted by Plato, who treats the division of labour as the foundation on which the division of society into estates is based.

This reference to Plato is backed up by a footnote, which reads:

With Plato, the division of labour within the community develops from the many-sidedness of the needs of individuals, and the one-sidedness of their capabilities. The main point with him is that the labourer must adapt himself to the work, not the work to the labourer, a thing which would be unavoidable if the labourer carried on several trades at once, thus making one or the other of them subordinate.

Marx then quotes a supporting passage from Plato's *Republic*, Book II, 370C. It's from part of the initial stages in the argument that is to dominate the whole *Republic*: Socrates has suggested that if they are to find the answer to the question of whether 'justice' is 'better' than 'injustice', they should look first at the nature of justice in the State, and this involves examining initially the 'origin of the city'—the reason why the State exists—which is 'the fact that we do not severally suffice for our own needs, but each of us lacks many things' and therefore 'one man calling in another for one service and another for another, we, being in need of many things, gather many into one place of abode as associates and helpers, and to this dwelling together we give the name of city or State' (369B).

I want to use this reference to Plato's argument by Marx in order to leave Marx himself for a while. Since Marx doesn't discuss the problem of literary value himself (in this kind of context, at any rate), it might be as well to look at Plato, who implicitly does, and then perhaps *return* to Marx with some clearer questions.

If therefore we now look at Plato's case against 'poets' in Book III of *Republic*, we find that he brings into play, as one step in his argument, precisely the point about the 'one-sidedness' of a man's capacities which Marx noted, but Plato elaborates it in an intriguing way. At 394E, he has Socrates say:

'This, then, Adeimantus, is the point we must keep in view, do we wish our guardians to be good mimics or not? Or is this also a consequence of what we said before, that each one could practise well only one pursuit and not many, but if he attempted the latter, dabbling in many things, he would fail of distinction in all?'

The reference back to 370C is clear, but it's also worth referring back to the original question which began this whole section about poets. At 376C Socrates, having established the kind of 'character' required in the ruling 'guardians' of the ideal republic, had asked: 'But the rearing of these men and their education, how shall we manage that?' The inquiry that follows is therefore to do with how the guardians will be educated; in our terms, we might formulate the question as: who is to educate them, and what should they read? In the rest of Book II Plato establishes that some poets sometimes 'tell lies about the gods' and that Book concludes:

'When anyone says that sort of thing about the gods, we shall be wroth with him, we will refuse him a chorus, neither will we allow teachers to use him for the education of the young if our guardians are to be god-fearing men and god-like insofar as that is possible for humanity.' (385C)

On Plato's premises, the conclusion seems fair enough: if poetry is like this it shouldn't be used in educating the guardians. But if we return to 394E the problem seems, at first, to have changed, for there Socrates seems to be asking whether the guardians should *be* poets, not merely whether they should *read* them: 'do we wish our guardians to be *good mimics* or not?' The Loeb translation, which I've been quoting, retains the sense of the Greek by using 'mimics' for *'mimetikous'*. Other translations at this point have, for example, 'Do we want our guardians to be capable of playing many parts?' (Cornford) or 'capable of playing many characters' (H. D. P. Lee). The difficulty of translation arises partly because the Greek word which is at the root of this notion of 'mimicking' is *mimeomai* (the verb) or *mimesis* (the noun), and these words, and their derivative forms, are normally translated into English as 'imitate' and 'imitation', the implication being that to 'imitate' is to produce an 'imitation', a copy of something, a representation. The word 'mimesis' has, I suppose, become familiar enough in English, if only through the title of Auerbach's famous book. But I think we tend to presume too quickly that 'mimesis' has only one meaning; we think of 'mimesis' in terms of, say, a painting being a representation of something, but if we think of 'mimesis' as meaning also a 'mimicking', it's clear that we don't think of a painting as 'mimicking' its subject. Let's pursue Plato's use of the word a bit further by going back to the beginning of his discussion of what we would probably call 'literary form'.

At 392D, we have this:

'Do not they [fabulists or poets] proceed either by pure narration or by a narrative that is effected through imitation or by both?' 'This too,' he said, 'I still need to have made plainer.' 'I seem to be a ridiculous and obscure teacher,' I said; 'so like men who are unable to express themselves I won't try to speak in wholes and universals but will separate off a particular part and by the example of that try to show you my meaning. Tell me. Do you know the first lines of the *Iliad* in which the poet says that Chryses implored Agamemnon to release his daughter, and that the king was angry and that Chryses, failing of his request, imprecated curses on the Achaeans in his prayers to the god?' 'I do.' 'You know then that as far as these verses,
　　　　　And prayed unto all the Achaeans,
　　　　　Chiefly to Atreus' sons, twin leaders who marshalled the people,
the poet himself is the speaker and does not even attempt to suggest to us that anyone but himself is speaking. But what follows he delivers as if he were himself Chryses and tries as far as may be to make us feel that not Homer is the speaker, but the priest, an old man. And in this manner he has carried on nearly all the rest of his narration about affairs in Ilion, all that happened in Ithaca, and the entire *Odyssey*.' 'Quite so,' he said. 'Now, it is narration, is it not, both when he presents the several speeches and the matter between the speeches?' 'Of course.' 'But when he delivers a speech as if he were someone else, shall we not say that he then assimilates thereby his own diction as far as possible to that of the person whom he announces as about to speak?' 'We shall obviously.' 'And is not likening one's self to another in speech or bodily bearing an imitation of him to whom one likens one's self?' 'Surely.' 'In such case then, it appears, he and the other poets effect their narration

through imitation.' 'Certainly.' 'But if the poet should conceal himself nowhere, then his entire poetising and narration would have been accomplished without imitation.'

The distinction, as it's used here, between 'narration' *(diegesis)* with and without 'imitation' *(mimesis)* may strike us as clear enough in itself, but we might still feel that to use 'imitation' in this sense is slightly odd. The Loeb translation has a footnote which tries to explain, but it seems to me still caught in a particular notion of what 'imitation' means in English:

All art is essentially imitation for Plato and Aristotle. But imitation means for them not only the portrayal or description of visible and tangible things, but more especially the communication of a mood or feeling, hence the (to a modern) paradox that music is the most imitative of the arts. But Plato here complicates the matter further by sometimes using imitation in the narrower sense of dramatic dialogue as opposed to narration.

I don't think Plato is 'complicating the matter' by his use of *mimesis* here (which the Loeb translates by 'imitation'); indeed it's arguable that this use of *mimesis* is a very ordinary one for a Greek. Cornford, in a note in his translation, puts the point very clearly:

Plato now passes from the content of literature used in school to its form. The Greek schoolboy was not allowed to repeat Homer or Aeschylus in a perfunctory gabble, but expected to throw himself into the story and deliver the speeches with the tones and gesture of an actor. (The professional reciter, Ion, describes how, when he was reciting Homer, his eyes watered and his hair stood on end, *Ion* 535 C.) The word for this dramatic representation is *mimesis*. This has also the wider sense of 'imitation', and towards the end of this section it is used of the realistic copying of natural sounds and noises in music. But at first Plato is chiefly concerned with the actor's assumption of a character. The actor does not 'imitate' Othello, whom he has never seen; he represents or embodies or reproduces the character created by Shakespeare. In some degree the spectator also identifies himself with a character he admires. Plato held that, in childhood particularly, such imaginative identification may leave its permanent mark on the characters of actor and audience.

We can perhaps see more clearly now why it is that Plato can argue from *this* notion of *mimesis* towards his conclusion at 395C; neither 'mimic' nor 'imitate' seems quite right (we seem to need a term like 'mimate'), but if we substitute 'mimic' for 'imitate' in the Loeb translation the argument at 395C might recover some of its force:

If, then, we are to maintain our original principle, that our guardians, released from all other crafts, are to be expert craftsmen of civil liberty, and pursue nothing else that does not conduce to this, it would not be fitting for these to do nor yet to mimic anything else. But if they mimic they should from childhood up mimic what is appropriate to them—men, that is, who are brave, sober, pious, free and all things of that kind: but things unbecoming the free man they should neither do nor be clever at mimicking, nor yet any other shameful thing, lest from the mimicking they absorb the reality. Or have you not observed that mimicking, if continued from youth far into life, settles down into habits and (second) nature in the body, the speech, and the thought?

What I'm suggesting, therefore, is that the idea of 'throwing oneself into the part', of temporarily 'becoming' the character who is speaking in the text, is crucial to an understanding of Plato's argument about the relations between literature, education and the 'politics' of his republic. This rather neglected element in Plato's objections to certain kinds of literature could lead us in various directions. For example, it might illuminate his own literary form! It could also help us to make sense of Plato's notion of what happens when a poet composes poetry, as in the famous passage in *Laws* 719C:

Whenever a poet is seated on the Muses' tripod, he is not in his senses, but resembles a fountain, which gives free course to the upward rush of water; and, since his art consists of *mimesis*, he is compelled often to contradict himself, when he creates characters of contradictory moods; and he knows not which of these contradictory utterances is true.

I think Plato means 'contradict himself' rather literally; insofar as the poet 'becomes' each character in turn, he does suffer something like a split self, a self in contradiction with itself. And it should now be clear that for Plato *reading* can involve a similar kind of *mimesis*—an assumption of another 'self', a process of *being* a 'mimic'. Which should bring us back to 'literature'.

But in fact I want at this point to take a sudden jump to what may seem an entirely unrelated subject: film criticism. What interests me here—and will eventually connect back to Plato—is that recent work in film-criticism, particularly, has tried to make use of certain notions drawn from Jacques Lacan's version of psychoanalysis, and one fundamental reason for that utilisation of Lacan has been that Lacanian psychoanalysis seems to suggest ways in which marxism and the 'theory of the subject' can be brought critically together. Let me expand that a bit. Most of the writers associated with the film journal *Screen* have sought to establish a connection between marxism and film-analysis, but the kind of marxism they prefer—basically that inspired by Louis Althusser—emphasises the key role of 'the subject' as the core-notion of ideology; to think in terms of individual human subjects, coherently unified individuals as the sources of meanings, the originators of action and discourse, is to think ideologically—to fail to recognise that the 'individual' is an ensemble of social relations, and that action and discourse are to be accounted for in terms of systems of relations (of production, of meaning, of significance) which are dominant over and actually constitute or construct the 'individual' and of which that 'individual' is largely ignorant or necessarily unconscious. I'm obviously simplifying, drastically, a complex and difficult case, but the case as a whole is not my concern at the moment. I want here simply to pick up some of the Lacanian notions that have been put to work in film-theory and then, later, suggest some possible parallels or applications in the field of 'literature' —which might, by a few crab-like steps, allow us then to return to Marx.

Let me begin with some standard classifications in film-theory. One can distinguish three different ways in which 'looking' is involved in a normal 'narrative' or 'fiction' film. First, the camera is 'looking' at something, whatever is in the field of vision of the lens at the time of filming—the 'profilmic event' which is filmed. Second, the audience in the cinema 'looks' at the screen, it watches the film. Third, in a typical commercial movie, the characters in the 'story' (the diegesis, what the narrative of the film unfolds) 'look' at each other. A fourth 'look', rare in commercial cinema, occurs when the audience is 'looked' at by a figure on the screen; Jean-Luc Godard might be instanced as a director who makes use of scenes involving a 'look' that approximates to this 'fourth look'. The implications of these distinctions between different 'looks' have been explored in a variety of directions: e.g. the way most commercial films try to ensure that the audience remains unaware of the fact of the camera or even of the screen; the audience, on the other hand, becomes preoccupied with the 'looks' of the characters. The distinction between these different 'looks' can to a certain extent be paralleled in at least one instance of painting. Michel Foucault, in his *Les mots et les choses*, has analysed Velasquez's painting *Las Meninas* in a way that can be adapted for my purposes here. We look at the painting. We see the interior of a room, in which the 'maids of honour' of the title are clustered round Margarita Maria, the young daughter of Philip IV of Spain and Queen Maria Anna. One of the maids is looking at the princess, but the princess herself is looking out 'at' us and so are some of the other people depicted. In particular, included in the scene is the painter himself, who stands with a palette and brush in his hands, facing a large canvas only the back of which is visible to us. The painter's look is towards us, hovering between his canvas and his subject—that subject being situated, logically, at the point where we stand. The looks of the painter and the princess, and others, seem to converge on the point from which we are ourselves looking. But as we look our eyes are drawn to the wall at the back of the room in the picture; that wall seems to be covered with pictures—then we realise that one of those 'pictures' is, after all, a mirror. And the mirror is so placed that we see a reflection in it, a reflection of two people apparently standing where we stand; the two figures in the mirror are also looking out at us, or back at themselves; they are the subject of the painter's look as he paints the canvas within the picture. There is clearly a kind of *vertigo* awaiting the spectator of this painting. The point at which the spectator stands is simultaneously the 'point' at which the painter stood for his own self-portrait in the painting and the point at which those two figures stand; if we see 'ourselves' in the mirror we also see the painter in the act of painting *us*, but we cannot see *that* portrait, only a self-portrait of the painter and a set of portraits of people looking at us being painted. The analysis could continue. One last point for now: the two figures visible in the mirror are, apparently, the royal parents, Philip IV and Queen Maria Anna—it is they whom we have replaced.

We can move from that to Lacan. One of the earliest and most fruitful notions that Lacan introduced into psychoanalysis is that of the 'mirror-phase'. Again, I will have to crudely summarise and simplify, as well as adapt. Lacan's essay on 'The mirror-stage as formative of the function of the "I"' suggests the following: that the human infant is always born 'prematurely', in that birth occurs well before the motor-coordination of the body has occurred, whereas other animals at birth have already reached a far more advanced stage of their motor-coordination; the effect of this is that the infant's initial 'experience' is of a 'world' in which the distinction between 'self' and 'not-self' is not yet clear, the 'body' is experienced as amorphic, unstructured, without clear demarcation of its limits or 'internal' coherence—the infant is unable to bring into fixed location with each other its own limbs and bodily parts, its very surface is a mystery to it. But when, at about the age of six months onwards, the infant first recognises its own reflection in a mirror, it sees 'itself' as a whole, a unit, complete and limited; its body is a coherent image, a symmetrical structure. The infant's response is worth noting: unlike, say, a cat faced with its own mirror-image, the human infant does not gaze fairly passively and quickly lose interest; it gesticulates, moves its arms, initiates a kind of *pas de deux* with its own reflection, discovers in movement the faithful accompaniment of its

ody by the mirrored body; it thereby discovers its identification with that
 to be reliable; indeed, in a stricter psychoanalytical sense the infant
s an 'identification, in the full sense that analysis gives to the term:
ly, the transformation that takes place in the subject when he assumes an
image' (Lacan). Above all, this moment of playing with its own image is a
jubilant moment for the infant, it acts with delight and fascination, with
burbling pleasure. But the infant's recognition of itself has, in a certain sense, to
be regarded as a mis-cognition, a mis-identification; there is a disparity, not
least in the aspect of motor-coordination, between what the infant bodily *is*
and what the infant sees itself *as*. And if we think of the infant as being held
before the mirror by its mother, there is also a certain interaction of looks at
work: the mother looks at the infant in the mirror and the infant in the mirror
looks back at the mother looking; the infant before the mirror looks at itself
looking at itself and at the mother looking at itself looking. Again, there is a
certain vertigo of identifications implied in this interaction of looks.

At this point, let me introduce another notion drawn from Lacan's work
which has been influential in film-criticism, the notion of 'suture'. In French,
and in English, the word, as a verb, means to stitch the lips of a cut or wound
after a surgical operation; the relevant sense of the word here is the sense of
closing up a gap by intermittent joins, a gap that is made only to be healed up;
the stitches hold in place two edges that will then fuse into a seam. In Lacan's
use, particularly as articulated by J-A. Miller, the term has a very complex and
technical application within psychoanalysis; but some film-theorists have
adopted the term, in a rather simplifying way, to analyse what happens as we
look at a film. In particular, think of a conventional way of filming a dialogue
between two people. First, we see person A as from person B's point of view,
then we see B as from A's point of view—the 'shot/reverse-shot' pattern
familiar in so many films. But in most instances of this shot/reverse-shot way of
filming a dialogue, what we in fact see is A as from B's point of view, but not
quite, since B's shoulder is often in the shot, visible in a lower corner of the
frame; we are seeing A as if from over B's shoulder, slightly behind B rather than
positioned exactly where B stands. But then, of course, when the reverse-shot is
given us, not only are we now looking over A's shoulder at B, but there is
nobody except B visible, just as in the first shot there was nobody visible
looking over A's shoulder. The position, in spatial logic, from which 'we' look
in either shot is shown, by the reverse-shot, to be empty, not occupied by any
spectator. Clearly, the means by which this is achieved is simple: the camera is
'removed'. But the effect of apparently occupying this position of an absent
spectator is curious: as spectators of the scene we are both there and not-there,
we are both 'B seeing A' and 'A seeing B' but neither A nor B, yet we are not any
visible C either: we are both present and absent.

This fluctuation, or oscillation, of presence/absence is claimed to be at the
source of our basic *pleasure* in watching a film; it is, so the argument or
implication goes, a peculiarly pleasurable experience to be so situated that we
are both present and absent, not simply in the sense in which having a 'cloak of
invisibility' might allow us a certain voyeuristic satisfaction, but more basically
in that our presence and absence are related to one another as a constant

flickering or 'suturing' of presence/absence, a constant movement between the two positions, and the pleasure is derived from that constant *loss* of presence and *regaining* of presence, as if we were constantly in a situation of being annulled, cancelled out, annihilated, yet constantly overcoming that threat and re-establishing our continued presence, existence, being-there. It is this aspect of the whole case that the dialogue shot/reverse-shot pattern brings out so clearly, which is why it has sometimes been offered as a paradigm example of the process of watching a film.

Now, I'm actually rather dubious about the application of this notion in film-analysis, and particularly hesitant about any generalisation from the dialogue set-up to other aspects of film. But what I want to suggest is that the linking of pleasure to 'suture', to this oscillating presence/absence, is an important insight, and that it is in relation to the process of 'reading literature', rather than of watching a film, that this connection might be more clearly substantiated. To do so involves shifting our attention from 'looking' on to 'speaking', or what Plato would term 'mimicking'.

Take the following as an example—John Donne's 'The Flea':

> Marke but this flea, and marke in this,
> How little that which thou deny'st me is;
> It suck'd me first, and now sucks thee,
> And in this flea, our two bloods mingled bee;
> Thou know'st that this cannot be said
> A sinne, nor shame, nor losse of maidenhead,
>   Yet this enjoyes before it wooe,
>   And pamper'd swells with one blood made of two,
>   And this, alas, is more than wee would doe.
>
> Oh stay, three lives in one flea spare,
> Where wee almost, yea more than maryed are,
> This flea is you and I, and this
> Our mariage bed, and mariage temple is;
> Though parents grudge, and you, w'are met,
> And cloysterd in these living walls of Jet.
>   Though use make you apt to kill mee,
>   Let not to that, selfe murder added bee,
>   And sacrilege, three sinnes in killing three.
>
> Cruell and sodaine, hast thou since
> Purpled thy naile, in blood of innocence?
> Wherein could this flea guilty bee,
> Except in that drop which it suckt from thee?
> Yet thou triumph'st, and saist that thou
> Find'st not thy selfe, nor mee the weaker now;
>   'Tis true, then learne how false, feares bee;
>   Just so much honor, when thou yeeld'st to mee,
>   Will wast, as this flea's death tooke life from thee.

Donne's poetry is, of course, often praised for the way it seems to capture the movement of speech: 'If it is a speaking voice that strikes us in the *Songs and Sonnets*, it is a voice with many inflexions and intonations . . .' (R. G. Cox). But it is, of course, *we* who have to *read* the poem with those shifting, constantly alive 'inflexions and intonations'. A 'good' reader of 'The Flea' will have to *say* the poem in a way that calls upon very subtle modulations of pace, tone, rhythm, etc. But what happens as we try to read the poem in that way? If I'm reading the poem alone, in the privacy of my own room—which is the characteristic situation in which we read poetry, if at all, today—I find myself speaking the poem aloud, or at least *sotto voce*; I also find myself glancing up from the page, my look goes towards another point in the room that is, in a peculiar way, 'occupied' by a projected 'Other' to whom this poem is addressed ('and now sucks thee', 'Oh stay,'); that 'Other' is not, of course, 'present' in the room, yet saying the poem expressively, dramatically, 'with feeling', seems to demand another presence. Indeed, this poem demands of that Other that she should participate in the dramatic movement itself—between 'And this, alas, is more then wee would doe' and 'Oh stay, three lives in one flea spare' the action of the Other is clearly implied: she attempts to kill the flea; and my 'Oh stay' has to be said as a response to that imagined, projected act—just as 'Cruell and sodaine, hast thou since/Purpled thy naile, in blood of innocence' has to be in response to the Other's act of killing the flea. But there is no other person in the room, only a projected and invisible Other created by me as reader, as performer of the poem. It is not that I suffer hallucinations while speaking the poem, though my eyes might even take on precisely the expression they would have if someone were there! This Other has, indeed, a curious ontological status it might be worth exploring further. But at the moment it is the 'I' who is speaking that interests me more. I find it difficult to read the poem, certainly aloud, without accompanying physical gestures, however minimal or re-strained and checked—a movement of the eyebrows, an angling of the head, a shrug of the shoulders. Yet, of course, these bodily 'reactions' (and the voice too is bodily) are not reactions to the 'Other', nor are they reactions to the 'text', inert marks on the page; they are constitutive of, part of, speaking (reading) the poem, and that is a controlled speaking, controlled in a peculiar sense. The 'words on the page' act, if you like, as a 'control' against which I measure my performance; my speaking those words in that order ('order' including punctuation marks, line-endings, etc.) is a kind of experiment, a testing out of ways of saying those words —I 'read' the poem in subtly or even markedly different ways each time. One might even suggest that I am a bit like the infant before the mirror, miming to my own movements, mimicking and adjusting to the 'ideal' image (the aural image?) I envisage for this poem, bringing my vocal gestures into line with that ideal yet obliterating the 'ideal' in the process of pursuing it. The 'perfect' reading of this poem always eludes me; it too is like an Other whom I both respond to and simultaneously project. The poem is not so much a mirror held up to life as a mirror of and for my own Other. Yet, at the same time, insofar as I operate the experiment I am aware of my speaking *as* an experiment, a finding-out, a discovery of something I am not wholly respon-sible for; I control the 'I' who speaks, that 'I' too is an Other. Yet it is 'my' voice, my physical voice and gestures, that are at work in the speaking, it is still 'myself' that is being controlled. It seems to me that this peculiarly oscillating 'I', flickeringly present as both I and Other, is best understood along the lines suggested by Lacan's notion of 'suture'. It is as if 'I' were both present and absent, looking over my own shoulder rather than simply identified with myself, yet unable to be seen even in the mirror I hold up to myself. These are visual metaphors, and unsatisfactory. Yet they perhaps capture—by analogy with the pictorial and filmic examples I explored earlier—something of the 'vertigo' that seems to be involved as soon as one tries to analyse the process of speaking, mimicking, this poem.

It would be possible to explore this process in a more strictly Lacanian way. I will simply indicate what I mean by quoting Jacques-Alain Miller: 'Suture names the relation of the subject to the chain of its discourse.' In other words, the notion of suture would lead us into an understanding of the activity of speaking and writing generally. I don't want, here, to develop that—partly because I don't have enough confidence in (my own grasp of) Lacan, and partly because I want to try to make clearer to myself some problems that I find I can't think about by simply taking over Lacan's approach and terminology. (It may also be that the kind of 'understanding' required can only be arrived at by and in a *process* of genuinely dialectical *practice*, though not necessarily by the style of process Lacan himself has adopted.)

Let me use Freud instead (if any Lacanians will excuse that 'instead'!). In chapter II of *Beyond the Pleasure Principle*, Freud gives the famous account of his grandson's game of *Fort/Da*—how the eighteen-month-old infant played with his toys by throwing them out of sight and having them returned, these actions being marked by the child's utterance of '*Fort!*' ('Gone!') and '*Da!*' ('There!'). The account, and Freud's explanation in this chapter, are presumably familiar. I want to pick out a footnote, which reads:

One day the child's mother had been away for several hours and on her return was met with the words 'Baby o-o-o-o!' which was at first incomprehensible. It soon turned out, however, that during this long period of solitude the child had found a method of making *himself* disappear. He had discovered his reflection in a full-length mirror which did not quite reach to the ground, so that by crouching down he could make his mirror-image 'gone'.

Clearly, this game gave the child a great deal of pleasure; Freud offers an account of why the game of *Fort/Da* with objects gave the child pleasure, but he doesn't actually comment on the pleasure to be derived from the mirror-version. It seems clear that what the child is doing is playing with his *own* disappearance in such a way as to control that disappearance, manipulate it; repeatedly he makes 'himself' vanish in order to reappear; he deliberately oscillates between 'presence' and 'absence', and the point of the oscillation is to constantly re-affirm, re-establish, his presence—not so much the repeated *fact* of his re-appearance but the repeated *act* of re-appearing; the pleasure occurs not by being-present or by being-absent but by being in *control* of being-present and of being-absent (the one necessary to the other). It is the 'I' who is in control both of the present 'I' (in the mirror) and of the absent 'I' (invisible, not-looked-at) who is the delighted 'I'. This 'third I' is the creation of the game itself, a peculiar I not otherwise available or known; in the intermittent, jubilant delight of that 'I' the split between I and Other is recuperated, fused, healed over, sutured.

But the game is perhaps a fragile one, in two respects. First, the child remains visible throughout to others, remains 'there', does not 'actually' disappear; an adult can spoil the game by registering the continued visibility of the child crouched below the mirror; this mirror-version is essentially a private and 'better', but still vulnerable, version of the familiar adult-child game of 'I see!'—where the child is dependent on the other continuing to call 'I see!' whenever the child chooses to re-appear. Secondly, and related to this, is the fact that it is 'only' the mirror-I who is under control, can be made to disappear; the ordinary I, this side of the mirror, remains, can only disappear from the mirror not from the real room. Insofar as the child is still held within the identification of the mirror-phase this is perhaps an impossible distinction for the child fully to make—Lacan dates the mirror-phase from six to eighteen months, and Freud's grandson was eighteen months old. But such refinements can be left aside.

What I want to suggest is that the *pleasure* of *reading* 'The Flea' combines both the pleasure of the moment of the mirror-phase itself and the pleasure of the *Fort/Da* mirror-game. By the 'pleasure of reading' I mean not the particular pleasures of reading *this* poem, but the pleasure at work, or released, in the *process* of *reading* itself, why we get pleasure from this kind of reading. Let me label that reading-pleasure 'extasie'—in homage to Donne's poem 'The Extasie' which puts into play some allied notions. (Indeed, I am tempted towards conducting my argument almost entirely in terms of some of Donne's poems—'Witchcraft by a Picture', 'A valediction: of my name, in the window', 'The Triple Foole'—but I'd better not.)

When I read 'The Flea' aloud I oscillate between speaking as 'I' and as 'Other' yet there is a kind of 'third I' who controls the fit or fusion between speaking I and speaking Other, 'measures' the one against the other, and uses as the norm for that measuring an 'ideal Other' whose voice would bear no trace of 'mine'; that ideal voice is perhaps experienced as a voice 'heard' but without physical embodiment, a voice audible only to the 'inner ear', the 'third ear', and my reading aloud of the poem may never measure up to that heard voice, though I try to mimic its subtleties, nuances, overtonal qualities, its many 'inflexions and intonations'; that is the voice I hear in 'silent' reading. What this process involves, then, is both a constant fluctuation in which I am absorbed by, dissolved in, taken over by, made absent by an Other who takes my place, replaces me, speaks instead of me, yet never fully so, since I am also simultaneously in control of that oscillating presence/absence, shaping my voice in a flexibly 'mimicking' way, and yet never fully in control either, since any final fusion escapes me: the Other I produce is never quite the Other that I hear. It is this peculiar equilibrium between presence and absence which I maintain, this playing of control against subordination, this maintenance of self-presence at the edge of self-absorption, of evanescence, that provides the 'extasie' of reading; I am split into I and Other only to re-assert the unity of that I that allows the splitting. Yet that unified I is itself under a double-demand, to maintain itself as intact, in control, over against the ideal Other and yet to reduce that ideal Other to the controlled Other who speaks in my voice. And in reading 'silently' I suppress the act of speaking aloud in order to effect an impossible fusion between the heard voice and the speaking I who does not speak, to identify the Other that I 'could' produce with the Other I hear—an attempted collapse of the actual into the ideal while preserving the insistence on the I who 'could' speak the perfect reading. But of course I could never speak aloud the voice I hear; while in silent reading the 'danger' of losing control, the threat of dissolution, is increased: 'I' fade into, am absorbed by, that heard Other I seek, im-mediately, to emulate: the reverse-shots no longer succeed each other but are superimposed.

It seems to me that it is this process which deeply *underpins* a dominant contemporary notion of 'literary value'. By that I mean that the possibility of such an oscillating and yet controlled, suturing, reading is felt to be a *sine qua non* for any claim of a text to being 'literature' at all, to having any value as 'literature' in the first place. What is deeply implicit in a certain tradition of criticism is the demand for that kind of 'extasie': unless a text can be read in that way, any further discussion of its *particular* qualities or 'value' is at best a reluctant discussion. Another, extreme but converging, way of putting that is to say that anyone who claimed that Donne's 'The Flea' was a 'good poem' because it could be used to seduce someone would be ruled out of court; what the literary critic is after isn't any particular *use* the poem might be put to, but a certain *frisson* to be got from *reading* it 'as a poem'. Or to put it another way, if a text can be read with (in) extasie, it can be discussed as 'literature'. There are two sides to this coin of 'value'. The first is precisely that 'literary value' is to be sought as a 'pure' value, divorced (initially or in principle) from 'non-literary' considerations, to be discovered not in 'what' the text says but in 'the way it says it', which is then seen as controlling and creating 'what is said'; from there the particular localisations of that 'way' can be explored, in terms of 'style', 'imagery', 'rhythm', 'tone' etc.—yet all these terms of analysis and comment are pointers to what is already 'known' to be there: 'literary value'; the details are a supportive spelling-out, not a demonstration or discovery (though they may be offered as such to someone else), and in most cases they can only be communicated to someone else not by formal argument or definition (what is 'tone'?) but by ostensive performance, by 'reading it *this* way'. The obverse of this is that since it is the *reading* that provides the extasie, 'literary value' can be assigned to texts of very diverse kinds by different readers, and their subsequent disagreements are not to be resolved by simply pointing to this or that feature of the text but rather by a persuasion directed at changing the way the text is read, by, in effect, shaping the other's reading to place him or her within the process of suture, to 'experience it for themselves'. In this way, 'literary value' is a quality 'immediately recognisable' yet simultaneously utterly elusive. Within critical discussion a particular text may have (it's a partly frivolous point) a certain kind of exchange-value—compare this with that, the effect here is similar to the effect there, this does less successfully what that poem achieves, etc.—but there can be no unit of value nor can one text be substituted for another text (each is 'unique'), since finally it is not texts that are the objects of the literary critical exercise but rather the process of reading;

29

ifies the attention paid to a text is that someone 'values' it—i.e. has
in extatic way.

aware that my case would have to be considerably elaborated in a
number of directions and that I would have to meet a number of problems
—not least those associated with a familiar kind of 'philosophy of literary
criticism'. All I can do here is make some limited suggestions and sketch out
four areas for further exploration.

First, it would be worth probing the way particular critics talk, when they do,
about what it is they are doing, because I suspect that quite often the *act* of
reading has an odd status in those accounts; to read in an extatic way seems
both the premise, the prior condition, of any commentary and the final effect of
any approving criticism, yet the actual process of reading is elided. (In specific
'practical criticism' or 'close reading' commentaries the text is simply inserted,
as quotation, into the analysis, with the assumption that it will be read in the
way intended—a variation of this procedure is, of course, my own use of 'The
Flea'; the difficulties this raises for 'close reading' of long novels are well-
known.) Consider, as an example, this passage from Leavis, from his
Education and the University:

For surely, as one might say to one's beginning students, it should be possible, by cultivating
attentive reading, to acquire a higher skill than the untrained reader has: a skill that will enable the
trained reader to do more with a poem than ejaculate approval or disapproval, or dismiss it with
vaguely reported general impressions, qualified with the modest recognition that (in Arnold
Bennett's words) 'taste after all is relative.' Analysis, one would go on, is the process by which we
seek to attain a complete reading of the poem—a reading that approaches as nearly as possible to
the perfect reading. There is about it nothing in the nature of 'murdering to dissect', and
suggestions that it can be anything in the nature of laboratory-method misrepresent it entirely. We
can have the poem only by an inner kind of possession; it is 'there' for analysis only in so far as we
are responding appropriately to the words on the page. In pointing to them (and there is nothing
else to point to) what we are doing is to bring into sharp focus, in turn, this, that and the other detail,
juncture or relation in our total response; or (since 'sharp focus' may be a misleading account of the
kind of attention sometimes required), what we are doing is to dwell with a deliberate, considering
responsiveness on this, that or the other node or focal point in the complete organization that the
poem is, in so far as we have it. Analysis is not a dissection of something that is already and passively
there. What we call analysis is, of course, a constructive or creative process. It is a more deliberate
following-through of that process of creation in response to the poet's words which reading is. It is
a re-creation in which, by a considering attentiveness, we ensure a more than ordinary faithfulness
and completeness.

What then, one might still ask, is the kind of 'attention' involved in an
'attentive reading'? Does 'reading' refer to an *act* of reading in the phrase 'a
reading that approaches as nearly as possible to the perfect reading' (and whose
is the 'perfect reading')? The last few sentences seem to oscillate between
'analysis' being a writing or talking about 'that process of creation in response
to the poet's words which reading is' and analysis being ideally a way of
actually reading the poem: 'It is a re-creation in which . . . we ensure a more
than ordinary faithfulness and completeness.' At the brink of this passage
hovers a dissolving of reading into writing, a notion of writing as a mode of
reading and vice-versa.

Second, there might well be an obverse side to the notion of reading as
extasie; for a text to allow or prompt or demand such a reading it might have to

have been *written* in a process akin to extasie: a kind of oscillating identification of the I who writes and the ideal projected or heard Other who speaks in the text but who is obliterated by the actual Other who is written. Only a detailed analysis could unpack this suggestion (the whole question of 'style' is involved) but such an analysis might easily begin from Plato's remarks about the poet 'seated on the Muses' tripod'. It would be interesting, for example, to compare the way in which Plato locates what I have called the 'ideal voice' as that of a god, with various modern accounts of literary creation in which the unconscious or the (impersonal) tradition are foregrounded.

Third, it is perhaps necessary to insist that my conclusion that the notion of 'literary value' (in the *sine qua non* sense) is rooted in a demand for an extatic reading is valid—if at all—within a particular history, of both 'literature' and 'criticism', and indeed within a history of the act of reading. The connections that would have to be explored are those between the emergence of our modern sense of 'literature' and 'the literary' some time between 1600 and 1800, the development of a particular mode of 'literary criticism' (in the nineteenth and twentieth centuries) tied to the 'experience' of 'literature', and the establishment of silent or solitary reading as the dominant habit of reading; the writings of John Donne and his contemporaries might figure in the account of all three aspects. Yet while acknowledging the historical relativity of my argument, it has to be said that I, at least, find myself already situated within that history—my 'responses' to 'literature', my sense of what 'reading a poem' involves, my habits of reading, have been intimately shaped by that complex history; if I want to grasp the presuppositions and limitations of that history, that might best be done by an internal critique rather than by an external assault or a mere proffering of an alternative. The key process within that critical tradition has come to be the process of reading 'attentively', 'responsively'. By attending responsively to that process of attending responsively I have perhaps clarified, in a provisional way, why it is that the notion of 'literary value', which appears to be the defining notion at the heart of 'literary criticism', is something of a screen-notion, in the sense in which Freud uses 'screen-memory': the 'primal scene' of literature is always an act of a reader rather than a mysterious attribute of a text.

Fourth, there is a certain parallel between the notion of extatic reading and a Lacanian way of talking about 'love'. In Lacanian terms 'love' might be regarded as the desire for the desire of the Other. Put that another way: the following is a peculiarly Lacanian dialogue:

John: I, John, love you Jane
Jane: No, I, John, love you Jane
John: Yes, I Jane love you John.

We perhaps ought to take seriously one way of talking about 'literature' as involving a 'love'.

Now let me return, finally, to Marx, with three concluding pointers.

First, I said earlier that Marx would look coldly on any attempt to somehow equate the notion of 'value' in his critique of political economy and the notion of 'value' in literary criticism. I also remarked that I thought that any attempt to push in the direction of Marx's question 'is value as such the general form, in opposition to use-value and exchange-value as particular forms of it?' would end in a *cul-de-sac*, in both political economy and literary criticism. But it is precisely *because* of that *shared cul-de-sac* that one can now suggest a certain equation between the use of 'value' in political economy and in literary criticism. For it is clear that the footnote query I quoted from the *Grundrisse*, about 'value as such', was a side-track for Marx, leading him away from what could be regarded as the key breakthrough in his critique of political economy: the recognition that 'value as such' has no content as a concept and that any attempt to talk in terms of 'value as such' was fundamentally misleading. (Parenthetically, it's worth registering in this context the difficulty of clarifying even the notion of 'use-value', and its converse 'need', in Marx.) One passage where the implications of this negative insight are clear enough is the following:

Men do not . . . bring the products of their labour into relation with each other as values because they see these objects merely as the material integuments of homogeneous human labour. The reverse is true: by equating their different products to each other in exchange as values, they equate their different kinds of labour as human labour. They do this without being aware of it. Value, therefore, does not have its description branded on its forehead; it rather transforms every product of labour into a social hieroglyphic. Later on, men try to decipher the hieroglyphic, to get behind the secret of their own social product: for the characteristic which objects of utility have of being values is as much men's social product as their language. The belated scientific discovery that the products of labour, in so far as they are values, are merely the material expressions of the human labour expended to produce them, marks an epoch in the history of mankind's development, but by no means banishes the semblance of objectivity possessed by the social characteristics of labour.

What Marx is pointing to here is that 'value' is not an attribute of an object but a form of relationship between social individuals, yet that fact is obscured for us precisely because we think of 'value' as somehow attached to *things*. Marx's own footnote to this passage captures the point succinctly:

When Galiani said: 'Value is a relation between persons', he ought to have added: a relation concealed beneath a material shell.

That 'concealment' is what underpins the whole of the analysis in this section of *Capital*, on 'The Fetishism of the Commodity and Its Secret'. In a similar way, one could claim that to speak of 'literary value' is normally to commit oneself to a 'Fetishism of the Text', in the sense that 'value' is then seen as somehow an attribute of the 'work of literature', the text, rather than as indicating a 'relation between persons'. But whereas the 'persons' involved in the relation of commodity-exchange are 'a buyer' and 'a seller', two 'distinct' persons, the 'relation' at work in reading extatically is between what I have termed 'I', 'speaking I', 'speaking Other', 'third I' and 'ideal Other', and, sometimes, a further projected Other (the addressed 'thee' of Donne's poem). These terms are clearly unsatisfactory, and this is partly because they tend to imply the presence (or presence/absence) of what we normally call 'persons'. And what we normally mean by 'person' is a unity of the 'I'. Of course, without that notion of the unified or fixed 'I' arguments about the somehow intrinsical-ly *one-sided* capacities of people are much harder to sustain—a point that

would take us right back to Marx's footnote on Plato's understand
'division of labour', and could also lead us into considering the way
reading and writing are a 'social product', a social 'labour', as 'langu
is.

That also brings me to my *second* point. Insofar as extasie involves
of identifications, identities, projections, it calls into question the very notion
of the 'unity' of the 'person' reading. To read Donne's 'The Flea' 'responsively',
'fully', 'appropriately' is to enter into a relationship with one's 'self' that
challenges the very coherence of that 'self'; it is to create in the process of
reading a palimpsest of 'I's and 'Others' in which the known, stable 'I' we
normally identify with, identify ourselves as, is constantly effaced and lost; yet
in the same movement, in a fluctuating and flickering way, that coherent I is
re-established, re-asserts itself as the locus of control over the evanescence and
vacillation. In subjecting my self to the reading I partially lose myself as subject,
experience the 'I' of the reading as constituted by and in the act of reading.
Much of the time, that stable, everyday I is dominant; in reading extatically it is
possible to glimpse the dissolution of that everyday I, to become aware of that I
as *always* constituted. The grammar of the language does not, finally, allow an
articulation of this dissolution, whatever the twists and turns of the offered
formulations; inexorably, the language leads back to the subject. Yet it is
possible to recognise that subject as a miscognition, and reading offers an
accessible instance of that recognition. (Remember that Aristotle thought that
writing might require someone 'with a touch of madness in him'.) Reading
therefore has an ambivalent significance for any marxist critique of 'the
subject': it both demonstrates or discloses the non-unity of the subject, opens
on to the absence of the subject, yet also offers a constant recuperation of that
unity: it is in reading that we can sometimes experience ourselves as most in
control of ourselves as sources of meaning, originators of discourse: it is *our*
reading, our emphases, tones, nuances, we offer; the poem means what we
make it mean, take it to mean. Yet at the same time in the same moment of
speaking, we can seem most intimately obliterated, effaced, replaced by
another voice which is not of our making but made by 'the poem itself'.

My *third* point is extremely tentative. In recent years, many attempts have
been made to bring marxism, psychoanalysis, semiotics, literary criticism and
film-theory into relation with each other. Often a hierarchy of relations has
been postulated in which, in principle, marxism joins hands with psychoanalysis and both are brought to bear upon the literary or film text, thereby
undercutting or replacing 'ideological' modes of criticism. It might now be
useful to explore the *self-contradictions* involved in reading in order to grasp
more clearly some of the concepts of both marxism and psychoanalysis, not
least the marxist concept of ideology. That approach may risk a collapse back
into discredited and discarded habits—of idealism, phenomenology, impressionistic vagueness, and, most heinous heresy of all, a lack of 'rigour'; it may be
a return to ideology, but it may also promote an internal critique of ideology,
a distanciation within ideology, an undermining of that subject which is not,
finally, to be fully eradicated or exorcised.

Simply as a recapitulating *coda*, let me finally offer three inter-echoing quotations for you to read, one from Marx, one from Lacan, and one from T. S. Eliot:

In a certain sense, a man is in the same situation as a commodity. As he neither enters into the world in possession of a mirror, nor as a Fichtean philosopher who can say 'I am I', a man first sees and recognises himself in another man. Peter only relates to himself as a man through his relation to another man, Paul, in whom he recognises his likeness. With this, however, Paul also becomes from head to toe, in his physical form as Paul, the form of appearance of the species man for Peter.

Capital

For it is at the level at which subjective 'synthesis' confers its full meaning on speech that the subject reveals all the paradoxes of which he is the patient in this singular perception. These paradoxes already appear when it is the other who offers speech: this is sufficiently evidenced in the subject by the possibility of his obeying this speech in so far as it governs his hearing and his being-on-his-guard, for simply by entering the other's auditory field, the subject falls under the sway of a suggestion from which he can escape only by reducing the other to being no more than the spokesman of a discourse that is not his own or of an intention that he is holding in reserve.

But still more striking is the subject's relation to his own speech, in which the important factor is rather masked by the purely acoustic fact that he cannot speak without hearing himself. Nor is there anything special about the fact that he cannot listen to himself without being divided as far as the consciousness is concerned. Clinicians did better by discovering verbal motor hallucination by detecting the outline of phonatory movements. Yet they have not articulated where the crucial point resides; it is that the *sensorium* being indifferent in the production of a signifying chain:

(a) this signifying chain imposes itself, by itself, on the subject in its vocal dimension;
(b) . . . .
(c) its own structure *qua* signifier is determinant in this attribution, which, as a rule, is distributive, that is to say, possesses several voices, and, therefore, renders equivocal a supposedly unifying *percipiens*.

'On the possible treatment of psychosis'

The point of view which I am struggling to attack is perhaps related to the metaphysical theory of the substantial unity of the soul: for my meaning is, that the poet has, not a 'personality' to express, but a particular medium, which is only a medium and not a personality, in which impressions and experiences combine in peculiar and unexpected ways. . . .

This essay proposes to halt at the frontier of metaphysics or mysticism, and confine itself to such practical conclusions as can be applied by the responsible person interested in poetry.

'Tradition and the Individual Talent'

Poisson: A Modest Review

Raymond Williams's new book is boldly, simply and ambitiously entitled *Marxism and Literature*. The title already indicates a problem. Consider those echoed titles of Williams's earlier books, *Reading and Criticism, Culture and Society, The Country and the City*; the 'and' in these phrases suggests a tension but also an overlap, a completion by interpenetration or mutual supplementation, a gesture towards possible wholeness. The other strain in Williams's titles suggests a movement, a process, a probable incompletion: *Drama from Ibsen to Brecht, The English Novel from Dickens to Lawrence, Long Revolution*. But the new title seems merely an inert juxtaposition, a rather wary bringing together of two terms that operate in different lexical worlds (not even a provocative gesture like *Modern Tragedy*, or *Keywords*, more like the statement of a problem, as in *Television: Technology and Cultural Form*). The new book is actually one in a series of 'Marxism and ——' titles, but—the thought arises—might it not equally be one in a series of '—ism and Literature' titles (Buddhism and Literature, Catholicism and Literature, Fascism and Literature)?

Characteristically, Williams anticipates the thought:

Even twenty years ago, and especially in the English-speaking countries, it would have been possible to assume, on the one hand, that Marxism is a settled body of theory or doctrine, and, on the other hand, that Literature is a settled body of work, or kinds of work, with known general qualities and properties. A book of this kind might then reasonably have explored problems of the relations between them or, assuming a certain relationship, passed quickly to specific applications. The situation is now very different.

But then, equally characteristically, Williams offers himself as the third term, linking the other two; he traces his own 'relation to Marxism and to literature which, between them, in practice as much as in theory, have preoccupied most of my working life'. The reading eye hesitates, and goes back. Williams's commitment to 'Socialism' has been an open secret, but that is not the same as a preoccupation with Marxism (at least in England, over a long period), and Williams's own relations with Marxism as a body of theory have only fairly recently been a matter of public explicitness. One's hesitation persists as one reads: Williams speaks of his work over thirty-five years as 'in direct if often unrecorded contact, throughout, with Marxist ideas and arguments', and of his present position as a 'new and conscious relation with Marxism', his present theory as 'in my view, a Marxist theory'. Insofar as

35

Williams's work over the years has represented, for many followers, a paradigm-shift, replacing and supplanting Leavis, he is right to suggest, modestly, that his 'individual history may be of some significance in relation to the development of Marxism and of thinking about Marxism in Britain'; the question then raised by these more explicit declarations might be whether the new book signals an epistemological break in Williams's own thinking. But to speak of an 'epistemological break' may be to speak as the kind of 'Marxist' Williams now sees himself as having once been, from 1939 to 41: 'it can mean that a style of thought and certain defining propositions are picked up and applied, in good faith, as part of a political commitment, without necessarily having much independent substance'.

These apparently preliminary remarks by Williams go, in one sense, to the heart of the book. For its main target is the practice of taking terms of *analysis* for terms of *substance*. One formulation can stand for many:

the analytical categories, as so often in idealist thought, have, almost unnoticed, become substantive descriptions, which then take habitual priority over the whole social process to which, as analytical categories, they are attempting to speak.

It is presumably not an accident, but a tactic, that Williams shows very particularly, in chapter 2, how *linguistics*, in its development from classical studies through nineteenth-century comparative philology to Saussure and beyond, has adopted a notion of language as

a fixed, objective, and in these senses 'given' system, which had theoretical and practical priority over what were described as 'utterances' (later as 'performance'). Thus the living speech of human beings in their specific social relationships was theoretically reduced to instances and examples of a system which lay beyond them.

Variations of this reversal are traced. Within the study of language itself, the 'referential' and the 'emotive', the 'denotative'/'connotative' and 'ordinary'/ 'literary' language distinctions came to act not as categories of analysis but as names for demarcated *areas* of language. In Marxist theory, 'base' and 'superstructure' came to indicate rigidly separated entities (whatever their dialectical relationships thereafter). In literary criticism, 'genre' assumed almost an independent existence, 'prior' to individual works. Williams's tactic against these hypostasised usages is to track their histories, recover their complex pedigrees, and in these frequent analyses of word-traces we hear most clearly the echoes and accents of earlier work—*Culture and Society* and *Keywords*. Interwoven with this strand are other echoes and repetitions of themes from earlier works: 'dominant, residual and emergent' and 'structures of feeling' are now titles of individual chapters, no longer phrases that play through other analyses but now the objects of analysis and quasi-definition themselves.

Most of this new book therefore induces a distinct sense of *déja-vu* for anyone who has followed Williams's previous work. What we seem to be offered is a shuffling of familiar pieces, an ordering of parts into a fairly predictable pattern. That pattern has its interest, of course; it becomes an intriguing question as to which theme or emphasis will link up next, as 'Base and Superstructure' leads to 'Determination' then to 'Productive Forces', 'Reflection and Mediation', 'Typification and Homology', 'Hegemony', etc.

And one notes, with the pleasure of recognition, where those remembered comments on Lukacs or Goldmann or Gramsci find their new place. In one sense, therefore, the new book offers a summary and summation of most of Williams's already published work—and as such is both too complex to further summarise here and, presumably, too familiar to require it.

But then the question arises as to how one receives, and judges, this summation. One approach to an answer lies in the significance of the many excursions into the history of key-words and of debates. What purpose do they serve in the text itself? One might see them as variations on a Cartesian circle: Williams himself speaks of a 'radical doubt', 'when the most basic concepts —the concepts, as it is said, from which we begin—are suddenly seen to be not concepts but problems, not analytical problems either but historical movements that are still unresolved.' But how can one begin to speak when the only terms available are themselves the problems? At times this dilemma can seem like a variant on an older idealist epistemological problem. Or one might see Williams as practising in these word-histories his own form of Whiggery: he presents an interpretation of others' positions so that they culminate, inescapably, in his own. Thus, after labelling his own current position 'cultural materialism', he can say of Marx's achievement: 'the stress on material history . . . was in one special way compromised. Instead of making cultural history material, which was the next radical move, it was made dependent, secondary, superstructural.' Others' positions become, similarly, 'not material enough' compared with Williams's own 'materialist' stance. But in either of these modes, Cartesian or Whiggish, these mini-histories of terms and positions would have to be seen as merely sleight-of-hand, a tactic or twitch of scholarship, since Williams's own eventual formulations and theories would in any case have to stand, finally, on their own merits, whatever the difficulty of a starting-point or their relation to others' positions.

But a more positive way of understanding these backward glances is to turn this last comment on its head and in so doing to grasp the word-histories as exemplifying the central and, to some extent, new positive thesis of the book. Against the structuralist-linguistics emphasis Williams now offers Volosinov and Vygotsky. The basic notion here is that of the 'multi-accentual' character of all language in practical use; since we always use language within a social, interactional situation, language is always a matter of differential emphasis, not merely in, say, pronunciation, but, crucially, in meaning. The relation between 'form' and 'meaning' within the 'sign' is not fixed (as notions of system or code tend to make it) but flexible, within an active social relationship between living people. We each, if you like, *bend* the language we speak our own way. And this is precisely what we see Williams himself doing: his interlocutors are previous theorists; he takes their terms and bends them to his own voice and meaning. The typography is the material index of this process: a particular term may appear as, say, 'material', *material* or, simply, material (without either inverted commas or italics); with the first it operates as someone else's usage; italicised, it registers Williams's modified emphasis; and it then takes its unremarked place as meaning something new. It's an often successful device: we do indeed find ourselves moving, as we read, across a range of meanings, beginning to read with Williams's own unique accentuation.

But, oddly, we can then see how this tactic unites the ploys of both idealist epistemology and Whiggish historiography. The first parallel is with Aristotle. In surveying the theories of his predecessors concerning a topic, Aristotle characteristically offers himself as the synthesis and does so by proposing a *terminology*; necessarily, that terminology is drawn either from those predecessors themselves or, by metaphor, from other fields of usage. Thus, he can 'solve' the problem of the One and the Many and Parmenides's paradox of becoming and being, by speaking of '*potency*' and '*act*'; but do these terms solve or merely dissolve the problem? Since, however, they *are* the 'concepts from which we begin', we cannot now think (metaphysically) beyond or without them. Yet Aristotle's initiating privilege cannot be repeated. Hegel perhaps tried, in his own Whiggish/Idealist blend of historiographical epistemology, to begin anew. But whereas Aristotle's syntheses remained inescapable common sense until Heidegger, Hegel's system seemed radically ambiguous even to his immediate disciples. The split into Left and Right Young Hegelians was crucially a matter of political interpretation of a densely ambivalent style of writing.

Consider now the case of Williams. He writes, for example: 'A Marxism without some concept of determination is in effect worthless.' He then surveys both Marx's various German terms and a range of English usages—for example, 'determination' of a calculation, a course of study, a lease, as setting bounds or limits, as external determinism, as determined laws. This section concludes:

This is where the full concept of determination is crucial. For in practice determination is never only the setting of limits; it is also the exertion of pressures. As it happens, this is also a sense of 'determine' in English: to determine or be determined to do something is an act of will or purpose.

This then allows Williams to achieve the required synthesis:

Determination of this whole kind—a complex and interrelated process of limits and pressures—is in the whole social process itself and nowhere else: not in an abstracted 'mode of production' nor in an abstracted 'psychology'.

But then this 'full concept' leaves *all* the *political* options open, in practice; the term 'determination' can receive equally the accentuation of a Stalin, a Sorel, or a Situationist.

That, Williams might say, is precisely what he intends. It is a constant emphasis of the book that 'situations, relationships and responses' are always 'varying and *in principle* variable' (his emphasis). Allied to this formulation is another, again italicised by Williams:

no mode of production and therefore no dominant social order and therefore no dominant culture ever in reality includes or exhausts all human practice, human energy, and human intention.

But then if we ask what *is* 'in reality' excluded in a particular case, the theoretical response can only be: 'It is an open question—that is to say, a set of specific historical questions'. This emphasis, against others, may be salutary; but then all historical (and philosophical?) questions become 'open questions' as all political options are 'open options'. When Williams says, of his discussion of 'commitment', that 'these qualifications are not meant to weaken the original claim, but simply to clarify it', we can sense the unease; but when he goes on to say that 'Alignment in this sense is no more than a recognition of specific men in specific (and in Marxist terms, class) relations to specific situations and experiences', the parenthesis is hardly a clarification of a formulation which has now weakened a polemical proposition into a toothless tautology. And it is then noticeable that 'class' is the one term that Williams nowhere in his book seeks to examine or define afresh—or even to dissolve. A Marxism without a specifiable historical method and without a specifiable political practice, but which still speaks in a 'class' accent, may not cease to be entitled 'Marxist'; but it may then be merely a matter of terminology, a *category* of analysis and not a matter of *substance*, whether we call that position 'Marxist' or not.

Whether we call a particular piece of writing 'Literature' or not may also be an open question. It has certainly had a historically variable answer, as Williams usefully shows in chapter 3. The emphasis of his final chapter, 'Creative Practice', is—refreshingly—on the creative character of *all* writing, as 'always in some sense self-composition and social composition'. But if we ask why we might *read* what is now, more narrowly, known as 'Literature' Williams again appears synthetically evasive. He writes:

Works of art, by their substantial and general character, are often especially important as sources of this complex evidence

for a 'cultural analysis' of the 'hegemonic in its active and formative but also its transformational processes'. On the same page he also writes:

The finite but significant openness of many works of art, as signifying forms making possible but also requiring persistent and variable signifying responses, is then especially relevant.

The second formulation *might* lead to an articulation of why reading literature might be not only a matter of 'evidence'—as, say, listening to the Archduke Trio is not only a matter of hearing evidence about the declining role of Archdukes in the Habsburg Empire. But Williams has little to say in this direction. He is right to protest that

it is still difficult . . . to prevent any attempt at literary theory from being turned, almost *a priori*, into critical theory, as if the only major questions about literary production were variations on the question 'how do we judge?'

and he is right to remark that 'genre-classification . . . can indeed be left to academic and formalist studies'. But to leave literature as either 'evidence', in however complex a form, or as an object for genre-classification, is perhaps still to leave open the most difficult question of all in this area: why we should read (let alone 'bless') the poets in the first place.

In *Marxism and Literature* Williams has perhaps tried to achieve a magisterial position and tone, a bending of a massively complex debate towards a resolution that transcends current polemical standpoints. For his own 'struggle at the roots of the mind', here as elsewhere, he deserves and earns much more than respect. But the resolution he offers may be only a matter of sustained resolve, his solutions only verging on the brink of dissolution, his synthesis only a matter, finally, of proposing 'terms of analysis as terms of substance'. But, to adapt yet another formulation from his own book,

this specific solution is never mere flux. It is a structured formation which, because it is at the very edge of semantic availability, has many of the characteristics of a pre-formation, until specific articulations—new semantic figures—are discovered in material practice.

Perhaps, however, until such 'new semantic figures' are made, in practice, aspiring critics and writers of this generation, 'Marxist' or otherwise, may still be left pondering bleakly those lines from Auden's *Homage to Clio*—and applying them ruefully to themselves:

> I dare not ask if you bless the poets
> For you do not look as if you ever read them
> Nor can I see a reason why you should.

Brontë's Entrée: A Note and a Query
On First Getting into Wuthering Heights

Emily Brontë's *Wuthering Heights* (1847) opens:

1801——I have just returned from a visit to my landlord

Why this opening? Why this date?

There is an immediate echo to that practice of writing 'to the minute' satirised by Fielding in *Shamela*; but that 'just' signals that we, the reader, have actually *missed* the 'minute' that is really important: it is not the return but the visit that intrigues us as we read this opening sentence. It seems, already, that we have arrived too late for the very first incident. The book seems already to have preceded us—and itself. But this is not *quite* a familiar plunge *in medias res*, since we soon discover that this was the *first* visit; like the narrator, we are *about* to embark on a new experience—except that he has already embarked, has already gone and made his visit, and returned to tell us all, whereas we are already one tiny step behind, a fraction tardy. It is that '1801' which serves to emphasise our slightly late arrival: it is as if we had just missed a whole century (the new one being rather too infant to offer a great deal as yet); behind '1801' stretches that enigmatic and mystery-filled line: 1799, 1798, 1797, ever receding further from our view. We are caught in history, stranded between two histories, one dead, the other barely born. '1800' would have been too much of a blank, at best an ambiguous threshold, a Janus moment; 1801 *confirms* our having missed a good deal, by as good as a century.

As we continue down the page, we are brought constantly to thresholds, as we arrive at the moment of the visit—to realise that it was nearly never made at all. It takes a certain 'perseverance' to push one's way, against surliness, clenched teeth, gates and barriers, into Wuthering Heights; but it is precisely the resistance that impels our progress:

The 'walk in' was uttered with closed teeth, and expressed the sentiment, 'Go to the Deuce'; even the gate over which he leant manifested no sympathising movement to the words; and I think that circumstance determined me to accept the invitation; I felt interested in a man who seemed more exaggeratedly reserved than myself.

When he saw my horse's breast fairly pushing the barrier, he did pull out his hand to unchain it, and then sullenly preceded me up the causeway, calling, as we entered the court.

Having got as far as the court, we pause to know where we are, and why 'Wuthering'. But then we further pause, to register another date:

Before passing the threshold, I paused to admire a quantity of grotesque carving lavished over the front, and especially about the principal door; above which, among a wilderness of crumbling griffins and shameless little boys, I detected the date '1500', and the name 'Hareton Earnshaw'. I would have made a few comments, and requested a short history of the place from the surly owner; but his attitude at the door appeared to demand my speedy entrance, or complete departure, and I had no desire to aggravate his impatience previous to inspecting the penetralium.

Like '1500', we can face either way, backwards or forwards into two rather different worlds; we are at a watershed between two life-styles. And hovering over that final noun is a sense, also, of *penetrate* which is to become slowly more apposite as we continue to probe gently forward into this tale of frustrated sexuality.

However, by now, we may feel that we have arrived; the pace quickens:

One step brought us into the family sitting-room, without any introductory lobby or passage; they call it here 'the house' pre-eminently.

We seem to be past the palimpsest of introductory passages; we begin to be introduced to the characters in more detail: Mr Heathcliff and the narrator himself, with his touchingly pathetic tale of unrequited and nervous romance. But then within a page both the visit and the chapter are over—and nothing of any great significance seems to have happened. Perhaps we didn't miss very much after all? As the chapter ends with the narrator deciding to make a second visit ('I shall go, nevertheless'), we can feel that we may be *about* to catch up with the story.

But chapter 2 opens: 'Yesterday'. Since that second visit was still in the future, perhaps it is now already over, and the blank space between the chapters covers it from us. We are momentarily re-assured: 'I had half a mind' not to go—but thresholds intervene again:

on mounting the stairs with this lazy intention, and stepping into the room, I saw a servant girl on her knees, surrounded by brushes, and coal scuttles, and raising an infernal dust as she extinguished the flames with heaps of cinders.

And the narrator departs for Wuthering Heights again—again, however, in the past tense. And again he has difficulties with chains, gates, doors, and refusals of entry—until a young man finally leads him, via a wash-house, into the same 'large, warm, cheerful apartment'. This time we have entered to find: a woman. And there new barriers appear:

I bowed and waited, thinking she would bid me take a seat. She looked at me, leaning back in her chair, and remained motionless and mute.
'Rough weather!' I remarked. 'I'm afraid, Mrs Heathcliff, the door must bear the consequence of your servants' leisure attendance; I had hard work to make them hear me!'
She never opened her mouth.

The narrator's attempts to break down this social barrier, to effect a polite introduction, result only in blunders and *faux pas*—which so accumulate, indeed, that by the end of the chapter his one wish is to *leave* Wuthering Heights. But here too he is prevented: this time the barrier across the threshold is a natural one: a blizzard. After the humiliating failure of his attempt to get away, he is finally, as the chapter closes, 'ushered to bed' in Wuthering Heights. There, in chapter 3, we join him—in a rather peculiar bed. Like the jewel in the chinese boxes, the bed is inside a 'case' inside a room inside Wuthering Heights. And also inside the closet are books and writings. We read them with him: names on ledges, names on fly-leaves, scrawls on margins, scribbles on blank pages of books. Here we do seem finally to have caught up with 'I': we read along with him (a *reading* 'to the minute'?), as the page is filled with what he reads—except that he reads it 'Yesterday' (or is it the day before yesterday now? are we actually falling behind?). Then we penetrate even further into private recesses: we move into the world of his dreams—which thereupon re-enact and re-orchestrate the difficulties of being carried over thresholds:

my companion wearied me with constant reproaches that I had not brought a pilgrim's staff, telling me that I could never get into the house without one, and boastfully flourishing a heavy-headed cudgel, which I understood to be so denominated.
For a moment I considered it absurd that I should need such a weapon to gain admittance into my own residence.

No weapon is needed to gain entrance however. Instead we come, suddenly, to a strange chapel in a hollow—to hear an endless, interminable sermon divided into 490 parts, 70 times 7, at the end of each of which he tries to depart. But the sermon then transgresses its own rule of arrangement; with the 'First of the Seventy-First', the crisis arrives—and the dreamer awakes. Only to relapse into another dream of entrances:

'Let me in—let me in!'

says Catherine Linton at the lintel. And only books can block up that hole in the pane.

Once Heathcliff has taken his place in the bedchamber, Mr Lockwood (for now he is given a name) descends cautiously 'to the lower regions' and finds himself back at the fire, now only a 'gleam'. As soon as possible he returns to his own lodging—and to the secure warmth of the fire the servant girl had been preparing when chapter 2 first opened. (Though even getting back to his own place is a lengthy and difficult business, a cold trudge through deep damp snow.)

In chapter 4 we are secure. For perhaps a page or so we seem to be up to date (but is this all still 'Yesterday'? when does Mr Lockwood *write* for us?): the motherly Mrs Dean arrives to minister to the exhausted narrator. And launches into her own story of past times ('waiting no further invitation') —precisely the story that precedes the opening. We listen, this time, with Lockwood. For twenty pages. Then the tale is broken off, interrupted by Mrs Dean herself, and we are reminded of the time it took—it is way past bedtime. Despite her protests Lockwood insists that Mrs Dean finish the course: he is hungry for more, with a fastidious and therefore intense hunger:

. . . One state resembles setting a hungry man down to a single dish, on which he may concentrate his entire appetite and do it justice; the other, introducing him to a table laid out by French cooks: he can perhaps extract as much enjoyment from the whole, but each part is a mere atom in his regard and remembrance.

Mrs Dean agrees to satisfy this slightly fetishistic appetite, and re-commences with a date:

43

instead of leaping three years, I will be content to pass to the next summer—the summer of 1778, that is nearly twenty-three years ago.

The gloss on the date reminds us that we still have a long way to go to get back to that '1801' where we began. Chapters 8 and 9 take us some little way—up to half-past-one on the morning of the fourth day.

But then, with chapter 10, we suddenly leap *forward*, some four weeks, weeks of 'torture, tossing and sickness'. And with this sickness we seem at last to be *almost*, as readers, *au courant* with *les actualités*. The reason for this sickness is partly that second visit to Wuthering Heights, so we are only faintly surprised when we read of a return visit:

Mr Heathcliff has just honoured me with a call.

But then that 'just' reminds us, once more, that we can never *quite* get up to date.

Clearly, the rest of *Wuthering Heights* continues with this game of chinese boxes and constantly procrastinated satisfaction; its construction remains one of embedding tales within tales, but by chapter 10 we have definitely 'got into' *Wuthering Heights*, even if it is mainly through the memories and good graces of Mrs Dean that, even now, we are allowed entrance into Wuthering Heights itself. We may, of course, feel that some of the features of the narrative-tense in these opening chapters betray merely the 'new' novelist feeling her way towards control of a familiar device, the normal past tense of the realist novelist; but it is worth asking how far Emily Brontë has deliberately built into her novel this whole opening sequence precisely as a pattern of frustrated entrances and exits, this 'preliminary' series of penetrations to the heart of the matter. For one of the problems that faces any writer, and any reader, is how to *begin*, how to get the fiction under way. By blocking the way initially Brontë seems to have set up a series of barriers we have to surmount, to push through. By beginning the tale just prior to our opening of the book, she arouses our curiosity at the same time as she partly frustrates it; and we, in trying to get back, drive forward, but that forward is always another step back (a rather Sternean thought!). It is—or can be—a seductive tactic for a novelist to adopt, and that tentative yet firm date '1801' is a beautifully appropriate 'come-on' to open with.

I want to conclude this note with two queries about possible influences. It would be interesting to know if Emily Brontë ever read Coleridge's *The Friend*. It had re-appeared in the year she was born (1818) and a young writer, attempting her first novel, might well have remembered reading in her childhood, or later, a striking passage from Section the First, Essay xi, of *The Friend*, 'Literature and the Public':

in the great theatre of Literature there are no authorized door-keepers: for our anonymous critics are self-elected. I shall not fear the charge of calumny if I add, that they have lost all credit with wise men, by unfair dealing: such as their refusal to receive an honest man's money, (that is, his argument) because they anticipate and dislike his opinion, while others of suspicious character and the most unseemly appearance, are suffered to pass without payment, or by virtue of *orders* which they have themselves distributed to known partisans.

Emily Brontë, particularly as a woman, may well have faced with some trepidation the task of penetrating, for the first time, the inner sanctum of 'Literature'—particularly when the pass was held by men. Her awareness of her difficulty was perhaps already signalled in her adoption of a male (or ambiguous?) pseudonym ('Ellis Bell'); entering literature, like entering marriage, often involves, for a woman, a new public identity. It's possible that this passage from Coleridge, with its metaphor of reviewers as 'door-keepers', may have sown a seed of an idea in the budding novelist's mind: to set up, in her own novel and under her own skilful control, a series of doors and thresholds through which the reviewers would themselves have to pass before they could assess their satisfaction with her.

My second query is so extremely tentative as to seem bizarre. It seems quite probable that a later novelist, also socially marginalised in his own way, Thomas Hardy, read *Wuthering Heights*; one could easily suggest that his very interesting choice of date-line for his 'The Darkling Thrush' was due to considerations similar to those of Emily Brontë. He dates this poem, concerned with a moment of passage from one century to the next, and which ends

> . . . I could think there trembled through
> His happy good-night air
> Some blessed Hope, whereof he knew
> And I was unaware

not 31 December 1899 or 1 January 1900, but 31st December 1900. On such fine balances and choices a real sense of the ambiguities and possibilities of 'history' depends. But there is another example of this kind of response to a date, in a perhaps less expected source. In 1901 a young literary critic called Lev Bronstein (and nick-named 'The Pen') wrote a somewhat disorganised and over-rhetorical essay entitled 'On Optimism and Pessimism, on the Twentieth Century, and on Many Other Things'. In it we read this passage:

The nineteenth century has in many ways satisfied and has in even more ways deceived the hopes of the optimist. . . . It has compelled him to transfer most of his hopes to the twentieth century. Whenever the optimist was confronted by an atrocious fact, he exclaimed: What, and this can happen on the threshold of the twentieth century! When he drew wonderful pictures of the harmonious future, he placed them in the twentieth century.

And now that century has come! What has it brought with it at the outset?

In France—the poisonous foam of racial hatred; in Austria—nationalist strife; in South Africa—the agony of a tiny people, which is being murdered by a colossus; on the 'free' island itself—triumphant hymns to the victorious greed of jingoist jobbers; dramatic 'complications' in the east; rebellions of starving popular masses in Italy, Bulgaria, Rumania. . . . Hatred and murder, famine and blood. . . .

It seems as if the new century, this gigantic newcomer, were bent at the very moment of its appearance to drive the optimist into absolute pessimism and civic nirvana.

—Death to Utopia! Death to faith! Death to love! Death to hope! thunders the twentieth century in salvoes of fire and in the rumbling of guns.

—Surrender, you pathetic dreamer. Here I am, your long awaited twentieth century, your 'future'.

—No, replies the unhumbled optimist: You—you are only the *present*.

A year later Lev Bronstein assumed a new pseudonym and pen-name, the name of one of his former jailers in Odessa: Trotsky. I find it interesting to speculate whether Trotsky ever read *Wuthering Heights*, that novel of enormous passion published just before the *Communist Manifesto* and on the eve of the revolutions of 1848—and, if he did, what he made of it. Do any readers know?

ANOMOLETTUS

READING LITERARY RELATIONS

A Study of the Reproduction
of the Social Relations
of Production of Literature

A text-book for use in schools and colleges

by

ANNE ARTHUR, B.A., M.A., Ph.D.

Sometime Research Fellow, University of Cambridge
One-time Temporary Lecturer, University of the West Indies
Part-time Tutor, Workers' Educational Association

Theoretical Parody Publications Ltd.
London 1987

CONTENTS

FOREWORD

This book is intended as a major contribution to a hitherto largely-neglected field, that of the marxist theory of literature. So little of genuine worth has been written in this field that my own modest contribution can be said to break completely fresh ground. It is written mainly for sixth-formers and under-graduates, since they constitute the largest single market for this kind of book, but I will be grateful to any one at all who buys it, or, even more, to any one who assigns it for reading on a compulsory course. The various parts of the book can be read in almost any order. Some sections may be found to be too difficult, others too easy; the reader is free to skip both, but I will welcome any suggestions or critical comments, so that subsequent editions can be improved and thus made accessible to an even larger market.

A.A.
Miami, 1st May

PART ONE: ANTITHESES

Some years ago he had embarked with great enthusiasm on an ambitious critical project: a series of commentaries on Jane Austen which would work through the whole canon, one novel at a time, saying absolutely everything that could possibly be said about them. The idea was to be utterly exhaustive, to examine the novels from every conceivable angle, historical, biographical, rhetorical, mythical, Freudian, Jungian, existentialist, Marxist, structuralist, Christian-allegorical, ethical, exponential, linguistic, phenomenological, archetypal, you name it; so that when each commentary was written there would be simply *nothing further to say* about the novel in question. The object of the exercise, as he had often to explain with as much patience as he could muster, was not to enhance others' enjoyment and understanding of Jane Austen, still less to honour the novelist herself, but to put a definitive stop to the production of any further garbage on the subject. After Zapp, the rest would be silence.

David Lodge, *Changing Places*

PART ONE

Part I, Main Course, Introductory Lecture: Figures and Models of Marxist Literary Criticism

A precise or *clear* man, in conversation or in composition, has a very important consequential advantage—more especially in matters of logic. As he proceeds with his argument, the person addressed, exactly comprehending, for that reason, and often for that reason only, agrees. Few minds, in fact, can immediately perceive the distinction between the comprehension of a proposition and an agreement of the reason with the thing proposed. Pleased at comprehending, we often are so excited as to take it for granted that we assent. Luminous writers may thus indulge, for a long time, in pure sophistry, without being detected.

Edgar Allen Poe

Recommended reading:
MARX, Karl, *A Contribution to the Critique of Political Economy* (1971)
GOLDMANN, Lucien, *The Human Sciences and Philosophy* (1969)
GOLDMANN, Lucien, *The Hidden God* (1964)
EAGLETON, Terry, *Myths of Power: a Marxist study of the Brontës* (1975)
BENJAMIN, Walter, *Understanding Brecht* (1973)
EAGLETON, Terry, *Criticism and Ideology* (1976)
ALTHUSSER, LOUIS, *Lenin and Philosophy* (1971)
ARTHUR, Anne, *Reading Literary Relations* (1987)

Let me open by reading you an extract from Karl Marx's Preface to *A Contribution to the Critique of Political Economy*, published in 1859.

The general conclusion at which I arrived and which, once reached, became the guiding principle of my studies can be summarized as follows. In the social production of their existence, men inevitably enter into definite relations, which are independent of their will, namely relations of production appropriate to a given stage in the development of their material forces of production. The totality of these relations of production constitutes the economic structure of society, the real foundation, on which arises a legal and political superstructure and to which correspond definite forms of social consciousness. The mode of production of material life conditions the general process of social, political and intellectual life. It is not the consciousness of men that determines their existence, but their social existence that determines their consciousness. At a certain stage of development, the material productive forces of society come into conflict with the existing relations of production or—this merely expresses the same thing in legal terms—with the property relations within the framework of which they have operated hitherto. From forms of development of the productive forces these relations turn into their fetters. Then begins an era of social revolution. The changes in the economic foundation lead sooner or later to the transformation of the whole immense superstructure. In studying such transformations it is always necessary to distinguish between the material transformation of the economic conditions of production, which can be determined with the precision of natural science, and the legal, political, religious, artistic or philosophic—in short, ideological forms in which men become conscious of this conflict and fight it out. Just as one does not judge an individual by what he thinks about himself, so one cannot judge such a period of transformation by its consciousness, but, on the contrary, this consciousness must be explained from the contradictions of material life, from the conflict existing between the social forces of production and the relations of production. No social order is ever destroyed before all the productive forces for which it is sufficient have been developed, and new superior relations of production never replace older ones before the material conditions for their existence have matured within the framework of the old society.

Marxist literary criticism has been haunted by this passage. But only by selected sentences of it. Those sentences have tended to be simplified and misread, not so much in explicit exegesis as in practical application. Two sentences have been crucial. The first is:

The totality of these relations of production constitutes the economic structure of society, the real foundation, on which arises a legal and political superstructure, and to which correspond definite forms of social consciousness.

In practice, a number of simplifying reductions have been substituted for this formulation. The sentence is 'remembered' as, say:

'the economic structure of a society is the real foundation on which arises a superstructure and a corresponding form of consciousness.'

This in turn can then become a formula, a fixed relation between definite elements. The original sentence, thus doubly transmuted, can then be thought of and even rendered as a diagram, a four-term hierarchy in which each 'level' 'arises from' the one 'below' it. Thus:

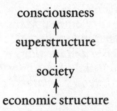

The relationship between these four labelled elements may then be acknowledged to be hazy. Are both 'economic structure' and 'society' to be included in 'the foundation', 'the base'? Or is the 'economic structure' the sole 'base' for a 'superstructure' which includes a loosely-defined 'society'? What precisely is the relation between 'superstructure' and 'consciousness'? How, overall, does the 'superstructure' relate to or 'correspond to' the 'base'?

At this point another selected phrase inserts itself:

the legal, political, religious, artistic or philosophic—in short, ideological forms.

This too is often rendered, more simply, as the single term: 'ideology'. Then the diagram can be readily modified, with 'ideology' replacing 'consciousness' in the four-tier hierarchy. The familiar but disabling formulae follow:– The economic base is 'real' and (or even because) it 'can be determined with the precision of natural science'. 'Marxism' can then be offered as the 'science' which gives a precise account of that 'economic base'. 'Ideology' is seen, by contrast, as a kind of illusion, a 'false' consciousness, neither itself offering a 'scientific' knowledge nor, quite, amenable to 'scientific' examination—since the second half of Marx's sentence peters out: there is no corresponding phrase to indicate that the 'ideological forms' can be 'determined with the precision of natural science'.

Then the second crucial sentence offers itself:

Just as one does not judge an individual by what he thinks about himself, so one cannot judge such a period of transformation by its consciousness, but, on the contrary, this consciousness must be explained from the contradictions of material life, from the conflict existing between the social forces of production and the relations of production.

Again, a selective, though more subtle, transformation of this sentence can insinuate itself. As a 'guiding principle' it can become something like:

'this consciousness must be explained from the contradictions of material life.'

Or more generally as:

'ideology is to be explained from contradictions in the (socio-)economic base.'

The royal road of 'Marxist method' is then declared open:– the 'ideological forms' can then also be 'determined with the precision of natural science', provided one can find a way of explaining those ideological forms by reference to the 'base' which can itself be scientifically accounted for by 'Marxism'.

But what then has happened to 'judging'? In Marx's own sentence a lop-sidedness was already apparent. One should not *judge* a period or an individual in terms of its or his consciousness. One should on the contrary *explain* a period's and an individual's consciousness in terms of its and his material life. But is explaining the same as judging? If marxist literary criticism, for example, is a matter of explaining, is it also a matter of 'judging'? Is marxist literary criticism a sub-branch of marxist history or marxist 'sociology', tying up a loose end, showing how 'even' literary works can be 'explained' by reference to 'the *ultimately* determining element in history' (to quote Engels writing to Bloch in September 1890)? Or, in another variation, is marxist literary criticism concerned with literary works as 'evidence' within a marxist analysis of the 'contradictions' in material life in a period? On either of these formulations the 'judgement' of literary works seems to be a different matter altogether. In any case, if one does not judge an individual by what he thinks about himself, how does an individual judge himself?

We can leave some of these questions on one side however. For *the* problem of marxist literary criticism has indeed tended to be seen as the problem of how one is to relate or connect a specific work of art, a particular literary text, to the 'society' or 'economic base' which has 'produced' it. The problem is seen as the closing of a gap between 'text' and 'society' by a series of causal levels or links in an explanation. Between the two pivotal terms other terms can be inserted in a kind of chain of 'mediations', thus:

society → class → ideology → author → conventions → text

The arrows in this chain indicate different and complex relations between the various mediating terms. These relations can be made clearer by re-arranging the chain as a diagram. This diagram gives us our *First Model* of 'marxist literary criticism', thus:

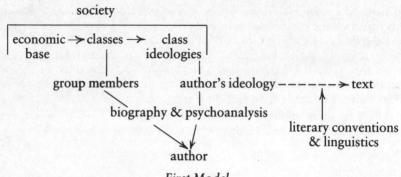

First Model

This First Model can be described as follows:—

(1) the economic structure of a society gives rise to 'classes', each of which is associated with a specific 'ideological form of consciousness';

(2) an author, by his insertion into a class (as a 'member' of a 'group' which is that 'class') or by a more mediated relationship to that class, has himself an 'ideological form of consciousness';

(3) one can explore the author's relation to a class and its 'ideology' by means of biographical evidence about (including perhaps psychoanalytical interpretation of) that author;

(4) his 'ideology' is 'expressed' or 'reflected in' his 'text', but that expression or reflection is also shaped by the 'relatively autonomous' contribution of the 'literary conventions' (and, on a different level, the linguistic features) which also characterise the text.

By tracing the links between these various 'mediations' one can finally establish the sought-for relationship between 'society' and 'text'.

But this kind of model has its problems. We can begin to explore them by asking first about one of the points of linkage in this diagram. What is the relation between the 'ideology' of an 'author' and the 'ideology' of a 'class'? The relationship is often seen as one of 'representativeness': that the author, in expressing the 'ideology' or 'world-view' of a class, offers a somehow peculiarly representative version of that world-view, a more articulated, coherent, or comprehensive working-out of that 'ideology'. If one asks 'more than what?', the comparison is then made with other expressions of that world-view by other 'representatives', by spokesmen or simply members of that class, in political speeches, essays, journalism, economic treatises, private letters, etc. These latter utterances are then sometimes offered as expressions of the 'real consciousness' of the class, while the artist's writing expresses the 'potential consciousness' of the class. That distinction rests ultimately upon the notion that the problems faced by 'the class' have a kind of 'ideal solution' which can best be articulated in fictional form, since the ideal solution is not available to the class in practical form. That ideal solution may then be itself analysed in terms of the contradictions it contains, and those contradictions, visible in the 'potential' synthesis, can be seen as resulting from the 'contradictory' position the class finds itself in within the system of economic relations which constitutes the infrastructure of a particular society.

This formulation implies that all members of a particular class face, in some sense, the 'same' basic problems, which can all be treated as, in the end, variations on one central problem: the location of the class itself within society. Then, since the author is himself a member of that class, he too faces those problems or that central problem. But the question then arises as to *why* a particular member of that class should have written a particular literary text in the first place: why *this* member wrote *this* text, why an individual found an 'ideal solution' to the problem(s) faced by the whole class, and found it by writing a text. At this point one has three options:–

(1) to leave a strange kind of gap in the chain of mediations;
(2) to take refuge in some circularly explanatory notion like 'genius';
(3) to have resort to very specific biographical explanations.

If the third of these strategies is adopted, a problem arises, since the more specific the biographical explanation is, the more difficult it becomes to claim a 'representativeness' for that individual's problems and solutions. The more a particular individual (say, Gustave Flaubert) is shown to be exceptional, unique, the more difficult it becomes to show, simultaneously, that the exception is a kind of norm, that Flaubert was, in some sense, a peculiarly 'representative' petty bourgeois.

What is at stake here theoretically is the very notion of 'class' as a 'group' composed of 'members'. If any one member can turn out to be 'representative' of the group, why could not any other member? If the 'solution' found by Flaubert was specific to Flaubert, if writing *Madame Bovary* was a specific answer to a set of specific questions which Flaubert faced (which can be explored at great length), why should not the specific 'solution' found by some other 'member' of the 'petty bourgeoisie' to *his* specific set of problems not equally be taken as 'representative': for example, in the literary sphere, the writing of a now-forgotten novel, or, in the 'practical' sphere, premature retirement from business?

What is therefore also involved is the status attributed to the literary work of Flaubert. Either the comparison between *Madame Bovary* and, say, Monsieur Desmoulins's premature retirement is a matter of usable 'evidence' (we can 'use' *Madame Bovary* as evidence in a way that we cannot with some other 'solutions'), or it is a matter of a 'judgement' of some kind between two 'solutions'—specifically, as between two novels that one is somehow 'better' than the other. But this second comparison either turns round in a circle (one is better than the other because it is more representative) or is a variation on the suitability of the text as evidence (another variation on the circle of representativeness: a better solution). Any third option introduces an element which seems to escape the chain of 'explanation' in this First Model: the problem of 'literary judgement', of whether one novel is better than another 'as literature'. A kind of sleight-of-hand can occur at this point, a collapsing of one question into another by a circular answer: a specific literary work can be claimed to be

61

'better as literature' than another *because* it expresses or contains a 'better' or 'more representative' solution to a class's problems. Thereby the whole chain of 'explanation' becomes almost a tautology: because an author wrote a work which, in expressing or formulating a better solution, is a better work of literature, that better author is more representative of his class, because he wrote a work which offers a more representative solution, so the problems which brought him to write that work were representative problems.

In analysing the texts and problems (or life) of a 'good' writer we are therefore necessarily analysing the (most?) representative problems of his class. The way is then open to a familiar kind of marxist preoccupation: with 'literary criticism', and with a criticism which focusses upon literary figures and works already acknowledged as 'great'. Even marxist history can then tend to become a branch of marxist literary criticism. Indeed, for a couple of generations 'literary' or 'cultural' criticism became almost the dominant mode in which marxist theory was articulated and developed in Western Europe.

A work of marxist literary criticism written in accordance with this First Model will often *present itself* in terms of a chain of explanation that stretches *from* 'base' *to* 'text'. But the working principle of any research actually conducted according to this model would seem, necessarily, to *begin* from the *text*, from a pre-judgement of the worth of the text, or from the author whose corpus of texts constitutes, inexorably, the culminating focus of the presented analysis. Actually to begin from the contradictions in the 'economic base' would raise, methodologically, the precise question such a model evades: who is 'representative' of a 'class'? (Formulations of method in terms of dialectical oscillation do not resolve the problem, since the dialectical movement occurs between two fixed points, both of which have been pre-selected, one of them by means of 'literary judgement'.)

The skeleton of this model can be clearly discerned in the extract from Lucien Goldmann I have handed out. The extract is from his *The Human Sciences and Philosophy*, pages 109 to 111 in the Cape paperback edition. The same problems are visible on a much larger scale in his *The Hidden God*, which you can consult in the library.

I draw your attention to this passage from Goldmann because it also discloses certain other problems to which I may return. One immediate problem is clear enough. In this summary passage there is almost no mention of the biographical relation of, for example, Pascal to the *noblesse de robe*. (The problems of that biographical connection are partly explored in chapter 7 of *The Hidden God*.) What happens instead is that the 'central idea' of Pascal's *Pensées* is juxtaposed, within the syntax of the first paragraph in the extract, to the 'tragic vision' of the *noblesse de robe*: ,

it is this class in France which developed the tragic vision wherein man appears torn between two contradictory claims that the world prevents him from reconciling. This is the central idea of Pascal's *Pensées* and of Racine's tragedies. Man is both great and weak. Great by virtue of his consciousness, his demand for totality and absoluteness; weak by virtue of the inadequacy of his powers to realise this demand. A 'reed', but 'a thinking reed'.

There are two points to be made about this juxtaposition. First, that the 'author' thereby evaporates, disappears from the argument to become simply the name on the spine of a book. Second, that book is then presented as a set of ideas, a series of propositions which can be summarised in a few lines. Insofar as the biography of the author is absent, a 'gap' in the chain of effects appears: a short-circuit is made between two other elements in the model: between 'class ideology' and 'text', or even between 'class contradictions' and 'text'. The advantages of this short-circuit are clear. The critic can leave open the question of the author's relation to the 'class' whose world-view is articulated in the text. The issue of biographical membership can then be left aside. The author can be postulated as simply expressing a viewpoint which he may or may not 'personally' 'share'. But if the biographical author is 'omitted', we are left with the text—and how is that to be regarded? The *dis*advantage of this omission becomes clearer if we consider another example of this approach in a particular critical work.

Terry Eagleton's *Myths of Power: a Marxist study of the Brontës* does not, at first sight, seem to 'omit' the 'author'. His introductory chapter tries specifically to place the Brontë sisters in a particular socio-economic and geographical location. Look at the first extract from Eagleton for yourselves. It's from pages 7 to 9 of his book.

Though Eagleton comes close in that passage to a *rhetorically persuasive* dissolution of the problem of 'representativeness', so that 'the Brontës' "eccentric" situation begins to seem curiously typical'—note the phrasing there—it seems to have peculiarly little bearing upon the rest of his book. For when he asks the more fundamental methodological question, his answer seems to short-circuit this biographical link. I quote:

Salutary though a reminder of the Brontës' historical situation may be, it leaves in suspension the problem of critical method—of how the fiction is to be rooted in, without being reduced to, specific social conditions. It seems clear that the connection we are pursuing here cannot consist in the mere relating of empirical literary facts to empirical social facts—cannot, that is to say, be simply a crude one-to-one correlation of literary and social detail, in the manner of some vulgar literary sociology. What must be in question here is some concept of *structure*. I am concerned in this study to identify in the Brontës' fiction a recurrent 'categorial structure' of roles, values and relations, and, since this informing structure seems to me distinctly ideological, to claim this as a primary mediation between the novels and society, a crucial nexus between fiction and history. I take the phrase 'categorial structure' from the Marxist critic Lucien Goldmann, who uses it to designate those shared categories which inform apparently heterogeneous works, and shape the consciousness of the particular social group or class which produces them. . . . By 'categorial structure', then, I seek to identify the inner ideological structure of a work, and to expose its relations both to what we call 'literary form' and to an actual history.

If we move from this passage to a later one, the implications of this paragraph are clearer. Chapter 5 is entitled 'The structure of Charlotte Brontë's fiction' and it opens with a summary version of the analyses given in the previous chapters. Again I quote:

The fundamental structure of Charlotte's novels is a triadic one: it is determined by a complex play of power-relations between a protagonist, a 'Romantic-radical', and an autocratic conservative. In *Jane Eyre* these roles are fulfilled respectively by Jane, Rochester and St John Rivers; in *The Professor* by William Crimsworth, Yorke Hunsden and Edward Crimsworth; in *Shirley* by Caroline Helstone, Shirley Keeldar and Robert Moore; and in *Vilette* by Lucy Snowe, Paul Emmanuel and Madame Beck.

From this it should be clear that what Eagleton means by a 'categorial structure' is something that can be rendered almost as a diagram of roles and functions, of tensions and contradictions. The text of each novel is seen primarily (in its 'deep structure') as a space, almost a pictorial two-dimensional space, or as an object with a specific shape. In the case of Charlotte Brontë that shape is a triangle:

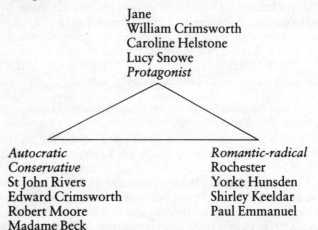

Jane
William Crimsworth
Caroline Helstone
Lucy Snowe
Protagonist

Autocratic	*Romantic-radical*
Conservative	Rochester
St John Rivers	Yorke Hunsden
Edward Crimsworth	Shirley Keeldar
Robert Moore	Paul Emmanuel
Madame Beck	

This structure or shape is then offered as more or less exactly congruent with the shape or structure of class-relations in the actual society. The 'power-relations' depicted in the text and the power-relations analysed in the society are not merely juxtaposed but potentially superimposed one on the other. Since it is the shape that is significant we can put, at any particular corner of the triangle in the diagram, not only a fictional character but also a 'real' representative of a 'real' class or fraction. It is not on the 'characters' or on the 'representatives' that the emphasis falls, but rather on the structure of relationships that link them.

This is, indeed, somewhat closer to part of Marx's formulation in the 1859 Preface:

In the social production of their existence men inevitably enter into definite relations, which are independent of their will.

But such an emphasis on 'structure' has its own problems. First, it does not seem to solve very satisfactorily the problem of 'connecting' Brontë's novels to the 1830s and 1840s as the time or conditions of their *production*, since a novel written in the 1970s *about* the West Riding in the 1830s and 1840s could presumably employ the 'same' basic shape or structure. Second, such a critical strategy can lead to a sense of the novel (and the 'society'?) as basically a static diagram, as something for which a summary or pictorial pattern can, finally, be substituted by the critic. Such criticism can then be accused of 'reductionism' and enough examples of that can indeed be held as hostages.

Such an approach can be distinctly reminiscent of an older form of novel-criticism, in which literary texts are presented in terms of 'themes', 'motifs' or 'ideas'. Goldmann's summary of Racine's plays as a set of 'ideas' directly comparable to Pascal's philosophical *pensées*, quoted earlier, is a case in point, and I've also included on the hand-outs a long extract from Marx's letter to Lassalle, 19th April 1859, which also exemplifies a similarly 'diagrammatic' approach. (Note that the letter was written in the year the Preface was published.)

The main problem about this method of criticism can be highlighted by reading you a passage from a music critic, Charles Rosen, in his *The Classical Style*:

In too much writing on music, a work appears like a large system of interrelationships in which the order, the intensity, and, above all, the direction of the relations are of secondary and even negligible, consideration. Too often, the music could be played backward without affecting the analysis in any significant way. This is to treat music as a spatial art. Yet the movement from past to future is more significant in music than the movement from left to right in a picture. That is why so many analyses of motivic structure are difficult to relate, not only to what is heard, but also to the *act* of listening; there is a difference between what one *can* hear, and how one listens.

This should remind you that a novel is *read*, in a movement in time. But what I have been calling 'diagrammatic criticism' tends to operate only upon the text conceived of as 'already read', as a completed work which we look back upon and the shape of which we then perceive as if we looked at the whole simultaneously. The obverse of this point is that such criticism tends also to treat the work as 'already written', as a text 'always' in a finished state, having already left the hands of its author. The author and the process of actually writing or reading the text can easily disappear, leaving the text as an object or structure in its own right, to be then related directly to the 'society'.

Eagleton's book on the Brontës partly exemplifies this. After the introduction locating the Brontës in their overdetermined social niche, the chapters that follow are focussed on the internal structure of specific texts. The result of this arrangement is that 'between' the introduction and chapter 1, on *Jane Eyre*, there seems to be simply a blank, a sudden shift in critical method, a total change of focus. The reader of Eagleton's book has then to be prepared to 'hold' the whole text of each novel in suspension, alert to enter it at any point which will yield a critical insight. The chapter on *Jane Eyre* begins:

Helen Burns, the saintly schoolgirl of *Jane Eyre*, has an interestingly ambivalent attitude to the execution of Charles I.

This is hardly the *first* thing that strikes a reader of *Jane Eyre*! To highlight such a detail is a tactic or mode of approach which, of course, Eagleton shares with many other critics, marxist and non-marxist.

The problems of 'the author' and of the process of writing do not disappear entirely from Eagleton's book. In chapter 5 he returns to them explicitly:

What is the relation between the 'structure' of an author's world-view and the 'structure' of his fiction? My own view is that the second is a mediated embodiment of the first—that a categorial structure creates or refashions the literary forms appropriate to it, and that 'form' is in that sense a consequence of 'structure'. Not, of course, a mere epiphenomenon of structure. Charlotte Brontë, like any author, inherited a complex, relatively autonomous legacy of literacy forms, but only some of these forms sufficed to articulate her ideological vision.

And:

The chief formal problem of all Charlotte's novels is how to resolve the tension between 'Romance' and 'realism'—to resolve it not only as *theme* but as *writing*.

Eagleton sees the solution of this formal problem in the use of first-person narration, most particularly in *The Professor*. But it is interesting that he discusses this not with reference to Charlotte Brontë finding a solution but in terms of 'the novel' doing so. I'll give you four instances.

The Professor 'solves' this problem at a stroke by suppressing the secret recesses of anguish and self-doubt, choosing instead a mode of subjectivity which tends to absolute control over an apparently recalcitrant but in the end magically pliant world.

For the novel fully to admit the experience of suffering and solitude into its world would be for it to risk collapse; it is only by a constant deflection of those facts that it survives.

The novel's apparently crass insensitivity to its hero's complacency . . . signifies well enough what the book has to sacrifice.

It is as if the book is half-aware of its protagonist's flaws but resolves to appear oblivious.

Of course one could read these formulations simply as acceptable figures of speech. But the accumulative effect of them (to leave aside Eagleton's intention) is certainly to posit the text as author of itself, as solver of its own formal problems. Charlotte Brontë evaporates, leaving the 'text' as autonomous and self-contained, even if 'it' cannot quite resolve all its own formal contradictions.

That this way of speaking is congruent with a short-circuiting of the chain of effects in the First Model at one point is clear. The 'text' is related directly to 'class ideology' or 'class contradictions'. But it can also be indicative of an emphasis upon another link in the basic chain. The link in question here is that between 'conventions' and 'text'. Eagleton himself initially retains a three-element link: between 'author', 'conventions', and 'text':

Charlotte Brontë, like any author, inherited a complex, relatively autonomous legacy of literary forms, but only some of these forms sufficed to articulate her ideological vision.

But in then eliding the role of the 'author' and speaking of the 'text' as itself the agent of its own production, he comes close to treating the text as the field or space of interaction and combination of certain 'inherited' literary forms without the role of an inheriting author being methodologically required at all. This tendency has of course been taken further and theoretically elaborated by other critics, and by Eagleton himself in later work. Consider for example the language of this passage from *Criticism and Ideology*:

Criticism is not a passage from text to reader: its task is not to reproduce the text's self-understanding, to collude with its object in a conspiracy of eloquence. Its task is to show the text as it cannot know itself, to manifest those conditions of its making (inscribed in its very letter) about which it is necessarily silent. It is not just that the text knows some things and not others; it is rather that its very self-knowledge is the construction of a self-oblivion. To achieve such a showing, criticism must break with its ideological prehistory, situating itself outside the space of the text on the alternative terrain of scientific knowledge.

I shall perhaps return later in this course to some of the problems endemic to this tendency. I might indicate them here, crudely enough, by asking why and how 'the text' appears at all, if the 'author' is at best only a catalyst for the combination and fusion of diverse literary conventions in search of a textual home, six literary figures or devices in search of a typewriter.

A different kind of emphasis on this link between 'author', 'conventions', and 'text' has, however, been suggested, in a more specifically marxist context, by Walter Benjamin. He can lead us to our Second Model.

Benjamin begins his essay entitled 'The Author as Producer' (1934) by posing the question often skirted by marxist literary critics: the question of 'literary value', in relation to the problem of political 'commitment'. He formulates the familiar terms of this debate thus:

> *on the one hand* one must demand the right tendency (or commitment) from a writer's work, *on the other hand* one is entitled to expect his work to be of a high quality.

Benjamin's 'solution' to this problem is given in the quotations I've selected from the same essay:

(1) I should like to demonstrate to you that the tendency of a work of literature can be politically correct only if it is also correct in the literary sense. That means that the tendency which is politically correct includes a literary tendency. And let me add at once: this literary tendency, which is implicitly or explicitly included in every correct political tendency, this and nothing else makes up the quality of a work. It is because of this that the correct political tendency of a work extends also to its literary quality: because a political tendency which is correct comprises a literary tendency which is correct.

(2) By mentioning technique I have named the concept which makes literary products accessible to immediate social, and therefore materialist, analysis. At the same time, the concept of technique represents the dialectical starting-point from which the sterile dichotomy of form and content can be surmounted. And furthermore this concept of technique contains within itself an indication of the right way to determine the relationship between tendency and quality, which was the object of the original inquiry. If, then, we were entitled earlier on to say that the correct political tendency of a work includes its literary quality because it includes its literary tendency, we can now affirm more precisely that this literary tendency may consist in a progressive development of literary technique, or in a regressive one.

What *counts* as a 'progressive development of literary technique' is left to some extent merely implicit in the essay. But some possible indications are given in these passages:

(3) Brecht was the first to address to the intellectuals the far-reaching demand that they should not supply the production apparatus without, at the same time, within the limits of the possible, changing that apparatus in the direction of Socialism.

(4) the barriers of competence must be broken down by each of the productive forces they were created to separate, acting in concert. By experiencing his solidarity with the proletariat, the author as producer experiences, directly and simultaneously, his solidarity with certain other producers who, until then, meant little to him.

(5) *A writer who does not teach other writers teaches nobody.* The crucial point, therefore, is that a writer's production must have the character of a model: it must be able to instruct other writers in their production and, secondly, it must be able to place an improved apparatus at their disposal. This apparatus will be the better, the more consumers it brings in contact with the production process—in short, the more readers or spectators it turns into collaborators.

(6) You may have noticed that the reflections whose conclusions we are now nearing make only one demand on the writer: the demand to *think*, to reflect upon his position in the production

67

process. We can be sure that such thinking, *in the writers who matter*—that is to say the best technicians in their particular branches of the trade—will sooner or later lead them to confirm very soberly their solidarity with the proletariat.

(7) Aragon was therefore perfectly right when, in another context, he said: 'The revolutionary intellectual appears first of all and above everything else as a traitor to the class of his origin.' In a writer this betrayal consists in an attitude which transforms him, from a supplier of the production apparatus, into an engineer who sees his task in adapting that apparatus to the ends of the proletarian revolution....

Will he succeed in furthering the unification of the means of intellectual production? Does he see ways of organising the intellectual workers within their actual production process? Has he suggestions for changing the function of the novel, of drama, of poetry? The more completely he can address himself to these tasks, the more correct his thinking will be and, necessarily, the higher will be the technical quality of his work.

A number of strands can be disentangled from these extracts. In speaking of 'changing that apparatus in the direction of Socialism' and 'adapting that apparatus to the ends of the proletarian revolution', Benjamin leaves open *what* 'changes' might further the 'ends' of revolution and what those ends might be. The 'direction' that leads to 'Socialism' can be seen as rather more definitely specified in the notion of breaking down the 'barriers of competence' and 'furthering the unification of the means of intellectual production'. But in what precise sense such 'unification' necessarily indicates the 'direction of Socialism' is left unclear. Nor is it clear who, precisely, are to count as 'the best technicians' in the 'trade' of writing, nor why, 'necessarily', *thinking* about 'his position in the production process' will ensure that, ultimately, 'the higher will be the technical quality' of a writer's work. Hovering over all these formulations is a kind of tautology, in which 'the writers who matter' are 'the best technicians' who are those writers who teach other writers. This argument could be read as simply saying that such writers are good (they *matter*) because they 'develop' literary technique. But then one might ask in what sense the 'development of technique' associated with, say, Joyce, Eliot and Pound (from whom other writers have certainly learned) constituted a *politically* 'progressive' development. That all three *'thought'*, in some sense, about their 'position within the production process' is clear, but it is also clear that this thinking did not lead all three 'to confirm very soberly their solidarity with the proletariat'.

If we try to rescue Benjamin from this problem by asserting that their 'development of literary technique' did not fulfill the other criteria (breaking down the barriers of competence, turning readers into collaborators, etc.), then it may legitimately be asked why *these* criteria are the sole appropriate ones for the development of *literary* technique. There is, it seems, however, a certain lop-sidedness in Benjamin's formulations which allows him to slide past this problem. He specifies that 'the tendency which is politically correct includes a literary tendency' and that 'a political tendency which is correct comprises a literary tendency which is correct'. But note that these two formulations do *not* commit him, by reversal, to the view that all 'literary tendencies' which include a 'development' of literary technique are 'included in' a political tendency which is 'correct'. Benjamin's position therefore seems to allow him to acknowledge a certain asymmetry in the relationship of 'literary value' to 'political commitment'. A 'work which exhibits the right [political] tendency, must, of necessity, show every other quality as well': *this* formulation, he says, 'is correct'; but that does *not* imply that every work which shows literary quality 'must, of necessity' 'exhibit the right [political] tendency' as well.

But if this asymmetry is the case, then the apparent tightness of Benjamin's argument somewhat dissolves. He claims in Extract (2) that 'the concept of technique represents the dialectical starting-point from which the sterile dichotomy of form and content can be surmounted'. But this 'sterile' distinction between 'form' and 'content' seems never, finally, to be exorcised from the deeper layers of the essay. This problem can be posed by giving you this crucial passage:

(8) Instead of asking: what is the position of a work *vis-à-vis* the productive relations [sic] of its time, does it underwrite those relations, is it reactionary, or does it aspire to overthrow them, is it revolutionary?—instead of this question, or at any rate before this question, I should like to propose a different one. Before I ask: what is a work's position *vis-à-vis* the production relations of its time, I should like to ask: what is its position *within* them? This question concerns the function of a work within the literary production relations of its time. In other words, it is directly concerned with literary *technique*.

The hesitation in this passage—'instead of this question, or at any rate before this question'—indicates the problem. If, *on the one hand*, Benjamin is *substituting* the question of a work's 'function within the literary production relations' for the question of 'the position of the work *vis-à-vis* the social production relations', then it seems that his question can have two rather different kinds of answer. *Either* a work may develop the literary techniques of its time and thereby have a 'progressive' function 'within the literary production relations' yet *not* constitute a 'politically' progressive development of technique (Eliot's work may be a case in point). *Or* a work may be 'progressive' both politically and 'within the literary production relations' (Brecht's work would be a clear case of this). Given these two possibilities, the concepts of 'literary production relations' and of the 'function' of a work 'within' those relations would have to be considerably clarified in order to discriminate more cogently between the work of a Brecht and the work of an Eliot. If, *on the other hand*, in order to so discriminate Benjamin can have recourse to *another* 'different' question, as he seems to at one point—'Let us ask ourselves *whose interests were advanced by this technique*' (the emphasis here is mine)—then he seems to raise the problem of the *relation between* the first question ('a work's position vis-à-vis the production relations of its time, does it underwrite them . . . or does it aspire to overthrow them?') and the second question (a work's *function within* the *literary* production relations). The second question may then be asked *before* the other, but both questions still have to be asked, so the term 'instead' is ruled out. But in discussing both the 'function within' in terms of technique and the 'position vis-à-vis' in terms of 'whose interests' (underwriting or overthrowing), Benjamin would seem, despite his claim, to have to distinguish once again between something like 'form' and something like 'content'. But *any* distinction between 'form' and 'content' would seem to threaten the basis of Benjamin's argument in the essay, since one could then

69

envisage a work as having a politically progressive 'content' but a 'regressive' literary 'form'. It was precisely *that* combination which Benjamin began by wanting to exclude. The political reasons for this exclusion are clear from Extract (9):

(9) we are confronted with the fact—of which there has been no shortage of proof in Germany over the past decade—that the bourgeois apparatus of production and publication is capable of assimilating, indeed of propagating, an astonishing amount of revolutionary themes without ever seriously putting into question its own continued existence or that of the class which owns it. In any case this remains true so long as it is supplied by hacks, albeit revolutionary hacks. And I define a hack as a man who refuses as a matter of principle to improve the production apparatus and so prise it away from the ruling class for the benefit of Socialism.

In speaking of such writers as 'revolutionary hacks' and of their work as 'so-called left-wing literature' Benjamin raises directly, again, the question of the relation between 'the author' and his 'text'. It is clear from his whole analysis that the decisive criterion of even political progressiveness is to be located for Benjamin in the 'technique' of the text rather than in the 'opinions' of the writer. But the relation between the writer's 'consciousness' and his techniques is not at all clear. If the writer 'addresses himself to these tasks' (the unification of the means of intellectual production, the organising of intellectual workers, changing the function of the novel, etc.), 'the more correct his thinking will be and, necessarily, the higher will be the technical quality of his work'. In this formulation the improved 'technical quality' of the work seems to derive from the writer's 'thinking' and, presumably, practical questioning of his position within the production relations. Again, it is that (practical) questioning which 'will sooner or later lead him to confirm very soberly his solidarity with the proletariat'. Benjamin thereby suggests an extremely close (and 'dialectical') relation between practical thinking, the technique of the work, and class-solidarity.

Behind this tight interrelation one can see glimmering a considerable modification of the First Model of marxist *criticism* I have explored up to now. What is almost implied is a reversal of the *methodological direction* within that First Model. For if one wants to relate the 'text' to the 'society' in the light of Benjamin's argument, the methodological starting-point would have to be the *'technique'* of a work and its 'literary' progressiveness compared with other techniques. In schematic terms, one could envisage the *direction* of the analysis in terms of the arrows in this diagram of the Second Model:

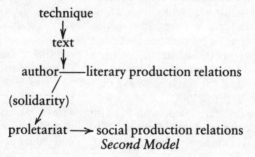

Second Model

70

The arrows in this diagram represent a line of 'mediations' in the process of analysis which 'links' the elements, but also, in some cases, a kind of causal relationship between some elements. It is the technique which 'makes' a text 'progressive'; the fact that the author of that text has 'produced' that progressive technique means that his (progressive?) position within the literary production relations involves him in or will *lead* him to 'solidarity' with the proletariat.

The difference between First Model and Second Model are interesting. The second model begins from a judgement of 'value' (the progressiveness of a literary technique), whereas the first model had difficulty in explicitly accommodating the question of 'value' at all. The First envisaged the relation between 'author' and 'class' as one of 'membership' of a 'group', whereas the Second seems rather to suggest a structural similarity of positions within different systems of production relations. It is not, however, clear whether this structural similarity can be equated with 'membership' of the *same group* (the 'author' as somehow a 'member' of the proletariat) but it does not seem to be a necessary implication. In the Second Model the text is not seen as 'expressing' the 'ideology' or 'consciousness' of the proletariat or any other group (and there seems therefore to be no problem of 'representativeness'). Rather, the text has to be seen as, if anything, involving the proletariat as 'collaborators' in its production. But this would imply a double-use, in rather different senses, of the term 'proletariat' and also, obviously, it raises the question of the relationship between the two sets of 'production relations'.

The questions raised so far indicate that this Second Model of marxist literary criticism suggests more problems than it solves. We can perhaps clarify some of them, and even begin to resolve them, by looking at a Third Model which can be seen as attempting to combine features of the first two.

In presenting, elaborating, and finally modifying this Third Model, I shall continue to make use of various blackboard diagrams. There is a danger in this form of schematisation: that of hypostasising the elements pictorially represented. But I intend them simply as instruments for thinking through certain quite complex theoretical problems. The simplifications involved will, I hope, be to some extent corrected as the argument proceeds, and as you do your own thinking during the course.

At a conference recently Terry Eagleton presented a basic diagram of the position which he has since elaborated in chapter 2 of his *Criticism and Ideology*. I'll begin from Eagleton's diagram on that occasion, and label it Third Model.

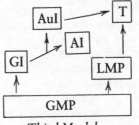

Third Model

The abbreviations here are:

GMP: General Mode of Production
LMP: Literary Mode of Production
GI: General Ideology
AI: Aesthetic Ideology
AuI: Authorial Ideology
T: Text

The relations between these elements, or terms, can be glossed as follows:

—The GMP of any social formation (or 'society') covers what one might describe as the general way in which the processes of production are organised in any particular society;
—The LMP denotes the particular ways in which the production of literature is organised in that society;
—GI denotes what has generally been referred to in marxist terminology simply as 'ideology', and this is pictured a 'arising from' the GMP;
—AI refers to the specific ways in which the area of 'the aesthetic' is articulated in a particular society, and this is seen as 'arising from' and linked to GI;
—Authorial Ideology (AuI) is related both to GI and to AI, and both AuI and LMP contribute to the constitution of the literary text (T).

Clearly, I am very much simplifying Eagleton's own more complex account in *Criticism and Ideology*. But I am doing so in order to leave open the possibility of gradual refinement in a direction which modifies and finally departs from Eagleton's own model, even in its more elaborated form. From now on, therefore, nothing I say should be attributed to Eagleton himself. Two amendments and two queries can immediately be offered.

Amendment 1: 'Within' GMP one can distinguish between Relations of Production (RP) and Material Forces of Production (MFP).

Amendment 2: If GMP and LMP are 'parallel' terms one could therefore suggest that 'within' the LMP there would be Literary Relations of Production (LRP) and Literary Material Forces of Production (LMFP). The precise meaning of these terms, if they have any, and the relationship between GMP and LMP can be left, for the moment, unclear (as in Second Model).

Query 1: If there is a specifiable LMP could there also be, say, an Educational Mode of Production, a Religious Mode of Production, a Sporting Mode of Production, etc. ? In other words, is the LMP distinct from the GMP in ways in which other areas of activity (or 'production'?) are not? This is a variant on the problem of parallel vocabulary: is 'production' in the phrase LMP more than a metaphor or analogue?

Query 2: This concerns what may seem initially a rather simple possible addition to the model. If the 'author' is present in the model in the form of AuI, could the 'reader' be present in the form of ReI? Or is 'Reader Ideology' simply to be included within Aesthetic Ideology? Or even simply included within GI? What is seen to be problematic by raising the question of the 'reader' is the precise relations between 'the author', AuI, AI, and GI and whether similar relations (whatever they are) would obtain between 'the reader', ReI, AI, and GI. If not, why not?

We can pursue first the implications of this second query.

In terms of the First Model, which also 'omitted' the 'reader', the question of the author and his relation to ideology was seen in terms of the author's membership of a class, the class-ideology of which he shared and articulated. 'Classes' do not appear in the Third Model so far. One could perhaps conceive of 'classes' as, in some sense, generated by or as aspects of the General Relations of Production. One might diagram this connection thus:

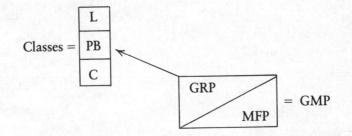

Abbreviations are:

    L stands for Labour or working class
    PB stands for Petty Bourgeois class
    C stand for Capitalist class

In terms of the First Model one could then place, say, Charlotte Brontë (CB) 'within' the PB category or box. But what then would be the relation between CB as PB and CB as 'author'? Moreover, what is the relation between CB (as PB and/or as 'author') and the LMP? If the LMP includes LRP do these also 'give rise to' what one would have to call 'Literary Classes'? But what would *they* be? And what would be the connections between 'the reader' and these 'Literary Classes', and between the Social Classes and the Literary Classes, and between the 'membership' of each (or both)? Does a 'Literary Class' have the same relation to the Literary Mode of Production as Social Classes have to the General Mode of Production?

Pursuing this line, one might ask further about the connections between GMP, Social Classes and GI (General Ideology). In terms of the First Model Social Classes would be a 'mediation' between GMP and GI, thus:

$$GI$$
$$\uparrow$$
$$Classes$$
$$\uparrow$$
$$GMP$$

But if we try to insert *this* pattern into the Third Model, where does AI fit? This raises in a different form the question of the relation between LMP and AI: does the LMP 'give rise to' AI (or perhaps to LI—'Literary Ideology') in the same way that GMP 'gives rise to' GI?

The problem here revolves round the relationship between GMP and GI and the meaning of both terms. We can try to clarify each of them separately and if possible return later to their interconnection. I will therefore offer two *clarifications*.

Clarification 1: 'Ideology'
An essay by Louis Althusser called 'Ideology and Ideological State Apparatuses' has suggested one way of thinking about 'ideology'. Althusser proposes that we should think of 'ideology' in terms of specific 'Apparatuses', and he distinguishes between the 'Ideological State Apparatuses' (ISAs) and the Repressive State Apparatus (RSA). The ISAs are those institutional structures of a society which are characterised by forms of persuasion (schools, churches, trade unions, political parties, communications media, and channels of culture), whereas the RSA is made up of those institutions which rely upon coercion (army, police, prisons). Althusser sees the primary function of both ISAs and RSA as that of maintaining and 'reproducing' the Social Relations of Production, though the normal function of the RSA is to maintain the conditions in which the ISAs can perform this function of reproduction.

Leaving aside the details and the problems of Althusser's own exposition, I want to adopt and adapt his terminology (without either committing myself to the rest of Althusser or attributing to Althusser the rest of what I say), in order to try to make it compatible with the notion of GI in Third Model.

If we try to 'insert' the notion of different ISAs into the Third Model, we might then speak of a Religious Apparatus and its accompanying Religious Ideology, an Educational Apparatus and its Educational Ideology, etc. One could then diagram 'GI' in more detail, thus:

Rel. App.	Rel. Ideol.
Educ. App.	Educ. Ideol.
Pol. App.	Pol. Ideol.
Cult. App.	Cult. Ideol.

= 'GI'

etc.

'Aesthetic Ideology' could then be located 'within' the 'Cultural Ideology' of the 'Cultural Apparatus'. But would that mean that 'within' Cultural Ideology, and further within Aesthetic Ideology, we could specify a 'Literary Ideology'? But in that case, would not Eagleton's 'LMP' be a corresponding element *'within'* the Cultural *Apparatus*? This might further imply that each Ideological Apparatus also includes an appropriate 'Mode of Production'. One would then have to speak of a Religious Mode of Production, an Educational Mode of Production, a Trade Union Mode of Production, and so on. (Remember *Query 1* earlier). But then the apparent 'parallel' between 'LMP' and 'GMP' in the Third Model would break down completely, since GMP *'gives rise to'* GI but is

74

certainly not *'within'* it in the way that it now appears that 'LMP' *is* 'within' 'Aesthetic Ideology'.

Clarification 2: 'General Mode of Production'

We can perhaps clarify some of the problems raised in *Clarification 1* by looking more closely at the notion of 'the GMP' and by concentrating first on the notion of 'production'. If I can speak, for my present purposes, of 'making a chair' as 'producing a chair', then the simplest way in which to envisage the basic elements involved in this process of production is thus:

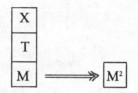

Diagram i

Abbreviations are:

X stands for the person making the chair;

M stands for the material X works on;

T stands for the techniques (of carpentry etc.) that X applies to that M in order to make the M into M²;

M² stands for the worked-upon-material, i.e. the chair.

The whole column (to be rendered/X/T/M) stands for the *action of making* ('X makes a chair', 'X applies T to M').

The double-arrows indicate that M₂ is the *product* of the *action* depicted in the column /X/T/M.

This basic pattern can obviously be elaborated on in familiar marxist terms. If X makes the chair for his own use, the chair can be said to have use-value (U-V) for him. But it may also have use-value for someone else (O Other). The chair might be given by X to O, or it might be bartered for something O has made (e.g. a table), in which case both the chair and the table would have an exchange-value (E-V). But the chair might be exchanged not for some *thing* (another M²) which O has made but for some service (an activity) which O offers to do for X. That service would then have a certain exchange-value for both X and O but a use-value only for X. X could however offer O not a chair but money (the general form of E-V) and the 'service' exchanged for that money could be for O to *make* something 'for' X. If what was made (M²) by O for X had a monetary value (E-V) for X which was greater than the money (E-V) given to O by X for making M², this exchange of O's work for X's money would result in an increase of money (of E-V) for X. One might risk calling the E-V which 'returns' to X as a result of this transaction 'E-V²'. (I hope you followed that. Would you like me to repeat it?)

The relationship between X and O sketched in this last transaction is clearly

75

that of Employer (E) and Worker (W) and one could diagrammatise the whole transaction thus:

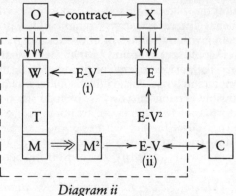

Diagram ii

Here the triple arrows indicate the taking up of positions within the whole system of the transaction;

C stands for Consumer (whoever it is that buys the product M_2);

The dotted-line box represents that area of the total transaction which can be termed the Relations of Production.

The 'relationship' between O and X is best understood as occurring 'prior' to their 'entering into' those Relations of Production, as a contract between them which 'gives rise to' the actual payment which occurs between and constitutes the basis of the 'relationship' between the Worker and the Employer. The term 'Material Forces of Production' (remember *Amendment 1*) might be seen as most clearly applying to M. But there are interesting problems here. 'T' has so far been used to denote 'Techniques', the *way* in which M is worked upon. But one could also extend 'T' to include also Tools (of whatever kind), the material instruments through which that work is carried out. Both T and M would thereby be included in the term MFP. Furthermore, insofar as the Worker is also a material force within this work-process the Worker too could be included within 'MFP'. (In some forms of work—e.g. 'heavy manual labour' —this is more obviously the case than in other forms of work.) That element of T which might more strictly be called Techniques can also be seen as a material force (e.g. the bodily skills of hand and eye of a lathe-turner).

Related to this point is that both M and T (as Tools at least) can be 'supplied' by X as Employer if X 'owns' both the required raw materials and the required manufacturing equipment. Equally, however, O could 'supply' not only T (as Techniques) but also the required tools and raw material if he were to 'own' them (e.g. an electrician supplying his own screwdrivers, or a home-weaver supplying his own material but using an employer's loom). But if O already *has all* the techniques, tools *and* materials necessary to produce M^2, there is no *need* for the contract with X in the first place in order to actually produce the product; there would be no need for an 'Employer' at all; M^2 can be produced and sold to C directly. This might still produce an increase in exchange-value for O, if E-V (ii) was greater than any 'costs' involved in 'using' and 'having' T and M in the first place. It is clear, then, that 'E' is a potentially *redundant* element within the whole transaction, and is 'necessary' only insofar as X is either supplier of T and/or M or as a required mediator between O and C. O could, logically, within this system of production relations, simply *'take the place of'* X if O could supply M and T for himself. What is clearly involved here is who 'owns' the various means of production in the first place, who can acquire them, and in what way. Thus the *Diagram ii* version of the 'GMP' is only one possible version of 'GMP'. The logically possible and historically actual transformations of *Diagram ii* are not my concern at this point, though we may return to some further features of the diagram later.

We have now tried to clarify the two terms 'GI' and 'GMP' in the Third Model. We can now try to clarify the relationship between them.

Clarification 3: Ideological Apparatuses and Relations of Production
It was suggested in *Clarification 1* and implied in *Query 1* that it might be a requirement of elaborating the notion of GI in Althusserian-influenced terms that we should speak in some sense of, say, an 'Educational Mode of Production' 'within' the Educational Apparatus. But would an Educational MP be analysable in the same terms as those used for the 'GMP' in *Clarification 2*? We can return here to the starting-point of that analysis of 'GMP'. If making or producing a table can be diagrammatised as in *Diagram i*, can the process of, say, 'teaching' be diagrammatised in a similar way. Could one suggest this as *Diagram iii*?

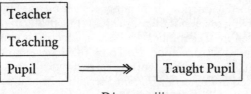

Diagram iii

But this apparent structural similarity is misleading, since if we revert to using 'X' and 'O', it is clear that their 'entering into' a teaching relationship could be diagrammatised as:

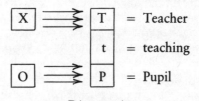

Diagram iv

77

Here O takes the place occupied by *Material* in the GMP *Diagram i*: the Other is, in some sense, the 'raw material' of the process of teaching. Since O does *not* take the place of M in the GMP structure it seems better to use a different shorthand for what occupies that position in the Educational MP in *Diagram iv*. Moreover, even though 'teaching' may involve 'techniques' and what might be called 'tools', since to retain the term 'T' as the term between Teacher and Pupil would also imply a closer similarity to the GMP process than has yet been established, it seems again preferable to use another term. For the moment, I shall use

    I instead of T, to indicate the subject of a sentence (I teach)
    P instead of t, to indicate a practice (the practice of teaching)
    Y instead of P, to indicate the 'object' of a sentence (I teach you).

One could then offer a general diagram for the various 'practices' that occur within and characterise the various Ideological Apparatuses, with I and Y designating certain roles or positions within those Apparatuses, for example those of Teacher and Pupil, Parent and Child, Priest and Congregation, etc. Thus:

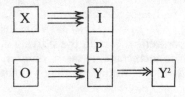

Diagram v

Before trying to elaborate this diagram, it is worth exploring another feature of the Ideological Apparatuses by raising a further question about the term 'ideology' itself. This will require a fourth 'clarification'.

Clarification 4: Ideology, Positions and Propositions

The term 'ideology' is most usually taken to refer to a set of beliefs, ideas or opinions. 'Ideology' would therefore refer, in the case of the Educational Apparatus, primarily to *what* is taught, to the content of courses or curricula, or, in the case of the Religious Apparatus, to the content of what is believed or preached. But it is possible to think of 'ideology' in rather different terms. I want to indicate this alternative by suggesting a fairly systematic vocabulary or terminology. (No lasting value is, however, intended for this terminology, outside of its function within this lecture.) Within an apparatus one can speak of:

(A) *Positions* (e.g. the 'position' of teacher, the position of pupil)
(B) *Propositions* (what is said, written, believed, thought, in that Apparatus).
    Propositions can include:
    (1) *Impositions:* Propositions which define, justify and account for the existence and distribution of the Positions within that Apparatus.

78

(2) *Expositions:* Propositions which make statements or convey attitudes, etc., concerning matters 'outside' that Apparatus.

A selective list of some possible kinds of Proposition and of related terms can
be offered:

A: 'Internal' to Apparatus

Positions: the reciprocal roles, functions, within apparatus
Practices: the activities specific to the apparatus

Propositions:

Impositions
Suppositions:	'definitions' of Positions
Presuppositions:	'definitions' of Practices (therefore of Positions)
Priorities:	'definitions' of the purposes of the Practices
Premises:	'definitions' of the purposes of the Apparatus (and therefore of its Practices, and Positions)
Paradigms:	an 'ideal image' of the Apparatus, in which Positions, Practices and Impositions cohere without strain or stress.

B: 'External' to Apparatus

Propositions made within the Apparatus with reference to another
Apparatus etc.

Expositions
Presentations:	conveying 'knowledge' or 'belief' or 'information'
Precepts:	endorsing the Practices of another Apparatus
Predispositions:	encouraging acceptance of Position-(ing) within another Apparatus. (These predispositions may become impositions within that other Apparatus.)

The terminological distinctions offered here are not meant to be either
comprehensive or particularly watertight. For example, one might add terms
like 'Preconceptions' (Expositional Presentations of one Apparatus appropriated by another Apparatus to support its own Presentations) or 'Models' (the
'ideal image' of some other Apparatus offered within an Apparatus by a
coherent combination of Expositions). But such a list is perhaps useful if it
highlights the *complexity* of the notion of 'ideology' and the corresponding
complexity of the possible interrelationships between different elements of
'ideology' and different apparatuses.

One aspect of the suggested terminology can lead us further into those complexities. In using these terms I am obviously bending certain familiar words. In particular, the word 'Proposition', covering both Impositions and Expositions, should *not* be taken as referring (only) to explicit statements. (It might even be better to use the term 'Pro-Positions'.) Particularly as regards Impositions, the Propositions *might* be *articulated as* statements or formulations, if, for example, an explicit challenge were offered concerning any Position or Practice. But in general 'Impositions' should be taken as referring *rather* to the structuring principles of the ethos of an apparatus: to 'enter into' a well-functioning apparatus is to be informed, imposed upon, shaped, positioned, by these *impositions in the actual working* of the apparatus. The 'internal social relations' of the apparatus are constituted by a constantly active and passive positioning in accordance with these explicit or implicit impositions; one could say that these 'Apparatus Relations' are constituted by the *structure of Positions*. The specific positions, practices and impositions of particular apparatuses could be considered in detail if we had more time; but a more general point can be made: that the constitutive apparatus relations of one apparatus may be more or less *congruent with, complementary to, compatible with, structurally analogous to*, or *homologous to* the constitutive apparatus relations of another apparatus or the relations of production in the GMP. Moreover it should be clear that those 'general' relations of production may themselves be the subject of implicit or explicit Impositions 'within' the process of production of the 'GMP' as well as the concern of the Expositions of various apparatuses. However, given the suggested terminology you should have no difficulty in extending and testing it for yourselves. All I want to do now is to make some very brief comments to highlight some of the implications of this alternative set of terms.

(a) The relation between the impositions and expositions of the various apparatuses may be one of consistency, compatibility, or interdependence with each other, both within and between apparatuses; or there may be various inconsistencies, incompatibilities, or contradictions.

(b) The emphasis in considering these interrelations between Ideological Apparatuses and Relations of Production often falls on explicit expositions (ultimately reducible to such 'core' ideological statements as 'Property is sacred'). But it is perhaps *primarily* in terms of the *impositioning* effected by apparatus relations that the contribution of the ideological apparatuses to reproducing the relations of production should be located. It is the *impositions* of an apparatus which can often be generalised as *predispositions* for positions and relations elsewhere.

(c) In particular, it is a characteristic feature of ideological apparatuses that the various positions within the apparatus constitute a hierarchy, some positions being 'defined' as *dominant* in relation to others, so that the dominant position (e.g. that of Teacher) is then seen as the 'active' pole of a power-relation, and the sub-dominant position (e.g. that of Pupil) as correspondingly passive.

(d) The suppositions and presuppositions can then serve to characterise this relative and uneven distribution of power as 'necessary', 'inevitable', or 'natural'. Since the apparatus itself *exists as* an organised structure of those positions and relations it becomes almost 'unthinkable' from *within* a well-functioning apparatus that such positions might be radically modifiable or unnecessary (e.g. that there could be an educational apparatus without the position of 'Teacher').

(e) One important aspect both of the hierarchisation and 'naturalness' of positions and one effect of impositions is a tendency for at least some occupants of the sub-dominant position to be impositioned as potential occupants of the dominant position within the same apparatus. Such impositioning can be regarded as instituting a *mirror-image relation* between dominant and sub-dominant positions: the pupil is impositioned as a mirror-reflection of the teacher, the child of the parent. The extent of such (selective) impositioning varies with each apparatus, but it may at times effect something akin to a replay of the mirror-phase for the occupant of the sub-dominant position ('his' mirror-image being now the 'teacher' who is already the achieved 'future' of the 'pupil').

(f) Anyone who accepts in practice (in the actual practices) the hierarchical positioning of apparatus relations tends then to be predispositioned to accept a congruent or parallel hierarchical positioning within another ideological apparatus or within general production relations, particularly insofar as explicit expositional predispositions reinforce this structural predispositioning.

At this point it might be worth trying to diagrammatise the analysis so far.

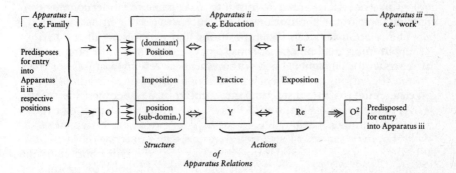

Diagram vi

Here the new abbreviations, Tr and Re, stand for Transmitter and Receiver of Expositions.

The column of Positions and Impositions *logically* 'precedes' the columns of Practices and Expositions, since those practices and expositions can be seen as 'arising from' the structure of positions. (Compare the role of the 'contract' in *Diagram ii.*) Obviously there is also a sense in which it is the *practices* which actually (in practice) 'position' the participants, though that positioning may have been prepared for by the predispositioning of another apparatus. Equally, the actual transmitting of and receiving of expositions occurs *as* a practice; the column of expositions has been singled out for clarity's sake. (It needs still to be remembered that these columns represent sentences of the form 'X *does* Y!)

'Entry into' the positions of an apparatus may also be brought about by coercion and those positions may also be maintained within an apparatus by a certain degree of coercion. But insofar as the Ideological Apparatuses are distinct from the Repressive Apparatus that distinction rests upon the relative importance and effectiveness of coercion; within an ideological apparatus coercion may achieve a 'formal' positioning but not effective positioning.

(*Parenthesis 1:* Insofar as the practices of an apparatus can be described as 'services', apparatus-relations might also take on the form of exchange-relations. (Remember *Clarification 2.*) For example, the pupil or some other agent such as the State might *employ* the teacher. The 'service' of teaching might also be seen as possibly 'producing' a 'product' with increased exchange-value: the pupil equipped with skills or techniques gained in the course of the teaching-process just conceivably *might* have a higher market-value than before. Such possible modes of 'insertion' into 'general' relations of production could easily be diagrammatised in detail, in accordance with *Diagram ii.* But I won't bore you with such refinements.)

What it *is* important to register at the moment is that these various clarifications have enabled us to see that what characterises an ideological apparatus is not a specific 'mode of production' but a *'mode of practice'* which constitutes the specific apparatus relations and positions. Insofar as ideological practices do have a 'product' that product is the *occupant* of one of the apparatus positions who has been *ideologised* by occupying it. Second, it is difficult not to conclude, in the light of these clarifications and considerations, that the notion of a 'Literary Mode of Production' in the Third Model was inadequate and confused. It is now time to return to literature.

We can return to 'literature' *via* a quotation from a rather interesting text:

MEMORANDUM OF AGREEMENT made this *1st* day of *April 1976* BETWEEN DR ANNE ARTHUR (hereinafter called 'the Author', which expression shall where the context admits include the Author's executors, administrators and assigns) of the one part and THEORETICAL PARODY PUBLICATIONS LTD., (hereinafter called 'the Publisher', which expression shall where the context admits include the Publisher's executors, and assigns or successors in business, as the case may be) of the other part WHEREBY it is mutually agreed between the parties hereto as follows:

1. The Author agrees to write the work at present entitled:
   Based on current work on 'The Social Relations of Production of the Literary Text'
2. The Author undertakes to deliver two copies of the final and complete typescript of the work ready for the printer and in house-style by *16 June 1979*.

. . . . .

6. The Publisher shall, unless prevented by war, strikes, lock-outs, or other circumstances beyond his control, produce and publish the work at his own risk and expense with reasonable promptitude. The Publisher shall have entire control of the publication; and the paper, printing, binding, jacket and embellishments, the manner and extent of advertisement, the number and

distribution of free copies for the Press or otherwise, and the price and terms of sale of the first or any subsequent edition, shall be in his sole discretion.

Even from this truncated extract it is clear that Anne Arthur (hereafter AA) has entered into an agreement with Theoretical Parody Publications Ltd. (hereafter BS, as the initials of the other signatory to the contract/Memorandum of Agreement). One could offer a diagram, along the lines of *Diagram ii*, to indicate the transaction thus commemorated:

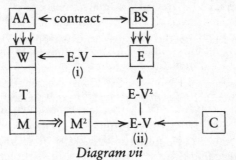

Diagram vii

M^2 would in this context stand for the 'product' of what I am currently writing; one might think of that product initially as a Manuscript. Insofar as you, for example, eventually read what I am writing you would occupy the position of C, presuming that you had bought your own copy of what I finally write. But of course you do not buy the manuscript (unless you are an American University Institute). So one has to insert another transaction into *Diagram vii*, thus:

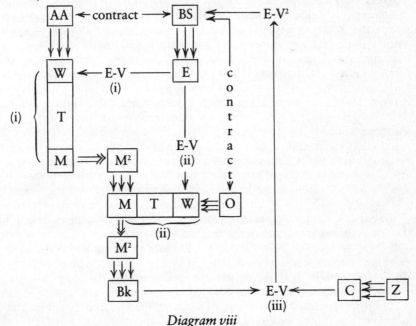

Diagram viii

Here, the column $/W/T/M/$(ii) represents the work of the *printers*, so that M(ii) is the material of their work, i.e. the manuscript which is the M^2 of column (i), while the M^2 of column (ii) is that manuscript as transformed by their work into the Book (Bk) which C actually buys (Z entering into this system of relations as C, as buyer).

Clearly this diagram could be transformed in various ways. There might be a direct 'contract' between AA and O (as in the case of eighteenth-century printer-publishers, or where AA has her manuscript published at her own expense, etc.). But leaving aside such transformations, the basic diagram needs some further comments and clarifications, and suggests some queries.

First, are the two columns of $/W/T/M/$ to be analysed in identical terms? If we consider $/W/T/M/$ (ii) first, the T here refers to various printing techniques, skills and tools and may include a certain element specified or supplied by E (remember clause 6 of the *Memorandum*). (I have, for simplicity's sake, presumed that BS also employs O, and therefore conflated two 'E' positions, although often BS will enter into another contract with X who 'supplies' W (ii) by employing O.) The M in $/W/T/M/$ (ii) is 'supplied' by the process in column (i), but is supplied *via* or because of the relation between W (i) and E. In that sense, one might claim that E also supplies M^2 (i) to column (ii).

In the case of $/W/T/M/$ (i), E may also supply various kinds of M (e.g. paper, illustrations) and even some elements of T (insofar as tools may include, e.g., a typewriter). But there are other elements in T (i) which W (i) supplies herself: what we can refer to for the moment as *'writing skills'*. There are also some elements in M (i) which W (i) supplies: what we can refer to for the moment as *'content'*.

At this point a clarification of the diagram might be useful. The *Memorandum* states in clause 1 that 'The Author agrees to write the work at present entitled: *Based on current work on "The Social Relations of Production of the Literary Test"*.' The grammatical hiccup in this formulation could be corrected, but the very problem this formulation pinpoints is that the Publisher may 'specify' the 'content' of a work but it is the Author who 'supplies' that content. Insofar as the relation between Author and Publisher includes this element of incomplete specification, one can consider certain variations: e.g. the more 'specific' the 'content' stipulated, the more one could speak of the Author as a *Hack* Author. One could make a similar point about T: the more certain writing 'skills' or 'techniques' are specified by the Publisher, the more, again, one might speak of the author as a hack. What is involved here is a *doubling* of positions: E can be seen as trying to a greater or lesser extent to 'occupy' the position of W. One might then compare this with certain relations of practice within ideological apparatuses—for example, where the pupil is treated as the mirror-image of the teacher.

If we now abstract from the Author-Publisher relation and presume that there is minimal specification of T and M by E, are we justified in speaking of $/W/T/M/$ (i) and $/W/T/M/$ (ii), of 'writing' and 'printing', in the same analytical terms? We can to some extent 'unpack' the abbreviations in column (ii)—into, say, editor, subeditor, designer, estimator, copy-preparer, keyboard operator, hand compositor, proofreader, etc. (for 'W'). The more we know about the

craft of printing, the more 'concrete' a description we can giv
authors, I have to admit my ignorance. (Benjamin's argı
relevant here.) But what kind of 'concrete description'
elements or terms in column (i)?

The problem here is best located in terms of M (i). If $M^?$
(or typescript), what is M (i)? What is the 'raw material'
by T (i) into M^2 (i)? In the case of the manuscript indicated by clause
Memorandum as the eventual result of Anne Arthur's labours, 'M' might be
variously described: in one sense, as previous books read by me (Lukacs,
Goldmann, Eagleton, Benjamin, etc.), or as notes, scribbles, drafts, jottings,
previously written by me, and particularly one specific previous manuscript of
mine (entitled *The Social Relations of Production of the Literary Text*). It is
tempting to locate the 'primary' 'raw material' finally 'embodied' in these
notes, etc., as 'ideas' (whether 'knowledge', 'opinions' or 'beliefs'). In this
particular case we could describe those 'ideas' in a variety of ways. One could
also 'judge' those ideas in a variety of ways. But one way of describing them
links back to some previous points. Insofar as those 'ideas' have been
developed within the context of the Educational Apparatus, they could be
described as Educational Apparatus *Expositions*: what I am writing could also
figure as *Presentations* in a lecture, for example. The 'Book' that is the final
product of the whole transaction of *Diagram viii* might, correspondingly, be
described as a 'text-book' for use within that Educational Apparatus.

Here we can introduce another modification of *Diagram viii*. If you look
again at that diagram, you might ask yourself where *you as reader* 'fit'. 'C'
denotes the purchaser of this Book, involved in a transaction with BS (which
probably occurs, of course, *via* another transaction and set of relations which
could be inserted into the diagram: between purchaser, bookseller, and 'E';
that system of relations could be further analysed.). But what is to be said of the
Reader rather than the Purchaser (since, for example, you may well not have
bought this book even though you are reading it)? And what is to be said of the
'relation', if any, between you, the 'reader', and me, 'the author'? If you were
attending a lecture given by me, the relationship would be an internal
(educational) apparatus relation and that could be analysed in terms of the
positions and relations constituted by that educational apparatus practice of
lecturing. (The practice of lecturing is, by the way, largely a redundant one
today, since the relations of intellectual production it exemplifies have been
rendered obsolete by developments in the material forces of educational
production—or so one might argue, in the light of Marx's 1859 Preface.) One
might therefore suggest that in reading this book you are being 'positioned' in a
mode analagous to the 'positioning' that occurs in attending (to) a lecture. One
might then speak of the Reader and Author of an educational text-book as
occupying TRANS-POSITIONS of the apparatus positions of Pupil and
Teacher. The 'relationship' between Reader and Author of such a text-book
might then be spoken of in terms of the *Transposed Practice* of the educational
apparatus. But where is that 'transposed practice' to be located? If 'Author' is a
transposition of Teacher, and Reader is a transposition of Pupil, one could
speak of the TEXT as a *transposition of a practice*. The Text can thereby be

...rly distinguished from the Book. The Book is a physical object, the product
of /W/T/M/ (ii); but the Text is not to be identified simply with that other
physical object the manuscript. The Text, in this terminology, might be
regarded as a *structure of impositions*: a *set of propositions* which constitute
'definitions' of the transposed positions (the Textual Positions) of the transposed practice. The terms 'propositions' and 'definitions' should here be taken
not so much as referring to 'statements' but rather as indicating 'designations':
though positions and practices are *able* to be 'defined' in verbal statements,
they can also be 'defined' or 'designated' (delimited, determined) *'in practice'*.
The overtones of 'in practice' are deliberate: it is in the *action* of a practice that
positions are primarily and most effectively designated or determined. But
there is also a sense in which statements or utterances can, in (their) effect, *be*
practical designations: the clearest cases are certain modes of address or
'interpellation', such as orders and commands. We might speak of such verbal
practices in terms of their *'propositioning'* of someone (and again the
overtones are deliberated ones).

But if we can now see that the M^2 of /W/T/M/ (i) is the *text* as a *set of
impositions*, a *combination of transposed practices*, as well as a set of
expositions, it is clear that 'T' denotes or includes the *activity of transforming*
certain apparatus practices into transposed practices and doing so by constructing a set of propositions *in language*, the effect of which will be to
'designate' the transposed positions. We might then speak of writing as a
(material) Technique which is *itself* transposed into a Practice, a way of
working with words, a way of working *on* written words, so that the particular
construction of words that results constitutes a written transposition of an
apparatus practice. We could call the result a *Textual Practice*. Equally, we
might say that *reading* is a *technique* of *reconstructing* the transposed positions
and practices designated in the propositions, a technique for *re-activating* the
Textual Practice.

(*Parenthesis 2: Linguistics* Any reader who is competent enough, or
interested enough, to do so may care to consider here the contribution that
linguistics might make to the study of how this trans(im)position(ing) is
achieved.)

Since both writing and reading are *activities* which occur in time, which take
time to perform, the trans-positionings that occur in the acts of writing and
reading are themselves *activities* of *construction*. In writing, the writer is
constructed as Author but that 'Author' is to be located only as the (re)con-
structed 'position' designated in the text. Equally, the one who reads is
constructed as 'Reader' only in the act of being pro-positioned by the text.
Clearly, this can be only a preliminary formulation. For the positions
designated in the practice of the text (the Textual Practice) may be 'designed' by
the writing as, say, transposed positions (Textual Positions) of 'Author =
Teacher' and 'Reader = Pupil'; but they may be *re-*constructed (or *de-*
constructed) in the reading as rather different transpositions—for example,
as 'Author = Pupil' and 'Reader = Examiner'. That is, the text may be
constructed as the transposed practice of delivering a lecture to a student,
but *re-constructed* as the transposed practice of a pupil submitting an

essay to a supervisor, or even (de-constructed) as the transposed practice of an insubordinate pupil parodying a lecturer.

Consideration of the possible complexities here can be postponed until next time, though the general point is an important one: that the text may 'posit' a particularly positioned Reader, but that positing may not be 'effective'. One reason for this lack of effectivity may be that the actual reader may not be *pre-dispositioned* to take up the position of the posited Reader. (For example, someone whose occupation positions him within the Educational Apparatus as 'Professor' is more predisposed to read *this* text from the transposed position of 'Examiner' rather than of 'Pupil'.) A variant of this situation is, of course, where a particular *Book* comprises *two Texts*, one of which *pre*-positions the actual reader into reading the other text from a particular Reader-position which may not be congruent with the implied Reader-position of the second text. (For example, a school-edition of a novel in which the Introduction or pre-text pre-(dis)positions the reader as 'Examinee'—thereby often killing the novel stone dead.) A single Textual Practice may, of course, combine a number of different Transpositions—part of the point of working at written transpositions of apparatus practices being to modify them and to permutate their combinations.

Now at this point you could, I'm sure, easily construct the *Fourth Model* for yourselves. All it involves is adding to *Diagram viii* the various relations and acts of author and reader that we've just been considering. In fact, you'll find *one* version of a Fourth Model on your hand-outs. You'll notice, I hope, that it represents only the system of relations appropriate to a *text-book* written and published under today's conditions; it would therefore have to be modified, as *Diagram viii* would be, for other—historical or possible—modes of organisation of the relations between author, publisher, printing workers, and purchasers. Since time presses and the hour is nearly up, while you look at the hand-out, I'll comment briefly on it; I'll then conclude by drawing your attention to some points of comparison between this Fourth Model and the three previous Models.

The *Fourth Model* indicates that there are four senses in which we could use the term 'author'. I have distinguished them typographically as:

(1) Author: a position within the relation Author-Publisher;
(2) *author*: the one who *writes* the text, the *writer* in column (i);
(3) AUTHOR: occupying a Textual Position as posited by the *author*;
(4) Textual Author: occupying Textual Position constructed by a *reader*.

There are also three senses of 'reader', distinguished as:

(1) *reader*: the one who *reads* the *text*, rather than 'reads' the Book;
(2) READER: the occupier of a Textual Position constructed by the act of *reading*;
(3) Textual Reader: the reader-position posited by the *author* in *writing*.

We can also see that a number of distinct *systems of relations* can be discerned. AA 'enters into' a system of relations, as Worker, with E (a system of Production). Z enters into a system of relations which connect with the system of production through the Bookseller (a system of Distribution). But AA and Z also enter into a system of relations with each other, which can be termed a *system of Literary Relations*: the relations between *author*, AUTHOR, *reader*, READER, Textual Author, Textual Reader, or, perhaps preferably, between, on the one hand, *author*, AUTHOR, Textual Reader and, on the other hand, Textual Author, READER, *reader*. It is this concept of a system of Literary Relations which perhaps allows the possibility of resolving some of the *problems* raised by the first three models of marxist literary criticism.

We can now compare this 'Fourth Model' with those first three. For speed of reference from now on I've re-labelled the models Models A, B, and C; the Fourth Model is therefore Model D.

Problem 1: 'Classes' and the location of 'the author'
Model A used the notion of class and the author's membership of or some other form of alliance with that 'group' which is a 'class'; one persuasive variation of this was the notion of a classic condensing of the Brontës' position in society. Model B indicated a structural similarity between the author's position within the 'literary production relations' and the role of the proletariat in the 'social production relations'. Model C included a location for 'authorial ideology' but the location of 'the author' was a problem.

Model D locates 'the author' in four different senses according to two different systems of relations (Author-Publisher, and Literary Relations), but *also* locates AA *within* an ideological apparatus; it does not deploy the notion of 'class'. But in locating AA as *both Worker* (in /W/T/M/ (i)) within a system of production relations (the final product of which is a Book) *and as Teacher within the Educational ideological apparatus*, Model D indicates a multiple positioning. It would be possible to locate AA also within other systems of relations or apparatuses (some of which might, in *other* texts by AA, be transposed)—e.g. in the positions of Mother (Family Apparatus), JP (Legal Apparatus), Employer (if AA owned a small firm), Employee (in a second but structurally similar or dissimilar system of production relations, if, e.g., AA were also a part-time telephone operator or secretary), etc. Such a multiple positioning might be analysed in terms of congruence/incongruence between the various positions, and also in terms of temporal distribution (across a lifetime or in the course of a busy week); a single text might also be constructed as a sequence of *different* transpositionings or as multiple but congruent transpositionings. The complexities here have some similarity to the complexities of 'condensing' in Model A, but they do not indicate any immediate sense in which the notion of 'membership' of a 'class' as a *group* could be used (though one might speak of 'AA' being 'classed' (or 'positioned') differently in different systems of relations, and for certain purposes of analysis one could *privilege* certain classings or specific combinations of classings). The positionings which are selected, or privileged, in any specific version of Model D would depend upon the particular case analysed: here, the privileging of the position of Teacher in the Educational Apparatus leads us to the second point of comparison between the four models.

Problem 2: Ideology and the Text
Model A saw the Text as 'expressing', 'articulating', 'embodying', etc., the ideology of the author, which was itself seen as related to the ideology of a class (cf. *Problem 3* below); a variant of this was a form of 'diagrammatic criticism' which saw the power-relations depicted in the text as structurally homologous to the power-relations between 'classes'. Model B indicated, not that a text might 'express' the ideology of the proletariat, but that a 'progressive' text might involve the proletariat as 'collaborators'. Model C spoke of 'Authorial Ideology' and 'Aesthetic Ideology' but the problem was raised (in *Query 2*) as to whether 'the LMP' 'gave rise to' the 'Aesthetic Ideology'.

Model D has emerged partly from elaborating the notion of 'ideology' in terms of the positions, practices, impositions and expositions of an ideological apparatus. Since Model D is specifically concerned with the writing of a text(-book) which can be analysed as the transpositioning of the mode of practice of the Educational Apparatus, that Text could be analysed as also transposing the Apparatus Ideology into a Textual Ideology: the apparatus and the text would then have a certain structural homology (and in some cases one might speak of the Text as offering a transposed Paradigm of the apparatus). Model D might also allow for a way of discriminating between two senses of 'collaboration' in Model B: insofar as /W/T/M/ (i) is an activity within a system of production which also includes /W/T/M/ (ii), various possible relations between W (i) and W (ii) and their respective Techniques might be elaborated, involving perhaps various possible combinations in a particular text of different *writing* practices and techniques with different *printing* techniques. But insofar as the Text is constituted as a set of impositionings, various variations are also conceivable in the *Literary Relations* between author/AUTHOR/Textual Reader and *reader*/READER/Textual Author. Involved in these Literary Relations might be certain possibilities of a different kind of 'collaboration', and this has some bearing on the relation between Apparatus Ideology, transposed apparatus practices, and Textual Ideology. In certain cases, elements of an Apparatus Ideology might be 'further' transposed *as* an 'Aesthetic Ideology' (e.g. the element of 'awe' transposed from the Religious Ideology as a component of the Aesthetic Ideology). But in the case of the Educational Apparatus version of Model D the Text is offered as a 'text-book', a book 'designed' and 'designated' for use within (variations of) the same educational apparatus; it will presumably, therefore, be 'consumed' and 'judged' in accordance with the Priorities and Premises of that apparatus rather than in accordance with any transposed version of them as 'aesthetic' criteria. One way of putting that would be to say that the *reader* will reconstruct the Textual Positions as 'Educational Positions' simply (though Z may not actually occupy any position within the educational apparatus him/herself).

Problem 3: 'Why write?': Problems, Solutions and Representativeness
Model A seemed to revolve round the notion of an author as facing problems representative of 'his' class and finding in his writing an 'ideal' solution to those problems, but left unclear why it is that the author writes at all; in a variation of

this 'the author' seemed to evaporate, leaving the text as posing and resolving its 'own' problems. Model B tried to establish a link between the 'technically progressive' writer and the 'politically progressive' writer but again left it unclear why the writer might write or why the writer might be technically and/or politically progressive, though it suggested a connection between these issues. Model C seemed not to be concerned with these issues in any explicit way.

In terms of the specific version of Model D, one clear answer to the question of 'why write?' is indicated in the presence of the 'contract' between AA and BS, and one could sketch variations of this 'contract' (and of the initiative for it) in terms of different systems of publishing (e.g. a patronage system, a state commission system, a hack system). But another answer is also indicated: that a Teacher should be *contracted* to write a text-book is an obvious case of apparatus and textual congruence, and one could analyse this kind of congruence further in terms of both positions and practices within an educational apparatus—the position of a Professor compared with that of a junior lecturer; the degree to which text-books are used within the various disciplinary practices of a specific educational apparatus and the significance of that for both Teacher and Publisher. One could indeed say that the very *use* of 'text-books' (or Casebooks, etc.) constitutes a 'solution' to certain problems of practice within the educational apparatus. More interestingly, the actual *writing* of a text-book can be seen as the transposition of certain *problems* of imposition and of practice within the educational apparatus, and the *task* of *writing* a text-book can be seen as constituted by two sets of problems: how to transpose the 'solutions' found to those problems of impositioning from the apparatus mode of practice to the textual practice; and, secondly, how to transpose certain problems of *exposition* from the apparatus practice to the textual practice. Those problems of exposition may be very similar indeed to the problems encountered within actual exposition within the apparatus (problems of 'knowledge', 'opinion', etc.); but the problems of *transposing im*positions may make *more* apparent and visible the problems of impositioning within the actual practice of the apparatus. By this I mean that there may be strains, tensions or contradictions *within* a *set* of impositions and also a certain tension or contradiction *between* particular *ex*positions and particular *im*positions. It may be that though contradictions between *ex*positions are fairly visible, the contradictions between *im*positions are less visible in actual practice but become more visible in their transposed form as *writing*. It is also worth suggesting that the task of *im*positioning has *priority* over the task of *ex*position, and that this too is peculiarly 'visible' in the transposed practice of a text.

Problem 4: Starting-points and Coventions
Model A offered itself as a method of analysis for answering the question of how a 'text' is related to 'society', but there seemed to be a methodological hesitancy as to whether that analysis 'began from' the text or from the society; a variation of this model began with an analysis of a particular society but then simply 'juxtaposed' the 'structure' of the text to the 'structure' of that society

without clarifying any 'causal' link between them. Model B suggested that the 'progressiveness' of a 'technique' might be the methodological starting-point. Both models also indicated a space for the operation of 'conventions' of literature. Model C implied that the 'ultimate' starting-point should be the 'GMP' but that the effective starting-point might be the 'LMP'.

Model D offers no explicit methodological starting-point, though the 'contract' between AA and BS seems the logical point of 'entry' into the diagram itself. It is, however, possible to conceive of different starting-points for the purposes of analysing different sections of Model D. For example, in Model D there is no specific 'location' of 'literary conventions', but insofar as Model D is concerned with the writing of a text-book one could locate the 'conventions' relevant to that text-book partly within the apparatus (the problem of transposing its 'conventions'; cf. *Problem 3*) and partly at the point of intersection or overlap between Literary Relations and Production Relations (Publishers too insist on the observation of conventions). Both Benjamin's comments on 'technique' and earlier comments on 'hack' writing are relevant to this sense of 'conventions'. But clearly, insofar as Model D is concerned with the writing of a text-book, there is a general problem about its applicability to what is normally meant (today) by the term 'literature' (poetry, novels), which the problem of locating 'conventions' partly raises. This question of the relation between Model D and 'literature' can lead us to two conclusions.

Conclusion 1: 'Literature' and 'Literary Relations'

One implication of Model D is that a text can be *written* and *read* as the transpositioning of an apparatus mode of practice. A text-book is a clear case of the transposition of an educational practice. But what of other kinds of text? Some seem obviously amenable to this kind of approach. For example, love-poems transpose some of the positions and practices of the Family Apparatus, and devotional poetry transposes one of the practices of the Religious Apparatus. It would, indeed, be easy enough to list many examples of the transpositioning of the practices of these two apparatuses. It might even be easy enough to think of examples where texts transpose practices found in a number of different apparatuses (the epistolatory novel might offer instances). We might also explore examples where a textual practice suggests a transposition of a practice in such a way that we are brought to extend our notion of what counts as an ideological apparatus (the relation of *The Spectator* to the eighteenth-century coffee-house style of association and conversation might be a case in point). Or we might recognise that certain textual practices have 'developed' from and through a whole series of transpositions of previous transpositions which were 'originally' generated from apparatus practices no longer extant because the originating apparatus is no longer available to us in the same form (much Greek and Roman poetry transposes social practices associated with forms of government or the apparatus of imperial administration; the analyses of Propertius, for example, in Francis Cairns's *Generic Composition in Greek and Roman Poetry*, are suggestive in this context). The general practice of 'story-telling' might be traced back to a variety of apparatus practices in this way (to the military apparatus of a tribal society or to the educational apparatus of a 'traditional' society). What is apparent from these pointers is that a great deal of 'literature' might be analysed not so much in terms of direct transpositions of Apparatus Relations but rather as *further* transpositions of *Literary* Relations established in *previous texts* ('modernist' literature offers numerous examples of this process). What remains worth emphasising generally, however, is that however 'remote' the 'connection' between a Textual Practice and a discernible Apparatus Practice, to *read* a text is to 'enter into' a set of Literary Relations just as to 'enter into' an apparatus is to 'enter into', to take up a position within, a set of apparatus relations. Here we might recall Marx's comment in the 1859 Preface from which we began:

In the social production of their existence, men inevitably enter into definite relations, which are independent of their will, namely relations of production appropriate to a given stage in the development of their material forces of production.

It is in the light of this remark that Model D might possibly be extended and elaborated to 'cover' a great many 'literary' texts.

Conclusion 2: 'Explanation' and 'History'
Clearly, Model D suggests a kind of 'explanatory' procedure: to 'explain' features of the text 'as' transpositions. But the common emphasis in much 'marxist' criticism has been to try to relate the 'text' to the *moment of its appearance* (*Wuthering Heights* to 1848, etc.). Model D suggests some ways in which this might be done fairly specifically, both in terms of the process of production of the 'Book' (which may have an important bearing on the 'Text' that is *written* or *read*, as for example in the case of Dickens's exploitation of serialisation or of the effect of Victorian illustrations in his novels), and in terms of the possible relation of the author to a particular apparatus at a particular biographical or historical moment. But, on the whole, Model D does not emphasise any particular 'causal chain' that links 'text' and 'society'; rather it emphasises the possibility of construcing and of re- or de-constructing *a set of literary relations* which may be relatively independent of any particular historical moment, in the sense that a *writer* can (re-)create an apparatus relation which may be anachronistic and a *reader* can 'revive' an ancient mode of textual practice (we can still *read* Propertius). This emphasis certainly goes contrary to a great deal of 'marxist' inquiry in the past; on the other hand, Model D is not incompatible with such characteristically 'marxist' preoccupations as the interrelation of 'causal instances' or the relation of 'ideology' to 'literature'; indeed, it seeks to suggest a more *precise* framework within which those preoccupations might be pursued.

However, I notice that the hour is now finally up, so I shall have to leave the justification of that last remark, together with the detailed *application* of Model D—which was what I intended to do this morning, but as usual I've gone on too long with the preliminaries—until some later lecture.

Thank you.

PART ONE

Part II, Optional Extra, Seminar Contributions: Voices Reading George Herbert's Dedication

This letter is written in a disguised voice!

Neddy Seagoon

'For I ain't, you must know,' said Betty, 'much of a hand at reading writing-hand, though I can read my Bible and most print. And I do love a newspaper. You mightn't think it, but Sloppy is a beautiful reader of a newspaper. He do the Police in different voices.'

Charles Dickens

HE DO THE POLICE IN DIFFERENT VOICES: Part I

T. S. Eliot

Almost any part of a double bind sequence may then be sufficient to precipitate panic or rage. The pattern of conflicting injunctions may even be taken over by hallucinatory voices. . . . if an individual doesn't know what sort of a message a message is, he may defend himself in ways which have been described as paranoid, hebephrenic or catatonic. . . . He cannot, without considerable help, discuss the messages of others. Without being able to do that, the human being is like any self-correcting system which has lost its governor; it spirals into never-ending, but always systematic, distortions.

Gregory Bateson

I was disguised as myself!!

Eccles

The Dedication
Lord, my first fruits present themselves to thee;
Yet not mine neither: for from thee they came,
And must return. Accept of them and me,
And make us strive, who shall sing best thy name.
   Turn their eyes hither, who shall make a gain:
   Theirs, who shall hurt themselves or me, refrain.

George Herbert

Chris's Dialogue
Q: That second line you just read out: 'Yet not mine neither: for from thee they came.' What do you mean by it?
A: Well, the dedication's addressed to God, and the line says that *The Temple* comes from God.
Q: You mean that God inspired it in some way?
A: Yes. Herbert's adapting the literary convention of the Muse inspiring the poet, and says that God's inspired him.
Q: You mean it's a convention; he doesn't really mean it?

A: Oh, yes, he means it. *The Temple* is inspired by God.

Q: Do you think that's true: that *The Temple is* inspired by God?

A: Yes.

Q: Why?

A: God tells me it is.

Q: ? ? ? Where, when, how?

A: There: in the text. It says: 'for from thee they came.'

Q: But that's what the *text* says, not God.

A: But God inspired the text, so it's God who says so.

Q: But that's nonsense! It's *Herbert* who says so.

A: Well, he should know, shouldn't he.

Q: How do you make that out?

A: Well, he tells us he was inspired by God, so . . .

Q: You're going round in circles! Herbert may be lying!

A: He wouldn't lie to God, would he, and the dedication's addressed to God, isn't it?

Q: Yes, but that's only a convention as well. It's really addressed to us.

A: No it isn't—it's addressed to God, and in any case Herbert wouldn't lie to us either about a thing like that.

Q: How do you know he wouldn't? He might think it was a 'white' lie that God would condone!

A: That would be an odd risk to take with God when you're dedicating your work to him. He's not lying. He's perfectly sincere.

Q: A sincere man can be mistaken. OK, he's not lying, but how do you know he's telling the truth?

A: Because the text tells me, and it's inspired by God.

Q: Come off it! If someone tells you he's inspired by God, do you believe him?

A: If it's true, I do.

Q: But how do you know it's true in this case?

A: Because Herbert tells me it is and he isn't lying.

Q: OK, but how does Herbert *know*?

A: You *know* when you're inspired by God!

Q: How do *you* know *that*'s true? Have *you* been inspired by God?

A: Yes—I've read *The Temple* so I've been, in a way, inspired by reading it.

Q: That's just playing with words, as well as going round in circles! How would *Herbert know* he was inspired?

A: Well, God wouldn't deceive him, would He?

Q: But you're *presuming* that God's inspired him—we only have his word for it.

A: No we don't: we have God's word—in the text.

Q: No we don't! In any case, 'The Dedication' isn't part of *The Temple* so even if *The Temple*'s inspired, this bit isn't, so . . .

A: Yes it *is* part of *The Temple*. You just don't believe that texts *can* be inspired by God.

Q: Even if I did believe that they could, why should I believe that *this* text was inspired by God?

94

A: Because I'm telling you it was.
Q: But who are *you*? ! !
A: I'm the author.
Q: You're not Herbert!
A: Well, I just said: 'Lord, *my* first fruits present themselves to thee,' so I
must be the author.
Q: Nonsense! You were just reading it out.
A: —to you.
Q: So what does that make me?
A: God.
Q: But I'm not God!
A: Then why did you listen?
Q: Because you read it out.
A: Do you think I shouldn't have read it?
Q: No. It's addressed to God.
A: Then why did Herbert print it; if it's printed, the reader will read it.

Q & A (The Reader):	Perhaps we shouldn't have read it?
Questioner:	*I* was just listening.
Apologist:	No you weren't. You were quoting it.
Quoter:	*You* were quoting it.
Answer:	*I* was *reading* it.
Q & A (together):	Perhaps we shouldn't have read it?
Herbert:	I told you whether you should read or shouldn't:
	'Turn their eyes hither, who shall make a gain:
	Theirs, who shall hurt themselves or me, refrain.'
Reader:	And which am I?
Herbert:	*I* don't know.
Reader:	Who does?
Herbert:	You—and God.
Reader:	*I* don't know.
Herbert:	Then ask God.
Reader:	?
Herbert:	It's all right. He'll tell you.
Reader:	How?
Herbert:	In *The Temple.* Come, enter in. Me thoughts I heard one calling, *Child*!
You (sotto voce):	But does God *exist*?
Me (puzzled):	Would that make any difference?

Chris: The question set for this seminar paper was: 'Can we read 'The Dedication' in George Herbert's *The Temple* as a poem?' I'm not entirely sure whether I was supposed to take that question too seriously, so perhaps you shouldn't take this paper too seriously, but it did make me think—as presumably it was meant to—about what I mean by 'reading a poem' and about the relation between religion, belief and literature. So I'll begin with a few general comments about 'religion and literature'.

We can schematically suggest a number of practices and relationships that might be regarded as characteristic of what is normally meant by 'religion' when the word refers to the Western Christian tradition: relationships between God and a believer, involving some form of 'revelation' from God to the believer and some form of 'prayer' from the believer to God; relationships between two believers, particularly those between a 'minister' of some kind and a 'lay' believer within a 'church', involving perhaps some form of 'preaching' from minister to layperson and in some cases a form of 'confessing' from layperson to minister; relationships between a believer and a non-believer, which may take the form of attempts by a believer to 'convert' a non-believer and, in some sense, one might speak of an 'internal' relationship 'within' a 'believer' between believing and not believing. Obviously, both this schema and, particularly, the terms I've used could be modified or elaborated. But this rough outline at least gives me a starting-point for considering some aspects of one connection between 'religion' and 'literature'.

That certain kinds of *writing* have a role or function *within* these relationships and practices is clear. One could instance the Bible itself or some other texts which are taken to be communications to the believer authorised by God, and such forms of 'revelation' can be discussed in terms of inspiration, prophecy or infallibility. In terms of 'prayer' one might instance not only, say, the 'Psalms' or the 'Our Father' from the Bible but also texts associated with liturgies; one might also include here a range of 'manuals' of private devotions, whether collections of actual prayers or 'exemplary works' such as Loyola's *Spiritual Exercises* or Law's *Devout Life*. These latter might be regarded more as 'preaching' texts, along with volumes of sermons and works of spiritual guidance; and one might include here a wide range of theological works of a more 'instructional' kind. Some works of theology or commentary may also be placed alongside texts associated more with the practice of 'conversion', such as apologetical works, tracts or even polemics. And there are obviously various ways in which 'confessional' works might be considered—spiritual autobiographies or accounts of personal conversion.

But if we ask whether such writings should be regarded as what we now call 'literature', we might find it difficult to make clear decisions in a number of cases—though we might find it easier to say that the 'Book of Job' and 'The Song of Songs' are 'literature' than to say that the 'laws' section of 'Deuteronomy' or the 'Letter to the Hebrews' are 'literature'. Similarly, though we might fairly readily think of Donne's *Sermons*, John of the Cross's *Songs and Romances*, Augustine's *Confessions* or Bunyan's *Pilgrim's Progress* in terms of 'literature', there are other sermons, hymns and spiritual autobiographies that we wouldn't naturally think of as 'literature'—or we might, faced with some such texts, resort to a distinction between 'good' and 'bad' literature or even 'writing'. Now, how do we regard George Herbert's *The Temple*? After all, it's been variously described as 'a manual of devotion', 'the seventeenth-century *Christian Year*' and 'a record of spiritual struggle', but also, obviously, as 'a collection of poems'.

Now, if I open *The Temple* at page 1 of my edition, I find a page—immediately before 'The Dedication'—headed 'The Printers to the Reader'. I want to pause over this page, because it seems to me to raise some of the problems of *reading* anything. This note from 'The Printers' opens:

The dedication of this work having been made by the Author to the *Divine Majestie* onely, how should we now presume to interest any mortall man in the patronage of it? Much lesse think we it meet to seek the recommendation of the Muses, for that which himself was confident to have been inspired by a diviner breath then flows from *Helicon*. The world therefore shall receive it in that naked simplicitie, with which he left it, without any addition either of support or ornament, more then is included in it self. We leave it free and unforestalled to every mans judgement, and to the benefit that he shall finde by perusall. Onely for the clearing of some passages, we have thought it not unfit to make the common Reader privie to some few particularities of the condition and disposition of the Person;

This is a fairly unusual kind of note, as it makes clear itself. But it is also a very familiar kind of writing in one respect. It's written in the first person plural (We) but addressed to 'the reader' not to 'you', and the text speaks of 'every man', 'he' and 'the common Reader'—i.e. the reader it addresses is put grammatically into the third person, not the second person. This is, when we notice it and stop to think about it, a slightly odd practice; compare it, for example, with the use of the second person when an announcer speaks on the radio to the listeners. But as a familiar writing practice, it is one that we transpose automatically; we read it as 'they' speaking to 'us': the written 'we' marks a position from which something is said, and the reader 'occupies' that position while adopting simultaneously the 'position' designated by 'he'. The reader in fact performs a complex operation of double-positioning and in a sense speaks to himself while listening to himself—though he 'speaks' in a 'voice' shaped by the rhythms, pace and tone of what is written.

If we now look at the first stanza of 'The Church-Porch', which follows immediately after 'The Dedication', we find:

> THOU, whose sweet youth and early hopes inhance
> Thy rate and price, and mark thee for a treasure;
> Hearken unto a Verser, who may chance
> Ryme thee to good, and make a bait of pleasure.
> A verse may finde him, who a sermon flies,
> And turn delight into a sacrifice.

The last two lines are a statement, but we tend to read that 'him' as almost implying a 'you'—i.e. as involving the reader of the poem in the possibility of 'a verse' finding *him*,—and, indeed, 'a verse' implies *the* 'verse' which the reader is reading. One reason, of course, for this way of reading the last two lines is the effect of the opening four lines of the stanza, which are addressed to 'thou'. Reading these four lines is, again, a matter of complex positioning: the reader 'speaks' the lines but at the same time occupies the position of addressee, but an addressee who is stipulated as enjoying 'sweet youth' and 'early hopes' —which the actual reader, of course, may not. But when we read that initial (capitalised) 'THOU' there is a momentary suspension: is this in some sense addressed to *me*, the actual reader or not? And if we consider the effect of that emphatically-placed '*Hearken* unto a Verser' we are tempted to say that the 'Verser' is George Herbert speaking in his own voice to me, the actual reader. But the use of 'a Verser' instead of, say, 'me', reminds us that the author of a poem may often adopt some kind of 'persona', a verbal 'mask' through which the poet speaks. By analogy, then, we might suggest that the effect of 'THOU, whose sweet youth and early hopes inhance' is to impose an '*impersona*' on the *reader*, so that as he 'listens' he occupies the position of the addressed 'thou' which is being addressed by the poet's 'persona' which, in reading, the reader also, in a sense, impersonates. What, though, would we say of the last two lines in that case? These lines have an almost epigrammatic form; they present a statement about 'a verse' and 'him'; they aren't an address from 'a Verser' to 'thou'—yet we might read them as still part of the preceding 'address' (the change in line-indentation, rhyme, etc., leaves this an open possibility). Then 'him' would be doubly specified: the impersona is given another characteristic: not only a 'youth' but one 'who a sermon flies'. That we *may* read these lines as simply postulating some 'other' character (*any* 'him' who flies sermons) is, of course, part of the point of the ambiguity: it poses a self-question to the reader—am I such a character?

To what extent can we say that the 'statement' in these last two lines is different from the statements in the Printers' note which follows the passage previously quoted:

Being nobly born, and as eminently endued with gifts of the minde, and having by industrie and happy education perfected them to that great height of excellencie, whereof his fellowship of Trinitie Colledge in Cambridge, and his Orator-ship in the Universitie, together with that knowledge which the Kings Court had taken of him, could make relation farre above ordinarie.

Obviously, these statements can't be regarded as implying an 'impersona' for the reader, in terms of the information they contain, but it's worth noting that this is not, as it's quoted, a complete grammatical sentence; it has to be read (though still ungrammatically) as a continuation of

Onely for the clearing of some passages, we have thought it not unfit to make the common Reader privie to some few particularities of the condition and disposition of the Person;
    Being nobly born. . . .

The paragraph-break here again indicates an option in reading; the previous paragraph has been an 'address' to the (third person) 'reader', 'every man', 'he'. The 'reader' postulated is anyone who reads the book. But the first paragraph ends with a kind of stipulation—the 'common Reader' who is presumed not to be already 'privie' to the details of Herbert's life which the note then goes on to specify. If the reader already is so 'privie', he may go on reading the rest of the note, but only b in some sense, and however minimally or perhaps subliminally, 'adopting' the implied impersona of one who isn't so 'privie'. The rest of the note speaks in an informative voice: it presents the history of Herbert's life and offers opinions. To some extent, we could say that the first paragraph speaks in the Printers' own voice, but the second paragraph speaks in a less specific voice: that of the biographer or informer. That voice might be compared to the one we would 'hear' if we read 'A verse may finde him, who a sermon flies' as simply giving us a statement of 'fact' or 'opinion' without being specifically addressed to us as 'him'.

If we bear in mind these obvious and basic points about the Printers' note and the stanza so far commented on, we can suggest a further set of comparisons when we look, now, at 'The Dedication' and consider the 'voice' or 'voices' in which we might read it. We could say, first, that the voice of the text seems to be very specific indeed: it is the voice of the *author* himself, the one who wrote *The Temple* ('*my* first fruits'). And, as it is a 'dedication', the addressee, the dedicatee, is clearly specified: it is God himself. But can we even attempt to 'imagine' God *reading* it—what 'voice' would He (She? It?) 'read' in? If we regard 'Lord' as a stipulation of an 'impersona' the reader is to adopt, how can anyone except God 'impersonate' *that* impersona? Of course, if we compare this dedication with a more familiar one—say, 'To my Wife'—it's clear that in reading 'To my Wife' we don't even try to impersonate the wife reading it: she is a specific, actual person and she is not me; nor can I impersonate the speaker whose wife she is: I am certainly not that specific person either. Such a dedication, one might claim, is neither addressed to me nor from me—unless I wrote the book I'm reading. But what happens if we do read a dedication from someone else to someone else? Does it give us information or make a statement, like the 'verse . . . sermon' epigram, or like the biographical details in the Printers' note? In one sense, it does (it 'tells' us that the writer is or was married), but we might compare it rather with *overhearing* information not intended for us, as in eavesdropping on a private exchange. Is this, then, how we should 'read' 'The Dedication' addressed by Herbert to God? (In which case, as often happens in eavesdropping, we find ourselves the subject, in part, of the conversation: 'Turn their eyes hither . . .'). But how does this notion of 'eavesdropping' square with our actual *reading* of 'The Dedication'—can one eavesdrop on what one is, in some sense, saying to oneself anyway?

Consider certain different kinds of text. If I pick up a private letter not written to me—I find it between the pages of a book, for example—and read it, I know that I am neither the writer nor the specified recipient. I am therefore in the position of an 'eavesdropper'. But what 'voice' do I read it in? Insofar as I *know* the writer, I might find myself 'mimicking' his or her voice, and insofar as I know the intended recipient I might try to 'imagine' how they might read it. But I am, biologically, historically, 'actually', neither the writer nor the intended recipient. I am in a curious position. Insofar as I 'listen' while I 'read', paying attention to what I read, I am rather like someone listening to someone else 'passing on' what *they* have overheard while eavesdropping, and that someone else might be regarded as 'rehearsing' what they overheard. But also, insofar as I try to occupy or intrude upon the positions of writer and recipient, I am having to attribute certain characteristics to both, to define them as possessing certain attributes proper to them. But if I don't *know* the actual people concerned, I have to more or less recover those attributes from my reading or interpretation of the letter—and even if I know one or both, I can hardly claim to know 'everything' about them (if only because I haven't read this letter before). I therefore have to select certain characteristics I take to be proper to them. But in doing so, I am 'dramatising' them, interpreting them as I might 'interpret' a role in a play-script. One might then speak of my trying to 'speak' in the writer's 'own voice' as my rehearsing, but I am not only rehearsing as speaker, but also 'as' 'listener'—I am doubly-positioned at least. And though I am being 'guided' by the text in attributing certain characteristics to both speaker and listener, I might be regarded as (with the help of the text) myself 'stipulating' a certain 'persona' for them both; in terms of what I 'know about people', I impersonate them both as certain *kinds* of people. I might then regard myself as occupying the same position as someone reading a text which both stipulates its own addressee as 'a certain *kind* of person'—an impersona—and itself speaks in a certain 'dramatic voice'—a persona. Of course I have to make my own decisions as to what that persona and that impersona are, but I would have to do that anyway in reading a text which did designate an impersona and persona.

If we now look back at the Printers' note to the reader, we can see that we read the first paragraph from our 'actual' position as 'listener'—i.e. the only attribute presumed in its addressee by the text is that of actually reading it. Insofar as we are doing so, we fit the specification! In 'listening' therefore while we read, we listen as ourselves, whoever specifically we may be. But insofar as in reading it we read in a certain 'voice', we have to rehearse a certain persona, that of the Printers. But of course we can't now *know them*, so the persona we attribute to them can only be a matter of more or less specific information, 'historical imagination', and the guidance of the text itself. But what happens when we read:

Onely for the clearing of some passages, we have thought it not unfit to make the common Reader privie to some few particularities of the condition and disposition of the Person;

—do we go on reading? The impersona designated is that of someone (a *common* Reader) not already 'privie'. Do I, this specific reader, meet that stipulation? If I do, then I decide that I will go on reading 'as' myself; if I don't, then I can only go on reading if I somehow adopt the impersona of a 'common Reader'. But there are a number of problems here. First, what is meant by 'common'—whoever is not already 'privie' to 'some few particularities' we are to be told? But we don't yet know what those 'few particularities' are to be; I might already know them or I might not, but I don't *know* that I *know* them until I know what they are; so I have to go on reading to find out. I might, of course, *believe* that I know them already—but only on the basis of the persona I have attributed to the Printers. In this respect, part of that persona is a stipulation of how much I believe they know about Herbert as compared with what *I* know, or think I know. Only if I believe that I know 'everything' about Herbert can I be sure that I know already whatever the printers are going to say. But how could I believe that I know 'everything' about Herbert—unless I was Herbert—or, perhaps, even unless I was 'God'. I might, of course, want to know 'how much' the printers know—but since they only promise 'some few particularities', that may not be as much as they know anyway. Second, there is not just a problem about deciding what the printers might mean by 'common' and 'some few particularities'; I have to decide what *I* mean by them in this context.

We can use a different example here (though the same point might be made in terms of the printers' note, it would simply take longer). When I read:

> THOU, whose sweet youth and early hopes inhance
> Thy rate and price, and mark thee for a treasure

how do I decide whether I meet this stipulation or not? I, momentarily at least, can take that 'Thou' as addressed simply to the reader, any reader, but then the 'Thou' seems to be specified. If I take all three stipulations in these lines together, I might be able to say pretty decisively whether I still have 'sweet youth' or not and whether I am marked 'for a treasure' or otherwise, but what of 'early hopes': did I or didn't I, do I or don't I? The problem that looms here could be phrased as: *'Can I class myself?'* Insofar as a stipulated impersona is constituted as a set of characteristics, one might say that it defines or indicates a *rule* about membership of a logical class: 'All Thous are: young, hoped early, and marked out for a treasure.' Now if, on the one hand, someone else makes up a rule about membership of a 'class' and tells me that, by that rule, I am a member of the defined class, and I say I'm not, his obvious reply is to say that *he* made up the rule so he knows whether I come under that rule or not; if I then point out some discrepancy in the wording of the rule which allows me to claim that the rule does not apply to me, and he then modifies the rule 'correcting' it to meet my objection, and then says that I do, still, come under that rule —obviously, such an exchange could go on for ever. If it's a rule I can simply ignore ('OK, you say I'm a sweet youth. So what!'), I will presumably abandon the exchange ('I'm going, mate'). If on the other hand, *I* make up a rule about membership of a logical class: 'All Xs get up at 7 am every day' and tell myself that I am an 'X' (i.e. I get up at 7 am every day), I can then adjust either the rule or the behaviour to ensure my continuing membership of that (continually refined) class. But when someone else makes up a rule about membership of such a class ('All Xs get up at 7 am') and assigns me to that class, I can't adjust the rule to fit my behaviour without its becoming a rule I have made up; I can only adjust my behaviour to fit the rule (which I may or may not want to do) if I am to 'remain' a member of the class designated by the rule. But what, thirdly, would be the case if I tried to both 'follow' a rule made up by someone else (i.e. adjusted my behaviour) and yet also made up the 'same' rule myself (i.e. I could modify the rule to fit my behaviour)? This situation is, of course, inherently unstable (even if possible): if I couldn't modify the rule, I couldn't claim to have made it up myself, but if I did modify it I couldn't claim to be following the 'same' rule that was made up by someone else. But *who* could decide that the rule I made up and the rule someone else made up were the 'same' rule anyway? Well, the reader of 'Thou whose sweet youth . . .' is in a position analogous to that third one mentioned. The reader both makes up the rule ('All readers/ addressees are "sweet youths"') since he speaks in the voice of the persona he has attributed to the 'author' *and* makes up the rule himself in deciding whether as 'reader' he fits it. If he decides that he doesn't, he modifies his behaviour (he adopts the impersona of one who does) in order to remain in that class (i.e. to go on reading). But this means that the reader is doubly-positioned: if he decides that he does not fit the rule and adjusts his behaviour accordingly, then he is no longer 'making up the rule' but rather following one made up by someone else; but he 'makes up' that someone else too since he 'plays' that 'someone else' (he speaks in the voice of the 'author'); but if he makes up the one who makes up the rule isn't he making up the rule as well, so he can modify the rule to fit his behaviour rather than his behaviour to fit the rule? At the same time, of course, it is he who 'decides' that the rule made up by the 'author' and the rule which classifies him as addressee are the 'same' rule—since it is he who makes the rules the 'same'.

All this may seem a long-winded, and rather idiotic, way of saying that the reader has to 'decide' what the text 'means' and that the author necessarily has to leave him to do so. It might also seem an indirect, and not very useful, way of talking about the problem of 'imaginative identification'. It is. But if we now go back to 'The Dedication' this roundabout way of analysing what happens, logically, when I read 'Thou whose sweet youth . . .' might be seen to be relevant. Try re-reading 'The Dedication':

> Lord, my first fruits present themselves to thee;
> Yet not mine neither: for from thee they came,
> And must return. Accept of them and me,
> And make us strive, who shall sing best thy name.
>> Turn their eyes hither, who shall make a gain:
>> Theirs, who shall hurt themselves or me, refrain.

How do I *read* it? Since, one might say, the text is spoken in Herbert's 'own voice' and I am not Herbert, I have to attribute to the speaker a certain 'persona' which I 'rehearse', on the basis of what I 'know' about Herbert (and the Printers' purpose in the note is to give even the 'common' reader some 'knowledge' on the basis of which to do that). But if the specified listener (implied reader/addressee) of this dedication is God, how can I, the reader, 'impersonate' God—and even eavesdropping involves attributing some impersona to the addressee. To a limited extent, I can attribute certain 'characteristics' to 'God' (by analogy of one kind or another) and I can also try to be guided by what I believe the 'actual' Herbert thought God's attributes were. The text itself might guide me in this: the designation 'Lord', for example, or the particular claim that 'from thee they came'. I might, for instance, 'interpret' this last phrase not as a claim that God had 'inspired' Herbert but as a more general claim that God is the 'source of all gifts'. But if I construct a 'set' of attributes for God in order to 'impersonate' that stipulated 'impersona', I probably (if I think within a particular Western theological tradition) run into some very specific logical problems. I can specify, uniquely, a particular human being (the 'actual' Herbert) by, for example, constructing a 'rule' for a 'logical class': 'All George Herberts: were born at time T in place P'—and the more precise I make that specification the more it could be said that I was specifying *the* George Herbert (not just 3rd April 1593 in Montgomery Castle, but, say, 9.36 am on 3rd April . . .). But this *kind* of specification involves a particular notion of 'space' and 'time' which—in the Western theological tradition —does not apply to God. I can also specify 'myself' (the actual reader) by saying 'I, here, now' (this precise time, 7.01 am, and this precise place, the top of Mount Everest), but by saying 'here, now' I specify 'my' location without further laborious elaboration. But—in the Western theological tradition —'God' is 'everywhere, always', so He, too, could be said to be 'here, now', as well as 'outside space and time'. Moreover, if I ask whether the 'speaker' of 'The Dedication' (the 'textual author', not 'George Herbert') occupies a point in 'space and time', I might answer, perhaps, that he (it?) does—as a set of material designations on *this* page (which does occupy a point in space and time); but is that set of designations a logical class of which there is only 'one member', or can the 'same' set of designations include a number of 'instances' (the 'same' words on *that* page)? This last question obviously raises the problem of how far a particular mode of production of a 'book' can ensure a 'material identity' of 'texts'. But I might also ask whether the *reader* of a text is a 'sole member' of a class—the *one* who is reading *this* text from *this* book here and now—and there can't be a 'material identity' of two actual readers. But—in the Western theological tradition—the term 'material' does not apply to God anyway. So, in trying to 'impersonate' 'God' in 'listening' to this dedication, in occupying the position of the implied reader, in attributing characteristics to 'God', those 'attributes' could include His being 'present' 'here, now' while 'I' read, but not 'in' space and time and not 'materially'. It's difficult to conceive of such a position. But we might—in terms of one Western philosophical tradition—conceive of my 'mind' as a non-spatio-temporal non-material 'locus', in which case 'God' *might* be said to 'occupy my mind' while I read. I might also, in terms of that philosophy, conceive of God, by analogy, as Himself a kind of 'mind'. And then could I say that while I read I read 'with the mind of God', or that while 'I' read God reads 'with my mind'? If *that* might be the case, then one could also speak of Herbert *writing* 'with the mind of God', or of God writing 'with the mind of Herbert'. And—in one theological tradition—that is precisely a way of talking about 'inspiration'. But if that could be the case, then one might say, in a hallowed phrase, that this dedication is a 'word of God'—which is precisely what the text claims to be (on one reading of 'for from thee they came').

This complicated way of unpacking some lurking problems has been intended to reveal a certain complicity between the assertions of this text and the deep formal structure of its literary relations, i.e. of the relations set up between its 'speaker', its 'addressee' and its 'reader'. In other words, if you try to take seriously what the text says and if you try to read it 'seriously', you are implicated in, drawn into, a whole set of basic philosophical-theological positions. Put another way, to probe the process of reading this text is to disclose some of the underlying premises of a certain religious 'ideology'.

If we do continue reading it, other facets of this ideology reveal themselves in all their tangled logic. Take the last two lines:

> Turn their eyes hither, who shall make a gain:
> Theirs, who shall hurt themselves or me, refrain.

How do I read these lines? Say I try to construct a set of stipulated characteristics for the implied reader and 'decide' whether I 'fit' them. Can I seek any guidance from the text as to what those characteristics might be? There are two sets of designations: 'who shall make a gain' and 'who shall hurt themselves or me', and they are posited as mutually exclusive categories. So I have to decide which of the two I fit. But how do I decide between them? I am caught here in a number of dilemmas. Let's play first with a fairly simple and superficial one. If I take it that 'who shall make a gain' is a 'good' set to be in, and (therefore) that I am 'in' it, I can go on reading *The Temple* 'as myself'. But if I decide that I am in the 'good' set, is it 'good' for *me* to decide that I am, since if we take 'good' as indicating 'morally good', we might feel ourselves a bit trapped as one theological tradition would murmur 'pride' at that point. Equally, if I decide that I am *not* in the 'good' set and am therefore morally bad, is that not a morally good (a humble) decision to arrive at, in which case how far does that good decision put me in the 'good set' after all? Alternatively, if I decide that I am in the 'bad' set, doesn't this mean that I should 'hope' to 'gain' from reading further—though *this* 'early hope' might be dashed pretty quickly by reading the next line again and deciding that since I am in the 'bad' set I should 'refrain'. The unavoidable difficulty of 'good' and 'bad' being 'moral' categories arises here from there seeming to be no third option: since these are the only two stipulations and are offered as alternatives, everybody must be in one or the other, but since the terms used imply a moral judgement everybody seems to be implicitly divided between 'the good' on the one hand and 'the bad' on the other. One must, in other words, come to some final judgement about oneself: a sheep or a goat, elect or damned. Luckily, another theological tradition might come to mind instead, best exemplified by the monk who was asked 'Which is the best book on humility?' and answered 'mine'. The burden of this (wiser?) tradition is that 'humility' is a matter of one neither presuming that one is saved nor presuming that one is damned, but is rather a matter of rightly judging oneself, knowing oneself for what one is—and if that includes having written the best book on humility it is a mark of humility to say so. But before the monk replies 'mine', he might ask: who decides that his *is* the best book on humility? And he might further ask, on re-reading his book rather more critically, whether *anyone* can 'judge' himself 'rightly'—which is partly a matter of whether only the 'good' can 'rightly' judge themselves but the 'bad' can't (it being a mark of goodness that one *can* judge oneself rightly). The wise monk might (and does, in one tradition) reply that one has to have an 'informed conscience'; but how do I examine my conscience to know whether it's correctly 'informed', and informed by whom? If it's informed by my confessor (say, some other monk) how do I know that *he* is appropriately informed —which is a matter of 'who judges the judge?' (as one spectator called out at the trial of the Chicago Seven—and was promptly done for contempt of court).

But all these questions are only variants on the question: can I *know* myself 'correctly', which is itself another variant on the question 'can I (logically) class myself?'

But in any case, and crucially, do the lines 'Turn their eyes hither . . .' invite me to judge myself? Since they are addressed to God, it is God who is being requested to make the decision, to decide whom to cast in either role. And 'God' would seem eminently qualified to decide, since—in one philosophical tradition—He is qualified as *the* Good and as Omniscient (He *knows* everything), while—in one theological tradition—He is *the* Judge. And it is God who, in the end, 'informs' the conscience and he can do so because he 'knows' me most intimately and can inform me about everything about me, which he does by 'speaking' not so much *to* my conscience but *as* my conscience or the Voice of God in me. Only God, in this tradition, finally knows what and who I *am*—and therefore only God can truthfully say 'I am who I am'. And since God knows everybody equally, only he can judge every person to be either elect or damned, either good or bad. But *I* don't know what his criteria are, unless he tells me. And in the text of 'The Dedication', of course, I am *not* told what the criteria are for judging between 'who shall make a gain' and 'who shall hurt themselves or me' since the text doesn't specify any further. So, if I read these lines, I have to attribute to the 'impersona' of God some criteria 'He' might hold concerning these two categories, and in the light of those categories I can then decide whether to go on reading *The Temple* or not. But since the text doesn't give me any further guidance as to what those criteria might be, in 'making up' a 'rule' for membership of these two sets I am not even trying to make up the 'same' rule as the textual author (Herbert?), since the textual author leaves it to the specified addressee to decide what those criteria might be (which is perhaps fair enough if the addressee is also the ultimate author of the text anyway). We might conceive of George Herbert as believing that the criteria he would use would be the same as God's, but since the text stipulates that God should do the action of choosing ('Turn' and 'refrain' are both requests or prayers), I can't decide whether Herbert (or his attributed persona) and I agree about what he means (Herbert, I mean); I have to refer to a 'third person', whom the text specifies as God. But how can I know God's mind in the matter?

Only if God acts to tell me. But the action he is requested by the text to perform is either to 'turn' my eyes as reader to the rest of *The Temple* or to 'refrain' my eyes from reading the rest of *The Temple*. But has he the power to do so? If I do go on to read the next lines in *The Temple*—i.e. 'Thou, whose sweet youth and early hopes' etc.—is it because God has made me do so, has made me 'turn my eyes' upon these lines? If I do read them, he certainly can't have 'refrained' my eyes—but does that mean that he hasn't got the power to do (in which case he isn't omnipotent) or does it mean that he hasn't answered the 'prayer' in the text (in which case he's a rather ungrateful patron), or does it mean that he has, somehow, answered that prayer but in terms that escape the dichotomy suggested to him: i.e. there *is* a 'third option' between reading and not reading *The Temple*?

There are various complicated possibilities here. If I have decided (how?) that I do *not* come into the category of those who will make a gain, and yet decide (do *I* decide?) to go on reading (in which case what 'gain' do I hope for?), but if, meanwhile, God has decided (would I know?) that I *do* come into that category, would I be disobeying my own rule but obeying God's in going on reading—in which case won't my obeying God mean that I will after all make a gain, and thereby contradict my own self-judgement? If, on the other hand, I have decided that I do come into the category of those who will make a gain, and therefore carry on reading, but in the meanwhile God has decided that I don't, will I be disobeying God's rule but obeying my own by going on reading—but if I am disobeying God's rule, won't that hurt me, so I've contradicted myself again. I'd better not explore all the possible permutations involved here, or I'd bore you (or amuse you) too much, but one recurrent element would seem to be the logical possibility of my continuing to read *The Temple* even though God and I disagree about whether I should. This possibility is a logical possibility, but is it an actual possibility? For if God 'decides' something, doesn't that—in one old tradition—constitute an *effective* decision? His word is a creating word; God only speaks performative utterances. And if he decides something about me and I nevertheless act 'otherwise', does that in fact also indicate a decision of his that I should act otherwise? In other words, who is responsible for my 'sin' of 'disobeying' God, and how did we get into the habit in the first place?

As an aside, and rather than quote the whole of *Paradise Lost* at this point, I'll quote here Herbert's *The Judgement*, one of the last poems in *The Temple* (just to show you that I *have* read it):

> ALMIGHTIE Judge, how shall poore wretches brook
> Thy dreadfull look,
> Able a heart of iron to appall,
> When thou shalt call
> For ev'ry mans peculiar book?
>
> What other means to do, I know not well;
> Yet I heare tell,
> That some will turn thee to some leaves therein
> So void of sinne,
> That they in merit shall excell.
>
> But I resolve, when thou shalt call for mine,
> That to decline,
> And thrust a Testament into thy hand:
> Let that be scann'd.
> There thou shalt finde my faults are thine.

Herbert leaves it (necessarily) to God to decide how to take that last line—and his own word for it. So do I.

But if a 'decision' 'either way' to read the last lines of 'The Dedication' runs the reader into some fairly complex problems, is there, after all, a 'third option'? Remember that God, being God, might refuse the apparently logically exclusive alternatives suggested by the text: turn, refrain. And insofar as I 'impersonate' God, I too might have to find that third way. One could perhaps suggest a third way: could I perhaps read this dedication not as an actual dedication addressed to God, but *as literature*? One might immediately ask, of course, whether God would then be 'responsible' for my reading a text as 'literature'. If he isn't, then 'reading literature' is the only (damned) thing in the world God is *not* responsible for, in which case reading literature is (perhaps) a sin (and criticism is maybe close to blasphemy). But if God is responsible for *everything*, he is also responsible for 'literature', in which case reading literature is (perhaps) reading God's word (and criticism is maybe close to commentary on the word of God). One might suggest moments in the history of Christian attitudes towards this peculiar activity called 'reading literature', in which both opinions have found their supporters. But what it would *mean* to read 'The Dedication' 'as literature', God knows. I don't.

But at least along the way I think I've discovered something of what's implicit in trying to read it at all: all the intertwined issues of Christian theology—God as omnipresent, omniscient, omnipotent, the good, the judge, the voice of conscience, the author of his word, the silent, the enigmatic. That'll do for one seminar paper.

*

Dai's Doodle

p = 'p is true'   not-p = 'p is not true'   (Asides)

He believes that p; but not-p.	He believes.
I believe that p; but not-p.	Credo quia absurdum?
He knows that p; but not-p.	He does not know.
He knew that p; but not-p.	He did not know.
He believed that p; but not-p.	He did believe.
He believes that p	He believes.
but I know that p.	How?
He believes that p	Why?
but I know that not-p.	Why?
I know that p, but I believe that not-p.	My son is dead.

He believes that p, but he knows that not-p;
therefore he makes-believe that p;
he tells me that p.
I believe him that p, but I know that not-p.

Is he
writing
fiction?
I suspend disbelief?

He knows that p, but he tells me that not-p.
I know that he knows that p
but he tells me that not-p.

He is lying.

I believe that he is
lying but I could be
wrong.

He believes that p, but not-p;
he tells me that not-p.

He is lying & telling
me the truth.

He believes that not-p, but p;
he tells me that not-p.

He is not lying & not
telling me the truth.

He believes that I believe that he knows
that not-p; but I believe that p;
he tells me that p; I do not believe him.

He believes that p, but he knows that not-p;
therefore he only makes-believe that p;
he tells me that p; I know that he only
makes-believe that p; therefore I make him believe
that I believe him. I don't know that not-p.

He tells me that p;
I believe in him;
therefore I believe that p.

But not-p.

He believes that God exists; he tells me
that he makes-believe that God exists;
I believe him; I make-believe that God exists.
I don't know that God does not exist.

He tells me that God exists.

Who is he?

*

Dai: I should think so too! I'm glad you warned us not to take your paper too seriously! But I must admit I'm a bit baffled as to which bits to take seriously at all. Somewhere in your paper there *is* a tricky and puzzling problem, which I've been trying to get clear in my own mind while you've been reading—I've been doodling away at the logic of 'belief'. It seems to me that you were confusing two rather different questions: what it means to 'make-believe' when we're reading a poem, and what it means to 'believe in' God; the fact that Herbert's

'Dedication' itself seems, to us, to couple these two problems together is what makes it peculiarly interesting, but I'm not sure that your implied conclusion holds: that somehow what's at stake is the question of whether 'literature' can exist at all. Eliot had somewhat the same thought, in his essay on Dante. Remember in the body of the essay he makes that very simple distinction between 'philosophical belief' and 'poetic assent', but then in a note worries about his position and actually ends up making it conditional on there being 'literature' at all—but in a way that implies that such a condition might well be shaky. I'll give you the two passages:

My point is that you cannot afford to *ignore* Dante's philosophical and theological beliefs, or to skip the passages which express them most clearly; but that on the other hand you are not called upon to believe them yourself. For there is a difference (which here I hardly do more than assert) between philosophical *belief* and poetic *assent*. I am not sure that there is not as great a difference between philosophical belief and scientific belief; but that is a difference only now beginning to appear, and certainly inapposite to the thirteenth century. In reading Dante you must enter the world of thirteenth-century Catholicism, which is not the world of modern Catholicism, as his world of physics is not the world of modern physics. You are not called upon to believe what Dante believed, for your belief will not give you a groat's worth more of understanding and appreciation; but you are called upon more and more to understand it. If you can read poetry as poetry, you will 'believe' in Dante's theology exactly as you believe in the physical reality of his journey; that is, you suspend both belief and disbelief.

But then, in the note to section two of the essay:

The theory of poetic belief and understanding here employed . . . is similar to that maintained by Mr I. A. Richards (see his *Practical Criticism* pp.179ff and pp.271ff.) . . . I am in agreement with Mr Richards's statement on p.271 (*op. cit.*). I agree for the reason that if you hold any contradictory theory you deny, I believe, the existence of 'literature' as well as of 'literary criticism'. We may raise the question whether 'literature' exists; but for certain purposes, such as the purpose of this essay on Dante, we must assume that there is literature and literary appreciations; we must assume that the reader can obtain the full 'literary' or (if you will) 'aesthetic' enjoyment without sharing the beliefs of the author. *If* there is 'literature', *if* there is 'poetry', then it must be possible to have full literary or poetic appreciation without sharing the beliefs of the poet. . . . If you deny the theory that full poetic appreciation is possible without belief in what the poet believed, you deny the existence of 'poetry' as well as 'criticism'; and if you push this denial to its conclusion, you will be forced to admit that there is very little poetry that you can appreciate, and that your appreciation of it will be a function of your philosophy or theology or something else. If, on the other hand, I push *my* theory to the extreme, I find myself in as great a difficulty. I am quite aware of the ambiguity of the word 'understand'. In one sense, it means to understand without believing, for unless you can understand a view of life (let us say) without believing in it, the word 'understand' loses all meaning, and the act of choice between one view and another is reduced to caprice. But if you yourself are convinced of a certain view of life, then you irresistibly and inevitably believe that if anyone comes to 'understand' it fully, his understanding *must* terminate in belief. It is possible, and sometimes necessary, to argue that full understanding must identify itself with full belief.

Now, you seem to be adopting a rather similar line, but turning Eliot on his head: since—you imply—there can't finally be a distinction between 'philosophical belief' and 'poetic assent', between 'taking the poem seriously' and becoming embroiled in the peculiar logic of the poem, there can't be 'literature', or at least that this example can't be *read* 'as literature'. Let me see if I can clarify why the problem arises but also why I think there is, finally, a difference between 'belief' and, if you like, 'poetic understanding'.

There's a nice story about a professor who once taught me theology. He was going through a 'crisis of belief' and every time he went to a eucharistic service he used to grapple mentally with himself as to whether he was sincere in going or not. By the time it got to the recitation of the Creed, he would be so exhausted by this battle with himself that he would be stretched out flat on one of the pews, and from there you'd hear, as the Creed began, his great booming voice: 'I BELIEVE IN GOD'—and then there'd be silence from him while the rest of the congregation continued to murmur their way politely through the rest of the Creed, until they got to 'and in Jesus Christ', at which point he would join in again, booming over everyone else 'AND IN JESUS CHRIST', and then, in a kind of choked self-silencing, he'd stop again, utterly exhausted by this effort of concentration and selective affirmation. These were the only two bits of the Creed he felt he could affirm without being intellectually dishonest.

Now, what interests me is precisely this sense of there being a difference between saying 'I believe in God' while honestly believing it and refusing to say the rest of the Creed because one doesn't *mean* it, 'believe it' or 'believe in it'. It's a bit like your reader *trying to mean* 'The Dedication'. But both of these instances seem to imply that saying something and saying that something with conviction, believingly, are different activities because the second is a kind of saying-plus-belief, a kind of two-tier operation: I both say 'I believe in God' and 'believe in God'. But as soon as you ask what that 'plus' is, you get into familiar difficulties. Rodney Needham's written a goodish book called *Belief, Language and Experience* which tries to tackle some of these difficulties. Among other things he traces the etymology and history of the word 'belief'; the complexity he uncovers is pretty unnerving—so that if I were asked what I 'mean' by the word 'belief', or, if you like, how the word 'belief' is used, I'd have considerable difficulty answering. But I think it's clear from Needham's analysis that to 'believe' (in) something can't be equated with having a *feeling* of 'belief', whatever else it may be. I'll come back to that later. At one point Needham draws an interesting parallel between affirming belief and Hume's analysis of 'making a promise', in the *Treatise* I, v. I'd better give you Needham's summary of Hume:

Hume thought the performance of promises to be one of the three 'fundamental laws of nature' on which the peace and security of human society entirely depended (1888: 526); and, since a promise is characteristically a declaration made by an individual, there would seem a reasonable supposition that its performance corresponded naturally to an act of the mind. But, as Hume proved, it is not itself a natural phenomenon. A promise is not simply a resolution, for that alone never imposes any obligation; it is not a desire to perform what is promised, for we may bind ourselves without such a desire or even with an aversion; nor is it, he argued, the willing of the action that is promised, for a promise always concerns some future time, whereas the will has an influence only on present actions. Therefore, Hume concluded, the act of the mind that enters into a promise 'must necessarily be the *willing* of that *obligation*, which arises from the promise' (516). We need not follow Hume in his subsequent argument about moral sentiments, but may come directly to his conclusion: 'A promise . . . is *naturally* something altogether unintelligible, nor is there any act of the mind belonging to it.' (517). Moreover, if there were any act of the mind belonging to the promise, it could not naturally produce any obligation, for promises have no force antecedent to human conventions. Thus 'promises are human inventions, founded on the necessities and interests of society' (519). The necessity comes from the fact that society depends on the mutual performance of services, but since these cannot be finished at the same instant, it is unavoidable that one party be contented to remain in uncertainty. A special form of words is hence invented by which we bind ourselves to the performance of any action, and on which the other party can rely: this form of words constitutes a promise, 'which is the sanction of the interested commerce of mankind' (522).

By Hume's account, therefore, a type of declaration which might seem to be the expression of a distinct state of mind, and intrinsic to the individual, is no such thing. It is instead the expression through the individual of a social institution, and it exists and has a special force because it is intrinsic to social life. The natural act of the mind which promises express is resolution (522), but the expression of a resolution is not commonly supposed to entail an obligation; so 'we *feign* a new act of the mind, which we call *willing* an obligation' (523).

Needham goes on: 'A promise is quite distinct from an inner state or experience: the whole point is that it must be public and conventional. It is a performative utterance, and there is no implication that it must be accompanied by any special emotion, etc.' Now, it seems to me that Needham, with Hume, has made one important point about 'promising': that it must be recognisable by someone else as being a promise, if only because it's normally (or necessarily) to someone else that we make a promise; and he's also used, almost *en passant*, Austin's term 'performative utterance' as the right term for promises. Needham is using Hume on promises to explore a similar case about 'believing', and this seems to imply that belief, or at least an affirmation of belief, must also be 'public and conventional', it must be recognisable as such by someone else, and that an affirmation of belief might be something like a performative utterance. It's not entirely clear to me just how far Needham himself wants to pursue these parallels, but there are two obvious difficulties about any such parallel that I want to explore myself. One is that you could argue that the 'someone else' who must be able to recognise your affirmation of belief *as* an affirmation of belief is, ultimately, God, and that could mean—on a certain understanding of God—that 'belief' needn't be humanly 'public' or 'conventional'; except that insofar as *you* have to recognise your affirmation to be one of belief *you* would need some 'public' rather than purely 'private' means of recognising it to be so. The case of my theology prof. is interesting here; the story partly makes sense because saying 'I believe in God' in a church during the communal recitation of the Creed *is* a public and conventional mode of affirmation. But is it a performative utterance and in what respects? It clearly isn't a performative utterance in the same way as making a promise or naming a ship is, since in those cases even if you said afterwards that you 'didn't mean it' you would still, according to the conventions, have made the promise or named the ship; you would, or could, still be held to your promise and the ship would still have the name you'd given it (though obviously there are differences between these two cases as well—it would be rather Goon-like to name a ship and then say 'But I didn't mean it'). But in the case of saying 'I believe in God' and then claiming you didn't mean it, it would be at least logically weird for anyone, including God, to 'hold you to it', even though that is precisely what some religious organisations try to do. (Though if you said you were lying, I suppose God could always reply that you were lying to yourself in claiming you were lying!) What I have in mind is that the crucial moment for saying 'I believe in God', or for reciting the Creed, is at baptism, as an affirmation that you are *entering* a community, a public act governed by liturgical conventions. Being baptised includes, not accidentally, both the making of a promise—to renounce the devil, world, flesh and all that—and the conferring of a name. But what is 'performative' about that utterance is precisely the joining of a group, a church, an *ecclesia*. It's here that I suspect your initial point about a religion as a set of practices and relationships was deficient. You talked about the relations between God and believer, priest and layperson, etc., but you left 'believer' unclear since you didn't talk about the act of *entering into* that set of relations and practices, the act of 'conversion'. But it's when we think about the act of religious *conversion* that the parallels and differences between religious belief and poetic assent become clearer. You see, a poem too could be regarded as a set of relations and practices, a kind of institution, which we 'enter into' by reading it. Remember that sentence of Wordsworth's in the preface to the *Lyrical Ballads*: 'It is supposed, that by the act of writing in verse an Author makes a formal engagement that he will gratify certain known habits of association; that he not only thus apprises the Reader that certain classes of ideas and expressions will be found in this book, but that others will be carefully excluded.' He even talks about this 'formal engagement' in terms of a 'promise' and a 'contract', though the precise terms of the promise aren't clear: 'I will not take upon me to determine the exact import of the promise which, by the act of writing in verse, an Author in the present day makes to his reader: but it will undoubtedly appear to many persons that I have not fulfilled the terms of an engagement thus voluntarily contracted.' Part of the point of the Preface is to argue for a new contract, a new expectation, a new promise—and he backs this up by pointing out how 'verse' has 'excited very different expectations' at different times. In other words, Wordsworth is trying to argue his readers, his *public*, into accepting a further change in the 'public' conventions; what the Preface is trying to do is ensure their conversion to those new conventions. But of course this very argument shows that the promise of poetry has to be learned, that 'literature' too is constituted by conventions and agreements and that these change, they 'hold' only for a certain period, which is why we have to 'learn' those of a past period. Also, what Wordsworth is asking for is a certain change in expectations for *these* poems, not for every poem written by other poets: while reading *these* poems, accept the terms of *my* engagement not somebody else's. And of course since those terms are new he finds he has to spell them out—that, for him, 'poetry is the spontaneous overflow of powerful feelings', and he asks his readers particularly that 'in judging these Poems he would decide by his own feelings genuinely, and not by reflection upon what will probably be the judgement of others.' It's *feeling* that Wordsworth puts at the centre of his notion of poetry: 'Another circumstance must be mentioned which distinguishes these Poems from the popular poetry of the day; it is this, that the feeling therein developed gives importance to the action and situation, and not the action and situation to the feeling.' Now, it seems to me that your way of talking about Herbert's 'The Dedication' is curiously Wordsworthian, partly because our whole notion of 'belief' has come to be essentially Wordsworthian: we tend to think that at the core of 'reading poetry', as at the core of 'religious believing', is a *'feeling'* which gives importance to the action and situation, rather than vice-versa. I suspect that's why Wordsworth is so often regarded as a 'religious poet' and why Arnold could even suggest that 'literature' might replace 'religion'. But isn't Herbert operating with a quite different notion of 'belief'? Feelings, of course, have an important place in his poetry, as presumably in his religious commitment, but it is the 'action and situation' that is important; to act in a certain way, to enter into or accept a certain situation, may give importance to, may even give rise to, certain feelings, but to think of the feelings as giving importance to the actions and situation would be, for him, inappropriate. Put that in terms of 'The Dedication': the dedication is precisely that, an *act* of dedication, a performative utterance, by saying it he does it; that act may or may not be accompanied by particular feelings (but what would a dedicatory feeling be?). The reader *can't* be in that situation, perform that act; what the reader *can* do is read or not read the rest of the volume, but to read it is to *act*, to enter on an engagement (and 'entry' is precisely what's implied by 'The Church Porch'), a commitment that implies consequences, just as 'entering the church' by being baptised is a commitment with consequences, involves living by certain rules of behaviour which you didn't 'make up'. And it's those rules of behaviour which are actually offered in 'The Church Porch': 'Beware of lust', 'Abstain wholly or wed', 'Drink not the third glasse', etc.—you stopped too early by only reading the first stanza. Insofar as 'The Dedication' *is* demanding a 'conversion' it's a public conversion according to conventions, rules of public behaviour, not some private feeling of 'believing in God'.

Now, having said that, can we read *The Temple* as 'literature'? What would that mean, in this case at least? *If* our notion of what's involved in 'reading literature' is basically a Wordsworthian one, then we can *try* to do what Wordsworth says the poet does: 'it will be the wish of the Poet to bring his feelings near to those of the persons whose feelings he describes, nay, for short spaces of time, perhaps, to let himself slip into an entire delusion, and even confound and identify his own feelings with theirs.' But if there aren't any 'feelings' involved—again, what's a dedicatory feeling?—we get into a tangle. So what are we doing when we read 'The Dedication' or 'The Church Porch' as literature? Wordsworth's phrase 'for short spaces of time' suggests one thing: that—to use Eliot's terms for a moment—'poetic assent' is precisely 'for short spaces of time', the time it takes to read the poem. Such 'assent' doesn't involve any long-term commitment to consequences in terms of the rules of behaviour governing our life, though it may lead to them if we are in some way 'converted' by reading something ('It changed my life' etc.). 'Poetic assent' doesn't involve any consequences because we don't just 'suspend disbelief', we 'suspend' the whole world, we put the whole world 'in brackets' while we read; to read a text as 'literature' is to enter into *that* situation—to perform an act of *epoché* curiously akin to that elusive device of the phenomenologists. But what does it mean to do *that*? One suggestion would be that it's to make a performative utterance that's governed by conventions but which *isn't* 'public' in the sense Needham, or Austin, intended. Use a parallel: if I make a promise to myself, I have to have available the public convention of 'promising' in order to do so, but whereas to make a public promise is to accept certain public consequences according to those conventions (not being trusted again if I break it, etc.), making a 'promise' *to myself* doesn't allow anyone else to insist on any consequences—which is why it's so easy to make and break promises to oneself (like 'I'll get up at 7 am every day'). If you think of the various 'utterances' that Austin discusses in connection with 'performatives', it's clear that many of them are both relational (I do something to, for, or with someone else) and *imply* some associated feeling (I apologise, I congratulate, I condole, etc.) —what he barbarously calls 'behabitives'—but the implied feeling isn't essential to the performative. Now, in real life we don't say 'I offer you my condolences' *in order to* have the feeling of sorrow, pity, or whatever; but it may be that, along Wordsworthian lines, someone might want to 'bring his feelings nearer to those of' someone condoling (why Wordsworth or anyone else should *want* to do such a thing is another matter); one way of 'condoling' someone is to write to them, of course, and given the association of the act of condoling with 'having a feeling', a 'good' letter of condolence doesn't just say 'I condole you', it attempts to enact feelings of sorrow, pity, regret, to communicate all the feelings one is conventionally supposed to have. Now it may be a curious thing to do, but one can imagine people reading letters of condolence not written to them, or by them, because 'the feeling therein developed gives importance to the action and situation' of reading the letter! In the case of declarations of love, it seems to be an extraordinarily common habit to read or listen to declarations not written to or by oneself—we call it reading love-poems or listening to Radio 1. What's involved in these instances is something like 'making a promise to oneself', at least in the case of reading (listening is rather different): a private act that only makes sense at all in terms of a public convention; to make a promise, or declaration of love, does logically require someone else to do it to, yet actually to make the promise or declaration to someone else involves one in possible *public consequences*; if all you want is the *feeling* and not the consequences, the only person you can involve is yourself, you have to keep the whole thing to yourself—which is maybe why reading literature is such a private activity these days, but that's another story. Now it may be that having got used to Wordsworthian premises, having learned those poetic conventions, we might try to extend them to other kinds of 'performative utterances' where feelings aren't involved at all—like warnings, advice, even assertions (like *Beyond the Fringe*'s reading of British Rail's 'Gentlemen lift the seat', as a loyal toast!)—but we would still be 'looking for' the feelings which *could* be associated with or accompany those utterances; it would still be the feelings that would 'give importance to the actions or situations'; so we might even try to read the warnings and advice in 'The Church Porch' as if they were expressing some elusively complex feeling —though I doubt if many readers have succeeded in doing so with that poem (they then write it off as an unsuccessful poem). I suspect that the Wordsworthian habit is now so engrained, or deeply learned, that we find it difficult, in England anyway, to 'read poetry' in any other way, however marginally satisfying the results. And it seems to me that that's eventually what you were doing, or trying to do, with 'The Dedication'. On the other hand, if you think of one kind of 'performative utterance' that Austin mentions in a footnote to *How to Do Things with Words*, a wholly different approach might be glimpsed:

I am told that in the hey-day of student duelling in Germany it was the custom for members of one club to march past members of a rival club, each drawn up in file, and then for each to say to his chosen opponent as he passed, quite politely, 'Beleidigung', which means 'I insult you'.

A whole mode of non-Wordsworthian reading is implied there! The point of the polite statement 'Beleidigung' is, of course, its consequences not its emotion; if one could create certain kinds of performative utterance, devoid of resonant emotion, and also without public consequences, one might have again shifted the conventions of 'literature', perhaps even with retrospective possibilities. Two examples spring to mind: in both cases fully to enter into the 'action and situation' the reader does actually have to *perform* not 'utterances' but *actions*. The first is quintessentially private, a literal playing with oneself; the second gains its point partly from the awareness that some time, some-where, thousands of other solitary people in quiet rooms will perform the same ludicrous actions—and there lies Samuel Beckett's promise of laughter. The first is from *Murphy*, his first published novel, the second from *Still*, one of his latest prose-pieces.

White (MURPHY)	*Black* (MR ENDON)
1. P—K4	1. Kt—KR3
2. Kt—KR3	2. R—KKt1
3. R—KKt1	3. Kt—QB3
4. Kt—QB3	4. Kt—K4
5. Kt—Q5	5. R—KR1

—and so on, including the notes.

Quite still then all this time eyes open when discovered then closed then opened and closed again no other movement any kind though of course not still at all when suddenly or so it looks this movement impossible to follow let alone describe. The right hand slowly opening leaves the armrest taking with it the whole forearm complete with elbow and slowly rises opening further as it goes and turning a little deasil till midway to the head it hesitates and hangs half open trembling in mid air. Hangs there as if half inclined to return that is sink back slowly closing as it goes and turning the other way till as and where it began clenched lightly on end of rest. Here because of what comes now not midway to the head but almost there before it hesitates and hangs there trembling as if half inclined etc. Half no but on the verge when in its turn the head moves from its place forward and down among the ready fingers . . .

—and so on, including the pauses.

Of course, to read Herbert's 'The Dedication', retrospectively, as a game of empty but amusing logical gestures would require a pretty perverse sense of humour.

*

LN: I *really* think you're being *extremely* inaccurate about Chris's paper. It's *basically irrelevant* to the argument whether we *feel* or *believe* anything while we read 'The Dedication'. What Chris is *really* looking for is a *theory* of reading, but, as usual, s/he's not been *rigorous* enough in the *analysis*. Feelings have got *nothing to do with* the problem of whether a *text* is *literature*; what we need is a *theoretical framework* in which we can *precisely locate* the *concept* of literature. There are some *totally untheorised* terms playing across Chris's discourse—terms like 'impersona', 'stipulated', 'postulated', 'overhearing', 'rehearsing'. The paper's logical *cul-de-sacs* about religious ideology are *interesting*, but they go *nowhere* because they're *utterly* premature; what s/he *should* have done was *elaborate systematically* that *part* of the argument about *reading*. I've drawn a small *diagram* which I want you all to look at. It should *clarify* the possible *permutations*. Of course, it's a very *provisional* sketch, what Althusser calls a *descriptive theory*, and it'll have to be *totally re-thought* at some point and somehow *integrated* with Pecheux's *discourse-analysis* and with Foucault's theory of *discursive formations*, and there's some recent work in Rumanian semiotics that I . . . Oh. Yes. The diagram. I've used some terms from recent work in some rather dubiously bourgeois sociology, but it's *basically* developed from Chris's own *vocabulary and systematises* that vocabulary at a *higher level*.

LN's Diagram

[Editor's Note: At this point the speaker apparently moved to the blackboard in order to draw the diagram mentioned. Unfortunately, this resulted in a loss of audibility on the tape-recording. For the next fifteen minutes or so, therefore, only fragments of the commentary are decipherable; these are given in full below, with ellipses indicated by (. . . zzzzz. . . . .). In these circumstances, it is particularly to be regretted that none of those present at the seminar transcribed the diagram concerned and that no reliable reconstruction of it has proved to be possible. It was, however, clearly concerned with the systematically possible relationships between different 'textual voices', in the activities of both writer and reader. This much at least is apparent from the opening remarks.]

(. . . zzzzz . . . . .) Let me explicate the diagram, concisely and systematically.

First, the *writer writing*. The writer *transimpositions* determinate apparatus positions and practices; they are reconstituted as *textual designations* ('the words on the page'). The particular apparatus is variable, and therefore so are the detailed inflections of the *textual voice*. But there are basically *three* modalities of textual voice possible, which I've characterised as *'own voice'*, *'dramatic voice'*, and *'voice-over'*. These are related to, or can posit, *four* categories of *textual reader* ('implied reader'): *'listener'*, *'addressee'*, *'understudy'*, and *'repetiteur'*. But not all categories of textual reader can be posited by each voice. There are *six* basic possibilities.

One: own voice/listener. Example: a private letter. I *write* a private letter to someone I know. I posit that specific someone as *listening* to my *own voice* in which I *pronounce* as *textual speaker*. The voice is a *private voice* and the relation between speaker and listener (the relation constituted *in* the text) is that of *confidant(e)*. In writing, I *presume* privacy, i.e. that no one apart from the specific reader will read the letter (no '*eavesdropper*'). Clearly, this suggests the (illusorily) close affinity between letter-writing and face-to-face oral communication: the text seeks to be transparent, a mode of *presence*, with the whole idealist metaphysics *that* involves (. . . zzzzz . . . . .)

However, (iii) cannot in practice occur without (iv), though they are analytically distinct. The writer, assuming a *dramatic voice*, posits the textual reader as, necessarily, adopting the *same* dramatic voice while s/he reads: the reader is posited as *understudy* to the *persona* which *stimulates* a *replaying* of the persona, a close *imitation*. The textual author acts as *actor-director*, demanding of the understudy more precise fidelity to the details and nuances of the role than that required for an *impersona*. An example of (iii) and (iv) clearly in operation together would be 'Bishop Blougram's Apology':

> So, you despise me, Mr Gigadibs.
> No deprecation,—nay, I beg you, sir!
> Beside 'tis our engagement: don't you know,
> I promised, if you'd watch a dinner out,
> We'd see truth dawn together?—
>   . . . You do despise me then.
> And if I say 'despise me',—never fear—
> I know you do not in a certain sense—
> Not in my arm-chair for example: here,
> I well imagine you respect my place . . .

The textual reader is here assigned two roles, *replaying* the *persona* in the Bishop's *dramatic voice*, while *attending to* that voice as Mr Gigadibs (stipulated as despising that persona yet deprecating that despising, etc.). In 'The Love-Song of J. Alfred Prufrock' we perhaps have (iv) with a variation on (iii): the persona talks to himself and himself plays his imagined impersonae ('Let us go then, you and I'; 'Oh, do not ask, "What is it?" '; ' "That is not it at all,/That is not what I meant, at all." '). In 'Gerontion' we perhaps have (iv) with (iii/a), if 'you' in the line 'I would meet you upon this honestly' is taken to be Christ rather than *specifically* the reader. (. . . zzzzz . . . . .)

What of a *voice-over* that isn't directed at a *stipulated class* of reader but at 'everybody'? Such a voice would be *broad-casting* to 'the public', but since a *public audience* is made up of *specific listeners*, each listener is *postulated* as a *'representative'* of that public, and, since the public is 'everybody', that includes the *presenter* as well, so the presenter *presents him/herself* as also a *representative* of the public. S/he therefore speaks in her/his 'own voice' but her/his *'own public voice'*, while the audience is postulated as listening *as themselves*, as each specific person yet also as undifferentiated everyone. The *Radio Times* reveals this structure clearly. For example:

10.30 MAIN NEWS
with *Angela Rippon*

Rippon is the 'presenter' of *The News*; we are 'with' her, since she too is a member of the public, and she too therefore 'listens to the news' while she 'reads' it. She, of course, only *reads* the news; whoever *writes* it is left coyly undeclared. (. . . zzzzz . . . . .)

Is this lengthy paragraph to be attributed to a *Radio Times* staff-writer, or to 'the presenter Anthony Smith', or to the producer David Paterson? We don't know who wrote the words—but they *present themselves* as written by somebody, so as we read them we *'repeat'* the style, tone, rhythm, of the way they're written, yet not in a dramatic voice (as understudy to a persona); we repeat them in *'our own voice'*. Insofar as the words are directed at 'everybody' as themselves, we don't need to adopt an impersona (Mr Gigadibs) either, so again we read *'as ourselves'*. Yet we didn't write the paragraph, so in repeating it as ourselves we *receive* it simply as *given*, as originating from no other source than the page itself, and since it is in 'our own voice' that we *'hear'* it, we tend to *endorse* it as what we *already know*: we are telling ourselves something that seems curiously familiar, or at least innocuous. To recognise explicitly that someone else, someone specific, is telling us this would be to turn this deeply ideological paragraph from *anonymous information* into challengeable assertion. The term I've chosen for this interesting, and wide-spread, anonymity, this reduplication of a non-dramatic voice in our own voice, is *'overhearing'*: we over-hear ourselves saying something. The reader in this case is a *'repetiteur'*—it seems an appropriate word to pinch from the French: assistant-master (in charge of Prep.), private tutor or coach, chorus-master (theatrical). No, I am *not* thinking of the overtones of French mistress. (. . . zzzzz . . . .)

But if Chris's points about reading are to have any general validity they must be *developed* to accommodate *all* texts, from a British Rail notice saying 'Passengers cross the footbridge by the line only' to George Eliot's *Middlemarch*. But in much of *Middlemarch*, unlike 'The Dedication', the reader is not being *addressed*, is not put in the position of impersona or even understudy. As s/he reads the text, s/he *over-hears* the text's *voice-over* and thereby is *positioned* as *repetiteur* of the text's *presenter*:

Miss Brooke had that kind of beauty which seems to be thrown into relief by poor dress.

This is information, anonymous knowledge, not addressed to anyone specific or to any class of reader but presented for everyone, anyone, to read; and I don't read it in anyone's voice except my own, I repeat it like a lesson remembered, or over-hear it while I (perhaps) *visualise* what is 'described':

Her hand and wrist were so finely formed that she could wear sleeves not less bare of style than those in which the Blessed Virgin appeared to Italian painters.

The peculiar *effectivity* of this mode of writing lies precisely in the *conflation* of the reader's own voice with that of the textual author; since the textual author has no definitely *dramatic* persona ('Here I am, an old man') and the textual reader has no *definite* impersona ('You despise me, Mr Gigadibs'), the conflation of tone, pace, 'style', is achieved without effort or dramatic exertion, easily, casually, intimately, 'naturally', 'immediately'. And the inclusion of dramatic voices—those of the 'characters'—*reinforces* the *union* of the *narrative-voice* with *my own voice*: as I read a dialogue passage interspersed by, supported by, narrative comment, the very demand of adjusting to the oscillating personae/impersonae relations 'between' the *character-voices* allows the non-dramatic narrative-voice to be assumed as almost wholly 'my own'. In that effect of 'overhearing' my 'own' comments lies the deepest *truth-effect*, the insidious credibility of the commentary, the unobtrusively acceptable 'knowledge' of the text, the barely-refusable status of the 'already-known' (. . . zzzzz . . . . .)

These 'textual relations' between textual voices and posited readers are in many cases transpositions of the adopted voices and posited relations in actual social relations, while those textual relations can themselves be further transposed by texts, as in much modernist writing. But, crucially, of course, the whole point about a 'literary' work, a work of 'literature', is the way in which *reading* it demands but doesn't guarantee a *reduplication* of the reader's voice with the textual voices: you don't read a novel or a poem, as you might read a letter or a public notice or a work of history or criticism, to get the gist of it, the *content* that a précis or second-hand account might give; a novel is constructed as a *play of voices*, as a particular and shifting set of relations between voice and reader (Thackeray knew this better than most). It's to *enter into* those relations and enact that play of voices that we read a literary text. Which also means that we can locate the *limits* of 'literature': only *some* textual relations can be transposed into 'literary' relations.

We can see this even more clearly if we now look at the *lower* half of the diagram, and analyse the *process of reading* as an activity of *re-impositioning*, of recreating (but not necessarily *complementing*) those textual positions, relations and voices. Again, we can approach this systematically, taking each textual relation in turn. Thus, if we go back to (i), *reading* a *private letter*, and

Phil: L!! Will you *shut up*! If you try to go 'systematically' and 'rigorously' through the rest of that grotty diagram, I'll strangle you. The things got more flaws in it than a skyscraper. It's not rigorous, it's not systematic, it's not even original. *And* you haven't read Wolfgang Iser and his mob. You could go on all day adding, defining, refining your terms and at the end of it all you couldn't *do* anything with them—I know you! All this pseudo-scientificity is worse than useless, it's just the latest way of *appearing* to be 'radical'. If you can somehow present yourself as taking up an intransigently systematic, rigorous stance about the concept of literature or realism or whatever, that's somehow supposed to guarantee a political intransigence. It doesn't even guarantee political coherence. In any case what you're offering are metaphors not concepts. You talk about locating the limits of literature. Rubbish. What would you do with Shklovsky's *Letters not about Love*; where would that fit into your neat little diagram? Don't answer, I'm not interested. Look, your *metaphors are* interesting, 'cos they're all we've got, but where you go barmy is in not grasping that we can *only think* in metaphors and metaphors can't be systematised; look what happened to Aristotle. Yea, I've read me Derrida. Take the metaphors seriously, think with them, and you might get somewhere. While you were jabbering on about theatrical voices and producers, directors, casting agents and all the rest, I was thinking about Diderot, Stanislavsky, Brecht. If you want to talk about *theatre*, read *them* and try and do some real acting. Then you might see that your 'distinctions' between 'own voice' and 'dramatic voice' simply don't work. Let me calm down. I'll read you something might show you what I mean. Are you sitting comfortably? Then I'll begin.

Phil's Description

'I was still in this state of inner division, uncertainty and ceaseless search for something I could not find, when I went into the general dressing-room where we would all have to put on our costumes and make-up together instead of by ourselves. The buzz and racket of the conversation made it difficult to concentrate. And yet I felt that this moment of my first investiture in that mildewed morning coat, as well as the putting on of the yellowish grey wig, beard, and the rest, was one of extreme importance to me. Only those material things could prompt me to find what I had subconsciously been searching for. On this moment I had pinned my last hope.

Our dressing-room resounded with exclamations, just as though the occasion were some ordinary amateur performance.

'Why, I'd never know you!'—'Don't tell me that's you?'—'Amazing!' —'Good work, I didn't think you had it in you!'—and so on indefinitely.

These exclamations drove me wild, and the remarks, tinged with doubt and dissatisfaction which fell to my share, quite disheartened me.

'Something is wrong . . . I don't know just what it is . . . who is he?' 'I don't understand, who are you supposed to be?'

How awful it was for me to listen to these remarks and questions when I had nothing to reply!

Who was I trying to represent? How did I know? If I had been able to guess I should have been the first to tell who I was.

And I heartily wished the make-up man in the nether regions. Until he had come along and transformed my face into that of a routine pallid theatrical blond I had felt I was on the track of discovering my secret identity.

. . . Finally they all went off to the school stage to be inspected by Tortsov. I sat alone in the dressing-room, completely prostrated, helplessly gazing in the mirror at my featureless theatrical face. Inwardly I was already convinced of my failure. I decided not to present myself to the Director but to take off my costume and remove my make-up with the aid of some horrid looking greenish cream which stood before me. I had already put one finger in it and begun to rub it on my face. And . . . I went on rubbing. All the other colours blurred, like water-colour which has fallen into some liquid. My face turned greenish-greyish-yellowish, like some counterpart to my costume. It was difficult to distinguish where my nose was, or my eyes, or my lips. I smeared some of the same cream on my beard and moustache and then finally all over my wig. Some of the hair clotted into lumps . . . and then, almost as though I were in some delirium, I trembled, my heart pounded, I did away with my eyebrows, powdered myself at random, smeared the back of my hands with a greenish colour and the palms with light pink. I straightened my coat, and gave a tug to my cravat. I did all this with a quick, sure touch, for this time I knew who I was representing and what kind of a fellow he was!

With my high hat on at a slightly rakish angle I was suddenly aware of the style of my full-cut and once stylish trousers, which were now so worn and threadbare. I made my legs fit the crease which had formed in them by turning my toes sharply in. This gave me ridiculous legs. Have you ever noticed how ridiculous the legs of some people are? I have always had a sense of aversion towards such people. As a result of this unusual posture of my legs, I seemed shorter and my gait was quite changed. For some reason my whole body was slightly inclined to the right side. All I needed was a cane. One was lying near-by so I picked it up although it did not exactly fit the picture of what I had in mind. Now all I lacked was a quill pen to stick behind my ear or hold in my teeth. I sent a call boy for one and while waiting for his return paced up and down the room, feeling how all the parts of my body, features, facial lines, fell into their proper places and established themselves. After walking around the room two or three times, with an uncertain, uneven gait I glanced in the mirror and did not recognise myself. Since I had looked into it the last time a fresh transformation had taken place in me.

'It is he, it is he!' I exclaimed, unable to repress the joy that was suffocating me. If only that quill would come, then I could go up to the stage.

I heard footsteps in the corridor. Evidently it was the call boy bringing me the quill. I rushed to meet him and at the door ran straight into Rakhmanov.

'What a fright you gave me!' burst from him. 'My dear fellow, who on earth is this? What a get-up! Is it Dostoyevskii? The Eternal Husband? Can it be you—Kostya? What are you supposed to be?'

'A critic!' I answered in a hoarse voice, and with sharp diction.

'What critic, my boy?' Rakhmanov continued his query, somewhat taken aback by my bold and penetrating glance.

I felt like a leech clinging to him.

'What critic?' I retorted with obvious intent to insult him. 'The fault-finding critic who lives inside of Kostya Nazvanov. I live in him in order to interfere with his work. That is my great joy. That is the purpose of my existence.'

I was myself amazed at the brazen, unpleasant tone and the fixed, cynical, rude stare which accompanied it, and with which I addressed Rakhmanov. My tone of voice and self-confidence upset him. He did not know how to find a new angle of approach and therefore was at a loss what to say to me. He was quite disconcerted.

'Let's go,' he finally said rather uncertainly. 'The others have long since begun.'

'Let's go, then, since they have long since begun,' I mimicked his words and did not budge but continued to stare brazenly at my disconcerted instructor.

An awkward pause ensued. Neither of us moved. It was obvious that Rakhmanov wanted to get this incident over with as quickly as possible but did not know how to go about it. Fortunately for him at this moment the call boy came running with the goose quill. I snatched it from his hand and stuck it between my lips. This narrowed my mouth into a straight, angry line. The sharpened point on one side of my lips and the broad flare of feathers on the other underscored the corrosive expression of my face.

'Let's go,' repeated Rakhmanov in a low, almost shy voice.

'Let's go!' My mimicking tone was caustic and brazen.

We walked onto the stage.

*

OK, that's from Stanislavsky's *Building a Character* and what's fascinating about it is that it's *true*. If you've ever created a role, or created anything, you can see what he's talking about. Kostya spent *days* before this exercise in a state of bafflement, inertia, distraction, self-division, as if he was almost possessed by some other personality yet not quite, as though he'd been drained of his own personality but without another one filling the emptiness —'it was as though I had forgotten something, could neither recall nor find it.' It's a *very* peculiar state. But what's really interesting is that what seems to be at stake is Kostya's own 'self'. It's very tricky to get this right. Stanislavsky sometimes gives the impression that an actor should 'lose himself' in a part. In *An Actor Prepares* he says '. . . the very best thing that can happen is to have the actor completely carried away by the play. Then regardless of his own will he lives the part, not noticing how he feels, not thinking about what he does, and it all moves of its own accord, subconsciously and intuitively.' But it's a lot more complex than that: even when Kostya was taken over by 'the Critic', he says, 'I still did not lose the sense of being myself. . . . Actually I was my own observer at the same time that another part of me was being a fault-finding, critical creature.' It's the old, old problem that Diderot explored in his *Paradoxe sur le comedien*; he too says that the actor 'must have in himself an unmoved and disinterested onlooker.' It's Brecht, of course, who's emphasised the Diderot approach this century, and Brecht's often sharply contrasted with Stanislavsky. He implies the contrast himself when he quotes Reumert:

If I feel I am *dying*, and if I *really* feel it, then so does everybody else; if I act as though I had a dagger in my hand, and am entirely filled by the one idea of killing the child, then everybody shudders. . . . The whole business is a matter of mental activity being communicated by emotions, or the other way round if you prefer it: a feeling so strong as to be an obsession, which is translated into thoughts. If it comes off it is the most infectious thing in the world; anything external is then a matter of complete indifference.

or Rapaport:

This is the central feature of our method of work on the part. . . . Take any object, a cap for example; lay it on the table or on the floor and try to regard it as though it were a rat; make-believe that it is a rat, and not a cap. . . . Picture what sort of rat it is; what size, colour? . . . We thus commit ourselves to believe quite naively that the object before us is something other than it is and, at the same time, learn to compel the audience to believe . . .

Brecht says that Rapaport is describing 'a course of acting, supposedly according to Stanislavsky's method', and against this 'supposedly' Stanislavskian method Brecht, of course, wanted his actors to develop an 'alienated' way of acting:

The actor does not allow himself to become completely transformed on the stage into the character he is portraying. He is not Lear, Harpagon, Schweik; he shows them. He reproduces their remarks as authentically as he can; he puts forward their way of behaving to the best of his abilities and knowledge of men; but he never tries to persuade himself (and thereby others) that this amounts to a complete transformation. Actors will know what it means if I say that a typical kind of acting without this complete transformation takes place when a producer or colleague shows one how to play a particular passage. It is not his own part, so he is not completely transformed; he underlines the technical aspect and retains the attitude of someone just making suggestions.

Brecht's own suggestions for practising and achieving this alienated acting include the rehearsal techniques of transposing speeches into the third person or the past tense, or speaking the stage directions out loud; but there's one suggestion he makes which I want to pick out:

The actor should refrain from living himself into the part prematurely in any way, and should go on functioning as long as possible as a reader (which does not mean a reader-aloud). An important step is memorizing one's first impressions.

When reading his part the actor's attitude should be one of a man who is astounded and contradicts. Not only the occurrence of the incidents, as he reads about them, but the conduct of the man he is playing, as he experiences it, must be weighed up by him and their peculiarities understood; none can be taken as given, as something that 'was bound to turn out that way', that was 'only to be expected from a character like that'. Before memorizing the words he must memorize what he felt astounded at and where he felt impelled to contradict. For these are dynamic forces that he must preserve in creating his performance.

Now you can probably see where I'm driving. It's when you think about *reading* that it's possible to push these different emphases of Stanislavsky and Brecht even further apart. What I mean is that for some people reading fiction seems to involve a complete identification, empathy, losing yourself, 'becoming' the characters or author, whereas other people want to hold back, observe, register what they're reading. The most extraordinary account of reading that I know seems almost to oscillate between these two attitudes, but to come down more with the first. Proust's *On Reading* talks at one point about the function of silence while we're reading:

. . . silence does not bear, like speech, the trace of our defects, of our grimaces. It is pure, it is truly an atmosphere. Between the author's thoughts and ours it does not interpose those irreducible elements of our different egotisms which refuse to submit to thought. The very language of the book is pure (if the book deserves that name), made transparent by the author's thought which has removed everything from it that was not itself, to the point of giving it back its faithful image; each sentence, in essence, resembling the others, for all are spoken with the unique inflection of a personality.

At another point he talks about the way reading can stimulate 'certain minds . . . which a kind of laziness or frivolity prevents from descending spontaneously into the deep regions of the self where the true life of the mind begins'; 'what is necessary', he says, in these cases, 'is an intervention which, while coming from another, takes place in our own inmost selves, which is indeed the impetus of another mind, but received in the midst of solitude. Now we have seen that this was precisely the definition of reading, and that it fitted reading only.' This 'definition of reading' almost collapses 'another mind' and 'our own inmost selves' into one, an absorption of the one into the other, though not quite. Now I think that Chris's account of reading 'The Dedication' tried to combine

Proust's emphasis *and* Brecht's—like Brecht's actor reading his part, she took nothing for granted, pulled up sharp, was astounded, contradicted, tried to make sense of the part she was being asked to play, but of course what she was basically astounded at was the notion—Proust's notion—of this intervention or impulse of another mind taking place in her own inmost self. Try to combine those two and you end up with Chris's dilemmas. I suspect though that Chris's paradoxes are related to Brecht and Proust in the same way that Brecht saw Vakhtangov's theatrical approach as related to Meyerhold and Stanislavsky: 'Viewed dialectically, Vakhtangov is the Stanislavsky–Meyerhold complex *before* the split rather than its reconciliation later.' Chris's dilemmas are the Brecht–Proust complex before the split rather than its reconciliation later. I'd better explain that a bit more.

You see, I think there's a deeply intractable problem about Chris's account, insofar as it aligns with Proust rather than with Brecht; it's the old problem of the 'self'. Like Proust, she seems to be operating with a notion of 'the inmost self' and it's the disorientation and disintegration of that self which the Brechtian part of her observes with such puzzlement: she can't pull the divergent bits of that self together, and she starts asking daft questions like 'can I class myself?' Basically, Chris's notion of the self is a Cartesian one, a self defined as a consciousness: all her dilemmas take place in her consciousness; reading for her is a 'purely mental state', as Proust calls it in *A la recherche du temps perdu*—remember that long passage where Marcel talks about the 'zone of consciousness', the 'abyss', that comes between him and reality except when he's reading, because then reality itself dissolves into consciousness. Now—to pick up a point of Dai's—Chris's notion of *meaning* is tied to this, so that she wants to mean what she says as if meaning were some kind of internal accompaniment of saying, an event in her mental self, in her consciousness. Well, that whole notion has been rightly hammered by Wittgenstein, Ryle and the Oxford lads; that kind of two-tier notion of meaning won't stand up any more. But what remains problematic is that there still *seems* to be a kind of doubleness at work, a two-tiered self, when we read, which Chris's account brings out very well—a disjunction between your real self, your actual everyday, ordinary self, with its everyday beliefs and feelings and what-not, and the beliefs, feelings, personality, that the reading self seems to have to adopt to read. Stanislavsky's pupil who finds himself turning into a Critic has the same problem—it's as if his 'real' self were somehow undermined and partly replaced by, or revealed as, another self.

But if we try to think about the self, the ordinary everyday self, *without* collapsing back into a Cartesian notion of consciousness, how can we think about it? It's here that 'the paradox of the actor' seems to bite very deep indeed. Because our very notion of 'self' seems already saturated with theatrical metaphors: the very word 'person' has overtones of 'persona', a mask, a theatrical role; we talk about 'playing a role', in such a way that almost everything we do seems to be a matter of role-playing; Shakespeare wasn't just being biassed towards his own metier when he gave us those inevitable quotes—'All the world's a stage', 'Life's but a walking shadow, a poor player/That struts and frets his hour upon the stage', 'I hold the world but as . . ./A stage where every man must play a part', 'this great stage of fools'; Ralegh had said it before him—'What is our life? a play of passion . . .'; the sociologists have said it, *ad nauseam*, since; even Sartre can't do without the stage—his *Kean* makes every existentialist seem like a bit-player looking for a decent role, an author in search of half a dozen characters; and if you probe Marx's or Freud's *metaphors* you come up with drama all over the place —we're all personifications of our economic positions, the unconscious is another scene, a representation in a hidden theatre. Goldsmith pinned us all down when he said that Garrick on the stage was natural, simple, affecting —but off-stage he was acting. We all see ourselves in Hamlet, but Hamlet sees himself as having to act a part—think of him in Act I, slipping in and out of character, his student-character, till his old college chums don't know whether he's gone mad or not. . . . If the notion of the self is an ideological one, its ideology is largely derived from the theatre, so it might be from Brecht's attack upon the theatre that we can develop an attack on the ideology of the self—think even of Brecht's early play *Man is Man* and the note to it: 'He is lived'. But I don't think that can be done just by a kind of psychological juggling with the self, a kind of merely psychological distancing from the roles we play, a standing outside of them while we play them, like Brecht's actors. It's important to do that, yes, if only because there's a parallel between Brecht's instructions to his actors and one aspect of relating 'theory' and 'practice' in politics: if you adopt a Stanislavskian attitude to politics, you throw yourself into the part, become 'committed', with all the 'right' and necessary emotions, passion, anger, and eventually hatred; that kind of spontaneity is real dramatic—but you may be playing the wrong script: think of *Measures Taken*. If on the other hand you remain detached, analytical, a spectator, then the nearest you'll get to political *action* is to write a few books of theory, all very useful, but without any direct point of purchase on political power—think of *Galileo*. You can't solve that dilemma simply by having it both ways or oscillating between the two, but you *can* treat *everything* you do, both action and theory, as *provisional*, as part of a script that can be re-written at any moment, a play in the making—think of the epilogue to *Good Person of Setsuan*: '*you* write the happy ending to the play'. That kind of 'provisional' attitude can even be maintained in relation to your own emotions, your own political anger—Brecht got close to expressing that in 'To Posterity':

> for we knew only too well:
> even the hatred of squalor
> makes the brow grow stern,
> even anger against injustice
> makes the voice grow harsh. Alas, we
> who wished to lay the foundations for kindness
> could not ourselves be kind.

OK, I'm getting away from reading, I know. But I'm trying to indicate why I think Chris's dilemmas arise from a *pre*-Brechtian attitude, so that I can point to a very different way of 'reading'. If you think about Brecht's practice in the theatre, there are at least three features of it that could perhaps be adapted to the practice of reading. First, his work is always collaborative, collective, not just in the sense of working with a theatre-group (the *Berliner Ensemble*) in rehearsing and producing plays, but in the very process of writing itself: almost all his writing was done in collaboration with others, picking other people's brains, having an open-door policy while he was writing, always, if he could, working with a group around him as he wrote. Second, he was constantly *re*-writing, revising, re-shaping, not just in the sense that every writer does—endless redrafts until there's a 'finished product'—but in a more radical sense of re-casting a script when it had outlived its usefulness, always regarding a version of a work as temporary, ready for this performance but not to be embalmed and fixed—think of what he did to *Threepenny Opera* when he wanted to make a film of it or when he wrote *The Threepenny Novel*. After Hiroshima he re-wrote *Galileo* and though he says 'we had to make only a few alterations—not a single one to the structure of the play', you get the impression that if structural changes *had* been needed, Brecht wouldn't have hesitated. Third, Brecht's attitude to his own plays was also the attitude he had to 'the classics'—he would rewrite, adapt, re-shape, re-*think* the plays by other authors that he produced himself, not just in the now-familiar sense of giving the play an 'interpretation' or 'cutting'; Brecht would write his own scenes and insert them, change the role of characters entirely, give them completely new lines—look at his adaptations of Lenz's *The Tutor*, Segher's *Joan of Arc*, Molière's *Don Juan*, Farquhar's *Trumpets and Drums*, or the process that went into his production of *Coriolanus*. Now the point about all these aspects of his work is that they aren't things that just went on in his head, if only because they involved lots of other people: they were collective and material activities in a public world; with Brecht, you always get the sense that writing, that *art*, is a form of practical *work*, not a private agony over a blank sheet of paper—that's perhaps what partly explains his rate of production, the speed at which he produced stuff: look at Volker's *Brecht Chronicle*! And in all this activity Brecht is reading a lot, researching his plays, looking at scripts, reading novels and classics for adaptation, keeping abreast of what's happening in literature generally, devouring books and manuscripts. But it's reading with an eye on *use*, a way of reading that treats texts the way a handyman treats bits of wood and odds and ends lying around the workshop, as raw material for his *bricolage*—to use that once fashionable Levi-Strauss term. Like the bricoleur, Brecht sees things from unexpected angles, finds uses for them they didn't have before, puts unexpected things together, in order to make *another* text, one that might have political edge in his own context, one that might help to change the theatre itself, and through that the audiences, and through them . . .

OK, what relevance can this have for our own kind of reading? Well, one thing is that most of us now read in *solitude*; we've become used to that notion of 'reading', and we actually think of most 'literary texts' in terms of private, solitary consumption, even though many of them weren't even designed that way—not even the great nineteenth-century novels: think of them being read out in the family or other gatherings, or, more generally, think of the public status given them by serialisation—a sense of large numbers of people reading each issue, each part-number, at the same time and discussing them; think of Dickens's public readings. And obviously a great deal of poetry, from Homer to Chaucer, was meant for public recitation, just as a lot of lyric poetry was meant to be sung in public or in a group—think of the context of troubadour love-songs. I suppose the nearest we get nowadays to that sense of a 'public' status for literature is in the serialisation of Dickens, Hardy, Trollope on TV, or at large rock-concerts, or, of course, in the theatre. But even in the case of plays the way we 'study' them tends to be by reading them, each of us individually. And literature generally *has* become something we 'study', at school or in universities; there's a long history behind that, but perhaps it's time we began to change that history a bit, to re-write the practice of reading and studying literature as more or less solitary individuals. I'm not sure it's possible to break that habit, or even to erode it—though you find something of what I'm after in writing workshops, or in the editorial meetings of small literary magazines; you also find it most obviously in oppositional theatre-groups, collectively creating a show. But can we introduce something of *that* into the everyday reading of literature, particularly in the 'study' of literature in education —particularly when the whole of education is still shaped by individual written performance, in competitive exams? Of course, there's some sense of collective, collaborative 'reading' when a text is discussed in a seminar or super-vision, but mainly that takes the form of comparing our individual 'readings', rather than using the text, collectively, to launch off from, find uses for, unexpected angles on, so that we can produce our own texts, do our own work.

I'll give you an example of the kind of collective and unexpected *bricolage* that can happen. Our theatre-group was thinking of doing a production of *Coriolanus*, so we started by having a close look at Brecht's 'Study' of the first scene and rewriting it, playing around with it. Then someone pointed out that the 'Study' had been written sometime around 1953, the year of the workers' rising in Berlin. And that led us to Gunter Grass's play, *The Plebèians Rehearse the Uprising*, about Brecht rehearsing *Coriolanus* during the rising. But then someone else decided to investigate the political context of Grass's work, in Germany from '64 to '66, and found out that Grass had made over fifty speeches for Willy Brandt during the '65 general election in West Germany; the money raised by those speeches was spent in providing five libraries for the West German Army (and one for conscientious objectors!), in order to help 'change the German Army into a civilised army'. And that led us on to the problem of *how* you could 'civilise' an army—which, after all, isn't that far from the problems explored in *Coriolanus*—so we ended up offering to do a show at our own local army barracks, and we re-wrote *Coriolanus* for that audience. We wanted to take the show to Northern Ireland after that, but it didn't work out. Or take 'The Dedication' itself. I was interested by Chris's quoting that note from 'The Printers to the Reader', in which the 'Printers' clearly interpret the dedication as claiming divine inspiration for *The Temple*. Now, in fact that note was almost certainly written by Nicholas Ferrar, not the printers—just as, incidentally, that 'sweet youth' *was* someone definite, Herbert's brother, Henry. But have you ever thought about the actual printers of *The Temple*? Their names are on the title-page of the first edition: Thomas Buck and Roger Daniel, printers to the University of Cambridge. Buck was one of the licensed printers in Cambridge from 1625 to about 1640, then his name disappears from the imprint and Daniel's appears by itself for a while; Daniel was in some kind of trouble with Parliament in 1642 and finally had his patent cancelled in 1650—at which point Buck's name reappears for a year or so; then in 1653 the London Stationers' Company, who'd been in a long struggle with Cambridge about the Stationers' monopoly being broken, more or less bought out the Cambridge printers and put a man of their own called Legate into the Cambridge print-shop as their agent; Cambridge cancelled Legate's licence in 1655 and appointed John Field instead, who had been printer to Parliament back in 1649—and the same year, 1655, Cromwell gave Field the monopoly on printing Bibles, together with Henry Hills, who'd been a Leveller in '48 and was also an official printer to the House of Commons, along with Giles Calvert and Thomas Brewster—and both those two were still going after the Restoration: they were both imprisoned in the early 1660s, and Calvert's wife had a secret press seized as late as 1667. . . . I could go on, but you get the point: the story of the *printers* in that period is fascinating, with a commercial monopoly battle going on between London and Cambridge and a political struggle going on over control of printing in general. Now, I'm not sure what *use* anyone could make of 'The Dedication', but it'd be fascinating to find out what happened to Buck and Daniel, and Calvert and Field, and Hills and Brewster, during the Civil War and after, so as to write, say, a play about the conflicts in the printing trade then and compare them with the conflicts in the printing industry today—the politics of control over the media and all that. If we did *that* we might *learn* something *useful*!

Pretty obviously, all this hasn't got much to do with what we normally mean by 'reading literature', but I'm suggesting that if you read with an eye to the *use* you can make of a text, all sorts of things turn up, and you find yourself trying to re-work the text in ways that actually teach you a lot more, in the end, than you would have got from 'reading' it the way Chris has—or, still more, than the normal kind of 'close reading'. I suppose what I'm after could be called *really practical* criticism! But I do think that if you believe that 'literature' is important, you can't just stick to criticism; you have to be able to cash that belief in action, and that means trying to *make* texts, *make* 'literature', write, use texts, in ways that actually connect to things that are important now. Otherwise you're back with Dai's Romantics, looking for private feelings, and then you get hang-ups about your private 'self'. So I want to rewrite Proust: 'reading *can* stimulate us to *action* when a certain kind of laziness or frivolity prevents us from engaging spontaneously with the complex *political* issues that are the true life of the society.' If we could regard reading in *that* way, then perhaps we could find a post-Proustian, even post-Brechtian way of regarding 'literature'. Certainly at the very least we need less *reverence* for the text, less of a fetishistic attitude; let's rewrite them, kick 'em around, see where they lead us, see what real use we can make of them in the public world, and that means, for me, within the political struggle. If we don't do that, then 'reading literature' is going to become more and more an empty activity, a mere private ritual, devoid of any real connection, a 'purely mental state'. About twenty years before Herbert was born, you can see a parallel to some of the problems we've now got about 'literature' in relation, then, to 'prayer'. Remember the *Second Admonition* to Parliament in 1572, against the revised *Book of Common Prayer*:

The Book is such a piece of work as it is strange we will use it, besides I cannot account it praying, as they use it commonly, but only reading or saying of prayers, even as a child that learned to read, if his lessons be a prayer, he doth not pray, even so it is commonly a saying, and reading prayers and not praying. . . . For though they have many guises, now to kneel, and now to stand, these be matters of course, and not any prick of conscience, or piercing of the heart.

The Puritans didn't try to rectify matters by activating their psyches while they mouthed the words of the Prayerbook. They turned to preaching, wrote their own prayers, spoke in tongues, discovered their *own* voices—and made a revolution, the only one we've had in this country! Herbert's whole project in *The Temple* makes some kind of sense if you put it back into that general context, as a rather liberal-conservative response to those ideological and political struggles of that revolutionary period; but what we need now isn't to spend hours trying to understand the logical intricacies of his 'Dedication'; what we need is real *practical dedication* to participation in our *own* revolutionary period, in our own ideological and political struggles, and if 'reading literature' can't be part of *that*, then it's just a way of being 'lazy and frivolous'.

George: Unfortunately, Phil, you've just spoiled what might have been an interesting case by falling into rhetoric, and rhetoric slides over problems, makes things just that bit too easy. You want us to dedicate ourselves, and somehow our reading, our really practical criticism as you call it, to the class struggle—you didn't actually say 'class-struggle', but I presume I'm right in thinking that that's what you meant. But what you seem to presume is that somehow we'll end up on the right side, your side, in that 'struggle'. And you obviously presume that you're on the right side already. But isn't that the real difficulty with the kind of activism you're actually advocating: that it turns into a rather blind kind of voluntarism: take the leap and you're there. Dai was talking about the conceptual problems of affirming specifically religious belief; well, your notion of political dedication reminds me of Kierkegaard's leap into faith. You seem to have forgotten your own comments about perhaps playing the wrong script, and the basic reason why you can talk about 'provisionality' one moment and apparently forget it the next is because you see 'political struggle' as, in the end, *external* to you, as something that happens elsewhere and that you have to join, dedicate yourself to. Yes, I'm being somewhat unfair, but all I'm doing is highlighting something that seemed to me to be subtly present in everything you've said about 'using' texts. On the other hand, what you said about the ideology of the self struck me as potentially very important, because it introduces a dimension that 'reading literature' *can* be relevant to. Let me put it in terms of some of the things you mentioned yourself. You talked about the Puritans making the only revolution we've had in this country. That statement would have to be qualified in all sorts of ways, but even if it *was* a revolution, we know that it was an increadibly complex period to *live* through. By that I don't just mean that it's not very easy to see it, then or now, cleanly as a 'class-struggle', or that the causes of the whole thing are immensely ramified, but rather that many of the people involved in what we used to call 'Puritanism' were very much preoccupied with their 'selves', or their 'souls', and they've left us records, diaries, autobiographies, tracts, sermons, which are above all concerned with the trials and tribulations of personal *conversion*, all the stages of awareness of sin, repentance, illumination, relapse, affirmation. The seventeenth-century civil war was fought out not just on battlefields or in the Putney Debates but also in men's 'souls'. One of the great metaphors of the time for spiritual, inner, conflict was 'civil war', and, as you said yourself, metaphors for thinking are important. That turmoil in the self, that self-division, that inner struggle, is something you seem to want to slide over. Even in your account of *Hamlet*, you turn Hamlet's play-acting into a pure device, even though you recognised yourself that play-acting *can* bring you close to a real kind of madness: isn't Stanislavsky's pupil in a state a bit like Hamlet's? You want us to get away from the writer's privatised agonies before the blank page, but you seem to think that political action doesn't, or shouldn't, have *its* own peculiar agonies! Yes, I'm slipping into rhetoric myself. But both your activists and theorists, your political Stanislavskians and political spectators, tend to forget about the subjective dimension of politics, that process of conversion, of real change at a very deep level that's required in any kind of 'political commitment'. In fact, there's now a species of theoretical voluntarism around which bypasses this whole problem, even more perhaps than the old-style activist voluntarism. I'll give you an example from a new journal I was reading recently; it's very sophisticated and very intelligent—a 'marxist journal in the theory and practice of psychology, psychoanalysis, linguistics, semiotics'. But in an article on 'Fetishism and Ideology' you get this kind of argument:

What is at stake in the displacement of an 'ideology' by a 'science' is not a movement of knowledge closer to a hidden reality, but a shift between two systems of concepts, implicated in different practices and with different effects. Thus the 'relations of production' are not existents in the real producing a set of phenomenal forms given to knowledge in the form of ideology, they are *concepts*, produced in a determinate discourse with a particular history, with its own conditions of existence, implicated in particular practices and exercising particular effects. The distance between 'ideology' and 'science', between 'phenomenal forms' and 'real relations', is not a distance between two realities, nor a distance between concepts and reality, but a distance between two discourses, and a distance between the political effects of these discourses.

The author may well be right—but how does that 'displacement' occur? I don't just mean 'how does the science displace the ideology?' I mean how did she, the author of the article, move from one to the other, and why? Because if 'the distance between "ideology" and "science" ' is simply a 'distance between two discourses, and a distance between the political effects of these discourses', how does anyone *cross* that distance, and how does anyone decide which of the two 'discourses' and their respective 'political effects' is to be preferred? You can't get out of that problem by attributing an impersonal status to 'discourse', as is sometimes done, if you want to continue to talk about 'Marxists' (as the article does) or about being a 'Marxist journal'. If being a marxist or being a marxist journal means anything, it means having chosen, in some sense, to cross that 'distance'—and 'science' *is* clearly being used by the author to mean, or include, whatever she means by 'marxism'. How, concretely and intellectually, does that 'crossing' occur? I know it's not an easy problem, and I'm putting it in a very simpliste way, but only because it's a problem that is too easily shrugged off or theorised away. Think what's happened in the last decade's debate about Marx's own so-called 'epistemological break'. For a while, there was a sustained argument about when, if at all, the 'break' occurred, the break out of 'ideology' and into 'science', and we had a few attempts to explain why the break occurred, if it did, when it did—but those explanations didn't get much beyond the old reliance on the conjuncture of 'the three sources of marxism' plus a dose of class-allegiance. And what we ended up with, after the 'break', was a self-justifying theory anyway, a theoretical practice that justified its own premises! After that, it was inevitable that we'd spend the next decade arguing about epistemology. Yes, I said 'we' because I suppose I, too, can't escape the argument, though it bores me stiff. And the reason why it bores me is because it's now infected almost every kind of political debate among marxists, at least among the 'theorists', while making them incapable of talking to anyone who doesn't talk about psychoanalysis, semiotics and epistemology. More important, because it points to a basic sleight-of-mind among today's marxists. It always seems, at least from the way they write, as if *they*'ve already crossed that 'distance', while 'ideological discourse' is always spoken, or more likely written, by somebody else—only too frequently by other self-proclaimed marxists they don't agree with. But that reduces 'ideology', like politics, to something external, something out there. One of the things I liked about that article, I must admit, is that it *didn't* see Marx himself as having escaped, at *any* point, into the clear light of scientific coherence. It very usefully analysed how '*Capital* is a text which is deeply fissured and multiply fragmented'. But if *Capital* itself is deeply fissured and multiply fragmented, mightn't it be possible that 'being a marxist' is always *also* a matter of being deeply fissured and multiply fragmented, and that's where a crucial part of the political significance of 'marxism' lies today? I'll put that less metaphorically. If 'ideology' has any real use as a political concept, and if being a marxist has anything to do with politics (which one can occasionally doubt these days), then the break from ideology to marxism can't be just an epistemological break. And if it's to be a political 'break', then it's going to be a very jagged one indeed, because 'politics', in my book at least, isn't just a matter of joining a political party, or taking part in industrial struggle, or writing theoretical articles, or supporting (critically) the armed struggle in whatever country you think appropriate. It's also, and dominantly, a matter of *how* you do those things and many others, and that criterion of 'how' may even prevent you, or save you, from doing some of them. Think of the effect that the women's movement has had, or perhaps had briefly, or perhaps should one day have, on what's meant by 'politics'. Since everything I do, from getting on a bus to going to a disco, from going to work to going to bed, can and normally does involve some kind of contact or relationship between men and women, everything I do has become, in principle and in the details of everyday living, politicised. The women's movement, whatever the theoretical and strategic problems of its relation to more 'traditional' political issues and perspectives, is clearly of enormous political significance if only because it brings politics into the heartland of the self. It's re-emphasised that everything we do is intimately political. A few years ago, all sorts of bad analogies were being offered between women's liberation and black liberation. I think that in one respect at least they're very similar: that everything a white does in a society where whites dominate blacks is political, every contact between white and black in America or South Africa or Britain has a political dimension. If the term 'ideology' doesn't include those constellations of feelings, attitudes, everyday responses, modes of thought, habits of action and reaction, that we can talk of in terms of 'white supremacy' or 'male supremacy', 'racism' or 'male chauvinism', then 'ideology' has become a very shallow and abstract term. Perhaps the term itself doesn't matter, though I'd like to think that 'ideology' can still carry *that* depth of meaning, instead of referring increasingly to what people 'think'. Because if we're going to talk still about 'bourgeois ideology' or 'capitalist ideology', then those terms have got to have the same full sense that the terms 'bourgeois' and 'capitalist' themselves have: a whole historical epoch, in all its subtle ramifications, is summed up in those terms in Marx. Yes, I know that all this is very familiar and that the problems of analysis *start* there, but I'm trying to redress a balance. You see, if you don't use 'ideology' with that kind of weight, your 'analyses' can get very remote or seem to most people to be very remote (and that's a crucial problem) from the day-to-day problems of living in a capitalist society. It's an old story that Lenin could analyse the economic problems of Czarist Russia starting from a glass of water on a peasant's table. Well, you can still analyse the economic problems of late international monopoly capitalism starting from what's on the table for a decent 'English' breakfast. But if you try to analyse the ideological and political problems of Northern Ireland starting from a pair of rosary beads in a Provo's pocket, you'll soon realise what's involved in 'ideology'. That's the kind of depth and real complexity I mean when I talk about ideology—and the obverse of that is what we mean by 'revolution'. Trotsky had the right idea when he wrote those articles in *Pravda* in 1923–24 on 'The Problems of Everyday Life', about politeness, drinking, swearing, how to address comrades, how to use libraries, and the rest. But that kind of analysis isn't being produced by our home-grown marxists any more. Is it any wonder they spend so much time talking only to each other! Yes, I'm off the point again, but you get my general point. I'll try and come back to literature and reading.

Well, all this was really sparked off by two things: Phil's leap into 'practical' criticism and—this may surprise you—a comment early on that Chris's question 'Can I class myself?' was a daft question. Well, I know Chris didn't mean it that way, but for me it has overtones of the political problem of 'class' and class-allegiance. Remember what I said about the way 'class-allegiance' is introduced, somehow or other, into accounts of how Marx 'broke' with his own early 'bourgeois humanism', 'Hegelianism', 'historicism' or whatever you want to call it? Connect that with what I also said about the Puritans and their preoccupation with 'conversion'. One of the most intractable problems in historical analysis of that whole period is just who *was* a 'Puritan' and what it meant, and if we can't sort that out now I doubt if it was any easier at the time. Incidentally, it still seems to me that it's the historians, not the epistemologists, who have given us the richest, and in the end clearest, accounts of what 'ideology' really amounts to. You could argue that a decent realist novelist or certain kinds of playwright can do the same, insofar as they operate a bit like historians. I'm thinking of, say, Caryl Churchill's play about the seventeenth-century, *Light Shining in Buckinghamshire*, with its real sense of the complexity of living through those years from 1640 to 1660, or, for a later epoch, the way in which David Hare's play for Joint Stock, *Fanshen*, based on Hinton's book about one typical village in China from 1946 to 49, gives some sense of what political conversion means: to 'fanshen' is to be converted, to 'turn the world upside down' as the Levellers called it. But the problem with such plays, and with historical works, and, in the end, with 'realist' fiction, is that they allow us to remain *spectators* of other people's changes. In fact, I think a whole case against 'realism', or at least against certain ways of reading realist fiction, could be based on that spectatorial attitude it invites in the reader. LN, you half-alluded to that attitude, I think, when you said of *Middlemarch* that we tend to 'overhear' what the text says while we in some way *visualise* what it describes. Well, I'm not sure I do 'visualise' in any precise sense, but I know what you mean. Basically, realist writing can put you in the same position as a play or a work of history does: you're 'looking at' events from a spectator's position. That poem of Ralegh's Phil quoted includes the lines 'Heaven the judicious sharp spectator is/That sits and marks still who doth act amisse'. Well, the great virtue of good realist works, and why Marx valued Balzac, and Lenin valued Tolstoy, is that basically they offer us a kind of historical understanding, perhaps the kind of intimate history the historian normally can't write because he hasn't got the documentation. (James said of Balzac that 'since history proceeds by documents he constructed, as he needed them, the documents too'.) But then, as readers, we *can* simply sit back and mark 'who doth act amisse'. The problem with realism isn't that the author is God but that he takes the reader up into heaven with him! Sorry, I'm riding another hobby-horse. I'll steer back again to class and reading, via history and Marx.

One of the things that is most difficult to grasp about *Capital* is the relationship between the 'history' and the 'argument' in it, or, if you like, the empirical evidence and the movement of the theoretical analysis. Because in the end Marx isn't offering us a history we can 'watch', partly because history in his sense can't in any way be visualised, and the reason why it can't is because what is crucial in history, for Marx, is a kind of 'logic' at work in it. I think *that* problem is at the core of those various metaphors in *Capital* about the 'appearance' and the 'essence', the 'phenomenal forms' and the 'real movements'. Quite often, 'ideology' is linked, in interpretations of Marx, with the 'appearance' or the 'phenomenal forms', as if what it was contrasted with was 'the real', so that the 'break' from ideology becomes a matter of grasping the 'real' movement 'behind' the appearances. In one sense, that's true, I suppose —that the 'real explanation', the *correct* explanation, of the relationship between capitalist-employer and wage-labourer is that the wage-relationship is an unequal exchange in which surplus-value is generated by the worker's labour-power but appropriated by the capitalist—that, crudely, is what 'really happens'. And, certainly, one can't *see that* happening, though one can grasp it conceptually, as a kind of logic, as an argument. It's then too easy, too simple, to say that 'ideology' is generated by what we *can* 'see happening'—and by lining up 'ideology' with 'appearance' one can get close to claiming that, particularly when 'ideology' is further linked with 'empiricism' as a merely 'perceptual' account of 'knowledge'. All sorts of wires get crossed at this point and it's very hard to disentangle them. But put it this way: the 'logic' that Marx discloses in history isn't, in the end, a conceptual logic, because the *major premise* of his syllogism isn't a proposition: it's a *distribution of power*. You can work out the logic of the exchange-relation involved in the wage-contract, and at that level it seems extremely easy to change it, to recognise how fundamentally *un*necessary 'the capitalist' is, or, if you like, the capitalist class. But, of course, it's far from easy to change it in practice, not just because coercive power, the state apparatus or whatever, is ranked on the side of the capitalist, but because of the grip of 'ideology', and what that means, in the end, is that 'ideology' too has the same structure: ideology too has a *logic*, the basic premise of which is a distribution of power. We need some way of really thinking that meshing of power and logic, if only to avoid two apparently opposite tendencies in thinking about 'capitalism', 'politics' and 'revolution'. The first is the belief that since capitalism is 'inherently contradictory' it will work out its own necessary destruction. That belief takes a thousand-and-one forms, from 'economism' to apocalypticism, but basically it's derived from a reliance on the 'logical' structure of Marx's analysis, from which one can indeed show the necessarily declining rate of profit or the increasing immiseration of the (Third World) proletariat. The second is the belief that what's crucial to political revolution is that people should see the 'contradictions', should understand the way in which they're exploited, and again that takes a multitude of forms, from the old debates about 'actual' and 'potential' class-consciousness to the latest varieties of vanguardism, since at the heart of vanguardism is a notion of 'taking power', in the sense of an attack on the centres of power, of State power. (That it's now not easy to locate the power to be 'taken' is a characteristic strategic problem of this perspective.) But for that you need specific people (the Party) prepared to *do* it, and their 'preparedness' is fundamentally a matter of 'revolutionary consciousness'. *Both* these perspectives tend to rely for their coherence on, at some point or other, the notion of 'class-struggle', which is why I'm intrigued by that question 'can I class myself?' On the first perspective, 'classes' are necessarily in conflict insofar as capitalism is logically self-contradictory, or, in another version, the very existence of 'classes', of capitalist relations of production, is logically in conflict with the development of the material forces of production, so that necessarily the maintenance of the one is at the expense of the other. Again, you can find more or less sophisticated variants of those two arguments but both of them rest in the end on a notion of 'class' in which, fundamentally, 'I am classed', the operation of 'classing' is performed by 'objective' factors. My position vis-à-vis the relations of production is not a matter of choice: we are all bearers of pre-determined class-positions. We may, by birth or otherwise, 'enter into' those positions but it's the positions we bear not the 'bearers' that are the motor of history. On the second perspective, the question of whether I can class myself seems to make a certain amount of sense, since if what's needed is the right kind of consciousness, the right kind of 'participation' in the 'class-struggle', then I can (have to, therefore must be able to) change my (class-)consciousness, align myself correctly with the right line in the class-struggle, take the right decisions, make the right moves—even if the 'I' here is subordinate to a collective decision. That's why vanguardism is so often allied with a rather curious kind of moralism, with accusations of deviationism, class-treachery, or just simple 'lack of dedication' and the need for 're-education'. That accusation is often formulated in terms of 'objective' factors or positions or effects, but it is so often the 'subjective' factor that is actually blamed. Yes, comrade, I'm deviating from the point again. But I'm not really. I'm getting there slowly—it *was* literature we were talking about?

Well, let's take the traditional problem of the relationship between 'ideology' and 'literature'. I said earlier that 'ideology', like the capitalist social formation itself, has a 'logic' the major premise of which isn't a proposition but a distribution of power. Here's a simple example of that kind of enmeshing of logic and power:

Zen Master brandishes large stick over pupil's head and says: 'If you say this stick is real, I'll strike you with it. If you say this stick is not real, I'll strike you with it. If you say nothing at all, I'll strike you with it.'

If you try to work that out as a problem of logic you'll be there for ever. The only 'answer' is to take the stick out of the Master's hand (though you don't need to hit *him* with it, necessarily). That's perhaps easy enough to recognise when it's written down—it may even be fairly easy to grasp when the actual stick is being waved over your head. But what happens when the Master sets an exam.-paper in which it states: 'If you say this exam. is real I shall fail you. If you say this exam. is not real I shall fail you. If you say nothing I shall fail you'? Does the pupil tear up the exam. paper? Of course, he could write about something entirely different, but the point is, finally, that the problem is only a problem because of the power of the Master over the pupil, to hit him or to 'fail' him. Gregory Bateson discusses the stick example in his account of the 'Double Bind', in order to explain what happens in a family which drives a child to schizophrenia. A double-bind has, for Bateson, a number of features: two or more people, one of whom is the victim; a 'primary negative injunction' ('don't

135

do X or I'll punish you', or 'if you don't do X I'll punish you'); a 'secondary injunction conflicting with the first at a more abstract level' (often communicated to the victim not by an explicit statement but by non-verbal means —posture, gesture, tone of voice); and a 'tertiary injunction' prohibiting the victim from escaping from the field covered by the other two injunctions. 'Ideology', it seems to me, has the structure of a double-bind, and that 'tertiary injunction' is where the 'distribution of power' premise is principally located, but not only in terms of someone else's power to prevent you from leaving the field. The reason you're trapped in a double-bind may quite often be because your *own* power is located within that field: to leave it would be to lose whatever power you yourself have. Obviously, this basic structure may have a number of variations: there may be more than one double-bind imposed on the same victim, all the injunctions may be more or less explicit, the primary injunction may come from one source, the secondary from another, *et cetera*. In all these cases, what you may have, abstractly, is a formal paradox or a logical contradiction, but what that means in practice, for the victim, is an insoluble dilemma, a self-contradiction. In some cases, you could say that the victim 'needn't' accept or obey the conflicting injunctions, but if the field of the double-bind is also the field which constitutes the very 'identity' of the victim, then 'leaving' the field means wrenching that 'identity'—which is why the family is such a paradigm of the field of the double-bind. Bateson also makes the point that the double-bind has to be a repeated experience, a 'recurrent theme' in the life of the victim, rather than a single traumatic event, but that when repetition has created an habitual expectation of double-bind any one element in the set of ingredients can be enough to 'precipitate panic or rage', or, presumably, apathy, catatonia. I'd like to develop the notion that capitalism is itself constituted as a double-bind, but I don't think I'll risk it. I *am* fairly confident, though, that a great deal of what's commonly meant by 'ideology' in the day-to-day politics of experience, of 'commonsense', can be analysed in terms of a double-bind structure—racism, male chauvinism, Parliamentarianism, 'a fair day's pay for a fair day's work', *et cetera*. And the point about at least some of these is that the 'victim' puts himself into a double-bind insofar as he won't leave the field of contradictory injunctions because he will lose his *own* power. The reason why I remain a male chauvinist (despite all the arguments) is that I would actually 'lose' a great deal of power, real economic, sexual, domestic, political power over women (what little I have) if I 'gave up' being a male chauvinist. The reason why most whites are, in the end, racist is because they won't give up the power of being 'white'—and that's not just tautologous (though the ultimate sticking-point in any ideological *argument* is normally a tautology) because 'to be white' means, in this world, now, to have the power, the privilege, that comes from being white. One can explain why it means that, historically, why that 'equation' holds in the actual world now and why it no longer holds quite as firmly as it once did, but one can't finally explain racism as an *illusion* about the real world. Racism rests on a partial perception and at an extreme sees the whole world in terms of the power that is at stake in that 'field', but that's precisely because it's the only 'power' which *is* at stake for many whites: they haven't got much power in any other field, basically because most

136

people don't have much power over their very survival, their means of life, of employment, the very forces of production which enable them to live. But what power they do have, they hold on to—and that includes, in this country, the power of simply being in the 'affluent' one-fifth of the globe.

Sorry, as usual I'm getting side-tracked, and I'm cutting corners in the process. But let me just make three points, or rather suggestions, and then I'll get back to literature. Very briefly, the relationship between ideology and the 'real world' isn't to be mapped on the model of 'two discourses' one of which is concerned with appearance and the other with reality, or one of which is epistemologically more valid than the other. Ideological discourse has the same *kind* of relation to the real world as the phrase 'leg of a chair' has to the leg of a chair. To call a chair-leg a 'leg' isn't a metaphor or simply an analogue. Though we can find other ways of describing what a chair-leg does, how it works, what it was made of, what its purpose is, etc., 'leg' is the only term we have for it, and the reason we call it a 'leg' is because we've *made* it in our own image, made it a leg in the first place. For it to be anything else we'd have to change the whole construction of chairs, and of ourselves too if we were actually to sit in those reconstructed chairs—though of course you can always tinker with the design of chairs and you can even now sit on the floor. (We're having rather similar problems with terms like 'chairman' at the moment, for not dissimilar reasons.) Second, as I indicated earlier, 'ideology' has to take the weight of a whole historical epoch, a whole mode of life, and that's partly because 'power', though crucially concentrated, is also dispersed. There are different kinds as well as levels of power at work in capitalist society and it's the relationship between those kinds as well as levels that is intractably difficult, even though the basic power remains what it always was: the power over survival itself, the very material conditions of existence. That basic material power was once the control over (possession of, ownership of) land and it still is to a large extent, globally, but increasingly the power over survival is located in the power over other forces of material production—'survival' can in this context be a relative term, while remaining, in the final analysis, an absolute. Third, to 'take power' can't be simply a matter of *taking* if 'ideology' in the sense of a double-bind rooted in one's own retention of power is at work. Taking power has also got to mean, in many cases, *eroding* one's *own* power, or, better, changing the nature of one's relation to the control of power, so that power *can't* be something you can keep for yourself. OK, OK, I began by accusing Phil of rhetoric! I'll take back that third, rhetorical suggestion—and offer you literature instead.

A work of literature can sometimes present or explore the double-binds I have in mind. Remember the scene based on the Putney Debates in that Caryl Churchill play I mentioned—where the Levellers are trapped, finally, not only by the contradictory 'injunctions' they are offered by Cromwell, Ireton, and God (via the Bible), operating in conjunction, nor simply by their own logical tangles about 'the people', 'property' and 'birthright', but also by accepting, literally, the terms of the debate in the first place, and the reason for their acceptance of a Debate (negotiations) rather than a military conflict, at that stage, was not only because they might well have lost the battle but because the Levellers and Agitators also needed, like Cromwell, a united Army to maintain the security of their own position in the first place. That moment in 1647 *is* a classic 'revolutionary' moment, but there were just too many real and intertwined double-birds to negotiate, including, as always, the real loss of power by the revolutionaries if they risked going further. (It's interesting that Milton's most profound insight into the 'Fall' concerns the real *risk* that Adam had to take to maintain his love of Eve—and that risk could only be a genuine one, against God, if he *lost*—but that's another story.) A novelist, too, can sometimes present us with an analysis of the roots of 'ideology', as I think John Berger does in his description of Umberto in *G*:

What Umberto calls madness is what threatens him. Not what threatens him personally—another merchant, a thief, the man who will cuckold him—but what threatens the social structure in which he lives as a privileged being.

His privilege is more important to him than his life, not because he could not survive without his American mistress, four servants at home, a fountain in his garden, hand-made silk shirts, or his wife's dinner parties, but because implicit in his privilege are the values and judgements by which he must make sense of his lived life. All values stem from his belief—that his privileges are deserved.

Yet the sense he makes of his life does not satisfy him. Why must liberty, he asks himself, always be retrospective, a quality already won and controlled? Why is there no liberty to pursue now?

Umberto terms madness that which threatens the social structure guaranteeing his privileges. *I teppisti* are the final embodiment of madness. Yet madness also represents freedom from the social structure which hems him in. And so he arrives at the conclusion that limited madness may grant him greater liberty within the structure.

He calls Laura mad in the hope that she will bring into his life a modicum of liberty.

That's an extra-ordinary perception of both the basis and the self-contradictions of ('petty-bourgeois'?) ideology, and, more generally, of the inevitably instrumental view of others that arises from any special pleading for oneself. But Berger—as is his aim—distances the reader from it, so that he or she can recognise it, analyse it as the text itself does: the *gaps* between the printed paragraphs hold you back for that pondered recognition. You were asking for a Brechtian way of reading, Phil,—you might do worse than start from an analysis of how *G* positions its reader.

But—to get finally to the point—what I want to establish is a different *kind* of connection between 'ideology' and 'literature', perhaps a complementary one to the Brechtian notions you were groping after, rather than a 'better' one, still less the 'only correct' one: there's no competitive ranking of approaches as far as I'm concerned. I can suggest the kind of connection I have in mind briefly, by going right back to Chris's paper. Surprised? Well, what it seemed to me that Chris was actually doing was uncovering the *logic* of the *double-binds* of 'religious ideology', not just in George Herbert but perhaps in the Christian religion generally—precisely as a 'logical structure the basic premise of which is a distribution of power'. I don't think, Chris, you used the term 'double-bind' but your analysis of the problems of trying to occupy *both* positions, being schizophrenically both addressee and addresser simultaneously, led you precisely into some of the classic problems of Christian theology—the omnipotence, omniscience, omnipresence of God, inspiration, belief, salvation, etc.—and the *way* you analysed them wasn't as *theoretical* issues, as 'theology', but precisely as someone caught in a double-bind, twisting and turning to get out of an insoluble dilemma. Like Beckett's reader playing chess against himself when the rules have gone crazy, I found your performance ludicrously funny at times. But I can see what you were trying to do, I think. A lot of the elements in your analysis could have been arrived at in a quite different way, by simply pointing to or explicating the 'meaning' of the lines and 'explaining' what Herbert 'believed'. But to try actually to *mean* such 'beliefs' yourself, to try to apply the claim that one was inspired to yourself, led you *into* the ideology of the text in a way that allowed you to disclose its structure as a series of double-binds, not just a set of historical 'beliefs'. Indeed, if you try to gain 'knowledge' of seventeenth-century religious belief by analysing what phrases like 'for from thee they came' *mean*, you won't get very far, but by trying to actually say them yourself and make rational sense out of them as something *you* said (in a different way, incidentally, from the way Della Volpe recommends) you ended up in the same dilemmas that underpin Herbert's beliefs, even if Herbert himself mightn't have recognised them as dilemmas. Partly because yours was an exercise in 'bad faith', in lying to yourself, rather than an expression of 'faith', you were able to uncover the logical structure of those beliefs. But then the crucial difference between you and Herbert, or between bad faith and faith, was that whereas you were only caught in the *logic* of the beliefs, the actual believer is caught in an enmeshing of logic *and* 'power' together. I mean that the basic 'premise' of religious belief is that the conditions of our very existence, not just of our survival, are under the power of someone else—'God'. It's our absolute contingency, the very fact of our existence, or anything's existence, that is the intractable dilemma at the core of religious belief, and once that contingency operates as a *premise*—not just as a propositional premise, but as the recognition, awareness, of ultimate powerlessness over the conditions of our existence—then the *logic* of religious ideology can be generated. That's why religious ideology is as difficult to 'break' as the ideology of the 'self': they both rest upon tautologies which seem necessary to any awareness at all—I can't be aware of anything without being aware of the 'I' as aware, and I can't be aware of that 'I' without being aware of its contingency; then you're straight back to Descartes, and behind him the Scholastics. The only way to 'eradicate' that movement of thought is to remove the premise, but you can't remove absolute contingency in the sense that you *can* remove the sources of relative powerlessness, those distributions of power that operate in other fields as the premises for other ideological beliefs. Which is why the 'omnipotence' of God is central to religious belief. What you can perhaps do is to trace the *shifts* in ideological beliefs, because insofar as they have a 'logic' that logic can have an internal history, a working out of its own contradictions: if 'history' has a 'logic', it may be that what one can call 'ideo*logics*' have a 'history' of their own.

What your analysis suggests, Chris, is that a 'literary' text might incorporate, might be structured upon, a particular *stage* in the history of an 'ideologic' and that a reading of the 'logic' of the text may reveal the logic of that ideology, that ideologic, precisely because a reading isn't enmeshed in the power-premise that gives rise to the ideologic: when I read a text I'm not actually *in* the double-bind the text articulates, because I'm not in the situation of powerlessness relative to power that the ideologic derives from. Or if I am so enmeshed in 'real life', I'm not while I'm reading. I think it was Dai who talked about the curious kind of *epoché*, of bracketing, that occurs as one reads. One aspect of that *epoché* is that to read is to 'enter into' a set of relations but they're not themselves relations of power. The text can't compel me to read it, even though we speak of a 'compelling' book or even of the 'power' of literature. I am always free to stop reading, even though there may be 'compelling' reasons for me to read, as in an educational system, but these reasons lie outside the operation of the text itself; at most I might be forced to go through the motions of reading—as a lot of 'education' actually persuades people to do. But if I'm right in suggesting that ideology is constituted by an enmeshing of power and logic, of a distribution of power and an ideologic which is generated from acceptance of that power, then it may be that a 'literary' text can re-work, re-construct, be structured by, or put into a kind of disarray, that 'ideologic'. A reader may then be able to grasp the structure of that ideologic, to see its contradictions in a way not normally accessible in the actual living of an ideological double-bind precisely because in the act of reading, the power-relation that supports the double-bind, that prevents one from 'leaving the field', is in abeyance. Think of the Zen Master with the stick; it's easy to 'see through' the problem posed when it's merely a puzzle I can play with, but when it's a dilemma I *have* to resolve it's less easy to recognise it for what it is—a deflection from the real problem of power and authority that the puzzle serves to conceal. Obversely, of course, one way of trying to 'escape' from a double-bind situation may be to 'escape' into *writing*: to put in abeyance the problem of power that fixes you in the double-bind, in order to work through, in the closed field of writing, a 'satisfactory' or acceptable resolution of the ideologic of that situation. It may be possible to trace that operation in at least *some* texts—unlike LN, I don't see why any method of analysis need apply to *all* texts. It may even be possible to explore the allure of 'being a writer' along similar lines: anyone whose identity is primarily constituted by the field of writing may be a full-time escapologist—which is not necessarily the same as being an escapist. To explore those problems may be more important than trying to 'relate' a text to its historical moment, since the derangement of an ideologic achieved in a text may be prompted by a paradox of power specific to a historical moment, or even the specific dilemmas of an individual, but the text may experiment with the internal possibilities and permutations of an ideologic in ways that realease it from the constraints of the actual double-bind operative at that (historical) moment. Certainly, I think myself that Chris's analysis of the double-binds of religious ideology in 'The Dedication' got us much closer to the 'history' of the seventeenth century as it was *lived* through, at least in terms of the central problems of religious belief, than any study of Phil's Puritan printers ever would. But at the same time, and more interestingly, that way of reading uncovered some of the *continuing* problems of religious ideology—after all, religious belief is still enormously significant and its basic logical structure is unchanged, even though different contradictions or different facets within the ideologic may be dominant at different times. I don't know whether that way of reading a text would be reading it 'as literature', but I suspect Chris was being put into a double-bind anyway by accepting the terms of the question in the first place. 'Can I class myself?' isn't, in the end, a daft question. 'Can I read "The Dedication" as a poem?' *is* a daft question.

Bert: 'Ave you finished then? Good God, at last! You know, Georgie, that was an unmitigated load of boring old crap. I haven't heard such ponderous inanities in a long time. 'Cutting corners' you called it! More like a slow-motion replay of a rained-off Test Match—every blessed ball bowled gently down the pitch, solemnly poked at for a long moment, then dismissed with infinite slowness into the covers. Can't you *follow through* an idea, George? Can't you bang just the occasional one to the boundary? Won't you at least *try* to smash a few googlies for six? It'd wake us all up anyway!

Look, there were just three interesting ideas in all that lot, but you didn't really *think* your way *through* any of them. One is worth a detailed look—your point about the state of 'marxist' theory in this country at the moment. The second, your argument about *power*, needs sorting out if it's going to be useful for anything. The third, your comments on Chris's analysis of 'The Dedication', you didn't take far enough. Can I backtrack on each of these points and try to show you what I mean? No offence, lad? Just trying to help.

First then, theory. You're dead right about the political problems the present spate of theory runs into, particularly all the guff about epistemology. Going back to the poverty of even radical philosophy certainly isn't a particularly promising direction for English marxists to take right now. It *might* be if we were fighting an entrenched and influential philosophical idealism of a *systematic* kind, but in this country we're not, and you can't fight the kind of 'a-political' and 'a-theoretical' idealist 'common sense' that *is* a problem in this country by the weapons of systematic philosophical criticism: your enemies don't read it and a lot of your allies *can't*. So how have we got into this position, with so much intellectual energy going into the sand? Let's try and answer that one first.

Remember, ten years ago, there was an influential theory around in England about the absence of theory in England—Perry Anderson's argument in his *Components of the National Culture*, that English 'culture' suffered from a double absence at its centre: we had no indigenous marxist theory and no classical sociology tradition, so we had no 'totalising' discipline of thought, unlike our friends, and enemies, in Germany, France, Italy. In all sorts of detailed respects, that was a shaky argument, and I'll come back to the most important ones in a minute. But the effect of its implicit recommendation and remedy was to lead a whole generation of English Lefties on to a continental trek, in search of that elusive 'totalising' theory. One version of Anderson's essay—the one he gave to the old Tawney Group—ended with the proposal to set up a New Left publishing house; from 1970 onwards we had one, New Left Books, with a whole series of eagerly-read (or eagerly-bought) *translations*—it wasn't till 1975 that the first English author appeared in the NLB list, Anderson himself. Just think back on that decade, '68 to '78—you're all just about old enough aren't you? It's a familiar point that anyone who relied on translations for their acquaintance with the European 'intellectual centre' (or even relied on *what* was translated to know what to bother to read in the original!), and tried to keep up with the translations, was, in effect, trying to assimilate fifty years of theoretical argument in one jump. 'Theoretically', you can do it—if you're a student, unemployed, self-employed, or a non-teaching academic; you *always* have to somehow master a long tradition in a very short space of time anyway: that's partly what education and reading are all about! But the 'peculiarity' of the English situation during that decade was two-fold.

First, that the 'assimilation' was very uneven, in fact pretty random, even at the level of what was published, so that, for example, *For Marx* was translated before *History and Class Consciousness, The Savage Mind* long before *Critique of Dialectical Reason*, criticisms becoming 'available' well before their targets were, and that whole upside-down pattern culminated, within a mere six years, in the whole process being pretty-near undercut by its own originating figure-heads almost before it had really taken root for a lot of people: Anderson's *Considerations on Western Marxism* and Althusser's *Essays in Self-Criticism*. By that time, of course, a new generation of translations was fluttering across the Channel: Lacan's *Écrits* partially stammered into English in '77. Obviously, I'm over-simplifying, and I'll come back to this in a moment; but that flurry of topsy-turvy assimilation is as interesting a cultural 'moment' as the 'dominance' of a previous generation of 'emigrés' analysed in Anderson's '68 essay.

The *second* 'peculiarity of the English' was that, complementarily, there was a sense of a very sudden *break* from whatever *did* exist in England of an 'indigenous marxism'; if you want to talk about 'epistemological breaks', you might well think about that one. Symptomatic of it was the shunting to the side-lines of the work of, say, Raymond Williams and Edward Thompson; even up to the late 'sixties, their work was part of the common debate on the Left; after about '70 you could run across young English marxists who'd never actually got around to reading them, because they were too busy with the Balibars; it became a bit like talking to someone standing on the top rung of a ladder who didn't know there were forty rungs below him, still holding him up.

The political effect of both peculiarities has again been two-fold. *First*, to displace tactical and strategic considerations, at the level of 'theory', on to the problems of the European Communist Parties, which are in various ways both different from and, in crucial respects, politically *less* difficult than the problems of the British political scene. Basically, the problems of a working-class movement which has had its 'own' party as the official government for ten out of the last fourteen years *and* has had the power to bring down the 'only' alternative government, by barely shrugging its shoulders, in '74, make the strategic problems of Eurocommunism etc. seem relatively minor by comparison—and I haven't even mentioned Northern Ireland.

Second, and complementarily, that continental drift in theory has helped to *widen* the 'gap' (or *further* widen it) between 'theory' and 'practice', or rather between the dominant concerns of current theory and the traditional problems of practice, for very much the reasons Anderson outlines in his *Considerations*: that 'Western Marxism' *and* its philosophical opponents are fighting on a displaced terrain, and not on the classic ground of marxist theory which is the intersection of politics and economics, not the intersection of philosophy and culture. There *has* been a revival of 'socialist economics' in England recently, but that revival has been comparatively little influenced by most of the books on the NLB list, so far, still less by any injection of semiotics or psychoanalysis. But it's still the case that you can tot up on one hand the number of analyses of Britain's political and economic problems, of any theoretical or strategic weight, that have appeared from the British Left in the last ten years. *NLR*'s own track record at that level has been pretty bad.

Now, given those general points, and given that your concern—and mine at the moment—is with the intersection of politics and culture, not directly with politics and economics or even economics and culture, the major problem is the 'epistemological break', in the sense I mentioned earlier: that quite deliberate effort on the part of a whole generation of young marxists to 'think European'. In itself, highly necessary, but we have to then get a bit clearer about both its origins and its pitfalls. So I want to go back *first* to Anderson's *Components* argument, and then, *second*, to the randomness and unevenness of assimilation I mentioned earlier.

Anderson argued that English culture had an absent centre, lacked a totalising discipline of thought. But, he said, 'the displaced home of the totality became literary criticism', in the work of F. R. Leavis. Rightly, he said that this was extraordinary, compared with the European role and status of 'Lit. Crit.'. On one side of the Channel English philosophy, after Wittgenstein, 'abandoned ethics and metaphysics, for the neutral investigation of language', while English literary criticism, through Leavis, 'assumed the responsibilities of moral judgement and metaphysical assertion'. On the other side of *La Manche*, France had 'a highly technical, hermeneutic criticism (Poulet and Richard) and an ontological and moral philosophy (Sartre)'. With the hindsight of ten years, one might say that what then happened in England, for a while, was that the neutral or technical 'investigation of language' derived from linguistics—after Saussure—combined with the 'highly technical' tradition of French literary criticism (really a form of *explication*)—after Roland Barthes—replaced Leavis and *his* tradition as the attempted totalising discipline. For a brief while, and still in some respects, semiotics attempted to become the 'centre'. On both sides of the water, it seemed, 'ontological' and 'moral' issues were effaced, with the slump in Sartre's status parallel to that in Leavis's. Once that implantation of Barthes into England had occurred, there was a relatively easy passage for the rest of the Sorbonne Circus, Althusser, Foucault, Lacan. And it wasn't surprising that the first fields to be occupied by this French invasion were those with more or less direct affiliations to the traditions of Leavisite criticism: film-criticism in the early days of *Screen*, the early work of the Birmingham Centre for Contemporary Cultural Studies, and, of course, 'literary criticism' itself. I'll not detail the subsequent stages of the English assimilation process now, except to say that the focal figure is no longer Barthes but Lacan; Althusser has remained central, if only through his epigones, but I'll come back to him later. It's Lacan that interests me for the moment. I want to raise three interlinked questions.

First, have or had 'ontological' issues been, in fact, erased? One of the figures who still remains unassimilated in England is Jacques Derrida, and it's not difficult to see why. Derrida has, over the years, exposed the 'onto-theological' elements in the work of Saussure, Lévi-Strauss and the great Jacques himself (Lacan, *and* Rousseau). In other words, Derrida has consistently probed the implicit 'idealism' of the whole range of inquiries founded upon 'semiotics'. (In addition, of course, it's a bit difficult to read Derrida if you've never worked on the Greeks, and classics has been a dead subject for years in England. But that's by the way.) I won't either summarise or assess Derrida's critiques now, because my main point here is independent of the correctness or otherwise of his various 'readings'. My main point now is that Derrida is a 'philosopher' deeply influenced by and indebted to Heidegger, and it is in terms of a strategy developed from and against Heidegger that Derrida operates; it's partly because of that, that Derrida has been able to disclose in Lacan's project its own 'philosophical' and ultimately 'metaphysical' underpinnings, and ambitions, since 'behind' Lacan's reading of Freud is the heritage of that partly Heideggerian reading of Hegel proposed by Kojève in the 1930s. *But in England* Heidegger remains almost totally absent from the theoretical debate. What I'm suggesting is that without a real encounter with the problems posed by Heidegger and after him Derrida, any assimilation of Lacan is more or less open to the charge of not having escaped 'metaphysics', of still, even if in a displaced mode, dealing with 'ontological' issues. I'll come back to the issues later, and why they're dangerous. I want to go back to Anderson on Leavis now.

My *second* question concerns Anderson's '68 analysis: was his thesis about the 'totalising centre' of European culture correct and, correspondingly, was his location of Leavis correct? I'd suggest that from the 1920s to the 1960s *neither* classical marxism *nor* classical sociology were really at the 'centre' of the European intellectual terrain. Both marxism and sociology were in fact transmuted into *philosophies* and only in that transmutation were they able to figure within the central intellectual debate, at the defining core of which was the philosophical lineage of Descartes, Kant, Hegel, Nietzsche, Husserl, Heidegger, Sartre—and, arguably, the single most influential figure in that debate for the twentieth century has been Heidegger. For two generations of intellectuals 'Marxism' was reformulated in a latent dialogue and contestation with a Heideggerian reading of Hegel, first in Kojève, then in Sartre. The phenomenon of 'Western Marxism' takes its shape from that dominance of 'philosophy'. (Incidentally, something similar seems to be happening to Freud's work now: psychoanalysis is reshaped as a philosophy; what's common to both castrations is the disappearance of any real concern with either marxism or psychoanalysis as concrete *practices*.) I can't offer details of this whole movement here; they would include, just as an indication, the transmutation of classical sociology into hermeneutics, in Dilthey, and then into epistemology in Lévi-Strauss, the intellectual filiations between Dilthey and Lukacs, the latent dialogue between *Being and Time, History and Class Consciousness*, and, eventually, Lukacs's own *Ontologie* (Goldmann's lectures on Heidegger and Lukacs make a stab at sorting this out), the critique of Heidegger by Adorno in *Jargon of Authenticity* but also the pull of Adorno's own *Negative Dialectics*, the influence of Heidegger on Bultmann and through him the whole development of twentieth-century theology leading through to the 'political theology' of Moltmann, Metz, Ratzinger—the last two being influenced by Rahner, whose own first book was heavily Heideggerian, etc., etc. One reason for not going into detail is that the central problems of that philosophical assimilation of marxism are still legible in today's marxist Lacanians and we can come back to them in a moment. But the *other* aspect of the question can now be clarified.

If Leavis, as Anderson argued, occupied the absent centre in England, was it *so* peculiar that he should? Anderson, interestingly, offers no explanation as to *why* Leavis did occupy that centre, except to remark that his claims for 'English' as the 'centre of humane studies and the university' should be seen 'not as a reflection of megalomania on the part of Leavis, but as a symptom of the objective vacuum at the centre of the culture'. That 'symptom' is a characteristic psychoanalytical-structuralist metaphor of the time, which leaves us without much explanatory illumination. Anderson does make two comments which, if followed through, might have begun to help. 'The paradox of this great critic,' he says, 'is that his whole *oeuvre* rested on a metaphysic which he could never expound or defend', and 'when challenged for the rationale of his critical statements, Leavis always replied that they did not properly speaking have an affirmative but *an interrogative form*; the latent form of all literary criticism was: "This is so, is it not?".' Anderson calls this interrogative technique of Leavis's criticism an 'epistemology' and says that it 'demands one crucial precondition: a shared, stable system of beliefs and values. Without this no loyal exchange and report is possible. If the basic formation and outlook of readers diverges, their experience will be incommensurable.' I think Anderson's terms 'epistemology' and 'metaphysic' are *both* misleading, and I'll try and say why, starting from that notion of the 'interrogative form' of criticism. What Anderson doesn't mention is that 'This is so, isn't it?' invites and expects the answer 'Yes, *but.* . . .'. (A point often made by Leavis himself—his practice arose out of a change in the social relations of the educational apparatus, which this balance of responses indicates and embodies; criticism too is a practice before it is a theory.) Implicit in that exchange is a *complex* notion of *language*, and it is not so much on a 'shared, stable system of beliefs and values' that Leavis based his actual critical practice as on a 'shared' *language*; for Leavis, the '*basic* formation' of all readers is given by language; language is both the object of the exchange (in both senses)—the 'words on the page'—and the *precondition* of the exchange, not simply in the sense that 'I gotta use words when I talk to you', but in the more complex Leavis sense that only an intimate inwardness to the English language, as shaped by its 'living speech' and concentrated in its literature, can 'qualify' one to take part in that exchange; 'doing criticism' is, in a profound sense, learning a language. That a particular language is the historical bearer of 'beliefs and values' (and *restricts* the possibility of certain beliefs and values) would certainly not be disputed by Leavis, but Anderson's emphasis on 'beliefs and values' at the expense of the central and passionate concern with language in its operation distorts Leavis's relation precisely to that Wittgensteinian 'linguistic philosophy' with which Anderson contrasts it—remember that Leavis regarded his mate Wittgenstein as having a 'naive' view of language. But it also obscures a fundamental affinity between Leavis and that real focus of European thought: Heidegger. For the concern that increasingly dominates Heidegger's work, from the early 1930s onwards, is *language*, language as the 'house of Being', language as the domain of poets, language as the crucial path to what is called thinking, key words as the recoverable traces of the pre-Socratic, the pre-metaphysical. (It is, of course, in that Heideggerian preoccupation with the *Ursprung* of language, of the *logos*, that a great deal of Lacan's own way with language is rooted; and, perhaps, Derrida's critique of Heidegger himself in terms of the occluded difference between the *written* and the *spoken* may be the best way of penetrating Leavis's fundamental limits.) That Heidegger's whole task, as he sees it, is to bring 'metaphysics' to its end, is one reason why Anderson is also misleading in claiming that Leavis's oeuvre 'rested on a *metaphysic* which he could never expound or affirm'. When Leavis did, in his last years, spell out the kind of 'thinking' he regarded 'literary criticism' as both demanding and provoking, it was to the anti-Cartesian philosophers Michael Polyani and Majorie Grene that he in fact appealed (which is indeed an index of the *real* poverty of English intellectual life). But to read that complex, and three-quarter baked, first chapter of *The Living Principle: 'English' as a discipline of thought* is to be reminded constantly, of the anti-metaphysical and anti-epistemological concerns of Heidegger—the *'ahnung'* of both thinkers is remarkably consonant. To quote one of Scotland's few authorities on Heidegger, Fergus Kerr:

To put the point provocatively and very schematically: most of what Heidegger can do for one, Leavis does as well or better; or, rather, since it is D. H. Lawrence whom he makes accessible and draws on, the creative-critical vision in *his oeuvre* is our best equivalent to Heidegger's *Seinsdenken*.

Kerr's account of the 'special kind of thinking which Leavis's work exists to promote' offers simultaneously an account of Leavis's reading of a poem and of Heidegger's *Gelassenheit* (that term he appropriated from Meister Eckhart, and which is echoed in that other mentor whom Leavis mediates who also captured a term from the Rhineland mystics—Eliot's *Erhebung*). In other words, the 'centre' of English culture, on this reading of Heidegger and Leavis, was not so very different from the 'centre' of European culture.

But that raises my *third* question, which again has two sides to it: what on earth does Anderson mean by this metaphor, which I've allowed and adopted so far, of 'centre', and *why* was it 'no accident that in the fifties, the one serious work of socialist theory in Britain—Raymond Williams's *The Long Revolution* —should have emerged from literary criticism, of all disciplines'? Both the metaphor of 'centre' and the formulation of the account of Williams highlight the method and the limits of Anderson's essay: it is, formally and explicitly, a 'structuralist analysis' of the intellectual map of Europe; *historical* questions, or any substantial explanation external to the internal trajectories and inter-defining relations of academic disciplines, are compressed to the point of being cursory. But what is a Lévi-Straussian 'structure' doing with a 'centre' in the first place? And to say that *The Long Revolution* 'emerged from literary criticism' is to excise a crucial political fact: the whole early history of the very *New Left Review* Anderson was writing in, and the origins of that *Review* in a crisis within, crucially, the Communist Party of Great Britain in 1956. The two points go together: in Anderson's compressed account of British nineteenth-century history, the emphasis lies on the dominance of a bourgeois-aristocratic fusion which constituted a ruling class which had no need of a totalising theory of its own society; only in one sentence is there a glimmer of a more substantial thesis:

There were social critics of Victorian capitalism, of course: the distinguished line of thinkers studied by Williams in *Culture and Society*. But this was a literary tradition incapable of generating a conceptual system. The intellectual universe of Weber, Durkheim or Pareto was foreign to the pattern of British culture which had congealed over the century. One decisive reason for this was, of course, that the political threat which had so largely influenced the birth of sociology on the continent—the rise of socialism—did not materialise in England. The British working class failed to create its own political party throughout the nineteenth century. When it eventually did so, it was twenty years behind its continental opposites, and was still quite untouched by Marxism. The dominant class in Britain was thus never forced to produce a counter-totalising thought by the danger of revolutionary socialism.

In that slide from 'the rise of socialism' to 'revolutionary socialism' is hidden a large argument, or assumption, which pivots round the twin claim that the British working class *'failed to create its own political party'* (as if *that* was what it ought to have done) and that when it did so 'it' (the party or the class?) was *'still untouched by Marxism'* (as if Marxism had the therapeutic powers of a mediaeval monarch). The implication is that what was fundamentally lacking in Britain was a *party* as the bearer of the Marxist intellectual challenge. But then the comparison with Europe would have to be posed rather differently: the claim that 'Marxism' and 'classical sociology' constituted the 'centre' of the European intellectual constellation would have to be unpacked into the claim that the crucial factor in European intellectual life was the presence of, presumably, the various Communist Parties of Europe. (A further, latent implication was perhaps that Anderson would eventually get around to reformulating his analysis in terms of the Gramscian notion of 'hegemony'.)

That such an account could be offered is undeniable, but it would raise two issues: the relationship of the intelligentsia to those Communist Parties *and* the kind of 'Marxism' to be found within those Parties. In fact Anderson's version of the impact of 'Marxism' on European theory is silent on precisely those two points, since the 'Communist Party' simply does not (and cannot) operate as a factor in his kind of analysis. The nearest we get to *explicit* mention of the CPs are phrases such as 'flourishing Marxist cultures rose in Germany, Italy and France', or 'the fifties and sixties saw a proliferation of Marxism on the continent: Althusser in France, Adorno in Germany, and Della Volpe in Italy all founded important and divergent schools', or, perhaps most 'symptomatically', the following: 'Marxism in the twentieth century, after the inevitable delay in its theoretical assimilation within the working-class movement which had been politically won to it, generated a new wave of major theory.'

That the CPs are 'absent' from the analysis doesn't mean that they're not taken for granted, of course. But one might suggest a rather different reason for this surely rather curious silence (involving periphrastic formulations like those quoted). Really to examine the relation between 'Marxism' and the European CPs would be to ask some rather harsh questions about those CPs in the light of 'marxism' itself, and really to ask questions about the relation between the European intelligentsia and the CPs would, eventually, be to ask questions about the relationship between the *English* 'Marxist' intellectuals, including the intellectuals of *NLR*, particularly perhaps its editor, and the *British* CP. But weren't the *origins* of *NLR* partly in the *break* from the British CP of most of its intellectuals? And wasn't that because of the Stalinism of that CP, because of the kind of 'Marxism' it proclaimed, because of the 1956 Soviet 'intervention' in Hungary—but *also* because, fundamentally, the British 'working-class movement' had *not* been 'politically won' to that CP, let alone its marxism? And incidentally, it's perhaps still worth remarking that 1968—the year of Anderson's essay—was not a particularly happy year for the European CPs anyway, especially in France and Czechoslovakia. I can't go into why the PCF 'failed' in France (or the PCI stumbled a year later in Italy), but at least it's worth asking why the CPGB 'failed' to hold its own intelligentsia, and, perhaps, later, why the British working class 'failed' to 'create its own political party throughout the nineteenth century' and hasn't been particularly 'won to' the CPGB—or *any* 'revolutionary socialist party'—in the twentieth century. I said that 'Stalinism' was one internal and external reason for the 'break' in 1956. That break wasn't an 'epistemological' break; it was fundamentally a 'moral' break, as anyone who reads the back sections of issues of *Modern Quarterly* for 1953 to 1955 can discern, or who even glances at *The New Reasoner* for 1956–7 can easily see. The central figures in that break were John Saville and E. P. Thompson, both working historians precisely concerned with the nineteenth-century British working-class movement. One of them was soon to write, in *The Making of the English Working Class* (1963):

I am seeking to rescue the poor stockinger, the Luddite cropper, the 'obsolete' hand-loom weaver, the 'utopian' artisan, and even the deluded follower of Joanna Southcott, from the enormous condescension of posterity. . . . Their aspirations were valid in terms of their own history; and, if they were casualties of history, they remain, condemned in their own lives, as casualties.

148

Put that now famous formulation alongside two poems published in Poland in the '50s, at a time when the only literature officially encouraged was 'concentration camp' literature:

> History's skeletons are recorded in round figures.
> A thousand and one becomes just a thousand.
> The odd one might never have existed.

and

> that old woman who
> leads a goat on a string
> is more necessary
> and more precious
> than the seven wonders of the world
> whoever thinks and feels
> that she is not necessary
> is guilty of genocide

It's difficult not to read both the historian's comments and the poets' lines as oblique judgements, also, on the era of Stalin.

It's also easy to see why, years later, E. P. Thompson chose Leszek Kolakowski, a hero of the second Polish October, as the formal recipient of his *Open Letter*.

In the year of that Polish October, that partial replay of the Budapest October of 1956 and partial rehearsal of the Prague spring of 1968, Raymond Williams, in *Culture and Society* quoted a passage from an essay entitled *Democracy*:

We cannot say that all men are equal. We cannot say $A = B$. Nor can we say that men are unequal. We may not declare that $A + B = C$. . . . One man is neither equal nor unequal to another man. When I stand in the presence of another man, and I am my own pure self, am I aware of the presence of an equal, or of an inferior, or of a superior? I am not. When I stand with another man, who is himself, and when I am truly myself, then I am only aware of a Presence, and of the strange reality of Otherness. There is me, and there is *another being*. . . . There is no comparing or estimating. There is only this strange recognition of *present otherness*. I may be glad, angry, or sad, because of the presence of the other. But still no comparison enters in. Comparison enters only when one of us departs from his own integral being, and enters the material mechanical world. Then equality and inequality starts at once.

The essay is by Lawrence and can lead us back to Leavis and Heidegger, and through them to a further two-fold question: *why* did Heidegger and Leavis provide the fundamental intellectual 'alternatives' to 'Marxism' on the continent and in England, and *why* does the British working class so consistently fail to produce or support a 'revolutionary socialist party'?

We can now ask, *if* 'most of what Heidegger can do for one, Leavis does as well or better', *what* can these two figures 'do for one'—which is one way of asking a question Anderson doesn't, finally, ask: why should the various modulations of Heideggerian thought have proved so attractive to the European intelligentsia, and *why* should Leavis have achieved such a peculiarly ambivalent status and stature in English 'culture'? One obvious clue is visible in the terms of that passage from Lawrence (whose *'oeuvre* is our best equivalent to Heidegger's *Seinsdenken*'). At a superficial level, both Heidegger and Lawrence can be appropriated by those who believe, or want to believe, that the central conflict in the twentieth century is between 'my own pure self' and 'the material mechanical world', between the integral individual and the 'forces' that want to 'reduce' the individual to a unit, a cipher, a faceless number, a mere letter A or B or C. In both Heidegger and Leavis there is an explicit 'attack' on what Heidegger calls 'technology' and what Leavis calls the 'technologico-Benthamite civilisation'.

The nuances needn't detain us here—the real complexity of Heidegger's notion of *Gelassenheit*, or the significance of Leavis's coupling of technology and *Bentham* (that 'genius in the way of bourgeois stupidity'—Marx). Such nuances are lost in the process of banalisation. What undergirds such banalising appropriation, however, is the 'real' and personal 'experience' of the appropriators, which is the 'experience', precisely, of a 'technologically' dominated world in which the 'individual' feels his or her life to be shaped by the impersonal, the mechanical. I needn't rehearse the familiar ideological themes. Nor need I elaborate the ideological version of the 'alternative' to this society: the vivid picture of regimented 'Soviet Civilisation' that has haunted the European press for decades. It's all too tediously familiar, and the 'illusions' are apparent. But there is a peculiar twist to the history of those 'analyses' of 'Western industrial society' and 'Communist Russia' (or more recently 'drably conformist China'). Faced with this long-established, deeply entrenched and well-cultivated fear and anxiety about the 'threat to the individual' in both 'Western' and 'Eastern' Europe, what current Marxist theories of an Althusserian or Lacanian variety are actually *seen* to be *offering* (and not only in their 'banalised' forms?) is precisely the eradication of the 'subject', the 'reduction' of the individual to a 'bearer' of a position within the relations of production, or within the chains of discourse, and all this in a style of abstruse technicism and in the name of 'science'. To put it crudely, if one 'marxist' reaction against Stalinism took the form of a moral emphasis on the uniqueness of the individual, one 'marxist' reaction against that moral humanism looks like a 'theoretical' spelling out of precisely the (moral) premisses of 'Stalinism' *and* of 'industrial capitalism'. I put it that way to emphasise the *practical*, the *political* difficulties in the way of offering *this* brand of marxism, in any generally accessible form, as the 'revolutionary theory' for a working class in an epoch scarred by concentration camps, genocide, and industrial and military dragooning into what are seen as huge homogenised 'masses'; the 'lived experience' of this period has been dominated for working-class people precisely by the fear of and resistance to being 'reduced' to a mere 'letter' in the insistent chains of some impersonal 'discourse' or imperialist 'system'. Obviously, to put it that way is to traduce rather than merely simplify, but I'm trying to take something like a historian's view from the future, in which the general shape of a moment is simplified to its essentials. I suspect, in other words, that *that* paradox will one day be the most apparent feature of the current relation of 'marxist theory' to 'the working class movement'. Meanwhile, I need to take the whole problem more 'seriously', I agree.

I suppose I do need to say a bit more about why I don't myself find Lacanian Althusserianism very attractive, or very rewarding intellectually—except as a fascinating intellectual game—and it's certainly nice to find punning back in favour after Lacan (you know the type: Lacan can, Kant cudn't, Foucault —oh!? Derridada, etc.). Anyway, there are two aspects to my disquiet. Both will take some time to spell out, so go to sleep if you like for a while. The first is a more theoretical objection, and focusses mainly on Lacan; the second is more directly political, and has more to do with Althusser. My first argument draws on two thinkers deeply influenced by Heidegger, Derrida and Alan Blum (not very well known here?), and also on some facets of Althusser and Lacan themselves; but I think it's my own argument in the end. I'll put it as simply as I can, using a very simple contrast to begin with.

Anyone who reads Plato and Aristotle is struck by two immediate differences between their works (as we've inherited them). Aristotle's works are 'systema-tic', characterised by a logical ordering, progression, and arrangement into clearly divided and sub-divided arguments, which combine together to unify the overall argument of each treatise and to establish the sequence of steps whereby that argument moves from its clearly stated initial problem or topic to its clearly stated conclusions. The treatises, though they were probably lectures at some time, have a *'written'* form (preserved perhaps through students' notes). Whatever the particular merits or defects of Aristotle's actual arguments, the intention of these works is clearly to provide a tightly interlocking system of inquiry, governed throughout by the rules of logic—Aristotle's own treatise on 'logic' being a key treatise.

Plato's works have a different structure and form. Though they were clearly *written*, they have the form of *'spoken'* dialogues. And their structure is clearly not systematic in the sense in which Aristotle's are. Rarely are all the facets of a question or topic followed through in such a way that the reader feels that all the logical possibilities have been considered. The device of having the interlocutors 'agree' tends to open a space for the reader, at each moment of 'agreement', to want to interject his own unmet objection: 'Yes, but . . .'.

Such immediate comparisons need, of course, to be elaborated and qualified. Though Plato's *Dialogues* are structured by a process of incremental agreement between the interlocutors, there is rarely, if ever, completely shared agreement by the end of the dialogue: some of the speakers may have left, others stopped contributing, others remain unconvinced, or there may in any case be no clear conclusion arrived at to the original problem posed in the dialogue. Yet at the same time a careful plotting or orchestration of each dialogue is apparent; the 'end' is already 'known' to the author. In the case of Aristotle, though each treatise has a clear central line of argument, there are constant 'objections' which are not answered in the course of the treatise but are despatched for suitable treatment to another treatise. Yet the treatises taken as a whole do not seem to have any progressively ordered relation to each other; the familiar order of the volumes in the Oxford edition, say, beginning with the 'logic' and ending with the 'poetics', gives a re-assuring sense of a clear starting-point and a 'sensible' order for study—until we actually begin to read the volumes, and find the cross-references multiplying. Admittedly, the crucial, underpinning treatises do seem to be the *Logic* and the *Metaphysics*, but which of these two guarantees the other? And anyway isn't logic one of the uses of language, which is treated in the *Rhetoric*, and doesn't the *Metaphysics* start from statements about the senses, about the human animal? Etc. In any case, don't many of the treatises begin with a summary of his predecessors' arguments, which provide an agreed starting-point, so wouldn't we have to read *them* first—wouldn't we at least have to read Plato first? So, where do we *begin*?

We can generalise the case of Aristotle in two crucial respects. Insofar as any argument is 'valid', it has to be so according to a 'logic'; but what makes the 'argument' of that 'logic' 'valid'? And if a 'system' of thought has no starting-point except outside itself, we cannot rely on its systematicity unless we can also rely on its starting-point, but that involves either an appeal to 'authority' or to another 'system'. The general direction of such comments is presumably familiar. My basic point, in *this* context, is that a 'theoretical' or 'scientific' system appeals to or includes a 'logic'. But given the 'crisis of logic', which has developed in the last hundred years, from Boole through Frege to Gödel, any theoretical system today is fundamentally unguaranteeable, as a *theoretical system*, including especially axiomatic systems (cf. the peculiar implications of Gödel's Theorem). Yet the implicit and sometimes explicit direction of the Althusserian trend is precisely to offer an axiomatic theoretical ('scientific') system of 'knowledge'. Any such attempt finally transforms itself, necessarily, into an appeal to '*authority*', normally, these days, to the authority of a *text* (so the footnotes multiply). In practice, few even among the most dedicated 'theorists' around today have the energy, or competence (training), to pursue their own debts back through the interminable chain of authorities, of texts. In any case such a project would, would it not, be a search for that transcendental signifier ruled out of play by Lacan and by Althusser. One fashionable response to this classic dilemma has been to treat the chain of texts (of signifiers, of discourse, of language) as an endless chain, a Möbius Strip impossible in principle ever to leave or ever fully to traverse; the effort of the 'theorist' or 'scientist' thereby becomes (in Barthes's words) merely to '*connect* to the historical chain of discourses, the *progressus* of discursivity'. But if the project of systematisation is, by its own account, bound to 'fail', why does the effort continue to be made?

Such a question invites an answer from the camp of Plato. The opposing (yet complementary) view would appear to affirm the transcendental signifier, the originator of discourse, the subject of thought, the expressive speaker, the 'I'. When Plato says that thought is the conversation of the soul with itself, we can all (presumably) pounce. But attend rather to what Plato *does*, as *writer*. It is not Plato who 'says' that in the dialogues. Plato constructs a conversation not in his soul but in his writing, a conversation between characters. (And

remember that Lawrence criticised him for not *really* making them characters.)
But why does Plato choose that method? One account would say, because it
allows him to explore a 'moral' notion of 'truth' or 'knowledge'; the reader is to
grasp the *relation* between the (moral, ethical) 'character' of each speaker and
the tenacity of his search for the truth; Socrates's main virtue then is
perseverance. Maybe.

What I, however, want to generalise out of Plato's method is a notion of
differences. There is already available the notion of 'differance'—Derrida's
term for the endless deferment of 'meaning', the hunt-the-slipper game of
signification where each signifier turns into a signified in turn as we hunt the
elusive traces of an always-already-no-longer-where-you-sought-it-now of
'meaning'. But 'differance' merely extends, endorses, and elaborates the
paradox of Aristotle's inter-textual cross-referring 'system'. At the core of
'differance' is the *materiality* of the sign, the 'precedence' of 'script' over
'speech' (it's not simply a matter of which order do you actually put the *books*
on the shelf in). That 'materiality' of the sign has now, of course, become itself a
'sign' of 'materialism', and therefore of 'marxism', for some of our Althusserian–Lacanian semioticians; and in delight at this magic allegiance a metaphor
is let loose: if the text is 'material', the 'author' is a mere fiction, or function, or
functionary, a name on the spine, a construct of the *ideology* of the idealist
expressive self; the 'death of the author' is proclaimed gleefully despite
protestations from numerous corpses, their only remaining function to be
spineless extras in a new epic, the *morte d'auteur*, written by scripts and
directed by trends. But both the author and the ideology of the self remain
stubbornly, if rather sullenly, on the set, ineradicable old hands.

The torsions I have in mind are plainly written in the following text, from a
decently obscure journal called *New Blackfriars* (January 1977):

It's of the essence of the ideological that in speaking, in constituting myself as a *subject*, I must
necessarily repress, remain in ignorance of, the very determinants of my discourse—determinants
which are visible only to *science*, to that science which is psychoanalysis. As 'I' speak—'I', the
coherent historical subject Terry Eagleton, *it*—the unconscious—speaks through me, constantly
disturbing and displacing my discourse. I am a subject only because I continually strive to *centre*
myself in a discourse which continually *decentres* me; struggling to become master of my words,
striving to see myself as the authentic source and origin of my meaning, I'm continually confronted
by those gaps, absences, contradictions and conflicts within my discourse which betray the
determining presence within it of the ideological, of the unconscious. These already *put me in
position*, ascribing to me a set of functions I can't escape, at the very moment my discourse struggles
to deny this fact by its apparent 'naturalness', its apparent susceptibility to my subjective control,
its 'obviousness' and spontaneity.

Further in the same piece:

It is important to see first of all that the validity of my discourse doesn't depend on me as a subject:
that, precisely, is the delusion of *ideology*, that what's valid is valid because of its rootedness in the
experience of the subject. Quite the contrary: validity, truth, science can emerge only by breaking
that fatal complicity between the subject and his discourse, by the subject *removing* himself from
any idea of being *author* of his discourse, recognising that, if he's to speak truly, scientifically, he
must become no more than the bearer of certain conceptual categories whose validity depends in
no way on himself. If what I say in this paper is to be scientifically correct, then I must become no
more than the 'space' within which a certain play of conceptual categories is brought into being. I

must break the complicity between myself and my discourse, which is never fully possible but which I can always strive towards, more or less successfully.

I suppose one could remark that this does rather sound like a mediaeval Rhineland mystic striving humbly to become the emptied space in which the Divine being can definitively whisper the truth—which may indicate something about mediaeval mysticism: could *kenosis* be a scientific procedure, I wonder? But it's probably more useful to ask what guarantees the 'validity, truth, science' that is to 'emerge' by 'breaking' that 'fatal complicity'. It would seem peculiar to claim, for example, that 'science' will 'emerge' by the 'subject' 'removing himself from any *idea* of being author of his own discourse'. Is that 'idea' merely a parapraxis, the unconscious speaking through the discourse? If so, the unconscious here speaks in idealist accents (or maybe the unconscious can itself commit the occasional parapraxis): removing the *idea* of gravity doesn't allow levitation to 'emerge' (unless you're a mediaeval mystic!). Later in the same article the text says:

The subject can't *know* the discourses which produce him, the deep structure and laws of the social formation, because the very process of being *constituted* as a subject involves the *repression* of that discourse, the misrecognition of those laws of the mode of production.

One might here ask, if the subject doesn't *know*, why or what *does* 'know' *that* 'the subject' does*n't* know? Does the unconscious know? Or perhaps 'marxism' knows? But does marxism know that it knows? Or perhaps marxism knows that '*it*' knows? Or perhaps *it* knows that marxism knows—or doesn't know? We've been in this hole before, a long time ago.

Most of Eagleton's article is taken up with an eloquent rendition of the Freud–Lacan variations on the 'way in which the category of the subject is constructed only on the basis of a repression of the determinants which went into its making'. This may seem to mean no more than that a concert pianist is ill-advised to think about carpentry while performing a Beethoven *adagio*. But clearly the text means more: the 'crux of this [repression?], of course, is the Oedipus complex', it says, in which the 'relation of unreflective unity' the baby lives with its mother is 'shattered by the recognition of *difference*, which is the inruption of the father into the mother-child relation'. The familiar chain follows: penis, lack, desire, the strings of absences and differences that constitute signification.

This beautifully *clear* article—Eagleton's very individual style at its best, a vivid lucidity—reproduces two strategies characteristic of the whole 'school' he here (re-)presents. One is the return to the Oedipus complex, to an *originating* explanation, without any *fully* intelligible account of why that structure of repression is so peculiarly persistent (the concept of the 'unconscious' *stands in for* such an account in this text), and, secondly, an admirable self-reflexiveness on the 'position' of the 'author', but no reflection on the physical, material situation of the speaker (the text originated as a paper to a small conference). By that I mean that Eagleton speaks of 'the science of psychoanalysis' as 'the science of what happens when the material body, equipped with its libidinal drives, is inserted into language', and as 'concerned with the utterly devastating consequences which ensue when the material body is inserted into language; for the body is never at home in language.' That repeated present tense, 'is inserted', seems actually to operate, in the text, as a past tense: the material body *was* 'inserted into language' at a traumatic moment, the recognition of (sexual) difference. But isn't the 'recognition of difference' a *continuing* feature of being in the same room as any body else, precisely because there are two *different bodies* (or more, at a conference, say) in the room, materially distinct, spatially differentiated, and formally different? And it's because each body is 'equipped with' a set of eyes and ears and a mouth, as well as 'libidinal drives', that the 'recognition' of each by the other is necessarily different, *formally* different, from the 'recognition' of each of itself (or of itself by each). The other body is necessarily registered as 'different' from *this* body *by* this *body*. To speak to someone else is always to speak from a different *material* 'position': the location of the mouth requires it. But what does this—fairly obvious and pretty basic—material difference have to do with the differance of signification, the problem of knowledge and the 'ideology of the subject'?

To try and make it clear, I want to pick up one of George's notions. He suggested that the structure of ideology was that of a double-bind, since a double-bind has a structure that makes a relationship or distribution of *power* the 'premise' of a 'logic'. He also said that he thought that 'capitalism' was shown as having the same double-bind structure in Marx's account in *Capital*. He then suggested that the reason (certain) 'ideologies' weren't simply 'misperceptions' of the real world but 'partial perceptions', was that they had a concrete 'premise' for their self-contradictory 'logics' in the actual 'power' that the sexist or racist stood to lose by changing his material practice (leaving the field or changing it) in order to resolve the antinomies in his 'ideologic'. Well, I'm not too happy with that way of analysing the problem. Let me worry it out by looking at George's two comments on language. He said that 'to be "white" means, in this world, now, to have the power that comes from being white'; now I agree that 'being white' in a society ruled by apartheid is to be, by that very fact, privileged. But the rule can only 'make sense' as a *rule* because 'to be "white" ' *also* means 'to be white', to have a *different* skin-colour from blacks. That difference is, very much, a matter, literally, of *perception*, a recognition of physical differences; that such perception is shaped, modified, sharpened, by a whole culture is clear—the Guatemalan *gaucho* or Colombian *campesino* seeing fifty-seven shades of brown in a horse's hide, etc., because the colour of a horse's skin makes a *material difference* in that kind of agricultural economy. But the double-signification of 'white', its operating as a signifier within one system and as signified in another, means that the informal 'logic' of racism has *three* terms, not two, which operate in a syllogism of confirmation, roughly:

> I am white;
> he is black;
> therefore: I must be 'White'.

What happens is that one kind of difference operates to confirm (and justify) another kind of difference. (The 'effect of the real' in literary or cinematic *mimesis* is achieved by a rather similar *doubling* of different codes.) That operation *does* have its 'major premise' in the actual distribution of power, in the social relations of production in the society; but it has its 'minor premise' in the existing social *language*, which makes available that double-signification of 'white'/"White"; that use of 'white' is, of course, an *imposition*, a rule of the language created by familiar processes, in law, education, the media, etc., all thereby serving—in their very use of *the language*—the specific interests of 'whites', though of some whites more than of others, etc. Once that '*super-*imposition', that double-signification, of *white* is established, 'confirmation' is easily available as a slippage-within-tautology ('white is White'), or as the confirmatory self-description ('I am white'—a fatal complicity of subject and discourse). But then, in order to describe oneself physically as white but *refuse* the ideological self-attribution of 'White', you need to make an explicit disclaimer: 'I mean I'm white only in a skin sense' (which of course you never are *only*). This distinction is, interestingly, easier to make in *writing*, by establishing typographical differences between the two senses. It's at the point where you *need*, politically *need*, a clearly *articulable* distinction between the two usages, that an account of the processes which constitute(d) that 'equation' becomes necessary also, in order to be able to *think* the difference and in order to be able to combat the confirmatory tautology if asserted by another. An example struck me the other day: the late Jomo Kenyatta once said in an interview, in the days of Mau-Mau, 'The British press have tried to paint me as black as possible.'

——Sorry! Forget all that. Scrub it out. Let me try again. Terribly sorry: lost me way a bit. I'll go back a few pages and start again. In the immortal words on the side of the grain-lifter: 'If at first you don't suck seed, try drier grain'——Where was I, then? Yes:

To try to make it clear, I want to pick up another theme in Eagleton's argument. Freud, as he rightly points out, is a deeply *tragic* thinker, because death (the death drive) threatens the whole enterprise. Eagleton allows the 'death-instinct' a momentary presence in his Lacanian re-write:

At the very heart of my discourse is a radical loss, for discourse is nothing but difference and absence; and just as the child, terrified by its first recognition of sexual difference, of the 'loss' of castration, the 'mutilation' of the mother, repressed this knowledge and believes contradictorily that all people have penises and some do not, so I, the adult, am continually tempted to repress that ceaseless movement of absence and difference—that movement of desire—through which my language conducts me, by erecting a *fetish* [sic], by fixing myself in some security as a subject through relating myself to some fetishised object which will be the guarantor of my security, of my being in place, of my imaginary, ideological relation of unity with the world. What I can't accept is that the world is independent of my consciousness, that the language I speak betrays, at every point, that *it* is speaking me; what I can't accept is that the world is independent of me, because that means I can die. As I hurtle from side to sign, caught up in that process of desire which language itself instigates, I want always to fold myself in some utter fixed fullness of sense and identity; driven as I am along that chain of absences which is language, I fight to return to some primordial plenitude of sense, some moment in which I cannot die because the world depends upon me. I'm torn, constantly, between the 'imaginary' and the 'symbolic'—between believing that my discourse is *my* discourse, and finding constantly that it's already structured, it already offers positions to me, which displace what I say, which outrun my conscious control. As the text of my speech unrolls, as I position myself as the author-subject of it, I find constantly that beneath the 'coherent' discourse I'm conducting is that true, invisible, scarred and mutilated discourse which is the unconscious, which is the sum of words which invade and contradict and escape all I say.

I'm not disputing this account, only probing it. Think of the logic of that phrase: 'all people have penises, and some do not'. Such a contradictory 'belief' seems a peculiar one to persist when we *know* the first part is 'false' in the 'real' world—and if that belief really is ineradicable then the liberation of women faces a prickly future, even a tragic one. But isn't there an older, ancient syllogism which it echoes: 'All men are mortal; Socrates is a man; therefore Socrates is mortal'. As a piece of common logic in a *textbook* that's perfectly sound and acceptable. But in the form, say, 'All animals die; I am an animal; therefore . . .'—the logical conclusion is somewhat more difficult to 'accept' (even the minor premise seems to stick in some throats—so does the major one, come to that!). There is always that tiny *trace* of a *refusal*, a fleeting urge just to check the conclusion one more time, bend it a little, query the validity of the syllogism, of the logic. The inexorable here seems an insult. All A will B; C is an A; therefore C will B. That's harmless, unless you happen to be the letter C and B means 'die'. But you don't just *happen* to be C. I'm suggesting that the fundamental 'repression' that shapes discourse is the repression of the knowledge of death, of final absence, the intellectual certainty that I will die, very soon. Because the logic of 'difference' requires the logic of 'same', and what makes us all similar is the body; all bodies die, every body dies. But—says the logic of *differences*—*my* body *cannot* be the *same* as every body else's, precisely because of the location of the eyes, hands, skin, body, that enforces the *recognition* of everybody else *as* everybody *else* in the first place (I am always in the first place). That fundamental, inescapable, mis-recognition that is *not* a mis-*perception* of the real world isn't (only) rooted in the Oedipal trauma; it persists as long as bodies persist. Which is for ever, within history; but they'll be somebody else soon. It would be interesting to detour here through mirror-stages, and the intimate intertwinings of sex, bodies and language, and the basis for various 'ideologies' in *this* difference that superimposes itself. But what interests me at the moment is the effect of this permanent (mis-)recognition on *conversation*, particularly intellectual conversation, and, eventually, on cognition.

A comment that George made, citing Bateson, may help: that a 'double-bind' has to be a *repeated* experience, a 'recurrent theme' in the life of the victim, rather than a single traumatic event; but that when repetition has created a habitual expectation of double-bind, *any one element* in the set of ingredients can be enough to 'precipitate panic or rage', that is, for the victim to trigger into play the rest of the double-bind process himself, or *on* himself. With that as a guideline, an Ariadne thread into speculation, consider the following suggestion: that *any* attempt to advance a coherent, logical, systematic argument acts, however latently, as the trigger for a double-bind process, both for the speaker and for the addressee. (In parenthesis: perhaps, George, Bernard Lonergan's term 'counter-position' might be better than 'double-bind'; a counter-position occurs between what you say and what you are; but let's stick with 'double-binds'.) There are various relatively superficial reasons why this should be so. For example, that fundamental mis-(re)cognition of *differences* needs 'confirmation' by the recognition of *other* differences, and since it is the intelligence (my relation to the shared language which articulates logics) that tells me that I *am* the *same* as the other, one tactically useful confirmation of differences occurs when the intelligence (*my* intelligence) can demonstrate its own difference from the other's intelligence, by a *difference of opinion* (a different relation to the shared language, a *contra*-diction), by saying *something* different, in content as well as form (everything *I* say is different in *form*, formally different, since 'I' say it). But the most amusing reason why coherence triggers double-bind (and thereby contra-dictory discourses) is that at the heart of coherence lies the logic of same/difference itself (or same/other), the principle (starting-point, axiom) of non-contradiction, of 'A is A', which also includes the logic of 'A is not B', but also includes the logical possibility of 'A is (a) B'—which therefore allows for the Socratic syllogism that tells me I *die*. To put the point in quasi-Gödelian terms: any completely systematic structure of propositions is capable of generating the syllogism which 'proves' that I die—which I *don't want* to prove, and which undermines *my* system. It is the refusal, the repression, the *negation*, of *that* which finally speaks in the evasions, avoidances, of any final coherence, which ensures that *anything* any body says will be contra-dicted, some time, since secreted at the heart of any assertion, any discourse, is a proof of my death. Which is why I am also drawn on to the path of, some time or other, contradicting what 'I' have said myself. Which is, I'm suggesting, the cunning reason for the endless chain of discursivity, the interminable path of thinking—or what is called thinking: the *progressus* of para-doxes, the history of dogmas. There is a further movement secreted in this progressus: that a *single* contra-diction, a contrary opinion, has to be defended, elaborated, made coherent by further, confirmatory, contra-dictions in the dialogue with the other; therein lies re-systematisation, de-systematisation, re-systematisation. If pursued, such a movement re-makes logic itself, throws the logic which coheres coherence into dispute, disarray, re-coherence. So we get that curious bass-line in the polyphonic history of 'ideas': the history of logic(s), the chain of epistemologies, the kaleidoscope of *epistémés*.

To the traces of Plato, Aristotle, Hegel, Husserl, Heidegger, etc., in this suggestion, might be added, as a mooring-point for our thread, the materialism of Marx: the central contradiction of 'language' lies not *within* its internal movements but *between* the social relations of its production (between the others to whom one speaks and writes, of whom one is one) *and* the material forces of its production (mouths, hands, bodies—those bodies one does not share, except occasionally, mouth to mouth or in peculiar positions). But marxism is not a philosophy of language; it is not, indeed, a philosophy. A marxist would ask of *that* account another account: of the conditions of its production. *Why* has that complex combination (or similar, different ones) of logic, psychoanalysis, and 'materialism' come into intellectual prominence in the late twentieth century? And why does it find its focus as well as its articulation in the often-punning play of language?*I* don't know; but a future marxist historian (if there are any) might well single out two features of this epoch.

The crucial development in the forces of production in the last thirty-five years has been the development of nuclear power. But the problem that nuclear power has posed, even in its un-developed state, from Hiroshima in 1945 to Cuba in 1961 to Windscale in 1978, has been two-fold: the potential death of *everybody* (all men are mortal—at the touch of a button) and the *stalemate* of political struggle (the Cold War, the *long-term* political implications of Windscale, etc.). A marxist who 'knows' that the class-struggle has never stopped short of revolutionary war has to face—if he or she is consistent—two *possible* prospects: endless *deferment* of that revolutionary war because of the risks of nuclear catastrophe, or an attempt to 'take power' which will 'succeed' *too late* (power as always-already-no-longer-where-you-sought-it-now)— not simply in the sense of that endless chase across the globe hunting and combatting the always-retreating, always-effective, absent/present control of international monopoly capitalism, but, more tragically, in terms of a moment of 'panic or rage', of misjudgement, of 'accident', as the threat to the identity of a class (structured on diminishing differences) approaches even imaginary success. Such thoughts must arise in any struggle for *theoretical strategic coherence*, any systematic scenario of 'revolution', any thinking through of political directions. But such thoughts have to be refused, repressed, forgotten, consigned back into the hopefully imaginary. But the generation that came to political awareness in the 1960s—who were *born into* a nuclear world—were the first in history to inherit the dilemma of *global* strategy in so acute a form, as so immediate a necessity, as the *only* context in which to *think*. Secreted at the heart of that dilemma is the impossible vision of simultaneity, the instant of full fusion, a single flash of final meaning: a shooting of *all* the clocks at once. But given the *double*-visions superimposed upon each other in that final reel of history, a certain playful yet serious contemplativity, *Gelassenheit*, seems the only possible response to that contradictory culmination of technological civilisation: the fission-chain.

Such a (semi-playful) account does not, however, satisfy. The conditions of production are more specific. And since my concern is Britain and the British assimilation of Lacanian–Althusserianism, it is the conditions of distribution that also intrigue me. I suppose one could argue that the peculiar *situation* of many British marxist intellectuals, old campaigners from the young 1960s, now marooned within the educational apparatus of the stagnant '70s, has some bearing on the question: that curiously irresponsible position of the State-financed, tenured, pensioned 'radical', who is paid by the labour of others to *think*; non-productive labour (in the *technical* sense, of course)

always echoes the position of the contemplative Guardian in a slave-society.
. . . But let that pass, with all nostalgia. Approach it from another direction.

As I write, there are dock-workers picketting the Polaris base in the Firth of
Clyde (one Polaris is beyond their reach, 'somewhere at sea'—and an RAF
V-bomber crashed, loaded, near Chicago today). Theirs is an 'industrial
dispute'. Navy personnel have already bypassed the picket once already in this
fight. (A report on the US Army published yesterday gave the average 'IQ' of
volunteers as 80. They too have been used as strike-breakers. Etc.) The
question on the picket-line is, as it always is, 'What do we do *next*?' The
'questions' of class-conflict are, also, immediately practical ones. Answers are
always found. But no 'revolutionary socialist party' in Britain seems to have
anything like a practical answer to the question: 'What do we do next, and *after
that*?' My own experience over twenty years is that no new *strategic*
perspectives have been developed by any revolutionary socialist party in
Britain within which the 'next tactic' makes sense. Yet the strategic perspectives of previous generations have been subjected to their familiar 'test-cases'
and largely found wanting or no longer viable. To 'connect' to the *progressus*,
to the historical chain of tactics, to the sequence of local, immediate struggles, is
not to make sense of the concept of *revolution*. In Britain in the last twenty years
some 'moments' in the history of 'the Left' are vivid and visible, moments when
certain lessons were learned: 1974, 1968, 1956. But one is less visible, though
important: 1963. The history of 'the Left' between 1956 and 1963 is marked by
a unique conjuncture of the development of a complex 'theoretical' current of
non-organised marxists ('Britain's largest unorganised party—the ex-
Communist Party') in sympathetic touch with the largest and least 'unpopular'
mass campaign of the post-war years, CND, with its demonstrations of
150,000 in 1961 and 1962 (slightly larger than the Vietnam Solidarity
Campaign demos of the late '60s). But the Campaign was a moral and not,
fundamentally, a political campaign. The task facing any marxist within that
current was to try to develop a political analysis that could successfully
politicise that single-issue, single-interest campaign. The failure is well-
known. But, to remind you, here's Stuart Hall, writing in *Sanity* in May 1963:

Can a political shape be imposed upon or arise from a movement which contains within its ranks
such garden varieties as anarchists, non-violent revolutionaries, proto-Trotskyists, New Left
socialists, soft-shoe communists, constituency Labour Party members, renegade liberals, pacifist
old-timers, beatniks and vegetarians, *Peace News, Solidarity, Sanity, Anarchy* and *War and
Peace*?

By any book, the answer should be 'No'. No single flag, no slogan, no ideology, no king, can
command the allegiance of so motley an army of the good.

New Left Review, whose first editor was the same Stuart Hall, between 1960
and 1963 was the 'Left' journal which most directly and theoretically agonised
over *that* problem. Here are two accounts of what happened to *New Left
Review* in 1963:

In January 1963, in circumstances which remain mysterious, the journal was purchased by an Old
Etonian who proceeded to dismiss the entire editorial board and change the journal in all but name.
The commitment to political involvement characteristic of at least the core of the old *NLR* was

completely jettisoned and in the first year of the new regime more space was devoted to tenor saxophonists playing in New York than to the British working class in its entirety.

David Widgery, *The Left in Britain 1956–1968*

We reached a point of personal, financial, and organisational exhaustion; and at this moment, the agent of history appeared, in the form of Perry Anderson. We were exhausted: he was intellectually fertile, immensely self-concentrated, decisive. We saw, in a partnership with him and his colleagues, an opportunity to regenerate the review and to recuperate our own squandered intellectual resources. We did not, as it happens, anticipate that the first expression of his decisiveness would be to dismiss the review's founders from the board.... Since taking on editorial control in 1963 Perry Anderson and his colleagues have conducted the review with system, conviction and decision. There was, however, a fracture in the passage from one tradition to another, which was never exposed to principled discussion. It was a very English transition: that is (according to one's viewpoint) gentlemanly and tolerant, or otiose and manipulative.

Edward Thompson, *An Open Letter to Leszek Kolakowski*

(One is, incidentally, rather reminded, reading this, of the poor deluded followers of Joanna Southcott.) The incident was 'mysterious' and the 'fracture' (an epistemological break?) was 'never exposed to principled discussion'. Both comments remain, fifteen years on, sadly true. Why? Let us treat this enigma, this silence, this suppression, as a 'symptom'. Of what? Of a fundamental blockage: the impossibility of extending the moral case against unilateralism into a total political programme and converting 150,000 heterogeneous adherents of the former into disciplined supporters of the latter. I say 'impossibility'. Not exhaustion or incompetence. What would have been involved would have been a revolution *against* the material needs, interests, hopes, expectations, of those who were to make that 'revolution'. *Fully to follow through the consequences of unilateralism* would have involved a fundamental threat to the material conditions of life of not just the 150,000 but most of the 50 million in Britain—a threat arising not (solely) from 'Soviet aggression' but from economic and other reprisals on us by our erstwhile 'allies'. To align with the 'non-aligned bloc' (the 'programme' of CND's *Freed From Fear* in 1961—the 'nonaligned bloc' being then India, Yugoslavia, Egypt, Ghana, etc.) was a liberal version of the para-doxical demand faced by any revolutionary socialist party in Europe and North America—a 'demand' it would have to make, in the first instance, of its own members. At the heart, the 'centre', of the strategic-theoretical *impasse* of the Old New Left was what one might call the 'imperialist differential'—and we have been in that hole before, from around 1850 to 1880. Labour historians can quarrel over the imperialist bonus to the British working class in those decades (and the related thesis of 'the labour aristocracy'), because the argument can go either way for that period; but that the 'differential' between the metropolitan worker and, say, the Bajan cane-cutter who produces the sugar the British worker puts in his tea (itself produced by Ceylonese plantation-workers on starvation rations) or the middle-class academic puts in his coffee (produced by a Brazilian Indian) —that *that* differential is now immense is undeniable. That the differential arises as one effect of the contradiction between the global material forces of production and the global relations of production may indicate an *explanation* of the impasse faced by a 'revolutionary party' in Britain, but an explanation, a scientific analysis even, doesn't *solve* the political, strategic impasse. (We all

know why a Labour Government 'failed' to prevent a nationalised international oil company from breaking its own sanctions against Rhodesia.)

But *if* European marxist theory *is* the theory 'of' the European working class (or
six-sevenths of it), it's not surprising, is it, that that theory, too, should have at
its 'centre' a *self-contradictory impasse*, a demand which it 'cannot' articulate,
which it has to suppress, to 'lose' in its own endless chains of discourse.

The silence about 'the Party' in Anderson's *Components* essay may be no more
than a local 'symptom' of a certain repressed moment of 'inruption' and
rupture in 1963, but that 'moment' may itself be no more than a 'symptom' of a
more general repressed discourse in which the key terms that form the 'chain'
could be rendered as: 'imperialist differential', 'revolution', 'too late', 'nuclear'. That 'ecology' and 'racism' are also characteristic currents in the Europe
of the '70s bespeaks the same emerging self-contradictions; when everywhere
is in the same chains we are all of us haunted by more or less the same
para-praxes. What is characteristic of Lacanian–Althusserianism is that it
takes the theoretical impasse of European marxism to its point of highest
theoretical development so far: into the contradictions of epistemology and the
proclamation that: 'The subject can't *know* the discourses which produce him,
the deep structure and laws of the social formation, because the very process of
being *constituted* as a subject involves the *repression* of that discourse, the
misrecognition of those laws of the mode of production'. One might now ask, *is*
it that the subject *can't* know the 'laws of the social formation' or, *rather*, 'can't'
know the *subject's own relation* to 'the laws of the social formation', his and
her own position within them—which (according to one's viewpoint) might be
seen more as that of 'ruler' than of 'subject'? I can see no reason to speak of
marxism or psychoanalysis as 'sciences' unless they *do* provide 'knowledge'
of the laws of the social formation and of the discourse of the unconscious (of
what the self leaves unsaid and why)—and 'knowledge' that is accessible to
knowing subjects, not just me but as many people as possible who resist that
knowledge. I can, however, I suspect, see a reason why the subject 'can't' know
his or her *position*, why that position 'has' to be mis-recognised. Eagleton
writes: 'I fight to return to some primordial plenitude of sense, some moment in
which I cannot die because the world depends upon me.' Perhaps a slight
re-writing will make my point: 'I fight to return to some primordial ignorance,
some permanent forgetfulness of the fact that I will die because I depend upon
the whole world'. Or one can perhaps further re-write thus: 'I struggle to arrive
at some moment in which, if necessary, I will die for the world—or at any rate
suffer a reasonably drastic change in the way I live now.' One can read those
latent reformulations, decipher that dilemma, equally in the angry but negative
expressions of ordinary motorists queuing at empty petrol-stations and in the
sophisticated but more positive prison reflections of Régis Debray, a *self-
analysis* that questions the motives for his being in the face of death in an
execution cell in Latin America in the first place. I suggest you read his *Journal
d'un petit bourgeois entre deux feux et quatre murs.*

Which brings me back to Debray's one-time teacher, Louis Althusser (a fair amount of the *Journal* is concerned with Debray's student formation), and to my second, more political, objection to Althusserian–Lacanianism. I'll be very brief indeed on this one. In fact, all I need to do is suggest that you also read two books by Althusser himself, *Essays in Self-Criticism* and *Montesquieu: Politics and History*—and that you read the first in the light of the second. But as a mere pointer to what I have in mind I'll single out one footnote from *Essays* and put it alongside some quotes from *Montesquieu*. The footnote reads:

For Marxism the explanation of any phenomenon is in the last instance *internal*: it is the *internal* 'contradiction' which is the 'motor'. The external circumstances are active: but 'through' the internal contradiction which they overdetermine.

Bearing that in mind, think of Althusser's own (brilliant) dissection of Montesquieu's *De l'Esprit des lois* (published in 1748). Althusser writes that:

the fundamental antagonism at that time did not counterpose the absolute monarchy to the feudal lords, nor the nobility to a bourgeoisie which was for the most part *integrated into the regime of feudal exploitation and profited by it*, but the *feudal regime itself* to the *masses subject to its exploitation*.

He then notes how those 'masses' slowly forced their way into the conscious-ness of 'history' and finally into the conceptual apparatus of 'political theory', though not, in fact, into Montesquieu's:

Not until the appearance of a poor priest from Champagne, like Meslier, . . . did this 'people', this 'common people' *(bas-peuple)*, enter as a *puissance*, first into pamphlets and finally into the concepts of political theory. Before this, it had only an allusive existence theoretically: as it does in Montesquieu himself. . . . But this *fourth puissance*, this subject of non-knowledge, passion and violence, nevertheless haunts the alliances of the other three [*puissances*: monarchy, nobility, bourgeoisie] as a *memory* does its loss: by its censorship.

Althusser concludes his analysis by claiming that:

By a unique historical *volte-face*, a man who looked towards the past seemed to open the door to the future. I believe that this paradox pertains above all to the *anachronistic* character of Montesquieu's position. It is because he pleaded the cause of *an outdated order* that he set himself up as an opponent of a political order which *others were to make outdated*.

At the end of chapter 3, 'The Dialectic of History', Althusser had already remarked that:

within him another man than the scientist took advantage of this ambiguity. The *man of a political party* which needed precisely the pre-eminence of the forms over the principles, and wanted there to be *three kinds of government*, in order that, protected by the necessities of climate, manners and morals, and religion, it could make its *choice* between them.

Consider now the case of Louis Althusser. *Montesquieu: Politics and History* was published in 1959, and Althusser has clearly moved on, theoretically, from his position then. But he remains, as he has done *since 1948*, 'the man of a political party'—a Party, the PCF, which has, again and again, wanted merely to 'choose' between 'different kinds of *government*', and has 'failed' repeated-ly. Perhaps its 'failure', even in its own terms, is intelligible: because that Party itself already stands *on the side of an outdated order*—and so, almost necessarily, do its *members*. In the torsions of that 'contradiction', deeply 'internal' to the political strategy of every European Communist Party (though not only the CPs), lies the 'motor' of their 'struggle'—a struggle to avoid the double-bind of 'revolution'.

What is then left, waiting, hopefully, in the wings, at the quiet margins of history and political theory, is that other *puissance*, those masses who live, and die, in their own fourth realm, their own dark world. *Politics and History*, published in the year of the Cuban revolution, of the formation of the NLF in Vietnam, of the last twitches of French terror in Algeria, can perhaps be read now, with hindsight, as a 'symptom' of a deeply persistent dilemma of strategy and direction, of allegiance and viewpoint. A spectre has been haunting European marxism for a long time now: not merely the spectre of *Eurocommunismo*, but the chill spectre of Euro*centri*sm.

Let me return to England, for a brief conclusion. It may be merely another minor symptom, but if you look down the list of NLB books, given in *NLR* 100, among the mere seven out of the first forty not so far reprinted or paperbacked are *Armed Insurrection* (published in 1970—the year armed struggle replaced the politics of People's Democracy in Northern Ireland, a mere hour's flight away) and Lucien Goldmann's *Immanuel Kant*. The second is the more interesting in this context, since Goldmann's argument is that Kant's philosophy is an expression of that 'tragic vision' which articulated the crisis of the bourgeoisie in the revolutionary epoch of the late Enlightenment. Goldmann starts his chapter on Kant's epistemology with an anecdote which may have a certain relevance. The chapter is entitled 'What Can I Know?'

Kant lays the philosophical foundations for the most profound and radical critique ever made of bourgeoise man. Perhaps the reader will allow me to explain how I first came to understand this. It was in a class-room, where I had just been expounding the general principles of Kantian ethics. A pupil delivered a vehement speech against this morality according to which, he said, his father, a most respected citizen, would be an immoral man. This was quite unacceptable to him. When, astonished, I asked him how he had come to that conclusion, the young man explained that his father, a shopkeeper, was every day in contact with a large number of people whom he did not otherwise know and who for him were no more than the means of earning a living and feeding his family. It would never have occured to him to treat all these unknown people as ends in themselves.

I must admit that I was taken aback by this reply. But my astonishment only increased when, on returning home and leafing through the writings of Kant, I found that Kant's first example of an immoral man corresponded more or less exactly to what my young pupil had said.

I wonder what Goldmann's reaction would have been had his pupil accused him, Lucien Goldmann, not only of being an immoral man for living in accordance with his own philosophy but also of being 'immoral' precisely according to the arguments of that philosophy. I offer this double-bind simply because I find it interesting that Heidegger's *Being and Time* was meant to culminate in an ethics and never did, and so was Sartre's *Critique of Dialectical Reason* and never did, and that Terry Eagleton's article from which I've been quoting begins with the comment that 'Marxism has had on the whole little to say about morality', but that it is 'in the provisional silence of those who refuse the term "morality"' that, perhaps, something of its true meaning may finally emerge'. That Western Marxism, and indeed European twentieth-century thought generally, has consistently been unable to develop, or refused to develop, a 'morality', may be a mark that 'European Marxism' is now the expression of another 'tragic vision'. Since 'morality' has been so long associated with that dead Queen of the Sciences, Theology, it may be yet another symptom that in his extensive and almost comprehensive survey of European and English intellectual life, in the *Components* article, Anderson simply omitted any consideration of theology. Yet as we reflect back upon 'Western Marxism' it seems that theological themes insinuate themselves at many points: Goldmann's major work was on the absent God of Jansenism, *Le Dieu caché*, Benjamin's mind is permeated by an Hebraic awareness of the silence and plenitude that speaks in the Word, the Text, and behind the neo-scholasticism of Althusser himself lies not only the *Tractatus Theologico-Politicus* and the *Ethica* of the seventeenth-century Amsterdam Jew, Baruch Spinoza, but also the Neo-Thomism of such mentors of his days in the *Jeunes Étudiants Catholiques* as Maritain and Gilson. Given the complex filiations between a form of theology at the centre of which is the word, *the* Book, and the peculiar importance of 'Literature' in European culture, it is again perhaps not surprising that, though Anderson's focus in that essay is explicitly on the 'culture' and 'disciplines' which 'provide our fundamental *concepts* of man and society', he omits 'creative literature' as well as theology. A Leavis would, of course, say that 'creative literature' provides us with *more* than 'concepts' of 'man and society', and that we *need* more than 'concepts'. Such a view might well be dismissed as 'idealist'—and indeed the final target of Anderson's coruscating critique is the residual idealism in Raymond Williams, derived from Leavis; the final footnote of the essay reads:

The influence of Leavis is discernible in its idealism *[The Long Revolution]*—corrected in much of Williams's later work. Leavis believed that 'to say that the life of a country is determined by its educational ideals is a commonplace'. (*Scrutiny*, No. 1, May 1932.)

It may then seem ever so slightly ironic that the first quotation in Anderson's own essay is from an article entitled *Problèmes Etudiants*, by Louis Althusser:

Louis Althusser has recently written that within the general system of higher education 'the number one strategic point of action of the dominant class' is 'the very *knowledge* students receive from their teachers'. This is the 'true fortress of class influence in the university'; it is by the very nature of the knowledge it imparts to students that the bourgeoisie exerts its greatest control over them'.

To believe that even *within* the educational apparatus it is *primarily* through 'the very *knowledge* students receive from their teachers' that class discipline is effected, shows more than residual traces of idealism. But I'd better leave these considerations and, finally, get back to literature and morality. I'm turning this into a lecture, and I don't want to end up doing *that*!

That comment of Eagleton's about morality is repeated in the last chapter of his book *Criticism and Ideology*, in which he uses the same kind of argument about 'aesthetics' and 'value'. According to Goldmann, of course, a work of *literature* may, equally with a work of philosophy, be the most coherent (and therefore in-coherent, self-contradictory) expression of a 'tragic vision'. Now, you know I'm not very keen on Goldmann's general method, but the idle thought does strike me that the logical outcome of the present spate of Althusserian–Lacanian marxism might well be a *novel*, or perhaps an instance of what Eagleton somewhere else calls 'that necessarily ironic genre', an autobiography. But I suppose it's already happened: if literature replaced theology and morality some time around Arnold's *Literature and Dogma*, and criticism replaced literature some time around Leavis's *Education and the University* (with Newman's *Idea of a University* and *Grammar of Assent* somewhere in between), criticism has become literature some time around Barthes's time, with *Roland Barthes par Roland Barthes* and *Fragments d'un discours amoureux* as the present last stage in this process without any goals. Of course, we're still faced with the question (which we can refuse) of whether to *read* such texts as those of Barthes, Lacan, Derrida, 'as literature', as their own kind of poems or novels—but perhaps that's now a daft question, as you said, George. Incidentally, that brings me back to the point I was going to make about your comments on Chris's reading of 'The Dedication'. (I haven't forgotten anything else I was going to come back to, have I?) I thought that your idea of *reading* the 'ideologic' of a text was quite interesting, but it didn't account for the *way* Chris did it. I think what she was actually doing was revealing 'what Leavis can do for you'—if you *push* him hard enough. There's a very curious notion of language at work, as I said, in Leavis's way of 'reading' a poem: he's very aware of the *text*, 'the words on the page', as *written*, yet he also, simultaneously, wants you to read it, often *aloud*, with all the flexible nuances and rhythms of the *spoken* voice. I think that's got something to do with his very *physical*, very *bodily*, sense of 'literature'—remember that marvellous Leavis *gesture*, the two-handed jab to the *gut*: 'It's down *there*!' Any rate, if you try to *read* like Leavis, with that incredible, even frightening *attention*, you have to somehow 'enter into' the poem—but in the same spirit as that phrase from Blake he was fond of quoting, where Blake says of his own writing:

> 'Tho' I call them Mine, I know they are not Mine.'

Well, I don't know, but I rather think that Chris was just taking *that* insight to its limits by taking seriously, literally, Herbert's lines about

> ... my first fruits present themselves to thee,
> Yet not mine neither.

It's the same problem, even though Herbert's is a theological or onto-theological way of putting it. Maybe there are other ways of really writing, or rather *reading*, and probing the ideologic of a text may be one. But perhaps in the end we have to recognise that most people read for *fun* anyway—certainly not to get 'concepts of man and society'. As marxists I think we ought to respect that, at least some of the time. And that notion of respect perhaps has important political implications. But I'm talking too much. Sorry to have gone rabbiting on. Our Zen Master has been very quiet, I notice. I wonder if he's got anything to add—or is the seminar over? Have you—is it?

I: Who? Me? You don't want *answers* do you? I mean, I've already given you a daft question, haven't I? Do you want a daft answer as well? In any case, judging by what you've just said, Herbert—yes, I *was* listening—I'd be *bound* to disagree with *all* of you, now wouldn't I? I won't even risk giving you another question, but I might add three more quotations, which I don't think any of you quoted, did you? Though you may remember them:

Briggs: So when I left I thought I must do something practical. I decided to bring the price of corn down. A few people eat far too much. So if a few people ate far too little that might balance. Then there would be enough corn and the price would come down. I gave up meat first, then cheese and eggs. I lived on a little porridge and vegetables, then I gave up the porridge and stopped cooking the vegetables. It was easier because I was living out. I ate what I could find but not berries and nuts because so many people want those and I do well with sorrell leaves and dandelion. But grass. It was hard to get my body to take grass. It got very ill. It wouldn't give in to grass. But I forced it on. And now it will. There's many kinds, rye grass, meadow grass, fescue. These two years I've been able to eat grass. Very sweet. People come to watch. They can, I can't stop them. I'm living in a field that belongs to a gentleman that comes sometimes, and sometimes he brings a friend to show. He's not unkind but I don't like to see him. I stand where I am stock still and wait till he's gone.

Claxton: There's an end of outward preaching now. An end of perfection. There may be a time.
I went to the Barbados. I sometimes hear from the world that I have forsaken. I see it fraught with tidings of the same clamour, strife and contention that abounded when I left it. I gave it the hearing and that's all. My great desire is to see and say nothing.

That's the ending of Caryl Churchill's *Light Shining in Buckinghamshire.*

The novel has declined as a coherent genre, not—as is often alleged—because it was the product of the rising bourgeoisie of the nineteenth century and could not survive it. The true reason is that it has disappeared into the abyss between everyday language and the technical discourses inaugurated by Marx and Freud. The sum of objective knowledge within the specialized codes of the human sciences has decisively contradicted and surpassed the normal assumptions behind exoteric speech. The result is that a novelist, after Marx and Freud, has either to simulate an arcadian innocence or transfer elements of their discourse immediately into his work. Hence the now entrenched bifurcation between pseudo-traditional and experimental novels. Both are doomed as genres (which does not exclude individual successes). The ingenuousness of the former is always bad faith; the past will never be recreated. The opposite solution—the inclusion of frontier concepts from Freud or Marx within the novel—has no viable outcome either. Ideas cannot be transposed into art without mediation. The missing mediation is—precisely, ordinary language. As long as this is untransformed at base, these concepts remain 'technical' and 'esoteric'. They run against the grain of spontaneous speech. Hence they are strictly *unusable* for the artist. If they are imported into the novel, they crush it: there have been no successful psychoanalytical tales. The novelist can only forge his art from the material of ordinary language. If there is a radical discordance between this and objective knowledge of man and society, the novel ceases. It has no ground between the naive and the arcane. The gap will only be closed by the reintegration of revolutionary ideas into unreflective linguistic practice, which would make possible a coherent novel once again. Such a change, of course, presupposes a changed society.

That's from another footnote in Perry Anderson's *Components*. You ought to read the rest of it.

Wahl: But I don't understand how others will reappear in your discourse . . .
Lacan: Look, the main thing is that I don't come a cropper!

That's from Lacan's *Seminaire XI.*

If you like, I'll give you an order instead of a question. Put those three quotations in their most suitable order.

And for your next seminar I'll simply supply you with a poem or two, without any questions attached. OK? Here they are:

Coy Supervision

Your tentative slow eyes widen in surprise
as we read together Marvell's *Mistress*:
a trembling in your thighs recoils against
that line about virginity, the worm that pries.
I coolly explicate the sense of 'quaint'
and slyly register your blushes,
how your eyelids flutter as you stutter out
unwelcome possibilities and hope
my coaxing voice won't ask that *you* articulate
the aptness of that choice.
I kindly let some other grope at *politesse* and taste—
he mutters on about the waste
he claims Marvell is postulating
in every unexpressed, suppressed desire—
but while I am debating some finer point of style
I notice that your eyes slide gently back to mine.

Bridgetown Housing, Barbados

Strange, the alchemy of encounter:
The spirit's mulatto architecture
Traces routes to others' entrances,
Compressing colour, time and distances
Into a local, battered splendour
We weave between—critic and defender
Of this old colonial faded style.
Our warmth increases every wandering mile,
Each new warren of the mind, the skin,
Evoking other slums in:
Liverpool, Alabama, Georgetown . . .
Our rage subsides, a thoughtful friendly frown
Appears instead; in dawn's half-lights
We stroll beyond these fading blacks and whites.

168

PART ONE:

Finals, Just Desserts, Examination Answers: Studies in Legal Fictions

A colleague had once declared that Philip ought to publish his examination papers. The suggestion had been intended as a sneer, but Philip had been rather taken with the idea—seeing in it, for a few dizzy hours, a heaven-sent solution to his professional barrenness. He visualized a critical work of totally revolutionary form, a concise, comprehensive survey of English literature consisting entirely of questions, elegantly printed with acres of white paper between them, questions that would be miracles of condensation, eloquence and thoughtfulness, questions to read and re-read, questions to brood over, as pregnant and enigmatic as *haikus*, as memorable as proverbs; questions that would, so to speak, contain within themselves the ghostly, subtly suggested embryos of their own answers. *Collected Literary Questions*, by Philip Sparrow. A book to be compared with Pascal's *Pensées* or Wittgenstein's *Philosophical Investigations*.

David Lodge

Course 007: Studies in Legal Fictions
Time allowed: THREE DAYS (take-away paper)

There are FIFTEEN questions. Candidates should answer QUESTION ONE *and* FIVE other questions, taken from any TWO other Sections. Not more than THREE questions may be taken from ANY ONE Section. Candidates are reminded that they are not permitted to duplicate *either* materials *or* methodological approaches in more than TWO questions but that they are encouraged to display throughout an overall epistemological consistency. Begin each answer in a fresh answer-book.

Section A: General Principles

1. 'The bases for our present legal procedures were first laid down in the mid-eighteenth century and were perfected by the late eighteenth century; from that short period stem almost all our current legal freedoms' (J. P. HERBERT). Support, refute or modify this claim with reference to *either* Fielding, *Tom Jones*, *or* Godwin, *Caleb Williams*.

Section B: Detection, Policing, Prosecution

2. 'The private detective has no private privilege before the law; his means and methods of pursuit and prosecution must be, in principle, as public as those of the police proper' (B. MALONE). Discuss the procedures of Poe's Dupin with particular reference to 'The Mystery of Marie Rogêt'.

3. 'His Majesty's Secret Service must be above suspicion—and beyond reproach' (H. M. CHARLES). How far does Sherlock Holmes go to meet these royal requirements in 'A Scandal in Bohemia'?

4. 'Anarchy is not merely thoughtless—it is unthinkable' (LORD CROMWELL). Would Father Brown agree? You may confine your discussion to 'The Blue Cross'.

5. 'The naked truth is never visible to a voyeur' (M. POWELL). Comment on the contribution of the cinema screen to our image of detection, with reference to *two* of the following: *Young Mr Lincoln, The Wrong Man, Peeping Tom*.

6. What confidence can be placed in the notion of a 'legitimation crisis'? Your answer should make some use of Raymond Chandler's *The Big Sleep*.

7. 'Everybody is always on trial' (*attributed to* J. S. KOBA). How far does this modern proverb illuminate *one* of the following *pairs* of novels:
   - (a) Robbe-Grillet, *Les Gommes* and *L'Année dernière à Marienbad*;
   - (b) Pinget, *L'Inquisitoire* and *Le Fiston*;
   - (c) Themerson, *Special Branch* and *Wooff Wooff or Who Killed Richard Wagner?*

8. Is *The Volunteers*, by R. H. Williams, a 'private eye' novel?

Section C: Accusation, Perjury, Confession

9. 'Only the accused knows, in the end, if he's guilty; that's the beauty of a British trial' (J. SAMSA). Is Kafka's *Der Prozess* truly British?

10. In what ways might the Soviet legal system be seen as having pioneered a genuinely contemporary concept of legality? You may *not* discuss Tertz, *The Trial Begins*, or Bienek, *The Cell*, or Koestler, *Darkness at Noon*, in your answer.

11. 'Normality is never on trial' (G. THORP). How far is this untrue in Nossack, *The Impossible Proof*?

12. 'Let no man be judge in his own case unless he be as just as what I am' (LORD JUSTICE DEVIAN). Does Camus's Clamence, in *The Fall*, judge himself, mercifully?

13. 'Accusation is the best form of defence' (P. C. REGINALD-NIXON). In the light of this remark, comment critically on the plays of Peter Handke, especially *Offending the Audience* and *Self-Accusation*.

Section D: Trials and Responsibilities

14. 'Athens had no trained legal experts—only trained democrats. And slaves. And women' (H. A. LENA). What relevance do the plays of Euripides have today?

15. List any *fifteen* plays by Brecht you consider appropriate.

*

Section A: General Principles

Question 1: Henry Fielding, *Tom Jones*

'Jesu!' said the Squire, 'would you commit two persons to the bridewell for a twig?'
  'Yes,' said the Lawyer, 'and with great lenity too; for if we had called it a young tree they would have been both hanged.'

Fielding, *Joseph Andrews*

i

In his influential essay, 'Ideology and the Ideological State Apparatuses', Louis Althusser seeks to advance a clarification and modification of Marx's architectural metaphor of 'base and superstructure'; he first sketches that metaphor thus:

Marx conceived the structure of every society as constituted by 'levels' or 'instances' articulated by a specific determination: the *infrastructure*, or economic base (the 'unity' of the productive forces and the relations of production) and the *superstructure*, which itself contains two 'levels' or 'instances': the politico-legal (law and the State) and ideology (the different ideologies, religious, ethical, legal, political, etc.).

Lenin and Philosophy, New Left Books, 1971, p.129 (cited hereafter as LP)

In this formulation 'law' appears within the superstructure but not as 'ideology'. As Althusser outlines his own 'descriptive theory' of 'the State' the position of 'law' becomes progressively unclear. He offers a distinction between the Repressive State Apparatus and the Ideological State Apparatuses; the former, in one formulation, includes 'the Courts':

Remember that in Marxist theory, the State Apparatus (SA) contains: the Government, the Administration, the Army, the Police, the Courts, the Prisons, etc., which constitute what I shall in future call the Repressive State Apparatus.

LP, p.136

On the same page, he states:

we can for the moment regard the following institutions as Ideological State Apparatuses . . . :
—the religious ISA (the system of the different Churches),
—the educational ISA (the system of the different public and private 'Schools'),
—the family ISA,
—the legal ISA,
—the political ISA (the political system, including the different Parties),
—the trade-union ISA,
—the communications ISA (press, radio and television, etc.),
—the cultural ISA (Literature, the Arts, sports, etc.).
I have said that the ISAs must not be confused with the (Repressive) State Apparatus.

But if 'the Courts' are listed with the RSA and 'the legal ISA' figures in the list of ISAs, is there not a certain 'confusion'? A footnote rather unhelpfully remarks: 'The "Law" belongs both to the (Repressive) State Apparatus and to the systems of the ISAs.' Subsequent lists of the ISAs sometimes include the 'legal' (pp.153, 156) and sometimes don't (though a casual 'etc.' can leave the list incomplete, as on p.143). The 'law' also seems, from one perspective, to stand 'outside' both RSA and ISAs and to make possible one distinction between them: Althusser justifies his use of 'State' in the term 'Ideological State Apparatuses', despite the apparently private nature of these institutions, on the grounds that 'the distinction between the public and the private is a distinction internal to bourgeois law, and valid in the (subordinate) domain in which bourgeois law exercises its "authority" ' (p.137); he adds: 'the domain of the State escapes it [bourgeois law] because the latter is "above the law": the State, which is the State *of* the ruling class, is neither public nor private; on the contrary, it is the precondition for any distinction between public and private.' It's not clear how far Althusser himself is employing the notion of the State being 'above the law'; if the 'law' is itself a State Apparatus, how far is the State to be distinguished from the Apparatuses which constitute it? Another distinction offered between RSA and ISAs is that the RSA 'functions massively and predominantly *by repression* (including physical repression), while functioning secondarily by ideology', while ISAs 'function massively and predominantly *by ideology*, but they also function secondarily by repression' (p.138). It's then, of course, difficult to know just what is distinctive about 'repression' if it only 'includes' physical repression; nor is it clear how 'ideology' is to be distinguished from 'repression' if *non-physical* 'repression' isn't 'ideology'. As we pursue the location of 'law' Althusser's distinctions become even more confusing. He distinguishes 'ideology in general' from (regional) 'ideologies' (pp.151, 156); but, according to his 'central thesis' (p.159), 'the category of the subject (which may function under other names: e.g., as the soul in Plato, as God, etc.) is the constitutive category of all ideology', even if 'it only appears under this name [the subject] with the rise of bourgeois ideology, above all with the rise of legal ideology' —and another unhelpful footnote adds: 'Which [which??] borrowed the legal category of "subject in law" to make an ideological notion: man is by nature a subject' (p.160). A number of questions arise: for example, is 'legal ideology' (only) a 'region' of *'bourgeois* ideology' (though the legal category of 'subject in law' would seem to predate even the 'rise' of 'bourgeois ideology')? And the crucial question—what does Althusser mean by 'subject'?—is never, to my mind, clarified in Althusser's text.

What particularly interests me here is the slippery status of 'law', 'the Law', 'legal ideology'—the different terms swim around in the text, and Althusser seems to have no clear idea of what he means by them or how, if at all, he differentiates between these terms, which perhaps isn't surprising since the legal process is never clarified or distinguished into its several practices, from legislation to sentencing. In a later text, *Reply to John Lewis*, Althusser is equally slippery: 'this bourgeois ideology', he says, 'is actually *in its deepest essence* [my emphasis] constituted by the ideological pair *economism/ humanism*' (*Essays in Self-Criticism*, NLB 1976, p.85. Cited hereafter as *ESC*); this 'pair' 'is a pair in which the two terms are complementary. It is not

173

an accidental link, but an organic and consubstantial one. It is born spontaneously, that is to say necessarily, of the bourgeois practices of production and exploitation, and *at the same time* of the legal practices of bourgeois law and its ideology, which provides a sanction for the capitalist relations of production and exploitation and their reproduction' (pp.85–6). 'Ideas,' he goes on to say:

find their foundations in the categories of Bourgeois *Law* and the legal ideology materially indispensable to the functioning of Bourgeois Law: liberty of the Person, that is, in principle, his right freely to dispose of himself, his right to his property. . . . This is the breeding ground of economism/humanism: the capitalist mode of production and exploitation. And this is the precise link by which, the precise place in which these two ideologies join together as a *pair: Bourgeois Law*, which at the same time both provides a real support for capitalist relations of production and lends its categories to liberal and humanist ideology, including bourgeois philosophy (*ESC* pp.86–7).

It's difficult to know precisely what all this means. 'Bourgeois Law', it seems, provides the 'categories' of 'economism/humanism', and 'bourgeois ideology' borrows from 'legal ideology' the 'category' of 'subject in law', yet 'ideology [in general] has no history'—even though the 'category' of 'subject' is the 'constitutive category of all ideology' and that 'category' 'only appears under this name' with 'the rise of bourgeois ideology'. Perhaps it is unfair to bring together in this way formulations from essays written three years apart, but the terminological counters that are being shunted around in the two essays seem to have at least a family resemblance to each other and one might therefore expect, if not compatibility between the essays, at least mutual illumination or specific clarification of differences. Yet all that remains, for this reader anyway, is a conceptual fog in what seems to be a crucial area for Althusser himself. Some of that fog might be cleared slightly by taking two other formulations by Althusser and trying to 'test' them. Though 'ideology in general' 'has no history', Althusser nevertheless thinks that 'it is possible to hold that ideolog*ies* have a history of their own (although it is determined in the last instance by the class struggle)' (*LP*, p.151). Presumably then, 'legal ideology'—if that is a 'regional ideology'—might have a history of its own. Secondly, Althusser remarks that 'in the pre-capitalist historical period which I have examined extremely broadly, it is absolutely clear that there was *one dominant Ideological State Apparatus, the Church*' (*LP*, pp. 143–4), whereas now, he thinks, 'what the bourgeoisie has installed as its number-one, i.e. as its dominant ideological State apparatus, is the educational apparatus, which has in fact replaced in its functions the previously dominant ideological State apparatus, the Church' (*LP*, pp. 145–6). There might therefore be a 'history' of changes in the relative dominance of ISAs—though it is perhaps odd that Althusser should credit 'bourgeois law' and 'legal ideology' with such significance in providing crucial 'categories' yet not discuss their 'dominance' in any period. Still, Althusser has a penchant for examining a historical period only 'extremely broadly', so perhaps a more detailed examination of a particular historical period can supplement, or even illuminate, his panoramic perspective.

In 1754 at Chelmsford the Chief Justice condemned a girl to hanging and dissection for murdering her baby. He had pressured the jury to bring in a simple verdict of guilty (at first they found her insane); but having exacted justice, he then expressed the helplessness of men before it: 'Before I pronounced the sentence,' he confided to his diary, 'I made a very proper speech extempore and pronounced it with dignity, in which I was so affected that the tears were gushing out several times against my will. It was discerned by all the company—which was large—and a lady gave me her handkerchief dipped in lavender water to help me.'

Douglas Hay, citing this incident, from the Harrowby MSS, vol. 1129, doc. 19(f), page 5, in his essay 'Property, Authority and the Criminal Law' in *Albion's Fatal Tree* (ed. D. Hay, P. Linebaugh, & E. P. Thompson, Allen Lane 1975. Cited hereafter as *AFT*) comments:

In its ritual, its judgements and its channelling of emotion the criminal law echoed many of the most powerful psychic components of religion. The judge might, as at Chelmsford, emulate the priest in his role of human agent, helpless but submissive before the demands of his deity. But the judge could play the role of deity as well, both the god of wrath and the merciful arbiter of men's fates.

AFT, p.29

Hay's essay examines the majestic ritual of the eighteenth-century English High Court circuit, the rhetorical power of the judge's Address to the Grand Jury and the righteous passion of his sentencing address to the condemned, the deliberate theatricality of the last-minute reprieve from the King, the paternalism and patronage of the gentry in supporting or ignoring petitions for mercy, and he places all these elements within a persuasive analysis of the crucial role of law, as legislative process and repressive practice, in eight-eenth-century England. At one point he analyses the relative strength accorded to religion and law in the ideological armoury of the ruling class, and concludes:

Religion still had a place within the ritual of the law: a clergyman gave the assize sermon, and others attended the condemned man on the scaffold. But we suspect that the men of God derived more prestige from the occasion than they conferred on it. A suggestion of this can be seen in an evangelical pamphlet published in 1795. In the metaphors of power, judges usually had been likened to God, deriving their authority from divine authority, mediated through the Crown. But the author reversed the metaphor in his attempt to resurrect religion: he likened the deity to an English high court justice, and called the Day of Judgement the 'Grand Assizes, or General Gaol Delivery'. The secular mysteries of the courts had burned deep into the popular consciousness, and perhaps the labouring poor knew more of the terrors of the law than those of religion. When they did hear of hell, it was often from a judge.

AFT, p.30

On the basis of Hay's analysis, we might suggest that—in Althusser's terms—in eighteenth-century England it was the legal apparatus which, for a time, replaced the religious apparatus as the 'dominant' 'ISA'. But we then have to be clearer as to what the term 'legal apparatus' denotes in the period. In terms of court-practice, some pointers may help to ward off a reading-back of twentieth-century practice into the eighteenth. Charles Cottu, a French judge who toured the Northern Circuit, recorded a reaction, as late as 1822, which can help us to avoid anachronisms:

The English appear to attach no importance to a discovery of causes which may have induced the prisoner to commit the crime: they scarcely even affix any to the establishment of his guilt. I am ignorant whether this temper of mind arises from their fear of augmenting the already excessive number of public offenders, or whether it proceeds from their natural humanity; it is however an undoubted fact, that they make no effort to obtain proofs of the crime, confiding its punishment entirely to the hatred or resentment of the injured party; careless too, about the conviction of the accused, whether his victim shall yield to feelings of compassion, or give way to indolence.

quoted by Hay, AFT, pp.40–1

Most prosecutions for felony in the eighteenth century were 'private' prosecutions, brought by the injured party, who could decide for himself upon the severity of the charge; the accused was not allowed a defence counsel to plead to the jury; character-witnesses for the accused often carried much more weight than any material evidence concerning his guilt or innocence of the particular crime; judges had wide discretion in sentencing, extending even to complete pardon; an 'appeal' against sentence primarily took the form of petitions to the king, supported by personal letters from sympathetic gentry or aristocracy, often based quite explicitly on considerations of patronage or kinship-ties. Hay interprets these various features of court-practice in terms of the complex patterns of local deference, loyalty and quasi-feudal dependency which still characterised the social and economic relations of rural and small-town life in eighteenth-century England. But, as he points out, these 'close and persisting personal relationships' did not obtain to the same degree in London, where, for example, 'judicial mercy . . . was more often a bureaucratic lottery than a convincing expression of paternalism' (p.55). One index to the difference between a rural parish and the metropolis was the prevalence in the capital of 'strawmen'—professional perjurers who could be regularly hired just outside the law-courts.

Hay's phrase 'bureaucratic lottery' hints however at a certain change which was becoming apparent in the legal-administrative procedures, and which was indeed to be advocated by the legal reformers: a regularisation and rationalisation of the relation between crime, charge and sentence. Romilly and Eden both appealed, more or less explicitly, to the model proposed by Cesare Boccaria in 1764: 'a fixed code of laws, which must be observed to the letter' (cf. p.57). But though English legal practice shied away from any such radical reform, it is arguable that a change of at least related significance did occur during the century. Towards the end of his detailed analysis of the origins and application of 'The Black Act' of 1723 (9 George I c. 22), E. P. Thompson remarks:

The Act registered the long decline in the effectiveness of old methods of class control and discipline and their replacement by one standard recourse of authority: the example of terror. In place of the whipping-post and the stocks, manorial and corporate controls and the physical harrying of vagabonds, economists advocated the discipline of low wages and starvation, and lawyers the sanction of death. Both indicated an increasing impersonality in the mediation of class relations, and a change, not so much in the 'facts' of crime as in the *category*—'crime'—itself, as it was defined by the propertied. What was now to be punished was not an offence between men (a breach of fealty or deference, a 'waste' of agrarian use-values, an offence to one's own corporate community and its ethos, a violation of trust and function) but an offence against property. Since property was a thing, it became possible to define offences as crimes against things, rather than as injuries to men. This enabled the law to assume, with its robes, the postures of impartiality: it was neutral as between every degree of man, and defended only the inviolability of the ownership of things.

Whigs and Hunters, Allen Lane 1975, pp.206–7 (cited hereafter as WH)

Thompson sees the early part of the century in terms of that 'recognised phase of commercial capitalism when predators fight for the spoils of power and have not yet agreed to submit to rational or bureaucratic rules and forms' (WH, p.197), when political and economic struggle within the ruling class is still shaped by networks of 'nepotism, interest and purchase' and fought out between followings of loyal dependents; the legal practices Hay analyses are in harmony with this phase. But there is then a paradox in the practice of 'the law': if 'the law' were to 'assume, with its robes, the postures of impartiality' (and if it did not it would be *less* effective as an 'ideological' weapon against the ruled) and if at the same time it was effectively to redefine 'crimes' as offences against 'things' rather than as injuries to men, there would have to be an abandonment of those courtroom practices which so clearly treated prosecution, trial and sentencing as shaped primarily by the initiative, partiality and discretion of the 'injured party'; in their stead would emerge a reliance not upon testimony of 'character' but on evidence of specific actions, and a shift from private pursuit and prosecution to 'impersonal' and 'public' policing and prosecution. In certain respects the conditions of life in London had already suggested the need for such shifts: the trade of perjury made it inevitable that magistrates should pay more heed to material evidence, while the need for a publicly-financed police force where no local gentry held sway had long been apparent.

At the same time there was a more general paradox at the heart of eighteenth-century legal practice, which Thompson outlines in his concluding remarks:

The work of the sixteenth- and seventeenth-century jurists, supported by the practical struggles of such men as Hampden and Lilburne, was passed down as a legacy to the eighteenth century, where it gave rise to a vision, in the minds of some men, of an ideal aspiration towards universal values of law. One thinks of Swift or of Goldsmith or, with more qualifications, of Sir William Blackstone or Sir Michael Foster. If we today have ideal notions of what law might be, we derive them in some part from that cultural moment. It is, in part, in terms of that age's own aspirations that we judge the Black Act and find it deficient. But at the same time this same century, governed as it was by the forms of law, provides a text-book illustration of the employment of law, as instrument and as ideology, in serving the interests of the ruling class. The oligarchs and the great gentry were content to be subject to the rule of law only because this law was serviceable and afforded to their hegemony the rhetoric of legitimacy. This paradox has been at the heart of this study. It was also at the heart of eighteenth-century society. But it was also a paradox which that society could not in the end transcend, for the paradox was held in equipoise upon an ulterior equilibrium of class forces. When the struggles of 1790–1832 signalled that this equilibrium had changed, the rulers of England were faced with alarming alternatives.

WH, p.269

Thompson himself, with the whole complexity of his study of the Black Act behind him, criticises 'a sophisticated but (ultimately) highly schematic Marxism' for which 'the law is . . . by definition a part of a "superstructure" adapting itself to the necessities of an infrastructure of productive forces and productive relations' (p.259); he proposes rather a complex and multi-faceted conclusion:

The law when considered as institution (the courts, with their class theatre and class procedures) or as personnel (the judges, the lawyers, the Justices of the Peace) may very easily be assimilated to those of the ruling class. But all that is entailed in 'the law' is not subsumed in these institutions. The law may also be seen as ideology, or as particular rules and sanctions which stand in a definite and active relationship (often a field of conflict) to social norms; and, finally, it may be seen simply in terms of its own logic, rules and procedures—that is, simply *as law*. And it is not possible to conceive of any complex society without law.

WH, p.260

But though Thompson's target here is, fairly transparently, Althusser, there is at least a certain congruence between his phrase 'its own logic, rules and procedure—that is, simply *as law*' and Althusser's rather hesitant recognition that, possibly, 'ideolog*ies* have a history of their own'. Thompson indeed seems to echo some of Althusser's hesitations and difficulties when he remarks 'The greatest of all legal fictions is that the law itself evolves, from case to case, by its own impartial logic, true only to its own integrity, unswayed by expedient considerations' (*WH*, p.250). The problem is, clearly, that neither Althusser nor Thompson can conceive of a 'history' of 'law', even of its 'own logic, rules and procedures', that would not be intimately shaped by a wider 'history'; yet at the same time even Althusser hesitates before any ultimate 'reduction' of the 'legal' to *total* determination by the class struggle. But if Thompson is correct that 'it is not possible to conceive of any complex society without law', then even a socialist society will be faced with the *problem* of the law's 'logic, rules and procedures'; if he is also right that we have inherited from the struggles of the past 'an ideal aspiration towards universal values of law', an aspiration which we discard only at great political risk, it may be politically important to try to grasp the 'history' or 'logic' of 'law'—if we can isolate it to grasp. Fully to 'isolate' legal ideology would be to produce a necessarily idealist account (perhaps a philosophy of law); it is in the practice of law that its problems of logic, rule and procedure always arise and are worked through—yet it is in the practice of law that it becomes inextricable from the wider history. How then are we appropriately to isolate 'law', 'simply *as law*'?

If we focus on one of the problems internal to legal practice which, it was suggested earlier, emerged in eighteenth-century England—the problem of *evidence*, of reconciling or combining reliance on 'personal' assessments of the accused's 'character' with an emphasis on 'impartial' and material evidence for the crime having been committed—we can perhaps recognise at least one instance of an attempt to probe the logic of that problem 'in isolation' from the concomitant pressures and considerations of actual legal practice: in the textual practices of *Tom Jones*.

iii

Dorothy George once remarked that Fielding's 'appointment as a salaried Justice of the Peace for Westminster in 1749 was in its way as epoch-making as the appearance of *Tom Jones* in the same year.' That comment suggests a biographical point of intersection between text and legal apparatus which need only be indicated here in a fairly sketchy fashion. Fielding first studied law at Leyden in his twenties (he was sent there in disgrace after an *affaire*), but his fairly successful period as a dramatist deflected him from any legal career for some time. Only after his satire on Walpole in his *The Historical Register for 1736* had prompted the retaliation of the Licensing Act of 1737 (under which all plays had to be licensed for performance by the Lord Chancellor), did

Fielding return to the law, studying for the next few years at the Middle Temple. In 1740, at the age of thirty-three, he was called to the Bar and went on the Western Circuit.

The same year, however, the publication of Richardson's *Pamela* tempted him back to literature, first with the parody *Shamela* and then with a novel which grew more serious and ambitious as he wrote it, *Joseph Andrews*, published in 1742. The death of his wife very shortly after may have contributed to his decision in 1744 to abandon literature again—the decision was made public in his preface in July 1744 to Sarah Fielding's *David Simple*. He devoted himself instead to serious preparation for an ambitious scholarly treatise on Crown Law, which was, hopefully, to make his reputation. The influence of these resumed legal studies can be seen in his next satire, celebrating the death of the old enemy Walpole, published in July 1745: *The Charge to the Jury: or, The Sum of the Evidence, on the Trial of A.B.C.D and E.F. All M.D. For the Death of one Robert at Orford*. This vein of political writing was continued in three anti-Jacobite pamphlets published the same year, and then from November 1745 to June 1746 he edited the pro-Government paper *The True Patriot*. Partly as a reward for this, and for his hand in *The Jacobite Journal*, Fielding was appointed Commissioner of the Peace for Middlesex in June 1747 and then Magistrate of the City and Borough of Westminster in July 1748. *Tom Jones*, which was perhaps begun as early as January 1745, was published in early 1749. Later the same year Fielding published two pamphlets which considerably furthered his legal reputation, at least in some circles: *A Charge Delivered to the Grand Jury* and *A True State of the Case of Bosavern Penlez*. The following year his *Enquiry into the Causes of the Late Increase of Robbers*, published with a considerable sense of timing in January 1750, was warmly praised by some members of the House of Commons Committee on Law Reform, which sat from February 1750 to June 1751. It is from that Committee that Radzinowicz, in his great history of English law, dates the 'movement for reform' in English criminal law.

Tom Jones therefore can, and should, be placed within this immediate context: it was written during those very years when not only Fielding himself but the House of Commons and Fielding's Government patrons were deeply preoccupied with questions of law and legal reform (and, incidentally, with improving the provision of law-enforcement in London). Fielding's predecessor as City Magistrate, Sir Thomas de Veil, had written his *Observations on the Practice of a Justice of the Peace intended for such Gentlemen as design to act for Middlesex or Westminster* as a result of reflecting upon his own term of office (a highly lucrative one in his case). It was published posthumously in 1747 and Fielding (who actually moved into Sir Thomas's old house) undoubtedly read it. It may not be too much to claim that *Tom Jones*, if it was not actually a kind of substitute for the finally unwritten treatise on Crown Law, was at least in part the result of and partial equivalent to 'Observations' not dissimilar to Sir Thomas's. It is time we looked at the text itself.

Early in *Tom Jones*, there is a characteristic paragraph:

As this is one of those deep observations which very few readers can be supposed capable of making themselves, I have thought proper to lend them my assistance; but this is a favour rarely to be expected in the course of my work. Indeed I shall seldom or never so indulge him, unless in such instances as this, where nothing but the inspiration with which we writers are gifted can possibly enable any one to make the discovery. (I, v. p.38; page refs. to Signet edition)

Since the 'observation' commented upon is hardly a 'deep' one, the playful irony is clear; but its reverberations are not, as yet. On the following page we read:

The sagacious reader will not from this simile imagine that these poor people had any apprehension of the design with which Mrs Wilkins was now coming towards them; but as the great beauty of the simile may possibly sleep these hundred years till some future commentator shall take this work in hand, I think proper to lend the reader a little assistance in this place. (I, vi. p.39)

The shift from 'sagacious reader' to plain 'reader' puts the actual reader in a dilemma of self-definition: if 'sagacious' he should not need the commentary in the next paragraph; as 'reader' he, of course, reads it. And when the simile is finally given in ultimately prosaic form, 'to say the truth, she was universally hated and dreaded by them all', that touch of authorial assistance only alerts us to be sceptical of its 'truth' since we have already been warned, however ironically, that only 'deep observations' will merit such assistance. Both the question of 'truth' and the distinction between kinds of reader are constantly being brought to our attention as we read. Book II, Ch. i, for example, speaks of not being afraid to leave 'a chasm in our history', where 'no matters of consequence occurred' (p.65); Book III, Ch. i, retrospectively notes that such gaps give the reader 'an opportunity of employing that wonderful sagacity of which he is master by filling up these vacant spaces of time with his own conjectures; for which purpose we have taken care to qualify him in the preceding pages' (p.97), and Fielding outlines how 'the judicious reader' will have filled in two of those gaps, 'as examples only of the task which may be imposed on readers of the lowest class', but, he warns, 'much higher and harder exercises of judgement and penetration may reasonably be expected from the upper graduates in criticism' (p.98).

Some of these 'harder exercises' clearly concern the 'truth' of what Fielding, as narrator, tells the reader: he attributes two motives to Jenny but adds, teasingly, 'But though this latter view, if indeed she had it, may appear reasonable enough . . .' (I, ix. p.48); he offers his own temptingly 'judicious' judgement: 'whether the captain acted by this maxim, I will not positively determine; so far, we may confidently say that his actions may be fairly derived from his diabolical principle . . .' (I, xiii. p.61); he alerts the unalert reader to apparent problems and suggests apparent solutions: 'I have thought it somewhat strange, upon reflection, that the housekeeper never acquainted Mrs Blifil with this news. . . . The only way, as it appears to me, of solving this difficulty . . .' (II, v. p.77); he even declares his own 'bias' in a way that reinforces the tactic of special pleading: 'Though I called him poor Partridge in the last paragraph, I would have the reader rather impute that epithet to the compassion of my temper than conceive it to be any declaration of his innocence' (II, vi. p.84). And, clearly, our judgement throughout is being invited, exercised, and manipulated concerning *what* is being narrated, the major incidents of the novel. But the hardest 'exercise' of all, perhaps, is most deeply buried in the text. In Book XII, Ch. viii, Fielding comments:

For instance, as the fact at present before us now stands without any comment of mine upon it, though it may at first sight offend some readers, yet upon more mature consideration it must please all; for wise and good men may consider what happened to Jones at Upton as a just punishment for his wickedness with regard to women . . . and silly and bad persons may comfort themselves in their vices by flattering their own hearts that the characters of men are rather owing to accident than to virtue. Now, perhaps the reflections which we should be here inclined to draw would alike contradict both these conclusions, and would show that these incidents contribute only to confirm the great, useful, and uncommon doctrine which it is the purpose of this whole work to inculcate and which we must not fill up our pages by frequently repeating, as an ordinary parson fills his sermon by repeating his text at the end of every paragraph. (p.554)

That 'great, useful, and uncommon doctrine' is, of course, never explicitly formulated, let alone frequently repeated. But the essential clue is immediately given, for those readers who still require a clue, at the beginning (of course!) of the next paragraph:

We are contented that it must appear, however unhappily Sophia had erred in her opinion of Jones, she had sufficient reason for her opinion . . .

Fielding has taken care to provide Sophia with 'sufficient reason' for her erroneous opinion, just as he has provided the reader with 'sufficient reason' for both agreeing and disagreeing with Fielding's 'own' judgements, interpretations and 'erroneous opinions'; but by this stage in reading the novel, we also realise that 'sufficient reason' is *never* 'sufficient' for proof, for 'truth' rather than 'opinion': we can never be sure that we know enough, or know the right evidence, for a final judgement, and yet we are forced to judge, always on insufficient 'sufficient reason'. We are forced to judge, to make up our own minds both in attributing motives and in reconstructing events, because the relationship with the narrator, established by the devices of style instanced above, puts us in that position—but the 'position' is not a single or simple one. At times it's as if we were judge or jury, weighing evidence and witnesses we have to recognise may be untrustworthy; at other moments, we find ourselves placed in the position of defence counsel, making a plea of mitigation or objecting to and protesting at a particularly tendentious interpretation of the 'evidence' by the prosecuting counsel (a role correspondingly assumed, at that same moment, by Fielding or one of his character-witnesses); and all the time we ought to know *ourselves* to be on trial, our own capacity for judgement is in the dock: are we a 'judicious reader' (III, i. p.98), an 'over-zealous' reader (III, iv. p.106) or just a plain, and inadequate, 'reader'? The only 'truth' we can be sure of is that Fielding puts that mildly accusing question to us; but we can't even be sure of the answer.

Tom Jones, then, can be read as creating a relation which shiftingly situates both 'author' and 'reader' in roles and practices whose closest analogue is the roles and practices of the legal apparatus, analysed not directly in terms of its repressive and ideological functions but (to use Thompson's formulation) 'simply in terms of its own logic, rules and procedures'; but at the same time, precisely in putting those roles and practices in a kind of constant disarray, the text discloses and produces possibilities not available in actual legal practice: we (both author and reader) have the option of switching and straddling legal roles and of subverting or endorsing legal practices within the operation of the novel. And these possibilities are open because, crucially, the relation is fictional and so are the case, evidence and witnesses we judge; our necessary judgements have no consequences except upon ourselves (the 'closure' of the novel ensures that our judgements do not affect what is 'already written', which itself in any case ensures a suitably 'happy ending') But this absence of responsibility then allows a further possibility: that the basic premise of the law's 'own logic, rules and procedures' can be put in question; precisely because the novel offers a fictional exercising of judgement (relaxation) and not an exercise in real judgement (responsibility) it can admit that legal judgement is based on insufficient 'sufficient reason' since 'the truth' can never be *known* to be known. But the law rests finally on the assumption that the truth can be made public, even if it is the 'private' truth of motive ('I swear to tell the truth . . .').

At this point, of course, the text, like the legal apparatus, is traversed by elements derived from a different ISA, the religious. If, as Thompson puts it, the law became in the eighteenth century 'the central legitimizing ideology, displacing the religious authority and sanctions of previous centuries' (*WH*, p.263), the logic of court rules and procedures still sought validation, foundation and legitimisation in religious ideology ('I swear . . . so help me God') since if perjury has no meaning neither do witnesses. *Tom Jones* recuperates certainty at the level of arbitrary 'given' character (Tom is ultimately good, Blifil irredeemably bad) and thereby links hands with a code derived from another tradition, the Literary Romance, and with one crucial element in the ideology of the Religious Apparatus. Fielding articulates both basic strategies in his 'own' comments on his relation to his readers:

Reader, I think proper, before we proceed any further together, to acquaint thee that I intend to digress through this whole history as often as I see occasion; of which I am myself a better judge than any pitiful critic whatever. And here I must desire all those critics to mind their own business, and not to intermeddle with affairs or works which no ways concern them; for till they produce the authority by which they are constituted judges, I shall not plead to their jurisdiction. (I, ii. p.31).

For all which I shall not look upon myself as accountable to any court of critical jurisdiction whatever; for as I am, in reality, the founder of a new province of writing, so I am at liberty to make what laws I please therein. And these laws my readers, whom I consider as my subjects, are bound to believe in and obey [. . . but . . .] I do not, like a *jure divino* tyrant, imagine that they are my slaves or my commodity. I am, indeed, set over them for their own good only, and was created for their use and not they for mine. (II, ii, p.66)

The limits are marked, but breakable: the reader is both subject of a benevolent creator who can ordain the constitution of his world as he sees fit, and is also (dangerously) a potential critic of the basic law of that world, the truth and authority of its creator. Yet the process of reading the text is, deliberately, a training in the undermining of the authority of that maker ('for which purpose we have taken care to qualify him in the preceding pages', p.97); in the curious 'social relation' which constitutes the text it is acceptance which is given, but scepticism which is produced. And in creating that fictional relation Henry Fielding, Gentleman, the concrete individual, can be seen as 're-working' the professional situation of Mr Justice Fielding, barrister and magistrate, towards an impossible resolution, a re-arrangement of role, practice and responsibility possible only for 'Henry Fielding', the writer of this novel. And to achieve that, he must in the process 'create' another, a reader who endorses and collaborates in that re-arrangement, that disarray of the apparatus, but who may, for that very reason, become even more subversive than its author. Whereas Mr Justice Fielding was clearly caught in certain acute contradictions in his own professional practice and opinions—visible in the tension between his strict application of the law as it stood, while acting on the bench, and his emergent awareness in his professional writings of a 'social' perspective on the causes of crime—the reader of *Tom Jones* is curiously privileged: while the reading process obtains, that transformation of the practices of the legal apparatus remains available to him, perhaps a promise of an eventual actual transformation.

v

This sketch of an analysis of *Tom Jones* is, of course, only a partial account. The complex interaction of religious and legal ideological elements in the text would have to be investigated further, and it would be necessary to place the whole novel within a much broader context of other literary texts—not least those other eighteenth-century literary works which reveal a preoccupation with facets of 'the law', ranging from *The Newgate Calendar* through *The Beggars' Opera* to Fielding's own *Jonathan Wild the Great*. One writer who might be interestingly compared with Fielding, on both counts, is Daniel Defoe, since a case can be made that at least some of Defoe's novels are constructed as reworkings of certain codes and practices of the Religious Apparatus (the relation of *Moll Flanders* to a tradition of 'case-law' in the theological-moral system of casuistry is an obvious example).

But what needs emphasis in this context is how closely the combination of 'religious' and 'legal' elements in *Tom Jones* reproduces the intersection of different practices in the London law-courts of the mid-eighteenth century. Like the reader of *Tom Jones*, the London magistrate, particularly, had to judge each character who came before him both in terms of their 'innate' moral character—perhaps visible to the trained and judicious eye even in their surface appearance, but, if not, able to be revealed by some superior person in a convenient note—*and* on the basis of whatever 'hard evidence' could be discovered. The one practice relied, in the end, on rank prejudice; the other claimed the authority of rational procedures. But neither, in the long run, provided the lower classes with sufficient reason for trusting in the omniscience and impartiality of 'the Law'. They had learned their lesson, in practice, only too well for that.

Section B: Detection, Policing, Prosecution

Question 2: Edgar Allan Poe, *The Mystery of Marie Rogêt*

The story is told of an automaton constructed in such a way that it could play a winning game of chess, answering each move of an opponent with a countermove. A puppet in Turkish attire and with a large hookah in its mouth sat before a chessboard placed on a large table. A system of mirrors created the illusion that this table was transparent from all sides. Actually, a little hunch-back who was an expert chess player sat inside and guided the puppet's hand by means of strings. One can imagine a philosophical counterpart to this device. The puppet called 'historical materialism' is to win all the time. It can easily be a match for anyone if it enlists the services of theology, which today, as we know, is wizened and has to keep out of sight.

Walter Benjamin, *Theses on the Philosophy of History*

In April 1841 *Graham's Magazine* published a short story by Edgar Allan Poe entitled 'The Murders in the Rue Morgue'. At a stroke, so the familiar account goes, Poe had invented the detective story, and his central character, C. Auguste Dupin, immediately established the prototype for a long list of fictional sleuths.

The second of the Dupin trilogy was published in the *Snowden Ladies' Companion* for November and December 1842 and February 1843; it was entitled 'The Mystery of Marie Rogêt: a sequel to The Murder in the Rue Morgue'. Of this second tale, Poe himself wrote, in a letter to Dr J. E. Snodgrass in June 1842:

The story is based upon that of the real murder of Mary Cecilia Rogers, which created so vast an excitement some months ago in New York. I have handled the design in a very singular and entirely *novel* manner. A young grisette, one *Marie Rogêt*, has been murdered under precisely similar circumstances with *Mary Rogers*. Thus under pretence of showing how Dupin (the hero of the Rue Morgue) unravelled the mystery of Marie's assassination, I, in fact, enter into a very rigorous examination of the *real* tragedy in New York. *No point* is omitted. I examine, each by each, the opinions and arguments of our press on the subject, and show (I think satisfactorily) that this subject has never yet been *approached*. The press has been entirely on a wrong scent. In fact, I really believe, not only that I have demonstrated the falsity of the idea that the girl was the victim of a gang, but have indicated *the assassin*. My main object, however . . . is the analysis of the *principles of investigation* in cases of like character. Dupin *reasons* the matter throughout.

It is the notion that Dupin '*reasons* the matter throughout' that can claim our attention first.

Six years earlier, Poe had already demonstrated what he regarded as the workings of 'reason'—the application of observation and logic to the solution of a 'mystery'—in his explanation of the 'mechanism' of a chess-playing 'Automation', in *Maelzel's Chess-Player* (*The Southern Literary Messenger*, April 1836). At one point in that essay Poe singles out an attempt at explanation by an anonymous writer who 'by a course of reasoning exceedingly unphilosophical, has contrived to blunder upon a plausible solution —although we cannot consider it altogether the true one.' Basically, this anonymous writer had tried to show that the partitions of the box, at which the automation chess-player sat, could be so manipulated as to conceal from view a hidden *human* chess-player, even during the 'demonstration' by Maelzel that the box did *not* contain any human agency. 'There can be no doubt', writes Poe:

that the principle, or rather the result of this solution is the true one. Some person *is* concealed in the box during the whole time of exhibiting the interior. We object, however, to the whole verbose description of the *manner* in which the partitions are shifted to accommodate the movements of the person concealed. We object to it as a mere theory assumed in the first place, and to which circumstances are afterwards made to adapt themselves. It was not, and could not have been, arrived at by any inductive reasoning. To show that certain movements might possibly be effected in a certain way, is very far from showing that they are actually so effected. There may be an infinity of other methods by which the same result may be obtained.... The probability of the one assumed proving the correct one is then as unity to infinity.

Poe counterposes to the anonymous writer's argument a two-fold strategy. First, he argues that the 'mechanism' of the Automaton *must* indeed be a human rather than a mechanical agency since the very nature of a chess game rules out a mechanical player:

Arithmetical or algebraical calculations are, from their very nature, fixed and determinate. Certain *data* being given, certain results necessarily and inevitably follow. These results have dependence upon nothing but the *data* originally given. And the question to be solved proceeds, or should proceed, to its final determination, by a succession of unerring steps liable to no change, and subject to no modification. This being the case, we can without difficulty conceive the *possibility* of so arranging a piece of mechanism that upon starting it in accordance with the *data* of the question to be solved, it should continue its movements regularly, progressively and undeviatingly towards the required solution, since these movements, however complex, are never imagined to be otherwise than finite and determinate. But the case is widely different with the Chess-Player. With him there is no determinate progression. No one move in chess necessarily follows upon any one other. From no particular disposition of the men at one period of a game can we predicate their disposition at a different period.... from the first move in the game of chess no especial second move follows of necessity. In the algebraical question, as it proceeds towards solution, the *certainty* of its operations remains altogether unimpaired. The second step having been a consequence of the *data*, the third step is equally a consequence of the second, the fourth of the third, the fifth of the fourth, and so on, *and not possibly otherwise*, to the end. But in proportion to the progress made in a game of chess, is the *uncertainty* of each ensuing move. A few moves having been made, *no* step is certain. Different spectators of the game would advise different moves. All is then dependent upon the variable judgment of the players. Now even granting (what should not be granted) that the movements of the Automaton Chess-Player were in themselves determinate, they would be necessarily interrupted and disarranged by the indeterminate will of his antagonist. There is then no analogy whatever between the operations of the Chess-Player and those of the calculating machine.

Second, to establish how the human agency is brought to bear, Poe offers a series of '*observations*' of the routine which Maelzel 'invariably' follows in exhibiting the interior of the box; Poe's explanation is deemed to be convincing because 'if it were observed that *never, in any single instance*, did M. Maelzel differ from the routine we have pointed out as necessary to our solution, it would be one of the strongest possible arguments in corroboration of it—but the argument becomes infinitely strengthened it we duly consider the circumstance that he *does occasionally* deviate from the routine, but never does *so* deviate as to falsify the solution.'

Poe's own solution need not detain us at all, but from this article on Maelzel's Chess-Player we can single out three strands: that a more or less correct solution may not be supported by correct reasoning; that a human agency is required by, and is implicated in, a pattern of unpredictable moves; and that only accurate observation can provide the data for a correct theory to build upon.

In 'The Mystery of Marie Rogêt' it is clear that Poe is attempting to apply a similar process of ratiocination to the solution of a crime; but the story in practice violates at least two of the principles *Maelzel's Chess-Player* relied upon. If a correct solution can be 'supported' by incorrect reasoning, a demolition of that incorrect reasoning does not thereby establish that the conclusion is incorrect; that Socrates is mortal remains true even if the argument offered in support of it is invalid (e.g. 'The gods are immortal; Socrates is not a god; therefore Socrates is mortal'). Yet Dupin spends quite some time in 'Marie Rogêt' demonstrating that the *argument* of the newspaper *L'Etoile* is fallacious; *L'Etoile* had sought to show that the body recovered from the river could not be Marie's; Dupin shows that their argument is incorrect, but this can in no way, of itself, show that the body recovered *is* Marie's. To 'establish' that, Dupin has to appeal to an identification by a witness—and at that point introduces another principle (the calculus of probabilities) to which we can return.

Within the text the ostensible reason for even entering upon the argument as to whether the body is really Marie's or not, is that G—, the Prefect, has made a 'liberal proposition' to Dupin for his help in solving the mystery, but Dupin distrusts G— sufficiently to realise that the (presumably pecuniary) proposition might not be honoured if the *precise* terms of the assignment are not met: to find the assassin of Marie Rogêt; a living Marie Rogêt or the assassin of someone else would not bring the reward. In the text, the reward offered to the public amounts to 30,000 francs, and the fact of this large reward is later to play a part in establishing that the murder was not committed by a gang. At this point, we have to take account of Poe's claim that 'Marie Rogêt' is based on the case of Mary Cecilia Rogers and that *no point* of relevance is omitted. Presumably, therefore, an equally large reward had also been offered in the case of Mary Rogers. In his letter to Snodgrass Poe claims to have indicated the assassin; he would therefore, according to his own reasoning, be in at least a very strong position to claim the offered reward—and this makes his offering of his solution to the Mary Rogers case as a public *fiction* rather peculiar. If Poe were really convinced by his own arguments, what was to stop him from publishing them as conclusive contributions to the *real* case? Fears of committing libel may have played a part, or even a reluctance to work outside the 'due process' of police arrest and formal trial; but there are other reasons, both why the parallels are not pressed to the point of actually identifying the murderer and why 'Marie Rogêt' is, necessarily, offered as fiction.

The ostensible reasons are clear in the text. The text in fact breaks off at the point where 'the murderer will be traced' and an editorial note (ostensibly by the editors of *Snowden Ladies Companion*) is inserted:

For reasons which we shall not specify, but which to many readers will appear obvious, we have taken the liberty of here omitting, from the MSS placed in our hands, such portion as details the *following up* of the apparently slight clew obtained by Dupin. We feel it advisable only to state, in brief, that the result desired was brought to pass; and that the Prefect fulfilled punctually, although with reluctance, the terms of his compact with the Chevalier. Mr. Poe's article concludes with the following words.—*Eds.*

Poe, in concluding the story, comes close to covering himself against any possible libel action by, first, a disclaimer and then by an appeal (again) to the Calculus of Probabilities: he notes the parallel with Mary Rogers, but adds:

But let it not for a moment be supposed that, in proceeding with the sad narrative of Marie from the epoch just mentioned, and in tracing to its *dénouement* the mystery which enshrouded her, it is my covert design to hint at an extension of the parallel, or even to suggest that the measures adopted in Paris for the discovery of the assassin of a grisette, or measures founded in any similar ratiocination, would produce any similar result.

For, in respect to the latter branch of the supposition, it should be considered that the most trifling variation in the facts of the two cases might give rise to the most important miscalculations, by diverting thoroughly the two courses of events; very much as, in arithmetic, an error which, in its own individuality, may be inappreciable, produces, at length, by dint of multiplication at all points of the process, a result enormously at variance with truth. And, in regard to the former branch, we must not fail to hold in view that the very Calculus of Probabilities to which I have referred, forbids all idea of the extension of the parallel:—forbids it with a positiveness strong and decided just in proportion as this parallel has already been long-drawn and exact.

But the notion that there might be even a 'most trifling variation in the facts of the two cases' brings us back to Poe's letter to Snodgrass. On the basis of the claims made there, one could say that Poe was satisfied that *no* 'trifling variation' could overthrow his analysis. But on what is that analysis based?

In a note added to the tale on its reprinting some years later, Poe states that it 'was composed at a distance from the scene of the atrocity, and with no other means of investigation than the newspapers afforded'. The strategy of the tale is to reproduce this dependence on newspaper reports: after Dupin has agreed to look into the case the narrating 'I' is sent to procure at the Prefecture 'a full report of all the evidence elicited, and, at the various newspaper offices, a copy of every paper in which, from first to last, had been published any decisive information in regard to this sad affair'. Though occasional appeals are made thereafter to the authority of the police file, the reader is not allowed 'direct access' to any documentary information apart from that contained in the newspaper reports, which are quoted at length. Clearly, the implication of this device is that the reader is on an equal footing with Dupin in trying to solve the mystery. But is that footing a secure one for either? At one point Dupin notes, of *Le Commerciel*, that its 'deductions from the premisses are philosophical and acute; but the premisses, in two instances, at least, are founded in imperfect observation.' But then even if Dupin's (and Poe's) own 'deductions from the premisses are philosophical and acute' the trustworthiness of *his* conclusions will depend on the 'observations' which found them—but he relies upon newspaper reports for his 'observations', his data. And, as Dupin himself remarks, 'we should bear in mind that, in general, it is the object of our newspapers rather to create a sensation—to make a point—than to further the cause of truth. The latter end is only pursued when it seems coincident with the former;' more specifically, he notes that the papers have been silent on a number of questions of importance: 'had the body been in any respect despoiled? Had the deceased any articles of jewellery about her person upon leaving home? If so, had she any when found?'

Clearly, the newspapers are *not* necessarily reliable as sources of 'observation' in the first place. We can see in this, perhaps, one reason why Poe, himself dependent upon newspaper reports, could not risk being publicly conclusive about the *real* case but resorted to a fictionalised version. But if the newspapers are not necessarily reliable, doesn't that raise a question about the strategy of offering long extracts to the reader? The problem here is that the ostensible strategy of the tale is the classic device of the 'detective story': that the *reader* is given *all* the necessary *clues* and is therefore in a position to test his or her own deductive powers against those of the detective. The implication that in the real case the newspapers may not have picked up *all* the clues is clear from the tale itself: not only that, but at least one reader of those newspapers is shown not to have noticed all the clues they do contain: the narrating 'I' claims to have acquired a copy of 'every paper in which . . . any decisive information' has been published, but when Dupin himself scours those same papers he selects five items which seem 'irrelevant' to the narrator (it was therefore a matter of chance that he procured *those* newspapers in the first place). Only in the light of Dupin's 'explanation' do these five 'extra' items come to appear relevant. But, of course, the *reader* is not taken into the *process* of *selection*; the singling out and presentation of precisely these items is already governed by the explanation which they are offered to us as supporting. In other words, the actual process which guides Dupin to *fix* upon *these* items as relevant is not given; all we are offered is the finished conclusion which shapes these items into a connected pattern. The peculiar problem here is that *if* these items are indeed relevant, then the explanation offered is 'reasonable', but only if the explanation is already regarded as reasonable can the items be singled out as more relevant than any others.

This interdependence of 'data' and 'theory' has some parallel with one aspect of the argument offered in *Maelzel's Chess-Player*, that a machine can only operate within 'algebraic' moves, whereas no move in chess *dictates* the next move. Given that the newspapers for the three weeks or so between the murder and Dupin's investigation had published numerous other items and had *not* published accounts of *all* the incidents that had occurred on or about the time of the murder, any process of 'reasoning' based upon the reports that happened to appear in the press could only be like trying to play chess against an opponent not all of whose pieces or moves are known to one. In other words, the 'reasoning' that Dupin is depicted as relying upon involves a large element of what we can call, for the moment, 'hunch' or 'intuition', while the 'observation' on which it is based is necessarily shaped to a large extent by what we can call, for the moment, 'chance' or 'accident'.

The reader, however, is not in the same position as Dupin; the reader is not, of course, given access to any 'extra' item in the newspapers which Dupin has already dismissed as irrelevant; the selection is already made for us, according to criteria of relevancy which are 'retrospective'—i.e. only when the explanation has already 'emerged' for Dupin does he offer these extra items for our consideration. Yet this practice is necessarily in contradiction with the principles which Dupin himself articulates to justify looking for those extra items in the first place:

Not the least usual error in investigations such as this is the limiting of inquiry to the immediate, with total disregard of the collateral or circumstantial events. It is the malpractice of the courts to confine evidence and discussion to the bounds of apparent relevancy. Yet experience has shown, and a true philosophy will always show, that a vast, perhaps the larger, portion of truth arises from the seemingly irrelevant.

But how then is Dupin different from a court? By singling out these items he too confines 'evidence' and 'discussion' to what appears relevant to *him*. Clearly, a *reductio ad absurdum* could be pursued here: at each point at which 'bounds' of relevancy are drawn, one could claim that the 'truth' will be discovered only by going outside those bounds to the 'collateral or circumstantial'. In terms of the tale, when Dupin says to the narrator 'I will examine the newspapers more generally than you have as yet done', it is open to the reader to wish to examine those same newspapers (the real ones in the real case of Mary Rogers) 'more generally' than Poe has done.

But even without this move, Dupin's principle runs into a certain contradiction. He extends his argument to cover the operations of 'science':

It is through the spirit of this principle, if not precisely through its letter, that modern science has resolved to *calculate upon the unforseen*. But perhaps you do not comprehend me. The history of human knowledge has so uninterruptedly shown that to collateral, or incidental, or accidental events we are indebted for the most numerous and most valuable discoveries, that it has at length become necessary, in any prospective view for improvement, to make not only large, but the largest, allowances for inventions that shall arise by chance, and quite out of the range of ordinary expectation. It is no longer philosophical to base upon what has been a vision of what is to be. *Accident* is admitted as a portion of the substructure.

But part of his own argument relies upon the exclusion of 'accident'. He argues that Marie must have intended to elope because she asked her fiancé to call for her at her aunt's after dark, thus allowing her till that time to arrange her elopement. That an accidental encounter with her former lover (or with anyone else) could have made her change her mind about going to her aunt's is simply not considered. The possibility of a *chance* meeting with her murderer has indeed to be ruled out for Dupin's whole thesis (linking the naval officer, Madame Deluc, and the boat) to hang together. (Of course, on his own principle that the more 'ordinary' a case, the more difficult it becomes to solve, a murder which arose from an entirely accidental encounter between two strangers would be insoluble—at least by ratiocination.)

Dupin completes the elaboration of his 'principle' with the comment that 'We make chance a matter of absolute calculation. We subject the unlooked for and unimagined to the mathematical *formulae* of the schools.' This formulation echoes three other points in the tale. The whole tale opens with the statement:

There are few persons, even among the calmest thinkers, who have not occasionally been startled into a vague yet thrilling half-credence in the supernatural, by *coincidences* of so seemingly marvellous a character that, as *mere* coincidences, the intellect has been unable to receive them. Such sentiments—for the half-credences of which I speak have never the full force of *thought* —such sentiments are seldom thoroughly stifled unless by reference to the doctrine of chance, or, as it is technically termed, the Calculus of Probabilities. Now this Calculus is, in its essence, purely mathematical; and thus we have the anomaly of the most rigidly exact in science applied to the shadow and spirituality of the most intangible in speculation.

The final paragraph of the tale returns to this 'Calculus' to justify the assertion that a single 'trifling variation in the facts of the two cases' would rule out a transference of the solution to one to the other. The passage quoted above concerning the 'long-drawn and exact' parallel continues:

This is one of those anomalous propositions which, seemingly appealing to thought altogether apart from the mathematical, is yet one which only the mathematician can fully entertain. Nothing, for example, is more difficult than to convince the merely general reader that the fact of sixes having been thrown twice in succession by a player at dice, is sufficient cause for betting the largest odds that sixes will not be thrown in the third attempt. A suggestion to this effect is usually rejected by the intellect at once. It does not appear that the two throws which have been completed, and which now lie absolutely in the Past, can have influence upon the throw which exists only in the Future.

This double appeal to the Calculus of Probabilities provides the tale with a framework of scientific and mathematical 'reasoning', insinuating that the reasoning exemplified within the tale is also 'scientific'. At one point Dupin does indeed appeal to scientific knowledge, in order to demolish *L'Etoile*'s assumption that a corpse will not float to the surface until six to ten days after being thrown into the sea, but this demolition—as we have seen—in no way contributes positively to the solution of the case. The calculus of probabilities is also appealed to within the tale in order to demonstrate that the accumulation of identifying features of the corpse constitutes 'proof not *added* to proof, but *multiplied* by hundreds or thousands'—but Dupin is in any case prepared to accept M. Beauvais's identification of Marie *without* any supporting evidence: 'Nothing is more vague than impressions of individual identity. Each man recognises his neighbour, yet there are few instances in which anyone is prepared to give a reason for his recognition. The Editor of *L'Etoile* had no right to be offended at M. Beauvais's unreasoning belief.' But if 'unreasoning belief' is legitimate in the case of identification, how far is it also legitimate elsewhere? Dupin himself rules out suspicion of Beauvais: 'In respect to the insinuations levelled at Beauvais, you will be willing to dismiss them in a breath. You have already fathomed the true character of this good gentleman. He is a busybody.' But what if the *reader* regards this 'fathoming' of 'character' as an 'unreasoning belief' and illegitimate?

My point is, of course, that if the 'reasoning' whereby Dupin arrives at his solution were truly a matter of 'scientific' calculation in the sense implied by the appeal to mathematics and calculus, there would be no need to have recourse to such agreed 'fathoming' at any point; yet, equally, insofar as Dupin's reasoning is based on a selection of data which derives (as far as the reader is concerned) *from* that reasoning, it is irrelevant whether the reader 'agrees with' the reasoning or not: the evidence offered the reader has already been shaped by that reasoning and would not be made available were it incompatible with the solution proposed. The reader, in other words, is not on an equal footing with

Dupin, though the whole strategy of the tale is to make it appear that he is; on the contrary, as readers we have to accept the *authority* of Dupin, both about the 'character' of suspects and about the 'relevance' of evidence. The tale itself indicates the model on which its own strategy is ultimately based:

That Nature and its God are two, no man who thinks will deny. That the latter, creating the former, can, at will, control or modify it, is also unquestionable. I say 'at will'; for the question is of will, and not, as the insanity of logic has assumed, of power. It is not that the Deity *cannot* modify his laws, but that we insult him in imagining a possible necessity for modification. In their origin these laws were fashioned to embrace *all* the contingencies which *could* lie in the Future. With God all is *Now*.

The law, the logic, of Dupin's 'reasoning' is God-like, at least in principle. That reasoning will embrace 'all contingencies' because it can, at will, 'control or modify' them; it has no need to, since the tale is, already, 'created' by its teller in accordance with that reasoning; nothing can lie 'in the Future', not even the throw of a dice, that has not already been 'fashioned' to fit that will, that 'reasoning'. What *distracts* the reader from this recognition that the tale and its God are 'two', the latter wholly controlling the former, is precisely the claim that *this* tale is modelled, point for point, upon the *real*: as we register the added footnotes which identify the characters and newspapers of the tale with their real-life counterparts in the Mary Rogers case we extend that identification to the whole tale, including the reasoning of Dupin: because that reasoning 'works' within the tale, it would 'work' also in the real world of actual crime and corpses. One important facet of the realist aesthetic of much nineteenth-century fiction is embedded here: that the 'fathoming' of 'character' and the (moral) 'reasoning' that works in the fiction also works in real life. But, more to my purposes at this point, some of the possible *permutations* of the operations of 'detecting crime' are also embedded in the tale.

It is clear that *only* in a fiction can the 'reasoning' fully shape the 'data' 'in advance'; Poe's recommendation that a writer should write 'backwards' is relevant here:

Nothing is more clear than that every plot, worth the name, must be elaborated to its *dénouement* before anything be attempted with the pen. It is only with the *dénouement* constantly in view that we can give a plot its indispensable air of consequence, or causation, by making the incidents, and especially the tone at all points, tend to the development of the intention.

'The Philosophy of Composition', 1846

It is also clear, in the tale, that the process of detection is not, whatever Dupin's or Poe's claims, a process of pure deduction from the data; at some point a 'hunch' intervenes, binding data and hypothesis together. It's also clear that if the observations on which the 'deduction' is founded are unreliable, the conclusion will be questionable. Within the 'bounds' of a *fiction* (everything within those bounds being 'relevant'), some 'observations' can be 'reliable', the reader can be offered 'data' which, within the conventions of the tale itself, is to be taken as trustworthy (that Poe's data is 'literally translated' from actual newspapers opens up the space for the reader to *question* his data in this tale). But where, in a real case of detection, is such 'reliable observation' to be located? Poe, Dupin and the reader are all in the same position of being 'at a distance from the scene of the atrocity, and with no other means of investigation than the newspapers offered', but those intervening sources of observation are themselves shown to be unreliable within the tale.

Think now of the position of a *jury* in an *actual* criminal case. They too are, necessarily, 'at a distance' from the scene of the crime; they too have to rely upon intermediary 'observations'; they too have to reconstruct the crime and decide upon the criminal on the basis of data offered to them, by the accused, by witnesses, by counsel, and—crucially in most cases—by the police. The police, now, are responsible for 'detection', for 'solving' a crime, for arresting the criminal; by that very fact, they are responsible for formulating the initial case against the accused, and the accused would not be in the dock (in theory) unless there were a *reasonable hypothesis* that he is the criminal. Yet at the same time the 'presumption' that formally operates in most legal systems is that the accused is innocent until 'found' guilty, the onus of 'proof' being upon the prosecution. But if the 'proof' in question cannot be a rigorously 'scientific' proof, but rather a 'hypothesis' that 'embraces all contingencies', that most closely 'fits' the 'evidence', then *endemic* in the process of detection-prosecution is a tendency towards *fiction*, towards a situation where the 'reasonable' hypothesis can 'control or modify' the 'data' 'at will', a process of selection and arrangement which operates retrospectively, a plotting back-wards. Endemic in the logic of detection-prosecution is a *fictional* urge: to 'plant evidence', to 'frame', to 'manufacture' a case, to 'fit' the already-selected 'criminal' to the crime, and vice-versa.

Within a detective fiction, while the convention holds that the 'observations' the reader is initially offered are indeed reliable, the reader and the detective-figure are, in principle, on an equal footing; the process of 'plotting backward' will be rendered visible to the alert reader, the 'data' allowing the 'hypothesis' to emerge increasingly into the open. It's perhaps worth suggesting that if that convention of reliability begins to crumble, the 'hypothesis' that controls the 'data' of the tale will become less visible, less open and accessible, more entirely a matter of the author's operating 'at will'. This permutation might be explored in a number of later texts (for example, those of Pinget), but it may also be worth suggesting that, similarly, if a convention that the *police* are 'reliable' begins to be eroded, the same kind of process may occur: the tendency towards 'fictional' control will be reinforced—either the 'hypothesis' will become increasingly comprehensive, extending to more and more 'collateral' circumstances, or the 'data' will become increasingly 'modified' to fit the hypothesis, and both these processes may become more covert, more con-cealed from even the alert inquirer. If, also, at the core of the data-hypothesis bond in detection is, necessarily, a 'hunch' or 'intuition', and if acceptance of a particular bonding of data and hypothesis depends upon a belief in the competence or authority of the 'detective', then an erosion of confidence in that competence or authority may reinforce a tendency to conceal the process of arriving at that hunch. There is a double paradox here: that an erosion of belief in authority may lead to a greater degree of imposed reliance on that authority, and that a suspicion of the unreliability of evidence may result in the provision of even less reliable evidence. Some facets of this 'logic', of these paradoxes or contradictions within the process of detection-prosecution, have perhaps been seen (or rather *not* seen) at work recently, for example in political 'deportation' cases (the inclusion of collateral circumstances, the extension of 'relevancy'), in trials concerned with the Official Secrets Act (the gap between any detailed evidence and the overall charge being filled merely by the authoritative assertion of a 'danger to security'), and in the operation of the emergency legislation in Northern Ireland (the word of a senior police officer taken as sufficient 'evidence' for internment). In some post-modernist detective fiction a related logic is clearly at work: as the relation between event and pattern becomes more and more a matter of authorial discretion, only an increased assent to authorial authority can entice the reader to trust in the eventual emergence of any pattern at all.

In relation specifically to Poe's tale, however, there are three further points worth brief consideration. The conclusion of Dupin's process of reasoning is not given in the tale; the 'editorial note' intervenes instead. But the added prefatory footnote states: 'It may not be improper to record . . . that the confessions of *two* persons (one of them the Madame Deluc of the narrative), made, at different periods, long subsequent to the publication, confirmed, in full, not only the general conclusion, but absolutely *all* the chief hypothetical details by which that conclusion was attained.' For the reader concerned with the verisimilitude of the tale, these subsequent confessions, operating from 'outside' the text, serve to confirm *in advance* (the footnote precedes the tale) the precise mapping of fiction onto reality, endorsing and ratifying the ratiocination of Dupin. However, for the reader concerned with the logic of the tale, the confessions can only be an 'accident': they lie outside not only the text but also the chain of reasoning of the text; a 'deduction' and a 'confession' may be in parallel, but the logic of a third-person account is not the logic of a first-person account (though certain strategies of detective-fiction may seek to fuse them: deduction by 'psychology', or, more radically, by the detective proving in the end to *be* the criminal). At the very least, the starting-points of a first- and third-person account are formally different, even though in the construction of the fiction ('plotting backward') they are the same: the logical starting-point is always a knowledge of the criminal. But what other 'confirmation' could there be, other than a confession? Given the problems of linking data and hypothesis, an 'intuition' is necessarily unreliable—only *knowledge* can bridge that epistemological gap, and only the criminal has that 'knowledge'; but unless we are ourselves the criminals, we have that knowledge only by proxy. We may, of course, arrive at the correct solution, even by incorrect reasoning; conversely, even correct reasoning may give us a wrong solution; only a form of knowledge that requires the mediation of neither observation nor reasoning could be self-validating. But, of course, even a confession may be 'false'. Most of us, however, would believe even a false confession—unless we had learned to suspect even the reliability of 'confessions' too.

Secondly, Joseph Wood Krutch remarked of Poe that he 'invented the detective story in order that he might not go mad'. It seems a bizarre comment, even if a certain amount of biographical data might support such an hypothesis. But considering the problems of 'scientific' reasoning that have been touched upon so far, the suggestion is worth considering. The text certainly reveals an awareness of the *paradox* of the 'Calculus of Probabilities': 'thus we have the anomaly of the most rigidly exact in science applied to the shadow and spirituality of the most intangible in speculation'. But it is not by mathematics or the calculus that Dupin arrives at his conclusions, but rather by a process that I have so far talked of in terms of data-hypothesis bonding, that bonding being achieved by a 'hunch' or 'intuition'. The last two terms seem unsatisfactory, but what others are we to use? The difficulty arises partly because the very process those terms point to is hidden from us, in the tale itself. Dupin reads all the newspapers 'more generally', we are told; he emerges from that reading with five items not noticed up to then by the narrator. Why *those* five items? They operate as crucial links in Dupin's chain of explanation, but how did he *recognise* them as such in the first place? The text does not, and arguably *cannot*, tell us. The actual *construction* of the hypothesis and its simultaneous (?) selection-and-connecting of the 'relevant' data (relevant now to itself, to the hypothesis) is a moment which is absent from the text. In one sense that 'moment' *must* lie 'outside' the text, since in this case we are not even given the final formulation of the hypothesis itself: that is covered over by the editorial intervention. The reader could, of course, ask him or herself in what sense that fusion of data and (an) hypothesis has occurred at all—for him or herself as a *reader*, trying to both match and anticipate Dupin's conclusions. But as far as the text is concerned there is only a jump in the chain of reasoning (signalled, perhaps, in a kind of displacement, by that *non-sequitur* of 'We have attained the idea either of a fatal accident under the roof of Madame Deluc'—the 'fatal *accident*' being introduced for the first time in this 'summing up'). If we allow the terms 'hunch' and 'intuition' to designate that *absence* 'in' the *text*, they may be acceptable enough. But if we introduce two other texts by Poe, as 'collateral' circumstances, we may see that there is a deeper problem.

In *Maelzel's Chess-Player* Poe argued that the chess-player must be manipulated by a human being since a machine could only handle strictly 'fixed and determinate' calculations, whereas in chess 'a few moves having been made, *no* step is certain', so that 'different spectators of the game would advise different moves' and 'all is then dependent upon the variable judgment of the players'. But why is the judgement of the players 'variable' and in what sense? And why couldn't a machine play chess? Clearly, whatever the answers to these questions, for Poe, the human brain does not necessarily proceed by 'fixed and determinate' calculations. In another text Poe tried to explore one process of the human brain, his own—in writing a poem. Poe's account of his writing of 'The Raven', in 'The Philosophy of Composition' (1846), is designed 'to render it manifest that no one point in its composition is referrible either to accident or intuition—that the work proceeded, step by step, to its completion with the precision and rigid consequence of a mathematical problem'. The essay reads, however, more like an account of someone playing chess, facing a sequence of choice-points at each of which, out of a possible set of options, the player chooses one; but at least in the account as given, the specific choices made by Poe are not arrived at by a comparative consideration of the merits of all the other possible choices. One example of this (absence of) procedure can suffice:

The sound of the *refrain* being thus determined, it became necessary to select a word embodying this sound, and at the same time in the fullest possible keeping with that melancholy which I had predetermined as the tone of the poem. In such a search it would have been absolutely impossible to overlook the word 'Nevermore'. In fact, it was the very first which presented itself.

That phrase 'presented itself' indicates the problem. If this was not 'accident' or 'intuition', it certainly wasn't arrived at 'step by step . . . with the precision and rigid consequence of a mathematical problem'. It was 'arrived at', perhaps, the way 'steps' are themselves arrived at in a mathematical problem, or the way a word is 'arrived at' when we speak, or, maybe, the way a word 'presents itself' when 'we' make a slip of the tongue, pen or typewriter. And we have *no full* account of how any of those processes happen, despite the efforts of Chomsky and Freud. But it is the ambition, the 'design', which governs this essay that intrigues me: the urge to give a 'scientific' account of the process of 'composition'. (That the essay could be considered the precursor of a long line of inquiries into the construction of poetry and that Poe's own *poétique* has its contemporary progeny, and that his Dupin story 'The Purloined Letter' has a certain status among today's Freudians, is not irrelevant).

Let me put alongside this ambition another, perhaps thinly-veiled, ambition:

There are ideal series of events which run parallel with the real ones. They rarely coincide. Men and circumstances generally modify the ideal train of events, so that it seems imperfect, and its consequences are equally imperfect.

The implication of that passage is that if 'men and circumstances' would somehow cease interfering, the 'ideal series of events' would have a free run in the world. It's a peculiarly idealist notion of history, among other things. It's also the view of some who seem to believe that they *know* what the 'ideal series of events' *is*, in other words, what the 'real' *ought* to be. In one sense, a commitment to an 'ideal train of events' seems inescapable, unless one is simply to be a fatalist. But there is perhaps a worrying overtone in this particular formulation, with its suggestion that a world *without* 'men and circumstances' would be a more 'ideal', a less 'imperfect' world. Such an ideal world is envisaged in a famous parable by Lichtenberg. It is the dream of a certain kind of scientist, whose admiration for the laws of physics and for mathematical order is tempered only by the realisation that 'men and circumstances' are, regrettably, not similarly 'fixed and determinate', or at least that to render them so would require the grasp of a law and order we do not yet have fully at our disposal.

These rather impressionistic reactions to that brief quotation are undoubtedly unfair to Novalis, from whom the passage is taken; but the passage was first selected by Poe—as the epigraph to 'The Mystery of Marie Rogêt'; and in that context some of the responses that 'presented themselves' seem not entirely inappropriate. For Dupin, at least, seems to prefer, on the whole, to live in an 'ideal' world, without the intrusions of men and circumstances:

Upon the winding up of the tragedy involved in the deaths of Madame L'Espanaye and her daughter, the Chevalier dismissed the affair at once from his attention, and relapsed into his old habits of moody reverie. Prone, at all times, to abstraction, I readily fell in with his humour; and continuing to occupy our chambers in the Faubourg Saint Germain, we gave the Future to the winds, and slumbered tranquilly in the Present, weaving the dull world around us into dreams. . . . Strange as it may appear, the third week from the discovery of the body had passed . . . before even a rumour of the events which had so agitated the public mind reached the ears of Dupin and myself. Engaged in researches which had absorbed our whole attention, it had been nearly a month since either of us had gone abroad, or received a visitor, or more than glanced at the leading political articles in one of the daily papers.

It would be interesting to know precisely what Dupin's 'politics' were. But it would be even more interesting to know just what Poe (or 'I') meant by that curious phrase quoted earlier: 'the insanity of logic'—or perhaps that was just a slip of the quill.

However, rather than take the option now of exploring those (related) problems, I want, thirdly and finally, to return to a phrase from *Maelzel's Chess-Player*. There, Poe had castigated the anonymous writer's method of explanation as 'a mere theory assumed in the first place, and to which circumstances are afterwards made to adapt themselves'. Poe should have attended to his own criticism. For there is a further 'gap' or 'absence' in the case of 'The Mystery of Marie Rogêt'—its absence from the January 1843 issue of the *Snowden Ladies' Companion* (cf. above). According to John Walsh, in his *Poe the Detective*, it was only after the publication of the first two parts that Poe became aware that the accumulation of evidence in the case of Mary Cecilia Rogers pointed not to a murder by a former lover, a naval officer, but rather to a bungled abortion. Publication of the third part of the tale was held back for a month while Poe tried to salvage his detective's 'reasoning'. But attempts to adapt the new 'circumstances' to the theory he had assumed in the first two parts could only result in that symptomatic *non-sequitur*, that sudden intrusion of a fatal *accident*, and in a specious 'editorial' intervention. Even six years later, however, Poe could still refer, with apparent authority, to the 'naval officer' whom his theory had once selected as the necessary criminal (letter to George W. Eveleth, 4th January, 1849). In a brief note, 'On Intuition', Poe once remarked: 'Great intellects *guess* well. The laws of Kepler were, professedly, *guesses*'; that 'professedly' marks his hesitation and reluctance in acknowledging that at the centre of the 'mystery' of 'reasoning' may be what we can still only call 'guessing'—and even a Dupin doesn't always guess well. Such an admission could only be a scandal to a mind so firmly wedded as Poe's was, professedly, to a mid-nineteenth century belief in 'the most rigidly exact in science'; it might even have led him to wonder whether his whole 'philosophy' was not, in a rather painfully literal sense, abortive.

Question 4: Gilbert Keith Chesterton, 'The Blue Cross'

A Dadaist is utterly unimpressed by any serious enterprise and smells a rat whenever people stop smiling and assume that attitude and those facial expressions which indicate that something important is about to be said.

Paul Feyerabend, *Against Method*

The Dadaists attached much less importance to the sales value of their work than to its uselessness for contemplative immersion. The studied degradation of their material was not the least of their means to achieve this uselessness. What they intended and achieved was a relentless destruction of the aura of their creations, which they branded as reproductions with the very means of production.

Walter Benjamin, *The Work of Art in the Age of Mechanical Reproduction*

. . . in accordance with then current Oxford practice, he [H. L. A. Hart] frequently likens laws to rules of games, as if laws constituted social life's contests in the way that rules constitute games; a sporting view of things, certainly.

Anthony Skillen, *Ruling Illusions*

Half-way through 'A Scandal in Bohemia' (1891) Sherlock Holmes

disappeared into his bedroom, and returned in a few minutes in the character of an amiable and simple-minded Nonconformist clergyman. His broad black hat, his baggy trousers, his white tie, his sympathetic smile, and general look of peering and benevolent curiosity, were such as Mr. John Hare alone could have equalled.

Twenty years later, the great Valentin, head of the Paris police and the most famous investigator in the world, encountered on an English train 'a very short Roman Catholic priest going up from a small Essex village'—and almost laughed:

The little priest was so much the essence of those Eastern flats: he had a face as round and dull as a Norfolk dumpling; he had eyes as empty as the North Sea; he had several brown-paper parcels which he was quite incapable of collecting. . . . He had a large, shabby umbrella, which constantly fell on the floor. He did not seem to know which was the right end of his return ticket. He explained with a moon-calf simplicity to everybody in the carriage that he had to be careful, because he had something made of real silver 'with blue stones' in one of his brown-paper parcels. His quaint blending of Essex flatness with saintly simplicity continuously amused the Frenchman till the priest arrived (somehow) at Stratford with all his parcels, and came back for his umbrella.

After Sherlock Holmes, the next major metamorphosis of Dupin thus emerged with Chesterton's Father Brown in 'The Blue Cross' (included in *The Innocence of Father Brown*, 1911).

Chesterton allows his readers to feel, at first, on more or less familiar ground: the debts to the now-lengthening tradition are registered, even if a certain shift is already visible:

The most incredible thing about miracles is that they happen. . . . there is in life an element of elfin coincidence which people reckoning on the prosaic may perpetually miss. As it has been well expressed in the paradox of Poe, wisdom should reckon on the unforeseen.

The due acknowledgement to Poe is made, with a certain grace and generosity, but Poe would not have been wholly happy with that term 'miracle' for his 'coincidences'; for Poe, any 'thrilling half-credence in the supernatural' prompted by 'coincidences of so seemingly marvellous a character' should quickly be quenched by studying the Calculus of Probabilities and acknowledging the abstract majesty of mathematics. And neither Poe nor Sir Arthur would have entirely approved of the next paragraphs:

Aristide Valentin was unfathomably French; and the French intelligence is intelligence specially and solely. He was not 'a thinking machine'; for that is a brainless phrase of modern fatalism and materialism. A machine only *is* a machine because it cannot think. But he was a thinking man, and a plain man at the same time. All his wonderful successes, that looked like conjuring, had been gained by plodding logic, by clear and common-place French thought. The French electrify the world not by starting any paradox, they electrify it by carrying out a truism. They carry a truism so far—as in the French Revolution. But exactly because Valentin understood reason, he understood the limits of reason. Only a man who knows nothing of motors talks of motoring without petrol; only a man who knows nothing of reason talks of reasoning without strong, undisputed first principles. Here he had no strong first principles. Flambeau had been missed at Harwich; and if he was in London at all, he might be anything from a tall tramp on Wimbledon Common to a tall toastmaster at the Hotel Metropole. In such a naked state of nescience, Valentin had a view and a method of his own.

In such cases he reckoned on the unforeseen. In such cases, when he could not follow the train of the reasonable, he coldly and carefully followed the train of the unreasonable. Instead of going to the right places—banks, police stations, rendezvous—he systematically went to the wrong places; knocked at every empty house, turned down every *cul de sac*, went up every lane blocked with rubbish, went round every crescent that led him uselessly out of the way. He defended this crazy course quite logically. He said that if one had a clue this was the worst way; but if one had no clue at all it was the best, because there was just the chance that any oddity that caught the eye of the pursuer might be the same that had caught the eye of the pursued. Somewhere a man must begin, and it had better be just where another man might stop.

And even though Sherlock Holmes might, just once, have been beaten by an ex-opera singer's 'wit', he would be unlikely to endorse Valentin's general philosophy of criminal composition:

'The criminal is the creative artist; the detective only the critic,' he said with a sour smile, and lifted his coffee cup to his lips slowly, and put it down very quickly. He had put salt in it.

Already in these first few pages of the tale, Chesterton has introduced a number of the variations that could occupy our attention in any study of the tradition from now on—not least of which ought to be the lacing of the detective-story with humour, from the whimsical to the wise-cracking to the metaphysically witty.

The bumbling Father Brown clearly shares some of the traits of his predecessors; he, too, is an unofficial amateur, though equipped with a surprising omnipresence and sometimes bizarrely appropriate knowledge; he too is celibate and apparently asexual; he too indulges, in this tale, in at least quasi-criminal actions, and he too seems to rely upon and appeal to a law which is superior to and can, if necessary, override the official law. But even in these characteristics Fr Brown is significantly different from Dupin and Holmes. His knowledge of criminal skills is derived not from cold observation or from collected data, but from an apparently warm and friendly relation with his 'flock':

'How in Tartarus,' cried Flambeau, 'did you ever hear of the spiked bracelet?'
'Oh, one's little flock, you know!' said Father Brown, arching his eyebrows rather blankly. 'When I was a curate in Hartlepool, there were three of them with spiked bracelets.'

His celibacy is not for the sake of solitude or to keep pure his ratiocinative processes, but rather to accommodate a more comprehensive love—and when he does speak of 'the softer passions' it is not with 'a gibe and a sneer' (as

Holmes did) but with delight and awesome wonder (as in *The Scandal of Father Brown* or *The Insoluble Problem*). His occasional misdemeanours are in a minor key, and mainly directed against property rather than people (a splash of soup on a wall, a delicately smashed window). And the law to which he has final recourse is a law of charity and forgiveness.

But it is the strategy of the tale itself that takes our analysis a step further. For we are positioned by this tale neither as admiring pawn (Holmes's Watson) nor as competitor (Poe's reader), but rather as alert and active follower. Our stand-in, Valentin, begins the chase from salt-cellar to high Hampstead Heath from sheer hunch; he follows not a chain of clues to be pieced together by reasoning but a succession of cues to be recognised, trusted in, and responded to; but the reader who merely follows unthinkingly, going along passively for an apparently interminable ride atop a crawling omnibus, until Valentin (inevitably) spots the next cue, is likely to kick him- or herself at the end for not bothering to grasp the *double* function of those cues: they both draw the detective after and confirm the criminal in advance—as Fr Brown explains:

'A man generally makes a small scene if he finds salt in his coffee; if he doesn't, he has some reason for keeping quiet. . . . A man generally objects if his bill is three times too big. If he pays it, he has some motive for passing unnoticed.'

Of course, GKC, having pulled this extra rabbit out of a hat that seemed long emptied, leaves the reader with a faint worry as to whether Fr Brown would care to justify all his other mildly outrageous acts as more than mere cues for Valentin. Not that it seems to matter much; the fun is in the chase itself, and it doesn't even seem a cheat when, Holmes-like, the tale gives information and deduction together, and the first c*l*ue last (' "that little bulge up your sleeve where you people have the spiked bracelet" ')—after all, the 'story' has to start somehow, and we knew whom we were chasing anyway, as soon as Valentin got off the boat: 'Flambeau was in England.' Nor does it seem to matter very much in which particular way Fr Brown foils the attempted theft, nor even whether Flambeau is arrested or not at the end. In fact, most of the elements that hold our interest in Poe or in Doyle seem only marginally relevant to *this* tale of a detective, a criminal, a crime (prevented) and a pursuit.

The comment that 'the criminal is the creative artist, the detective only the critic' provides the appropriate prompt. The interest of the tale, if it has one, lies, it seems, in its 'aesthetic' (or even Aestheticist) appeal—though its artistry may seem a touch artificial today; there is a somewhat Decadent dependence on insistent alliteration, a kind of fervour of 'fine' writing, an over-reliance on assonance and simile:

Between the silver ribbon of morning and the green glittering ribbon of sea, the boat touched Harwich and let loose a swarm of folk like flies . . .

Such writing is rightly suspect, perhaps. But in Chesterton's slightly strained, though sometimes attractive, striving after 'effect', we should at least be prepared to recognise the precursor of some later developments in detective fiction: we don't read Pinget for the plot and we do indeed read Robbe-Grillet for the writing. But it's not only the writing, the pervasive and possibly irritating trickery of style, that is governed by 'aesthetic' considerations. If we react with any degree of pleasure to the list of Flambeau's 'crimes', for example, it's because they appeal to a certain kind of imaginative delight in the absurd or ludicrous: the child, or the anarchist, in us responds favourably to

how he turned the *juge d'instruction* upside down and stood him on his head, 'to clear his mind;' how he ran down the Rue de Rivoli with a policeman under each arm . . .

And some of us are prepared to suspend any rational objection when we read that

It was he who ran the great Tyrolean Dairy Company in London, with no dairies, no cows, no carts, no milk, but with some thousand subscribers. These he served by the simple operation of moving the little milk-cans outside people's doors to the doors of his own customers.

We might even feel that this particular example indicates a fairly acute grasp of some important principles of commerce. In general, however, we are clearly in the same kind of world as that of a cartoon comedy, a two-dimensional and rather vividly-coloured fantasy, in which some of the things we might, in our more carefree moments, like to do ourselves can actually happen:

'Sorry to confuse your accounts, but it'll pay for the window.' 'What window?' I says. 'The one I'm going to break,' he says, and smashed that blessed pane with his umbrella.

When the sober British police inspector asks 'Are we after escaped lunatics?', he is almost on the right track; but the more appropriate term might be 'fools'. The tale suggests a suspension of the ordinary rules of behaviour, a reversal of the everyday, which has affinities with that sacred suspension of power-relations known in mediaeval Europe as the Feast of Fools, when the first are put last and the weak have a crack at ruling the strong, when the lowest novice becomes the Lord Abbot and the Boy-Prince reigns. It's deeply appropriate that Fr Brown should leave behind him a trail of reversals: salt swapped for sugar, tangerines labelled nuts and nuts labelled tangerines, a broken window paid for before it is broken, a parcel inquired for before it is lost, and a thief attempting to steal his own parcel. The Feast of Fools was indeed an escape, from hierarchy and oppression, but only a limited and temporary asylum, a merely momentary image of an impossible but promised Utopia. And Fr Brown's antics too have their limits, though rather interesting ones.

Perhaps the only time the reader is offered a clue, on equal footing with both Fr Brown and the listening Valentin, is in the 'innocently clerical conversation' on the darkening heath—and Valentin, at least, misses the point:

The taller priest nodded his bowed head and said: 'Ah, yes, these modern infidels appeal to their reason; but who can look at those millions of worlds and not feel that there may well be wonderful universes above us where reason is utterly unreasonable?' 'No,' said the other priest; 'reason is always reasonable, even in the last limbo, in the lost borderland of things. I know that people charge the Church with lowering reason but it is just the other way. Alone on earth, the Church makes reason really supreme. Alone on earth, the Church affirms that God Himself is bound by reason.'
The other priest raised his austere face to the spangled sky and said:
'Yet who knows if in that infinite universe——?'
'Only infinite physically,' said the little priest, turning sharply in his seat, 'not infinite in the sense of escaping from the laws of truth.'
Valentin behind his tree was tearing his finger-nails with silent fury. He seemed almost to hear the sniggers of the English detectives whom he had brought so far on a fantastic guess only to listen to the metaphysical gossip of two mild old parsons.

As Fr Brown is later to point out, Flambeau here gives away his disguise as a priest, since to attack reason is 'bad theology' (whatever your brand of 'theology' happens to be). Unlike Poe's narrator, Fr Brown would not agree that God, creator of the world, 'can, at will, control or modify it'; God, too, for Fr Brown, is 'bound by reason', by the 'laws of truth'. The truth, even the most scandalous, can hold no terrors for God's undercover agents: 'Has it never struck you that a man who does next to nothing but hear men's real sins is not likely to be wholly unaware of human evil?' But then it becomes rather important to know what is comprised by 'reason', what is legislated for in those 'laws of truth'. Fr Brown continues the argument:

Reason and justice grip the remotest and the loneliest star. Look at those stars. Don't they look as if they were single diamonds and sapphires? Well, you can imagine any mad botany or geology you please. Think of forests of adamant with leaves of brilliants. Think the moon is a blue moon, a single elephantine sapphire. But don't fancy that all that frantic astronomy would make the smallest difference to the reason and justice of conduct. On plains of opal, under cliffs cut out of pearl, you would still find a notice-board, 'Thou shalt not steal.'

It's an intriguing piece of rhetoric. It reverses (once more) familiar expectations, this time of 'science': that the world as scrutinised by physics and chemistry is universally shaped by the same basic principles, whereas norms of behaviour, rules of conduct and codes of morality, are relative, specific to the societies which generate and rely upon them. It is Flambeau who can conceive of quite different worlds, wonderfully alternative universes, but for Chesterton himself, Flambeau's creator, there is a rational limit to *social* experiment: 'The French electrify the world not by starting any paradox, they electrify it by carrying out a truism. They carry a truism so far—as in the French Revolution' —but no further. Even Proudhon's mildly paradoxical thought that property might *be* theft is beyond the ken of this 'reason'. Of course, however, if there were neither property nor theft, there could be no detective story, even in fantastic vein, centred on the attempted theft of a cross 'made of real silver "with blue stones" '. And with property, inevitably, goes not only theft but policemen: 'even as he turned away to collect his property, the three policemen came out from under the twilight trees'.

But Flambeau's gesture of greeting to Valentin at this climactic point reminds us once again that we do not take this story of crime and detection too seriously: 'Flambeau was an artist and a sportsman. He stepped back and swept Valentin a great bow'. Crime, in this tale, is a game to play, a matter of art and sport; the law is necessary to the game not as its governing rules (to break the law is certainly not to 'cheat' in this game) nor is breaking the law the object, quite, of the game (the goal is the cross itself); the law has a rather curious status: it defines the character of some of the moves (some are within the law, others not), and it defines one of the teams (Valentin *is*, in colloquial parlance, 'the law'), but its main function is to get the game going, to say which team starts with the ball in the first place (as, in chess, it is always White who gets the first move). And just as the law acts as a necessary but curiously irrelevant premise to the play of the text, so it seems a necessary premise for the game of crime—yet one that must always have an air of artifice. One has the constant impression that GKC's story could actually get along quite nicely even if there were no law, no crime, no punishment, no criminal, no policeman; the chase could find some other object. Nevertheless the story, as written, relies upon the law: *this* story needs the law, even if it suggests some possible, wild reversal of the whole genre: a detective tale without a crime, a criminal, a detective or the police.

There is in fact a real paradox imaged in 'The Blue Cross'. It is always possible to recognise both that 'the Law' is only constituted by particular laws and that those laws are created and enforced primarily to maintain and safeguard a particular distribution of power and of property which is arbitrary, in the sense that there can be no entirely *rational* justification for any specific differential allocation of power and privilege; any such rationales can always be challenged in the name of a different or 'higher' rationale. But then *any* *system* of law, not only all particular laws, can seem an arbitrary and unjustified encumbrance; one response to that realisation is then a more or less explicit wish for a society that could operate *without* 'law', an an-archy (literally, a society without a chief magistrate) where *nobody* 'reigns'. It is only in fantasy, by a suspension of the real, by the use of a playful and perhaps child-like imagination, that we can envisage such a Utopia; yet it is perhaps partly by that constant recourse to 'dreams' in which not 'law' but art and game (which may have their own 'laws') provide the principles which shape society, that we can continue to affirm that 'somewhere a man must begin, and it had better be just where another man might stop'. The utopian, anarchist tradition may at times be caricatured as limited to slightly lunatic gestures, like smashing windows or throwing soup at the wall, but without such hankerings after *bouleversement*, after a permanent festival of the oppressed, it is doubtful whether even 'plodding logic, . . . clear and common sense French thought' will ever electrify the world.

What blocks the 'progress' of 'reason' is sometimes brute force—at the point where Fr Brown resorts to his rhetorical defence of universal reason, Flambeau 'without changing by the faintest shade his attitude or voice' simply says 'Just hand over that sapphire cross of yours, will you? We're all alone here, and I could pull you to pieces like a rag doll.' But at other times it is the elaborations of 'reason' itself that drive the reasoner into an impasse, Chesterton has two interesting remarks in an essay of 1908 entitled 'Orthodoxy':

Everyone who has had the misfortune to talk with people in the heart or on the edge of mental disorder, knows that their most sinister quality is a horrible clarity of detail; a connecting of one thing with another in a map more elaborate than a maze.

and:

Imagination does not breed insanity. Exactly what does breed insanity is reason. Poets do not go mad; but chess-players do. Mathematicians go mad, and cashiers; but creative artists very seldom. I am not, as will be seen, in any sense attacking logic: I only say that this danger does lie in logic, not in imagination. Artistic paternity is as wholesome as physical paternity. Moreover, it is worthy of remark that when a poet really was morbid it was commonly because he had some weak spot of rationality on his brain. Poe, for instance, really was morbid; not because he was poetical, but because he was specially analytical. Even chess was too poetical for him; he disliked chess because it was full of knights and castles, like a poem. He avowedly preferred the black discs of draughts, because they were more like the mere black dots on a diagram.

The reference to Poe's preference for draughts is to the opening of 'The Murders in the Rue Morgue', and we might easily go back here to that famous opening. But let me move in a different direction instead.

Paul Feyerabend opens his *Against Method: outline of an anarchist theory of knowledge* thus:

The following essay is written in the conviction that *anarchism*, while perhaps not the most attractive *political* philosophy, is certainly excellent medicine for *epistemology*, and for the *philosophy of science*.

The reason is not difficult to find.

'History generally, and the history of revolutions in particular, is always richer in content, more varied, more many-sided, more lively and subtle than even' the best historian and the best methodologist can imagine. History is full of 'accidents and conjunctures and curious juxtapositions of events' and it demonstrates to us the 'complexity of human change and the unpredictable character of the ultimate consequences of any given act or decision of men'. Are we really to believe that the naive and simple-minded rules which methodologists take as their guide are capable of accounting for such a 'maze of interactions'? And is it not clear that successful *participation* in a process of this kind is possible only for a ruthless opportunist who is not tied to any particular philosophy and who adopts whatever procedure seems to fit the occasion?

Feyerabend's first quotation in that passage is from V. I. Lenin, *Left-Wing Communism—an infantile disorder* (1920), and it is worth giving a bit more from that polemical pamphlet of Lenin:

History as a whole, and the history of revolutions in particular, is always richer in content, more varied, more multiform, more lively and ingenious than is imagined by even the best parties, the most class-conscious vanguards of the most advanced classes. This can readily be understood, because even the finest of vanguards express the class-consciousness, will, passion and imagination of tens of thousands, whereas at moments of great upsurge and the exertion of all human capacities, revolutions are made by the class-consciousness, will, passion and imagination of tens of millions, spurred on by a most acute struggle of classes. Two very important practical conclusions follow from this: first, that in order to accomplish its task the revolutionary class must be able to master *all* forms or aspects of social activity without exception (completing after the capture of political power—sometimes at great risk and with very great danger—what it did not complete before the capture of power); second, that the revolutionary class must be prepared for the most rapid and brusque replacement of one form by another.

Feyerabend continues to interweave Lenin and a transposition of Lenin in 'quoting' this passage:

First, that in order to fulfil its task, the revolutionary class [i.e. the class of those who want to change either a part of society such as science, or society as a whole] must be able to master all forms or aspects of social activity without exception [it must be able to understand, and apply, not only one particular methodology, but any methodology, and any variation thereof it can imagine] . . .

Lenin himself goes on to discuss the need for both 'legal' and 'illegal' revolutionary work, for work even in 'non-revolutionary bodies':

Inexperienced revolutionaries often think that legal methods of struggle are opportunist because, in this field, the bourgeoisie has most frequently deceived and duped the workers (particularly in 'peaceful' and non-revolutionary times), while illegal methods of struggle are revolutionary. That, however, is wrong. The truth is that those parties and leaders are opportunists and traitors to the working class that are unable or unwilling (do not say, 'I can't'; say, 'I shan't') to use illegal methods of struggle in conditions such as those which prevailed, for example, during the imperialist war of 1914–18, when the bourgeoisie of the freest democratic countries most brazenly and brutally deceived the workers, and smothered the truth about the predatory character of the war. But revolutionaries who are incapable of combining illegal forms of struggle with *every* form of legal struggle are poor revolutionaries indeed. It is not difficult to be a revolutionary when revolution has already broken out and is in spate, when all people are joining the revolution just because they are carried away, because it is the vogue, and sometimes even from careerist motives. After its victory, the proletariat has to make the most strenuous efforts, even the most painful, so as to 'liberate' itself from such pseudo-revolutionaries. It is far more difficult—and far more precious —to be a revolutionary when the conditions for direct, open, really mass and really revolutionary struggle *do not yet exist*, to be able to champion the interests of the revolution (by propaganda, agitation and organisation) in non-revolutionary bodies, and quite often in downright reactionary bodies, in a non-revolutionary situation, among the masses who are incapable of immediately appreciating the need for revolutionary methods of action.

Lenin then cites Britain as an example of where 'no one can tell in advance how soon a real proletarian revolution will flare up . . . and *what immediate* cause will most serve to rouse, kindle and impel into the struggle the very wide masses, who are still dormant. . . . It is possible that the breach will be forced, the ice broken, by a parliamentary crisis, or by a crisis arising from colonial and imperialist contradictions, which are hopelessly entangled and are becoming increasingly painful and acute.' Quite rightly, Lenin does not speculate further.

It is a familiar story that Lenin gave up playing chess, as too much of a distraction from the tasks of revolution. It's also a familiar fantasy that when living in Zurich in 1916–17, on the eve of the actual but unexpected revolution, Lenin may have been writing his *Imperialism: the highest stage of capitalism* across a library-table from James Joyce, then completing *Ulysses*, while the two of them might even have dropped into the Café Voltaire to see what those anarchist artists Tzara and Ball were up to. Such a marvellous coincidence as Lenin's flat being just across the street from the home of Dada was bound to attract an author of travesties. But it is even more provoking of wild laughter that the latest twist in that supremely meta-methodological discipline, the philosophy of science, should have produced a self-declared Dadaist (cf. Feyerabend's footnote to his use of 'anarchist' in his sub-title—a footnote to a title-page being a pleasantly Dadaist gesture). Perhaps the reason for that declaration of Dadaism is ultimately to be located in that curiously persistent problem of bonding 'data' and 'hypothesis': either the one is already shaped inextricably by the other or an unbridgeable 'gap' erupts 'between' them. And one curiously persistent feature of models of 'revolution' derived from the Bolshevik moment of 1917 is that they seem to require a moment of absolute 'rupture', a sudden and total break in the familiar chains that bind the future to the past (such a 'rupture' could only be recognised or validated as a 'revolution' *retrospectively*). Those who back away from 'anarchy' **may** have to per-manently postpone such a revolution. It's an intriguing **and rather** pleasantly fantastic thought that at some particular moment the *juge d'instruction* should have to be, very suddenly and perhaps very sharply, turned upside down and stood on his head 'to clear his mind'—or change it. Such a 'crime' might indeed be an image of a non-ordinary law, a paradigm of the politics of the extra-ordinary, an echo and anticipation of the Festival of the oppressed.

Question 6: Raymond Chandler, *The Big Sleep*

In October 1949 Raymond Chandler, in a letter to James Sandoe, complained:

> As for mysteries, that's hopeless. There don't seem to be any worth the trouble [of reading]. It would be an excellent thing right now if someone would come along with a good cool analytical mystery, the hell with suspense and witty dialogue, and let us look at the fundamentals for fresh. The whole form has lost its way, the emphasis has gone to inessential matters.
> *Raymond Chandler Speaking*, ed. D. Gardiner & K. Sorley Walker, London 1962, p.59.
> (Cited hereafter by page number only.)

The same year, in 'Casual Notes on the Mystery Novel', Chandler re-stated some of the 'fundamentals' of the genre:

> The mystery must elude a reasonably intelligent reader. This, and the problem of honesty, are the two most baffling elements in mystery writing. Some of the best detective stories ever written do not elude an intelligent reader to the end. . . . But it is one thing to guess the murderer and quite another to be able to justify the guess by reasoning. (p.65)

Chandler was very much concerned with the problem of what he calls 'honesty' in constructing the tale: the reader must be given 'the sort of facts which can be reasoned from', and must have a fair chance of making the right inferences. But two comments in this connection are worth linking: 'Inferences from the facts are the detective's stock in trade, but he should disclose enough of his thinking to keep the reader's mind thinking along with him' (p.66); 'There must come a time when the detective has made up his mind and has not given the reader this bit of news, a point as it were (and many old hands recognise it without much difficulty) when the detective suddenly stops thinking out loud and ever so gently closes the door of his mind in the reader's face' (p.68). But, as has been clear since the days of Poe's Dupin, there is a sense in which the detective *cannot* disclose his 'thinking', but only the results of that thinking; he may register that curious *moment* of insight for the reader but only retrospectively can he offer an account of it. (Fielding's send-up of *Pamela* might be recalled at this point.) There is a clear moment of insight in Chandler's novel of 1940, *Farewell, My Lovely*:

> I nodded across the office at Mr Rembrandt, then I reached for my hat and went out. I was half-way to the elevator before the thought hit me. It hit me without any reason or sense, like a dropped brick. I stopped and leaned against the marbled wall and pushed my hat around on my head and suddenly I laughed.
>
> (chapter 15)

The same thought may have struck the reader long before (that Marriott got Marlowe's card from Mrs Florian), but until it strikes Marlowe the reader can't take the next step—only Marlowe can pick up a phone and *confirm* the link between Marriott and Mrs Florian. The reader is always, sometimes irritatingly, dependent upon the detective's reasoning and the 'disclosure' can't, unfortunately, be mutual; the problem is, in other words, not so much that the reader *guesses* while the detective 'reasons' but that the reader has no way of shaping events in order to 'test' a guess that presents itself without 'any reason or sense'; the reader can't prompt the detective. Which is one further reason why Chandler was correct to comment, in 1940, *à propos* of Christie's *Ten Little Niggers*:

I'm very glad I read the book because it finally and for all time settled a question in my mind that had at least some lingering doubt attached to it. Whether it is possible to write a strictly honest mystery of the classic type. It isn't. To get the complication you fake the clues, the timing, the play of coincidence, assume certainties where only 50 per cent chances exist at most. To get the surprise murderer you fake the character, which hits me hardest of all, because I have a sense of character. (p.48).

It's not surprising to find Chandler, after this comment, remarking in 1944 that 'I really don't seem to take the mystery element in the detective story as seriously as I should' (p.49), or, in the same year, that 'the detective or mystery story as an art-form has been so thoroughly explored that the real problem for a writer now is to avoid writing a mystery story while appearing to do so' (p.48). In 1947 he seems to have considered a new twist in the tradition: 'No, I am not working on a story of murder without detection. I have such a story in mind, but have not got down to it yet' (p.217), and in 1949 he was still hankering after a development in the genre that would not 'fake the character' but would rather 'fake' being a 'mystery' at all: 'I am not satisfied that the thing can't be done, nor that sometime, somewhere, perhaps not now or by me, a novel cannot be written which, ostensibly a mystery and keeping the spice of mystery, will actually be a novel of character and atmosphere with an over-tone of violence and fear' (p.56).

ii

A decade earlier he had already written of *The Big Sleep*, his first novel, published in 1939, in similar terms:

I was ... intrigued by a situation where the mystery is solved more by the exposition and understanding of a single character, always well in evidence, than by the slow and sometimes long-winded concatenation of circumstances. (p.209)

Dupin had, long before, relied upon a similar 'fathoming of character', albeit marginally; in *The Big Sleep* such 'fathoming' is not difficult: from the very first chapter the (nympho-)mania of Miss Carmen Sternwood is apparent to all but the dimmest. But the strategy of the text is then to lead us into a tangle of ramifications, elaborations, mystifications, weaving together in a complex pattern a pornography racket, a blackmail racket, a gambling racket, police corruption, homosexuality and an assortment of violent deaths (Geiger, Brody, Owen, Jones, Canino). The thread we are ostensibly following through this maze derives from a possibly blameless request that some gambling debts, though 'legally uncollectable', should be honoured. But it is hardly 'deduction' or 'inference from the facts' that keeps Marlowe in touch thereafter with the varied goings-on; coincidences of timing, chance encounters, and some implausible luck keep the story moving, and the reader tails along, waiting, like GKC's Valentin, to see what bizarre incident will happen next. Within that general play of 'collateral' events, Marlowe does do some clearing of the 'fog' (cf. p.65) by putting twos and twos together, but his main weapon is a fast tongue rather than a scientific calculus; the set-pieces of the book are conversational sparring matches in which the object is to trick the interlocutor, either into divulging information that could have been kept concealed or into being misled by varieties of verbal deception; and, occasionally, a gun can enforce a degree of suitable loquacity. But does it matter, in the end, whether all the loose-ends in this by-play are tied neatly into a final bow? In 1949 Chandler wrote:

I remember several years ago when Howard Hawks was making *The Big Sleep*, the movie, he and Bogart got into an argument as to whether one of the characters was murdered or committed suicide. They sent me a wire asking me, and dammit I didn't know either. (p.221)

That such a question can remain unanswered in the novel indicates one function of the complex 'plotting' that occupies most of the book: it serves to distract the reader from concentrating on the 'real' question which structures the quest—'who killed Rusty Regan?' But that is only the 'real' question in the sense that to answer it is to finish the novel; once that hidden (yet insistently raised and repressed) enigma is resolved the story is over. Yet, in principle, the alert reader could ask that question by chapter 2, guess the answer by chapter 3, and be able to 'justify' it by, at the latest, chapter 24 (the incident with the naked Carmen that clinches Marlowe's account in the final chapter). But were the novel, or Marlowe, or the reader, to arrive at 'the answer' by chapter 24, the novel would nevertheless not have 'finished', since much of the collateral 'plot' is still only half-unfolded; equally, 'solving' the various subordinate mysteries in no important way contributes directly to arriving at the solution to Regan's disappearance. The 'answer' given in the last chapter is not, therefore, either the final step in a chain of deductions (clues) nor the last in a causally connected sequence of events (cues); the story is finally given shape not so much by a 'solution' of its 'problem' as by a 'resolution' of its 'suspense': the pattern of expectation is not so much 'where does that clue lead?' but simply 'what is going to happen next?' (which partly accounts for the sense of awkward 'second start' in chapter 20)—and the logic of such suspense leads simply to the continual question 'how is it going to end?' And we know the answer to *that* question only when it ends. But whereas a solution to a problem can be correct or incorrect, an 'ending' can only be 'satisfactory' or 'unsatisfactory'. Our criteria for judging the shape of this tale are, necessarily, 'aesthetic'. The structure of Chandler's novel offers a variation on the data-hypothesis bond; we accept the 'relevance' of so much that is 'marginal' in the book insofar as we are satisfied by the totality; we retrospectively allow the 'collateral' insofar as we are convinced by the 'whole'. But that is primarily a matter of the *effect* of 'closure' achieved by the final pages, even by the final sentence: 'I never saw her again'—the whole story, with all its still trailing elements, is signalled as conclusively over, done with.

With Chandler, the detective story aims for the 'organic', for the 'form' of 'good fiction':

The mystery novel must have a sound story value apart from the mystery element. The idea is revolutionary to some of the classicists and most distasteful to all second-rate performers. Nevertheless it is sound. All really good mysteries are reread, some of them many times. Obviously this would not happen if the puzzle were the only motive for the reader's interest. The mysteries that survive over the years invariably have the qualities of good fiction. (p.64)

Another note elaborates one aspect of this position:

The mystery novel must punish the criminal in one way or another, not necessarily by operation of the law courts. Contrary to popular belief, this has nothing to do with morality. It is part of the logic of the form. Without this the story is like an unresolved chord in music. It leaves a sense of irritation. (p.66)

It then follows that the *form* of punishment has also to be appropriate, part of the overall pattern. Yet at the end of *The Big Sleep* Miss Carmen Sternwood is not, in any normal sense, 'punished'. Part of the reason is that she herself is 'not normal' (ch.22). Since the tale revolves round the 'exposition and understanding of a single character', it is perhaps not surprising that the 'ending' should be 'appropriate' to the character involved. But could not some readers be rather irritated at this somewhat lop-sided 'resolution', at the thought of Rusty Regan's murderess being merely 'taken away' to be 'cured', privately and unofficially, while another murderer, the homosexual Carol Lundgren, is given no such chance.

iii

The problem at this point could be posed in more general terms. Even if a rational chain of detection, from facts to inference, from crime to criminal, could be constructed, could that chain be extended to embrace the specific 'punishment' that follows? Should, for example, the punishment fit the crime or fit the (character of the) criminal? Or is 'punishment' itself an 'inappropriate' term? And how do we decide? One aspect of that general problem was explored by Max Weber in his analysis of bureaucracy:

The more complicated and specialized modern culture becomes, the more its external supporting apparatus demands the personally detached and strictly 'objective' *expert*, in lieu of the master of older social structures, who was moved by personal sympathy and favor, by grace and gratitude. . . . As a rule, only bureaucracy has established the foundation for the administration of a rational law conceptually systematized . . .
    The 'rational' interpretation of law on the basis of strictly formal conceptions stands opposite the kind of adjudication that is primarily bound to sacred traditions. The single case that cannot be unambiguously decided by tradition is either settled by concrete 'revelation' (oracle, prophetic dicta, or ordeal—that is, by 'charismatic' justice) or by informal judgments rendered in terms of concrete ethical or other practical valuations. This is 'Kadi-justice', as R. Schmidt has fittingly called it. Or, formal judgments are rendered, though not by subsumption under rational concepts, but by drawing on 'analogies' and by depending upon and interpreting concrete 'precedents'. This is 'empirical justice'.
                    From Max Weber, ed. H. H. Gerth & C. Wright Mills, London 1948, p.216.
                                                    (Cited hereafter as *W*.)

The 'ideal type' of judge within a bureaucratic, rational, formal legal system can be described in a way that echoes Watson's description, in 'A Scandal in Bohemia', of Sherlock Holmes as a perfect reasoning machine with none of the softer passions:

The conception of the modern judge as an automaton into which the files and the costs are thrown in order to that it may spill forth the verdict at the bottom along with the reasons, read mechanically from codified paragraphs—this conception is angrily rejected, perhaps because a certain approximation to this type is implied by a consistent bureaucratization of justice.
                                                    (*W*, p.219)

'In principle', indeed, 'the idea of "a law without gaps" is vigorously disputed', writes Weber; but if there are indeed 'gaps' does that not undermine the whole 'principle' of a rigorously rational system? And how are they to be 'filled'? Could one have a blending of 'rational law' with 'Kadi-justice' or with 'empirical justice'? But if Kadi-justice appeals to 'revelation', what is the source of that 'revelation'? And what is the 'empirical' basis of 'empirical justice'? One suggestion might be that both Kadi and empirical justice implicitly appeal to 'Literature', to sacred texts and even, more or less directly, to 'fiction'. (An essay by Roland Barthes, *Dominici, or the triumph of Literature*, in his *Mythologies*, explores this possibility in relation to legal judgements in modern France.) If therefore we now explore 'rational law' we may in fact find ourselves back with the other brands.

Weber writes: 'The only decisive point . . . is that in principle a system of rationally debatable "reasons" stands behind every act of bureaucratic administration, that is, either subsumption under norms or a weighing of ends and means' (W, p.220). But whose 'norms' and whose 'ends'? (In *The Big Sleep* Carmen is 'not normal'—but by what norm?) Recently, the question of the 'norms' which underpin and justify a whole system of law has been explored by the 'critical criminologists'; the logic of their case is that legal 'norms' have to be situated within a total context, that what is required is a 'fully social theory' which can embrace not only 'the political economy of crime' but also 'the political economy, the social psychology and the social dynamics of social reaction to deviance' (*The New Criminology*, by I. Taylor, P. Walton & J. Young, London 1973, p.276. Cited hereafter as *NC*). Nothing less, in fact, than a total theory of society is required. (It is perhaps of interest that at this point in their argument they refer to the work of a novelist as the best-available instantiation of such a 'total theory', cf. *NC*, pp.277–8.) But such an account is also required, logically, by any application of law which seeks to take notice of all the 'individual circumstances' of a case, or fully to take cognisance of the 'character' of the accused—if, as Dupin pointed out, 'it is the malpractice of the courts to confine evidence and discussion to the bounds of apparent relevancy', any court which seeks to extend the area of 'relevance' beyond the 'recognised and *booked* principles' of evidence, can have no fully rational grounds for setting new bounds. On the other hand, if the notion of 'norms' is itself driven back through the hierarchy of bureaucratic 'means and ends', the only 'logical' stopping place tends to be that mysterious 'reason' known as *'raison d'état'*, which perhaps is not so very different from the 'revelations' of Kadi-justice: 'oracle, prophetic dicta or ordeal'.

Foucault's work on the history of crime and punishment (*Discipline and Punish*, London 1977, especially Part 4) suggests one 'solution', in principle, to this 'anomaly of the most rigidly exact . . . applied to . . . the most intangible in speculation' (to adapt Dupin): what he calls 'the normalisation of the power of normalisation'. If the 'criminal' does not act in accordance with the 'norm' or, to put it more generally, is 'not normal', the 'humane' form of eradication is to 'normalise' him, by punishment, coercion, imprisonment, retraining, psychological readjustment, re-education, or whatever means will achieve that end. But if some methods have proved successful in normalising the criminal *after* his crime and capture, would it not be more sensible to apply those methods *in advance* to potential criminals? And since no one can be sure *who is* a potential criminal until a crime has actually been committed, and even then there is no guarantee that the real culprit will be detected, the logic of this solution is to extend normalisation techniques developed for 'criminals' to everyone. That way crime might be finally eradicated—and, with it, the need for law: the dream of anarchy would be finally realised! (At the same time, however, such an extension of normalisation techniques might have a tendency, if successful, to create more deviants—since the 'bounds' of the 'normal' would tend to encroach more and more upon previously 'collateral' matters.)

Foucault locates the linchpin of what he calls the 'carceral texture of society' in the 'model prison'; in its combination of total surveillance and 'scientific' human micro-engineering the ideal prison of the humane reformers has indeed threatened to become the model for a whole society—though eventually, perhaps, and for that very reason, a rather redundant model:

now, as medicine, psychology, education, public assistance, 'social work' assume an ever greater share of the powers of supervision and assessment, the penal apparatus will be able, in turn, to become medicalised, psychologised, educationalised; and by the same token that turning-point represented by the prison becomes less useful when, through the gap between its penitentiary discourse and its effect of consolidating delinquency, it articulates the penal power and the disciplinary power. In the midst of all these mechanisms of normalisation, which are becoming ever more rigorous in their application, the specificity of the prison and its role as link are losing something of their purpose.

Discipline and Punish, p.306

Perhaps Carol Lundgren, in a more enlightened and humane text, would indeed have also been sent to be 'cured' as simply 'not normal'—perhaps even before his crime.

The real problem remains, of course, even with this 'solution' of extensive normalisation apparatuses: what is to count as 'the norm'? Weber pointed to one awkward facet of this problem:

The propertyless masses especially are not served by a formal 'equality before the law' and a 'calculable' adjudication and administration, as demanded by 'bourgeois' interests. Naturally, in their eyes justice and administration should serve to compensate for their economic and social life-opportunities in the face of the propertied classes. Justice and administration can fulfil this function only if they assume an informal character to a far-reaching extent. It must be informal because it is substantively 'ethical' ('Kadi-justice'). Every sort of 'popular justice'—which usually does not ask for reasons and norms—as well as every sort of intensive influence on the administration by so-called public opinion, crosses the rational course of justice and administration just as strongly, and under certain conditions far more so, as the 'star chamber' proceedings of an 'absolute' ruler has been able to do. In this connection, that is, under the conditions of mass democracy, public opinion is communal conduct born of irrational 'sentiments'. Normally it is staged or directed by party leaders and the press.

W, p.221

iv

If we now ask 'what is the norm?' in the text of *The Big Sleep*, the obvious answer has to be that Marlowe himself is: not a formulaic norm which might be rationally challenged or reformulated, but rather a living norm which is 'attractive' or 'sympathetic' to the reader; it is Marlowe's *character* which seems to offer us access to the undeclared norms that govern this book. (Poe, interestingly, wrote: 'the depicting of [Dupin's] character consituted my design.') But Marlowe's 'character' is by no means presented to us as 'normal': Marlowe is curiously unmotivated by those 'normal' passions of sex (like his predecessors—note the attitude behind the comment 'I'm unmarried because I don't like policemen's wives') and of money:

I am so money greedy that for twenty-five bucks a day and expenses, mostly gasolene and whisky, I do my thinking myself, what there is of it; I risk my whole future, the hatred of the cops and of Eddie Mars and his pals, I dodge bullets and eat saps, and say thank you very much, if you have any more trouble, I hope you'll think of me, I'll just leave one of my cards in case anything comes up. I do all this for twenty-five bucks a day—and maybe just a little to protect what little pride a broken and sick old man has left in his blood . . .

The Big Sleep, ch. 32. (Cited hereafter as *BS*)

It's worth elaborating for a moment Marlowe's relation to money. The plot 'begins' with Marlowe 'calling on four million dollars' and with him investigating a possible blackmail attempt; the final chapter sees Marlowe himself accused of wanting to blackmail those same millions—'I suppose you want money,' says Mrs Regan. But Marlowe, without even the motive of blackmail, keeps quiet about Carmen's murdering Regan and by his silence bends the law himself. His relation to money is indeed in parallel to his relation to the law: unlike both, say, Eddie Mars (whose wealth is basically 'illegitimate') and General Sternwood (whose wealth is basically 'legitimate'), Marlowe makes his living by a legitimate activity that yet operates askew to the law, in both senses: he is not part of the *organised* forces of 'law and order' (cf. his own comments on the Missing Persons Bureau, for example), though neither is he involved in organised crime. His 'crimes' arise from operating outside the rules of organised law-enforcement (cf. for example ch. 18), just as his self-employment is a way of avoiding the constraints of an 'organised' job (he was fired for insubordination). In many respects, then, Marlowe slides *between* familiar pigeon-holes; the exchange between Marlowe and Mrs Regan suggests the basic ambivalence:

You think he sent that loogan after you?
What's a loogan?
A guy with a gun.
Are you a loogan?
Sure, I laughed. But strictly speaking a loogan is on the wrong side of the fence.
I often wonder if there is a wrong side.
We're losing the subject.

BS, ch. 23

If we now go back to the more general subject of 'norms' and 'law', it may be possible to locate these features of Marlowe's 'abnormal' character and position within a wider framework.

v

Jürgen Habermas has suggested, in his *Legitimation Crisis*, London 1976. (Cited hereafter as *LC*) a different 'solution' to the problem of 'validating' a basic 'norm' in society. He argues that the liberal-capitalist state was able to appeal not to a transcendent or revealed norm nor to an arbitrary *raison d'état*, but to a 'self-evident' norm embedded in its economic organisation:

Bourgeois ideologies can assume a universalistic structure and appeal to generalisable interests because the property order has shed its political form and been converted into a relation of production that, it seems, can legitimate itself. The institution of the market can be founded on the justice inherent in the exchange of equivalents; and, for this reason, the bourgeois constitutional state finds its justification in the legitimate relations of production. This is the message of rational natural law since Locke. The relations of production can do without a traditional authority legitimated from above.

LC, p.22

But then Marx's analysis of this alleged 'exchange of equivalents' struck a double-blow at bourgeois ideology:

In Marx, therefore, theoretical analysis of the value form has the double task of uncovering both the steering principle of commerce in a market economy and the basic ideology of bourgeois class society. The theory of value serves, at the same time, the functional analysis of the economic system and the critique of ideology of a class domination that can be unmasked, even for the bourgeois consciousness, through the proof that in the labour market equivalents are not exchanged.

LC, p.26

In late capitalism, however, with the growing control of the 'market' by monopolistic company decisions and with the increasingly open contribution of the State to the maintenance and reproduction of the 'relations of production', the 'self-legitimation' of the market has ceased to be viable even in the eyes of its exponents; once again there is a need for explicitly *political* articulation and justification of 'ends and means'. But the relatively simple contrast, as formulated by Weber, between 'the propertyless masses' and the 'propertied classes' is complicated by the effects of State intervention and by a differential relation of workers to employers, particularly in the area of the monopolies. Habermas summarises some of these complications thus:

During the sixties, various authors, using the United States as an example, developed a three-sector model based on the distinction between the private and the public sectors. According to the model, private production is market-oriented, one sub-sector still being regulated by competition while the other is determined by the market strategies of oligopolies that tolerate a 'competitive fringe'. By contrast, in the public sector, especially in the armaments and space-travel industries, huge concerns have arisen whose investment decisions can be made almost without regard for the market.... In the monopolistic and the public sectors, capital-intensive industries predominate; in the competitive sector, labor-intensive industries predominate. In the monopolistic and public sectors, companies are faced with strong unions. In the competitive sector workers are less well organised, and wage levels are correspondingly different.

LC, p.34

The combined effect of strong unions in certain sectors, the relative independence from market constraints of monopoly companies, and the politically-guided interventions of the State, is that in *some* sectors and for *some* workers the liberal-capitalist thesis of 'exchange of equivalents' is no longer operative, and—it is implied—the Marxist analysis of 'the value form' therefore no longer strictly obtains:

'Price setting', which replaces price competition in the oligopolistic markets, has its counterpart in the labour market. Just as the great concerns quasi-administratively control price movements in their markets, so too, on the other side, they obtain quasi-political compromises with union adversaries on wage movements. In those branches of industry belonging to the monopolistic and the public sectors, which are central to economic development, the commodity called labour power receives a 'political price'. The 'wage-scale partners' find a broad zone of compromise, since increased labour costs can be passed on through prices and since there is a convergence of the middle-range demands of both sides on the state—demands that aim at increasing productivity, qualifying labour power, and improving the social condition of the workers. The monopolistic sector can, as it were, externalise class conflict.

LC, p.38

There are, however, two distinct ways of *perceiving* these 'changes'. One, which might be economically appropriate to some sections of the population still operating in the 'competitive fringe' or outside of any organised employment at all, would be to see both the 'control' of the monopolies and the 'quasi-political compromises' effected by strong unions as forms of 'blackmail' against *them*; the rhetorical vocabulary is familiar, and is activated in editorials and press reports ('public opinion') whenever there is a major strike in an important industry: 'Blackmailing the community', 'Holding the Country to Ransom', etc.; in such formulations the 'victims' of the 'blackmail' are alleged to be everyone, including 'the State', the monopolies and even those other trade unionists who happen not to be on strike themselves at that particular moment. In Britain, the 1974 miners' strike and the consequent General Election made the logic of this perspective clear, in the rhetorical question: 'Who Governs?' But that question is in any case the question underpinning *any* discussion of *raison d'état*, of social 'ends and means', of fundamental legal 'norms'. The alternative way of perceiving a situation of 'quasi-political compromise' involving monopolies, unions and government, could also be formulated in terms of 'blackmail': that the price of the unions' silence on more fundamental issues (including who actually *does* govern) is a relatively privileged 'political price' for *some* workers' labour power, at the expense perhaps of other workers, those in less organised areas and in sectors (or even countries) which are difficult to unionise or less likely to be the beneficiaries of State intervention; crucially, such 'compromises' may serve as a *substitute* for any fundamental shift in or challenge to the continuing power of the monopolies, including their power over State interventions and 'government'. The logic of this perspective would perhaps be embodied in the often rhetorical question: 'Who are the class traitors?'

It would be possible to discuss at least some aspects of this analysis of late capitalism in terms of structural parallels within *The Big Sleep*. For example, the position Marlowe occupies *vis-à-vis* the other main protagonists in the plot is somewhat parallel to the position that might be felt to be their own by someone who regarded *both* the unions *and* the large capitalist companies as tarred with the same brush, as operating 'legally' but 'illegitimately': the difference between Eddie Mars and General Sternwood would then be seen as a matter of degree, even though Sternwood is much the more 'respectable'; equally, the official forces of law and order (the State apparatuses) would be regarded as at best incompetent, almost certainly hand-in-glove with those they are supposed to control, and at worst corrupted and controlled themselves. What is then seen as needed in such a situation is precisely for someone (a Marlowe) to take the law into their own hands. Thus one could fairly easily outline a case for regarding Marlowe's ambivalent attitudes as reproducing in large part the dilemmas and reactions of a traditional stereotype of the petty bourgeois *proto-fascist*. But equally, and quite differently, one could regard Marlowe's final option of 'silence' as echoing the 'political compromise' of the *'reformist'* within a system which is rejected at one level of response but basically endorsed, perhaps rather cynically admired, and ultimately even protected at another level. And one could also sketch another alternative interpretation which would place Marlowe as a *conservative moralist* marooned ineffectually, for the most part, in a world where the values of truth, personal honesty and a basic sense of what is right and wrong have been for so long flouted or only hypocritically retained that the only possible response is to withdraw to the marginalised role of independent moral arbitrator. The very ease with which such apparently contrasting sociological 'equivalents' for Marlowe could be offered indicates that analysis along such lines would be lop-sided or wrong-headed; though it also perhaps suggests that the manifest differences between the proto-fascist, the reformist, and the decent moral conservative are differences only within a fundamentally shared perspective. However, to understand *why* the figure of Marlowe might be metamorphosed into such ostensibly diverse forms might be to uncover a potentially important *permutation* in the logic of norms and normality.

vi

But what would it mean to 'understand the figure of Marlowe'? The type of analysis gestured at above approaches the text as a pattern of interrelated positions—those of Marlowe, the racketeers, the clients, the police—structurally homologous to some positions occupied or postulated in the 'actual' shape of a society, specifically a late capitalist society. But 'Marlowe' is, from another angle, only a name for the narrative strategy of the text: at one level, 'Marlowe' is the narrating 'I', the offered and endorsed viewpoint of the text upon its proceedings; at another, 'Marlowe' is the *raison d'être* of the text: the plot, the characters, the action of the text serve to create and define the 'character' of 'Marlowe' as the unifying 'theme' of the whole reading experience of a Chandler novel. Our understanding of, and judgement upon, 'Marlowe' is the central component in our understanding of, and judgement upon, the novel as a whole; but equally our response to the novel is almost wholly shaped by our response to 'Marlowe'. Obviously Chandler's novel is no different in this respect from many other novels narrated by their central protagonists. But since the 'content' of *The Big Sleep* is made up almost entirely of matters of 'law and order', of crime, corruption and violence, our response to those matters is also almost wholly shaped, in the reading experience, by our response to 'Marlowe'. But on what is that response based? Primarily, it is based on 'aesthetic' considerations—which need only at this point be indicated by differentiating them from 'moral' or 'rational' considerations: whereas in reading Poe or Conan Doyle we are mainly drawn into the process of 'ratiocination', and whereas in really encountering violence, corruption or crime we might be preoccupied by the 'moral' questions they pose for us, in reading Chandler we are primarily invited to *appreciate* the craft of the language, the skill of the construction, the orchestration of the action, the 'resolution' effected by the final chord. We are to *enjoy* the whole experience. Though the novels regularly 'deal with' such matters as criminal or police brutality, the corruptions of the powerful or the 'law-abiding', these are proposed for our relaxed pleasure not our urgent response. The overall effect a Chandler novel aims for, and often achieves, is for the reader to close it with a sense of aesthetic satisfaction, of closure and finality, to recognise that this indeed is 'where it ends'—till the next novel.

I want to emphasise the obvious, but difficult, point that there is something deeply problematic about this textual strategy (though it is a totally familiar one, Chandler being merely a major exemplar in a long tradition). What is problematic is not that we should respond to such a novel according to primarily 'aesthetic' considerations, but rather that—once the fairly short-lived experiment in purely 'ratiocinative' detective fiction had lapsed—a reliance on familiar aesthetic criteria seemed the only possible alternative. It is at this point that the real difficulty arises: for is there not a parallel *in these terms* to the shifts that Habermas's analysis of late capitalism indicates: that once the short-lived liberal-capitalist 'equilibrium', with its 'self-justifying' synthesis of economics, politics and morality (normality) had passed, any re-assertion of a 'rational' or even 'moral' basis for a system of law seemed untenable, and what did indeed take its place, for a time, in much of Europe, was an appeal to 'norms' which can in one sense be termed 'aesthetic', those norms embodied not in a formulated code but rather in a living focus and exemplar, a Führer. There is a crucial insight into Fascism in Walter Benjamin's remark: 'The logical result of Fascism is the introduction of aesthetics into political life'; his own analysis, limited to certain elements in Fascism, can help us to probe further. In 1936, in *The Work of Art in the Age of Mechanical Reproduction*, he argued:

Fascism attempts to organise the newly created proletarian masses without affecting the property structure which the masses strive to eliminate. Fascism sees its salvation in giving these masses not their right, but instead a chance to express themselves. The masses have a right to change property relations; Fascism seeks to give them an expression while preserving property. The logical result of Fascism is the introduction of aesthetics into political life. . . .

All efforts to render politics aesthetic culminate in one thing: war. War and war only can set a goal for mass movements on the largest scale while respecting the traditional property system. This is the political formula for the situation. The technological formula may be stated as follows: Only war makes it possible to mobilize all of today's technical resources while maintaining the property system. It goes without saying that the Fascist apotheosis of war does not employ such arguments.

Among the 'arguments' that Fascism *did* employ was an appeal to *nationalist* fervour, but the concept of 'nation' has been, since at least the time of Herder, an aesthetic one: what 'defines' a 'nation' is a shared 'culture' rather than a geographical boundary, and what is meant by a 'culture' is inherently indefinable: the German or English 'way of life' is known only from the inside, by an intimacy of experience that cannot be fully articulated; what it means 'to be English' cannot be formulated with any precision; yet such phrases appeal to a sense of agreement: *'we know'* what it is to be 'English'—if 'we' *are* 'English'. But of course the difficulty is that we thereby presume a 'norm' which we cannot even articulate in order to justify it; we may never be able to *say* with full conviction what constitutes a 'normal' Englishman, but we harbour the deep delusion that, damn it all, *some* things just *aren't* normal for any normal English person—faced with the infinitely diverse activities, tastes, habits and life-experiences of fifty million people, a leap is made to the overarching hypothesis of some peculiarly 'English' characteristic which they share, and which rules them out of consideration if they don't; there is an even deeper delusion, often, that being 'English' is the *normal* thing for everyone to be—even Germans. It is this fundamentally 'aesthetic' notion—neither rational nor moral nor immediately political—that not only underpins the appeal to militaristic nationalism (that patriotism which both justifies and makes possible war between 'nations', reshaping millions of different people into demarcated but homogenised national armies) but also fuels a deeply entrenched mode of reaction to developments *within* 'nations': by an appeal to 'our English way of life' everything from changes in spelling practices to new fashions in dress, hairstyle or behaviour, from emerging forms of political agitation or economic struggle to ancient ways of making love, can be castigated and rejected as peculiarly 'offensive'—even when not (by some oversight) actually illegal or (was God nodding?) clearly immoral. The most dangerous manifestation of this irrational reaction is, of course, racism, not only in its more overtly and crassly 'cultural' forms (an outraged horror at an unfamiliar musical convention) but in its most genocidal: one reason for the extermination of six million Jews was that their very existence radically challenged the equation of 'culture' and 'nation' while at the same time embodying an intensive version of that equation.

The ramifications of this 'aestheticisation of politics' are apparent in many of the more intolerant and fearful twitchings of the middle-class backlash in England today, from the arrogant antics of Mary Whitehouse to the synthetic posturings of Margaret Thatcher. But the campaign to create in Thatcher the quintessentially 'British' woman is no accident: as in Nazi Germany, the logic of an appeal to an inexpressible 'nation' can only culminate in a politics of personality, in an 'image' in flesh of the *living* norm for a whole society. And, as in Nazi Germany, control over the mass media, the mass reproduction of images, is inevitably a crucial weapon in the aestheticisation of politics: it is in the daily dramatisation of a dramatised society that aestheticised politics finds its most pervasive expression. Benjamin, at the beginning of his 1936 essay, quotes a prophetic comment of Valéry: 'Just as water, gas and electricity are brought into our houses from far off to satisfy our needs in response to a minimal effort, so we shall be supplied with visual or auditory images, which will appear and disappear at a simple movement of the hand, hardly more than a sign'; Benjamin's own concluding sentences in that essay are even more prophetic:

'*Fiat ars—pereat mundus*', says Fascism, and, as Marinetti admits, expects war to supply the artistic gratification of a sense perception that has been changed by technology. This is evidently the consummation of '*l'art pour l'art*'. Mankind, which in Homer's time was an object of contemplation for the Olympian gods, now is one for itself. Its self-alienation has reached such a degree that it can experience its own destruction as an aesthetic pleasure of the first order. This is the situation of politics which Fascism is rendering aesthetic. Communism responds by politicising art.

In that final comment the work of, above all, Bertolt Brecht is broached; it was perhaps Brecht who found the most important way of developing beyond the ratiocinative element in art that had emerged so single-mindedly in Poe, without collapsing back into a safely 'aesthetic' response to crime, violence and corruption. Brecht's own direction had already been signalled in the title of his 1927 essay *Shouldn't we abolish Aesthetics?*

The logic of the aestheticisation of politics leads not only to a politics of personality but to a legislation of personalities: as the ineffable norm of national normality becomes the linchpin of a pervasive ideology, the pressure grows to extend the legal net to cover (once again?) more and more facets of life-style: if explicit criminalisation is not achieved, the grounds for suspicion of criminal intent are gradually extended to cover more and more 'questionable', 'undesirable', 'unconventional' modes of life and thought. That, in England now, someone is young, black and unemployed can be sufficient grounds to justify a body-search or arrest 'on suspicion'. That, in Germany now, someone once lived in the same house as a member of the KPD (Communist Party) can be sufficient grounds for depriving them of a teaching post. That, in the Soviet Union now, someone has given an interview to an American journalist can be sufficient grounds for suspecting their sanity. At the same time, the aestheticisation of politics can increasingly diminish the possibility of any publicly canvassed alternative mode of political analysis: when 'scientific' psephology is the media's substitute for investigation of political demands, and the melodrama of personality-clashes in the Commons replaces any coherent presentation and explanation of policies, the likelihood of even any feeble continuation of a 'system of parliamentary democracy' must be called in question. But in any case, one of the functions of the 'quasi-political compromise' of 'parliamentary democracy' is to obscure the basic structural contradiction of combining late capitalism with a non-totalitarian political system.

According to Chandler, 'All of my novels started from some known or unknown fact. Most of my work came from knowing or hearing of an inside news story that could not be published. Then fiction took over.' It was presumably not only Marlowe who, in *The Big Sleep*, was protecting the rich from the disclosure of their crimes. It was once the ambition of fiction, and the hope of aesthetics, that in art the truth might be made public and apparent. As 'fiction' takes over in the late twentieth century its function may be, increasingly, to leave the truth concealed. Perhaps in that context it may be the critic who takes on the peculiarly ambivalent role of a private eye.

Section C: Accusation, Perjury, Confession

Question 9: Franz Kafka, *Der Prozess*

Kafka's *The Trial* begins: 'Someone must have been telling lies about Joseph K., for without having done anything wrong he was arrested one fine morning' (*The Trial*, translated by Willa and Edwin Muir, Penguin edition, 1966, p.7; cited hereafter by page number only). Necessarily, Kafka is himself telling a kind of 'lie', since here he is asserting as 'true' something he knows not to be true: fiction is not truth—though neither is it untruth. But it is not necessarily Kafka who tells us that 'Someone must have been telling lies' and that K. was arrested 'without having done anything wrong', since the whole novel is written in a curious third-person subjective, from the viewpoint of the third-person singular that is 'he': the reader is formally restricted, by this textual strategy, to K.'s perspective throughout. Which means that K. may possibly be the 'someone' 'telling lies', since the question seemingly at issue is whether K. *has* done something 'wrong' or not. But even if we *knew*, from outside K.'s perspective, that K. had indeed committed some 'crime' we could not therefore conclude that K. was 'lying' in telling us (if he does) that he had done nothing wrong, since there is one difference between 'wrong' and 'crime' and another between 'telling a lie' and telling an 'untruth'. Fiction is a kind of 'lie' because we tell it 'as true' knowing it to be untrue; but we may even tell an untruth without lying provided we believe it to be true, just as we can lie while telling the truth provided we believe it (erroneously) to be untrue. We therefore have a logical criterion of lying even if we have no logical criterion of truth; but we have no empirical criterion of someone else lying (since the liar may be lying in telling us that he was or wasn't lying, and only he can tell us), even if we claim to have an empirical criterion of truth.

On the logic of these problems the novel is constituted; on the logic of the same problems every legal trial which depends upon the distinction between perjury and 'telling the truth' is vulnerable: when the accused pleads that he is 'not guilty' we, as jury, do not immediately believe him (otherwise there would be no trial); when a witness states his testimony we presume to believe it (otherwise there would be no witnessing). The relation between 'truth' and the various participants in a trial is curiously and interestingly diverse, yet for a trial to operate at all we must accept the risks of systematic and collusive lying among witnesses while discounting the plea of the accused as simply a necessary gesture in a ritual. (Perhaps only a 'show trial' which rests on an alternative notion of 'objective guilt' may escape these dilemmas.)

218

Throughout the novel, however, because of its third-person subjective viewpoint, we seem, as reader, to be allowed privileged access to precisely that area closed off to a law court: the mind of the accused. Surely we can therefore judge whether K. is *lying* or not, even if we cannot judge whether he is telling the truth. But because K. is never told of what he is accused, our privileged position does not allow us, or K. (unless he is lying), to know *what* it is that would crucially condemn him (at least as a perjurer) if he did lie. What we do know is that K. asserts that he wants to be acquitted and to be declared innocent. But there is another distinction between being acquitted and being innocent: given the problems (among others) of lying and perjury, it is possible both for the innocent to be found legally guilty and for the legally guilty to be in fact acquitted. Logically, indeed, only the accused could really judge his own innocence or guilt—of perjury at least. It is not necessary to his guilt or innocence that he be tried and found either legally guilty or legally not guilty. To believe that it is necessary is to believe an untruth; to believe that it is not necessary and to assert that it is, even to oneself, is to lie. But a legal system, one might insist, cannot be concerned with guilt and innocence, only with the legal declaration of guilty or not-guilty; but then, of course, a legal trial cannot establish for the accused his guilt or innocence; any accused who thinks that it can is misled, and one who knows that it can't and yet insists that it can is lying. And yet what are guilt and innocence if they are not to be equated with legal guilt and non-guilt? But if they are so equated a court has nothing to discover; it has only to pronounce. And if they are not so equated, what is it that a court finally pronounces upon? It seems necessary to assert that legal guilt is and is not to be equated with that guilt which is not merely legal guilt—but then no judgement can resolve its own ambivalent relation to the judgement it pronounces.

Kafka's novel twists some of these threads tighter at a moment when K. tells us, and himself, that he is lying. When the Priest finishes his last interpretation of the Parable of the Law, the text reads:

'I don't agree with that point of view,' said K., shaking his head, 'for if one accepts it, one must accept as true everything the doorkeeper says. But you yourself have sufficiently proved how impossible it is to do that.' 'No,' said the priest, 'it is not necessary to accept everything as true, one must only accept it as necessary.' 'A melancholy conclusion,' said K. 'It turns lying into a universal principle.'

(p.243)

The exchange is a characteristic spiral of logic. K. concludes that if *everything* is to be accepted as necessary but not necessarily as true, then something may be necessary without being true, indeed *everything* may be necessary without being true: 'the lie' may indeed be 'the order of the world' (to adapt the translation of this same phrase by Douglas Scott and Chris Waller in their translation of *The Trial*; Picador, 1977, p.246), even if we cannot know whether it is—though if it *might* be, we would have to proceed on the assumption that *nothing* is true. (Such a world would be, perhaps, an anti-world to one of Hegel's.) But, of course, K.'s own conclusion depends upon a self-contradictory premise: if the priest's words are taken to apply to the world, rather than to the text of the parable, then they defeat themselves: if *everything* is to be accepted as *necessary*, it must also be *necessary* to accept everything as true—*and* as not true. Alternatively, if it is not necessary to accept everything as true, we do not have to accept as true the claim that everything is necessary. And then to assert that something, or anything, is necessary may be to lie, not just to tell an untruth. In any case, in saying that 'it turns lying into a universal principle' K. is already equivocating: 'K. said that with finality, but it was not his final judgement' (p.243). And immediately after, we are given an instance of him lying that something is necessary: the priest asks K. 'Do you want to leave already?', and 'although at that moment K. had not been thinking of leaving' he answers 'Of course, I must go'—yet a moment later we read: 'his immediate return to the Bank was not so necessary as he had made out, he could quite well stay longer'. Meanwhile, ' "You have to leave now," said the priest. "Well, yes," said K., "you must see that I can't help it." "You must first see that I can't help being what I am," said the priest' (p.244—an overtonal rather than literal translation). K., we know (we think), is lying. The priest, we may suggest, is telling an untruth: 'I can't help being what I am.' If that were true, K. too, presumably, could not 'help' being what he is—in which case either he cannot be 'guilty' or his guilt is 'objective', determined in advance by what he cannot help; if we have to accept *everything*, including our own guilt or innocence, as unavoidable, as necessary, then we can make no sense of 'guilt' and 'innocence'. On the other hand, if we *can* 'help' being what we are, then what we are is not necessary, including what we are or do at any particular moment: to claim that we *have* to do *anything*, even to return to a Bank on time, would then be untrue; we do not even *have* to *be* at all, our very existence or continued existence is not *necessary*. Indeed, the possibility that hovers is that *nothing* is necessary at all.

Though perhaps there is one exception: it may not be necessary that we be born, but once we are born it is necessary that we die. The penultimate untruth—or desparate lie—that K. tells concerns the ancient, fatal syllogism: 'Logic is doubtless unshakable, but it cannot withstand a man who wants to go on living' (p.250). It can. It does. And as he dies K. utters the final self-deception: ' "Like a dog!" he said.' But he doesn't, and cannot, die 'like a dog', since, as Erich Fried—pursuing this logic—has written:

> A dog
> that dies
> and that knows
> that it dies
> like a dog
>
> and that can say
> that it knows
> that it dies
> like a dog
> is a man

Erich Fried, *On Pain of Seeing*, London 1969, p.11

One of the reasons why K. does not die like a dog is that (according to Wittgenstein at least) 'a dog cannot be a hypocrite, but neither can it be sincere'

(*Philosophical Investigations*, p.229), and in judging his own dying to be like a dog's K. is perhaps sincere but, more likely, a hypocrite; he cannot be neither.

It would be possible both to pursue further the relations between truth, lying and necessity in *The Trial* itself and to examine related strands in Kafka's other work—for example in *The Judgement*, or *In the Penal Colony*, or, especially perhaps, in *The Castle*, where K.'s claim (lie?) that he is the Land Surveyor is the first of many exaggerations and deceptions which structure the life of the village and of the novel, and which are doubled in the exaggerated significance attached to the 'castle' by critics. One could also analyse Kafka's own desparate attempts to be 'honest' about his own relationships in his correspondence with Milena and with Felice, or in his *Letter* to his father. His whole relationship with his father, and the connections between fatherhood and the 'law', could also be examined. Kafka's legal education, apprenticeship and work is obviously relevant (think of the attempted precision of his reports for the insurance company); so is his grasp of the 'religious' problem of 'The Fall' (think, for example, of the typical remark: 'Original sin, that old injustice committed by man, consists in the complaint unceasingly made by man that he has been the victim of an injustice, the victim of original sin'). It would also be feasible to sketch an analysis of *The Trial* in terms of the different ideological apparatuses focussed upon in each chapter, the whole under the dominion of 'the Law'. But though these facets are important, the *central* strategy of *The Trial* is to place the reader, alongside K., at the point where the 'logic, rules and procedures' of 'the law' converge: the position of the accused.

The 'accused' is a *necessary* premise for those rules and procedures, for that logic, to operate at all; but it is not necessary for the accused to be anyone in particular—the trial can, and will, proceed even if the accused is 'the wrong man'; it is not even legally necessary for the accused to be present at the trial, or even known (one can be accused 'with persons unknown'): a mere 'K.' or even a number can suffice on occasion. And perhaps, so long as there *is*, somewhere, an accused, there needn't, after all, be any specific accusation; certainly, the 'wrong' accusation is no impediment to the logic of the court: the rules of logic are not contingent upon any specific content. As we read *The Trial* we ourselves perhaps necessarily supply a content for that unformulated accusation: we too are caught within the process of the text, we too begin to 'tell lies' about 'K.', perhaps to accuse him (in our 'interpretations') of crimes, or wrongs, or faults, which we guiltily feel ourselves to be accused of by the novel, or which we (innocently, and erroneously) think are somehow 'necessary' crimes. At that point we should perhaps recognise that *we* have placed *ourselves* in the dock with K.; prosecutor and accused change places, or perhaps their functions fuse—as in the initial plea of some accused: 'Guilty'. It is the logic of that situating which we can see being worked through in novels subsequent to Kafka.

(Unfinished—no time)

Question 12: Albert Camus, *La Chute*

For if the Idea of Beauty appears only in dispersed form among many works, each one nevertheless aims uncompromisingly to express the whole of beauty, claims it in its singularity and can never admit its dispersal without annulling itself. Beauty, as single, true and liberated from appearance and individuation, manifests itself not in the synthesis of all works, in the unity of the arts and of art, but only as a physical reality: in the downfall of art itself. This downfall is the goal of every work of art, in that it seeks to bring death to all others. That all art aims to end art, is another way of saying the same thing. It is this impulse to self-destruction inherent in works of art . . . that is constantly stirring up the aesthetic disputes that are apparently so futile.

Theodor Adorno, *Minima Moralia*

Fully to situate Camus's *The Fall* (1956) would involve considering, at least, his pre-war membership of the Algerian Communist Party, his passion for truthful reporting while working for *Alger Républicain*, his treatment of the relationship between a moment of 'crime' and the procedures of the law-court in *L'Étranger* (1940), his involvement with the Resistance and, particularly, his dispute with Mauriac over the capital punishment of French traitors after the war, his quarrel with Sartre over Sartre's reaction to *L'Homme Revolté* (1951)—during which Sartre described Camus's position as that of a paternalistic 'advocate' for the oppressed, the impact of Kafka's work on Camus's 'philosophy', the general impact of Koestler's *Darkness at Noon* (published in France in 1946) on the French debate about the Soviet concentration camps (cf. Merleau-Ponty's *Humanism and Terror* for something of that debate) and —perhaps most centrally—Camus's political silence on the Algerian situation from 1945 to 1954 and his opposition to the FLN thereafter (cf. Conor Cruise O'Brien, *Camus*, London 1970, pp. 64–75). But it is on the strategies and tactics of the text itself that I want to focus.

One immediate indication of the basic strategy is retained in French even in the English translation (by Justin O'Brien, Penguin edition, 1963, cited hereafter by page number only): the shifting terms of address used by Clamence to his listener—*Monsieur* (p.5ff), *Monsieur et cher compatriote* (p.13ff), *cher Monsieur* (p.16ff), *mon cher compatriote* (p.33ff), *cher ami* (p.54ff), *mon cher ami* (p.57ff), *mon cher* (p.72), *cher ami* (p.78), *mon ami* (p.87), *très cher* (p.100) and, finally, *cher maître* in the closing words of the book. That gradual increase in familiarity is an index to the relationship that is courteously and skilfully established and confirmed and it is one not only between Clamence and his silent listener but also between Clamence and the reader, who, in 'silently' reading the monologue of *The Fall*, enacts the voice of Clamence, plays the role of the speaker to whom the reader also 'silently' listens; the reader is positioned as both of the actors in this dramatic monologue that is a 'dialogue of a special kind'. From the opening of the text the reader is offered a double-role which he remains as free to refuse as a bar-room customer approached by a stranger: 'May I, Monsieur, offer my services without running the risk of intruding?' (p.5). To accept such an offer is always a risk; to go on reading is always a risk. Mockingly, the reader, in the guise of that silent drinker in an Amsterdam bar, is given his opportunity for refusal: 'Now I shall withdraw, Monsieur, happy to have been of help to you. Thank you; I'd accept if I were sure of not being a nuisance. You are too kind. Then I shall bring my glass over beside yours' (p.5). From that moment it will take more than discourtesy or rudeness to slide away; it will soon take a kind of cowardice. Within a page our own reactions are being both responded to and prompted by the text: 'If that be foolish. . . . Ah, I see you smile at that use of the subjunctive' (p.6); and soon we are offered a description which we, perhaps, uneasily, admit does, more or less, in a way, fit us:

Pleased to know you. You are in business, no doubt? In a way? Excellent reply! Judicious too: in all things we are merely 'in a way'. Now, allow me to play the detective. You are my age in a way, with the sophisticated eye of the man in his forties who has seen everything, in a way; you are well dressed in a way, that is as people are in our country; and your hands are smooth. Hence a bourgeois, in a way! But a cultured bourgeois! Smiling at the use of the subjunctive, in fact, proves your culture twice over because you recognise it to begin with and then because you feel superior to it. Lastly, I amuse you. And be it said without vanity, this implies in you a certain open-mindedness. Consequently you are in a way . . . But no matter. Professions interest me less than sects. Allow me to ask you two questions and don't answer if you consider them indiscreet. Do you have any possessions? Some? Good. Have you shared them with the poor? No? Then you are what I call a Sadducee. If you are not familiar with the Scriptures, I admit that this won't help you. But it does help you? So you know the Scriptures? Decidedly, you interest me.

(pp.8–9)

By this stage we know that our interlocutor calls himself a 'judge-penitent' (p.8), which may merely suggest a penitent judge, or perhaps a modern version of a friar-penitent, but hints in either case at a curious fusion of roles normally separated: someone positioned simultaneously as judge (about to judge) and as penitent (the accused already found guilty and undergoing penance). We have been steered away from judging in the first few pages ('Mind you, I'm not judging him', page 6; 'Still, let us take care not to condemn him', page 7), but now we are explicitly invited to judge the judge-penitent himself: 'As for me . . . Well, judge for yourself.' (p.9).

At the second meeting (perhaps with that mockingly polite invitation still in our ears—'Try it!', page 14), we are given more upon which to judge, as Clamence unfolds the story of his life in Paris, a life that he can summarise at this stage in ostensibly self-satisfied phrases:

. . . just imagine, I beg you, a man at the height of his powers, in perfect health, generously gifted, skilled in bodily exercises as in those of the mind, neither rich nor poor, sleeping well and fundamentally pleased with himself without showing this otherwise than by a happy sociability. You will readily see how I can speak, without immodesty, of a successful life.

(p.22)

No reader can, I presume, get this far without a certain unease or even repulsion at Clamence's self-description: the whole portrait has a subtle tone of corruption about it, an ideal turned into a perversity; like J. H. Newman's description of the liberal English gentleman, this portrait seems pervasively yet never precisely askew to the model it simultaneously evokes yet undermines. The question that is being put to us already is: 'by what standards are you judging?' For in the complex interplay of this whole passage (pp.15–32) a number of possible grounds for an adverse judgement are both suggested and allowed for in advance: if we sense that Clamence is selfish, he counters with Aristotle—'I enjoyed my own nature to the fullest and we all know that therein lies happiness, although, to soothe one another mutually, we occasionally pretend to condemn such joys as selfishness', and we are forced to ponder that 'pretend'. If we lean towards pride or hypocrisy as Clamence's crucial fault, we have to recognise that the hypocrisy and pride are accompanied by a peculiar honesty and humility, since it is Clamence himself who paints this double-faced portrait. In any case, *which* Clamence are we judging? If we feel that the Clamence of his 'Edenic' period (cf. p.22) is to be judged severely, or even adversely, is it not the Clamence now speaking who allows us to see that—and doesn't that rather qualify our judgement? The tactic of this section is perhaps signalled in those two separated but mutually-echoing comments: 'we have to have judges, don't we?' (p.16) and 'it set me above the judge whom I judged in turn' (p.21); we feel called upon to judge this self-portrait while sensing that the man who provides it has already, like a subtle Titorelli, forseen and reckoned with our judgement. And if we settle back to follow this complex game with mere accepting amusement, we are ambushed in our smile by the comment: 'My reflection was smiling in the mirror, but it seemed to me that my smile was double . . .' (p.31). And this sense of the complex joke being against us is uneasily confirmed by the last few sentences of this section:

If pimps and thieves were invariably sentenced, all decent people would get to thinking they themselves were constantly innocent, *cher Monsieur*. And in my opinion—all right, all right, I'm coming!—that's what must be avoided at all costs. Otherwise, everything would be just a joke.
(p.32)

As the monologue of the third meeting develops, the tactic of the text becomes even clearer: the examples of behaviour we feel called upon to disapprove of multiply and begin to rouse uneasy echoes of our own behaviour; each reader is being prompted to a self-recognition in at least some of the incidents and attitudes that are laid before us—and each will respond to a different pattern in this skilfully constructed account. No reader will have experienced quite the same rankling humiliations or utilised exactly the same devious strategems as Clamence, but the details of the text serve by this stage very much as cues to our own memories, trailers for those 'little films' we too run 'a hundred times' in our imagination—or which we slyly censor even in our private cinema. The invitation is by now explicit:

if everyone told all, displayed his true profession and identity, we shouldn't know which way to turn! Just fancy visiting cards: Dupont, jittery philosopher, or Christian landowner, or adulterous humanist—indeed, there's a wide choice. But it would be hell! Yes, hell must be like that: streets filled with shop-signs and no way of explaining oneself. One is classified once and for all.
    You, for instance, *mon cher compatriote*, stop and think of what your sign would be. You are silent? Well, you'll tell me later on.
(p.36)

When, finally, we are given the incident at the 'centre' of Clamence's memory—the girl on the bridge, the fall, the hesitation, the turning away—its details are specific (so specific as to leave judgement, like decision, finely poised in welcome doubt), but its significance is general; we could all disclaim any definite action, any particular commission; it is harder to maintain our innocence when accused, however implicitly, of inaction, of hesitation, of turning away, of the sin of *omission*.
    The next two sections can be slid over quickly here—they offer themselves,

to some extent, precisely as temptations to that response: 'the question is how to slip through and, above all—yes, above all, the question is how to elude judgement' (p.57). But the final section repeats and makes explicit the strategy of the whole:

I know what you're thinking: it's very hard to disentangle the true from the false in what I'm saying. I admit you're right. I myself . . .

(p.88)

That broken, suspended phrase allows us to register, quite clearly, the Camus who offers himself as, in part, Clamence. One of the temptations of the text is to read it as autobiographical, as confessional, in however displaced a fashion, for Camus himself; it is a comforting way of distancing Clamence from ourselves. The paragraph continues on a different tack:

You see, a person I knew used to divide human beings into three categories: those who prefer having nothing to hide rather than being obliged to lie, those who prefer lying to having nothing to hide, and finally those who like both lying and the hidden. I'll let you choose which case suits me best.

(p.88)

The reader has also, by this stage, to choose which category suits the reader best—or if he rejects the categories offered, to decide what he would say instead. For it is clear that the grip of the text has been all along designed to close upon the reader:

in short I adapt my words to my listener and lead him to go me one better. I mingle what concerns me and what concerns others, I choose the features we have in common, the experiences we have endured together, the failings we share—good form, the man of the moment, in fact, such as reigns in me and in others. With all that I construct a portrait which is the image of all and of no one. A mask, in short, rather like those carnival masks which are both lifelike and stylised so that they make people say: 'Why, surely I've met him!' When the portrait is finished, as it is this evening, I show it with great sorrow: 'This, alas, is what I am!' The prosecutor's charge is finished. But at the same time the portrait I hold out to my contemporaries becomes a mirror.

(p.102)

By this mirror-portrait,

I provoke you into judging yourself, and this relieves me of that much of the burden. Ah, *mon cher*, we are odd, wretched creatures and, if we merely look back over our lives, there's no lack of occasions to amaze and scandalise ourselves. Just try. I shall listen, you may be sure, to your own confession with a great feeling of fraternity.

(p.103)

But, of course, Clamence cannot listen to our confession. The whole operation of the text, as text, is necessarily one-sided. But to *read* the text is to enter into a complex dialectic, a dialogical relation with ourselves, the end-term of which may well be a curious kind of confession. At the centre of that dialectic is Clamence's 'judgement' on Clamence, not only the Clamence of his Edenic days but the Clamence who speaks in the present: 'I haven't changed my way of life; I continue to love myself and to make use of others' (p.104). But we also, as reader, are provoked to judge Clamence's judgement of himself, and insofar as we recognise the distance between Clamence and Camus we are faced with the task of understanding Camus's judgement on his own character Clamence (and perhaps also the judgement on an earlier, or

225

present, Camus expressed through that character); but we have also, then, to judge those judgements of Camus—while at the same time Camus is, by the very complexity of his text, testing our own capacity for judgement: at what points, and for what reasons, do we stand back from Clamence and refuse his attitudes, opinions, judgements? The crucial question is: for what reasons? If we can articulate the grounds of our 'judgement' in this multi-layered (OK: multi-lawyered) case, what are they? One might even ask what *kind* of 'grounds' are they? Or do we have any at all?

One easy, distancing, response is to treat the novel firmly as a disguised polemic, with pre-chosen and safely remote targets: as, for example, 'a satirical portrait of left-wing intellectuals as Camus saw them, lost in the nihilistic desert of 20th century ideologies, led astray by their own systematic abstractions' (Emmett Parker). The epigraph from Lermontov lends some support to this kind of reading:

Some were dreadfully insulted, and quite seriously, to have held up as a model such an immoral character as *A Hero of Our Time*; others shrewdly noticed that the author had portrayed himself and his acquaintances. . . . *A Hero of Our Time*, gentlemen, is in fact a portrait but not of an individual; it is the aggregate of the vices of our whole generation in their fullest expression.

But that 'shrewdly' may rather register an ironic anticipation of a predictable interpretation, while that final sentence merely brings us back to the problem of judging the 'vices' we are invited to recognise—and of judging them to be vices in the first place. If we duck the problem of 'judging' then we are perhaps reproducing the 'fall' that is at the centre of the novel: we take note of the problem, recognise it as a difficult and demanding problem, and then turn away. The logic of that refusal is either to decline the instrusion of Clamence in the first place (never really to *read* the text) or to close the novel merely with the relief of having it behind us, a safe and distanced memory of reading ('Fortunately'); on the basis of either response we can, coolly, skilfully, professionally, 'place' the novel in its 'historical' context, as time passed, as past time.

Another, familiar, response is to opt, respectfully, perhaps 'critically', for an 'aesthetic' judgement upon *The Fall* 'as a novel'—to quote, for example, Sartre's moving and eloquent tribute:

One lived with or against his thought, such as he revealed it to us in his books—*La Chute*, above all, perhaps the most beautiful and the least understood—but always through it. It was a singular adventure of our culture, a movement whose phases and final term one tried to guess.

—and to pick out that phrase, 'the most beautiful and the least understood', and, after some suitable elaboration, to leave it, more or less, at that. Such an 'aesthetic' or 'literary critical' response must seem inadequate; but perhaps it holds a clue to the paradox and the pressure of the actual reading experience of the novel. At one point in the text we are reminded of a certain kind of 'aesthetic judgement'. Clamence justifies his retention of the painting of *The Just Judges*, the stolen panel from the Van Eyck altarpiece *The Adoration of the Lamb*, and offers, among other reasons, the claim that

among all those who file past *The Adoration of the Lamb* no one could distinguish the copy from the original.

(p.95)

226

To file past the copy in reverent admiration, accepting the pre-packaged judgement of the guide-book, is merely to consume a cultural commodity, to clock up an item in a tourist's educational schedule. Of course, those who have the expensive privilege of not merely filing past might protest that *they* at least, the dedicated experts, can indeed 'distinguish the copy from the original': given the very materiality of the art-object in this case, a 'copy' could be easily detected by the useful, though of course ancillary, scientific tests of the auctioneer; and given the other 'authentic' panels of the polyptych any well-trained art-historian could heuristically sketch the missing components and assess a forgery against that absent ideal, even if the missing bit had never been known to them (though in this case, as Camus perhaps knew, the Van Eyck altarpiece is noticeably 'incoherent' by the received standards of the art-historians of the period). But if our task is neither to nod with second-hand awe nor to carbon-date an expensive investment, what is our response to be? If we seek to make that kind of 'judgement' known as 'aesthetic', what is the basis for our judgement?

Walter Benjamin, meditating on that ancient distinction between the 'original' and the 'copy' (Plato in his own way was concerned with it), has probed the effects of dislodging the art-object from its cultic niche and function; he argues that the 'aura' of the original is dissolved in the era of technical reproduction, leaving behind only muffled and ambivalent traces in the practices of cultural exhibition (one aim of which is, arguably, to enhance the 'aura' of the original precisely as 'an original'); more crucially, when the processes of artistic production render the notion of *any* 'original' unintelligible ('to ask for the "authentic" print makes no sense'; did it ever make sense to ask for the "authentic" *Hamlet*?—for different reasons), 'the total function of art is reversed: instead of being based on ritual, it begins to be based on politics' (Benjamin, 'The Work of Art in the Age of Mechanical Reproduction'). But before we return to Benjamin's insight here, it is worth detouring through a phase he does not consider. The 'novel' is already an example of a 'work of art in an age of mechanical reproduction': it never made any sense to ask for the 'original copy' of *Tom Jones*.

At the moment of the appearance of *Tom Jones* one kind of response to it was already formed and waiting, a reaction exemplified in Samuel Johnson's comment, recounted by Hannah More:

I never saw Johnson really angry with me but once, and his displeasure did him so much honour that I loved him the better for it. I alluded rather flippantly, I fear, to some witty passage in Tom Jones: he replied, 'I am shocked to hear you quote from so vicious a book. I am sorry to hear you have read it; a confession which no modest lady should ever make. I scarcely know a more corrupt work.'

Sir John Hawkins spelt out the basis of Johnson's reaction in a celebrated piece of invective against *Tom Jones*:

a book seemingly intended to sap the foundation of that morality which it is the duty of parents and all public instructors to inculcate in the minds of young people, by teaching that virtue upon principle is imposture, that generous qualities alone constitute true worth, and that a young man may love and be loved, and at the same time associate with the loosest women. His morality, in that it resolves virtue into good affections, in contradiction to moral obligation and a sense of duty, is that of Lord Shaftesbury vulgarised, and is a system of excellent use in palliating the vices most injurious to society. He was the inventor of that cant-phrase 'goodness of heart', which is every day used as a substitute for probity, and means little more than the virtue of a horse or a dog: in short, he has done more towards corrupting the rising generation than any writer we know of.

Hawkins and Johnson, in accusing Fielding of *philosophical naivety* about the nature of morality (like Rubashov in *Darkness at Noon*, perhaps, they do not accept that 'subjective' intention or personal character can take precedence over the 'objective' principles by which we should be governed), are also condemning Fielding's novel. That interpenetration of moral and 'critical' judgement is, of course, inherited, endorsed and perpetuated in an English critical tradition that passes through Arnold to Leavis—Leavis's refusal to give the ultimate 'grounds' of his criticism was due, in its way, to a sound eighteenth-century instinct, just as his sense of personal 'authority' has one of its roots in that eighteenth-century practice, instanced in a letter of Goldsmith's in 1758, of awarding poets marks out of 20 for 'Judgement'—the critic himself necessarily scoring the maximum. T. S. Eliot indicated one undercurrent in this censorious tradition when he remarked: 'I view Johnson's *Lives* as a master-piece of the judicial bench'. Fielding himself had already recognised the parallel (it is more than a parallel for him):

I must desire all those critics to mind their own business, and not to intermeddle with affairs or works which in no ways concern them; for till they produce the authority by which they are constituted judges, I shall not plead to their jurisdiction.

Tom Jones, I, ii

I shall not look upon myself as accountable to any court of critical jurisdiction whatever; for as I am, in reality, the founder of a new province of writing, so I am at liberty to make what laws I please therein.

Tom Jones, II, ii

One effect of that tradition of interweaving 'aesthetic, 'moral' and 'judicial' criticism is perhaps to allow political judgements to appear in 'criticism' in a disarmingly disguised form—as in the judicial pronouncements of the Old Bailey, or the moral judgements of the BBC censors, or the aesthetic policy declarations of the Arts Council; but another effect has been to help engender an apparently opposite reaction: the radical separation of the 'aesthetic' from any other kind of judgement, including 'moral' and 'political' (precisely the rationale of the Arts Council). In its more sophisticated form—popularly articulated by Oscar Wilde in the preface to *The Picture of Dorian Gray*—this latter reaction proposed *l'art pour l'art*; in its popular form—still sophisti-catedly articulated by a host of smoothly privileged pundits—this reaction led to an enthroning of 'taste'. Benjamin sketches another, and more basic, reason for this double-faceted counter-tradition:

Taste develops with the definite preponderance of commodity production over any other kind of production. As a consequence of the manufacture of products as commodities for the market, people become less and less aware of the conditions of their production—not only of the social conditions in the form of exploitation, but of the technical conditions as well. . . . In the same measure as the expertness of a customer declines, the importance of his taste increases—both for him and for the manufacturer. For the customer it has the value of a more or less elaborate masking of his lack of expertness. . . . It is precisely this development which literature reflects in *l'art pour l'art*. This doctrine and its corresponding practice for the first time give taste a dominant position in poetry. . . . In *l'art pour l'art* the poet for the first time faces language the way the buyer faces the commodity on the open market. He has lost his familiarity with the process of its production to a particularly high degree. The poets of *l'art pour l'art* are the last about whom it can be said that they come 'from the people'. They have nothing to formulate with such urgency that it could determine the *coining* of their words. Rather, they have to choose their words. . . . . The poet of *l'art pour l'art* wanted to bring to language above all himself—with all the idiosyncracies, nuances, and imponderables of his nature. These elements are reflected in taste. The poet's taste guides him in his choice of words. . . . At the end of this development may be found Mallarmé and the theory of *poésie pure*. There the cause of his own class has become so far removed from the poet that the problem of a literature without an object becomes the centre of discussion.

Charles Baudelaire, London 1973, pp.104–6

This passage is best understood not in terms of its 'juxtapositionism'— commercial developments 'and' literary developments—but rather as indicating a specific series of shifts 'within' the cultural apparatus; it echoes Brecht's note on 'The Reading of Plays', concerning *Threepenny Opera*:

Its publication represents little more than the prompt book of a play wholly surrendered to theatres, and thus is directed at the expert rather than at the consumer. This doesn't mean that the conversion of the maximum number of readers or spectators into experts is not thoroughly desirable; indeed it is under way.

Adorno suggests a perhaps more generous account of *l'art pour l'art* than Benjamin: that, to adapt E. P. Thompson's phrase about law, it was concerned with art's 'own logic, rules and procedures—that is, with art simply *as art*'. In his *Philosophy of Modern Music* Adorno offers an account which is partly complementary to Benjamin's (as concerned with changes in artist-audience relations) but which, in considering also a later phase, and a different art-form, partly disputes Benjamin's implicit evaluation and certainly refuses Brecht's optimism:

From the middle of the nineteenth century on, good music has renounced commercialism altogether. The consequence of its further development has come into conflict with the manipulated and, at the same time, self-satisfied needs of the bourgeois public. The pathetically small number of connoisseurs was gradually replaced by all those who could afford the price of a ticket and wished to demonstrate their culture to others. An abyss developed between public taste and compositional quality. . . . Radically modern music could no longer count on . . . support. Quality may be determined according to the same standards in advanced works as well as in traditional works—perhaps even more easily—despite the limitations of these standards. The prevailing musical language no longer removes the burden of accuracy and integrity from the shoulders of the composer. At the same time, the self-appointed mediators have sacrificed their capacity to make such judgements. Since the compositional procedure is gauged simply according to the inherent form of every work—not according to tacitly accepted, general demands—it is no longer possible to 'learn' definitively what constitutes good or bad music. Whoever would pass judgement must face squarely the immutable questions and antagonisms of the individual compositional structure, about which no general music history can teach. No one could be better suited to this task than the progressive composer, whom discursive reasoning most eludes. He can no longer depend upon mediators between himself and the public. Critics live literally according to the 'high reason' expressed in the song by Gustav Mahler: they evaluate according to what they do and do not understand.

Philosophy of Modern Music, London 1973, p.8

These comments of Adorno bring us back to one phrase in Sartre's remark about *The Fall*: 'perhaps the most beautiful and the least understood'; for Adorno, a 'critic' will only venture to evaluate positively what he 'already' understands, but such a critic is debarred from that very 'familiarity with the process of . . . production' which is the only basis for 'understanding' when the object of evaluation is 'the inherent form' of 'the individual compositional structure', its peculiar 'questions and antagonisms'; it is, for Adorno, the 'radical' composer who (despite Benjamin's counter-case) is most 'expertly' concerned with the 'material' which is 'included in the process of ... production' of art, whether that 'material' be musical or linguistic. But to speak of 'the inherent form' (as Adorno does) and of the 'material' (as I have just done) of a work of art is to reintroduce a distinction which Benjamin at least struggled to reject: that between 'form' and 'content', precisely the distinction which is at issue in the conflation of 'moral' and 'aesthetic' judgement and which haunts the long debate about 'politics' and 'art'.

At this point it is worth returning to *The Fall*. I suggested earlier that the problem posed for the reader by the strategy of the novel is that in reading the novel he is drawn into a complex dialectic of judging judgements and is thereby invited to reflect upon the grounds of his own judgement. Towards the end of the penultimate meeting Clamence speaks of himself as 'Elijah without a messiah', 'showering imprecations on lawless men who cannot endure any judgement', and he comments:

He who clings to a law does not fear the judgement that puts him in his place within an order he believes in. But the keenest of human torments is to be judged without law. Yet we are in that torment.

p.86

The 'torment' that faces the critic who attempts to 'judge' a work, the 'inherent form' of which is closed to him, is that of 'judging without law', of attempting to come to a 'judgement' while being ignorant of the 'law' that governs the object of that judgement. (One could reformulate along these lines Fielding's remarks about critics and about making what 'laws' he pleases in his new province of writing.) But the same could be said of the composer himself, on Adorno's account: for if 'the prevailing musical language no longer removes the burden of accuracy and integrity from the shoulders of the composer' and if 'the compositional procedure is gauged simply according to the inherent form of every work' and if, finally, 'whoever would pass judgement must face squarely the immutable questions and anatagonisms of the individual compositional structure', then how is the composer to 'judge' his 'own' composition and what would it mean for him to do so? In the actual *process* of *production* the composer would seem to face most acutely that 'torment' of judging (and of being judged) 'without law', without the *already* achieved 'inherent form' of the 'compositional structure' which provides its own 'logic, rules and procedures'. There is, of course, a readily-available 'Romantic' version of that 'torment': the agonies of creation, the struggle with the inner soul seeking expression; and in that hybrid character Adrian Leverkühn we can discern a daemonic variation of that torment. But there is always a more prosaic and certainly more practical question the artist has to answer: at what point is the work finished, when is the process of production over? One way of approaching that question is to explore the problem of the 'unity' of the work of art (a problem that could be formulated in terms of a 'missing' panel from a polyptych).

Adorno remarks that 'no one could be better suited to this task [of 'judgement'] than the progressive composer, whom discursive reasoning most eludes'. Adorno's own favoured candidate as 'progressive composer' is Schoenberg, and a comment by Heinze-Klaus Metzger on Schoenberg's *First String Quartet, in D minor, opus 7,* may help us to grasp the kind of *non-*'discursive' 'reason' which informs it:

By using multiple counterpoint on a small fund of basic material Schoenberg achieves a wide variety of motives and thematic figures. No generally applied method is used; the dialectic between particular and general is always real, and is never allowed to relax into a harmonious balance. The result, so far as the overall form is concerned, was a work which is simultaneously in one movement and in four movements, one in which the usual four movements of large-scale cyclic sonata form are compressed into a single one, in such a way that their relationships to one another constitute a sonata form of a higher logical order. Thus for example the 'slow movement' takes on the function of a 'second subject' within the overall sonata, and the development technique which proliferates throughout the whole work . . . like the localized transition sections, is always logically polyvalent, having a function both in terms of each particular formal part of lower or higher significance, and within the larger sections or the overall form. This state of affairs, taken in conjunction with the inexhaustible contrapuntal combinations, sometimes leads one to think of Freud's concept of over-determination, in which case the compositional economy of the work could also be interpreted as a criticism of this compositional economy; perhaps the most fruitful aspect of a dialectic whose task, according to Adorno, is to break through the constrictive nature of logic with the aid of logic's own means.

Sleeve-note, *DGG 2530 329*

Picking up the allusion to Freud, and the final comment about a 'dialectic' that seeks to 'break through the constrictive nature of logic with the aid of logic's own means', we might recall Freud's own comments on the relation of the dream-work to 'logic':

We are here interested only in the essential dream-thoughts. These usually emerge as a complex of thoughts and memories of the most intricate possible structure, with all the attributes of the trains of thought familiar to us in waking life. They are not infrequently trains of thought starting out from more than one centre, though having points of contact. Each train of thought is almost invariably accompanied by its contradictory counterpart, linked with it by antithetical association.

The different portions of this complicated structure stand, of course, in the most manifold logical relations to one another. They can represent foreground and background, digressions and illustrations, conditions, chains of evidence and counter-arguments. When the whole mass of these dream-thoughts is brought under the pressure of the dream-work, and its elements are turned about, broken into fragments and jammed together—almost like pack-ice—the question arises of what happens to the logical connections which have hitherto formed its framework. What representation do dreams provide for 'if', 'because', 'just as', 'although', 'either—or', and all the other conjunctions without which we cannot understand sentences or speeches?

In the first resort our answer must be that dreams have no means at their disposal for representing these logical relations between the dream-thoughts. For the most part dreams disregard all these conjunctions, and it is only the substantive content of the dream-thoughts that they take over and manipulate. The restoration of the connections which the dream-work has destroyed is a task which has to be performed by the interpretative process.

The Interpretation of Dreams, ch. VIc

For Freud, 'the incapacity of dreams to express these things must lie in the nature of the psychical material out of which dreams are made'. But in discussing the procedures, devices, rules by which the dream-work operates —displacement, condensation and overdetermination—and in probing the 'psychical material' out of which they are 'made', Freud too seems to operate with a distinction between 'content' (manifest, latent) and 'form'; for Freud the dream-work *is* the 'dream' yet he can also write that the dream-work 'is under some kind of necessity to combine all the sources which have acted as stimuli for the dream into a single unity' (Standard Edition, IV, p.179). The problem here is not what is that 'necessity' that governs the operation of the dream-work, but rather how we are to conceive of that 'unity' demanded by that 'necessity'. Insofar as the 'dream-work' achieves its object, insofar as it makes sense to speak of '*a*' dream, how are we to speak of the 'unity' of that dream?

Benjamin writes of the poets of *l'art pour l'art* as having 'nothing to formulate with such urgency that it could determine the *coining* of their words', their 'choice of words' being 'made only among words which have not already been coined by the *object* itself'; to coin a word is always to seek to escape the pull of existing words, to wrench and dislocate the language of our thought. We need a word (a 'concept') which is neither 'form' nor 'content', which allows us to speak of that 'unity' which is the object of the dream-work and its product, a word which may also enable us to speak of the art-work's achievement of 'unity'. Freud speaks of the aim of the dream as 'wish-fulfilment'; we can take one overtone of that term, together with a pun on 'content', and speak of the 'contentment' sought by the dream-work; and we can take the chiming word 'containment', as indicating that the 'dream' 'contains' its 'content' not as a container but rather in the way a quarrel is 'contained', made tolerable, held in check, without being resolved or defused —anger or impatience which is 'contained' is only partially repressed. And, finally, we can take the overtones of 'pressure' in 'repressed', together with an undersense of 'select' or 'sieve', and speak of the 'strain' which characterises the dream-work. Fusing these terms, a verbal noun can be coined: '*constraint-ment*'—an action, process, work, whose gradually achieved effect *is* constraintment, the *dream-work* arrives at *self-constraintment*. Condensation and displacement are devices, tactics, which serve and are parts of the process which is self-constraintment; the dream-work's self-constraintment is always precarious, however, since the necessity for it, what makes it necessary, is finally insatiable, uncontainable, discontented, unconstrainable: the 'dream' is a moment of truce in an *agon* the only end of which is death and which started with birth itself.

If we think of the art-work also in these terms, or with this term, Adorno's phrase 'the immutable questions and antagonisms of the individual compositional structure', and Metzger's 'dialectic' which seeks 'to break through the constrictive nature of logic with the aid of logic's own means', can lead us back to the 'logical' problem which confronts the reader of *The Fall*. It would be possible to formulate that problem in familiar 'logical' terms: is it possible to make a ('legal') judgement 'without law'? That problem, in its manifold variations, could be tracked through the well-worn debates in the philosophy of law, or pursued into political or moral philosophy, or elaborated according to endless constitutional permutations on the 'separation of powers'. The logic of the ideology of law has its own interminability. But the task of the 'text' of *The Fall* is not to 'answer' the 'immutable questions and antagonisms' that arise within that ideologic; it is to 'arrive at' their self-constraintment, to 'hold' the conflict of 'thoughts and memories of the most intricate possible' kind;

those 'trains of thoughts and memories' which are self-constrainted as *The Fall* can be traced back through Camus's other writings, his life, his 'whole generation', the whole history of an epoch, just as the trains of thoughts and memories which traverse our different 'readings' of *The Fall* could also be traced till they are lost over numerous personal and epochal horizons: those trains start out 'from more than one centre, though having points of contact' and 'each train of thought is almost invariably accompanied by its contradictory counterpart, linked with it by antithetical association'. A certain kind of 'criticism' seeks to trace those chains and trains, those thoughts and memories; such criticism is interminable. There is another kind of 'criticism' which seeks to 'understand' the 'logic' that is at work in the process of self-constraintment, or which is itself in the process of self-constraintment; in doing so, such criticism may lay bare the ideo*logic*al questions and antagonisms, contradictions and conundrums, which formed the 'framework' for the *work* of constraintment; 'the restoration of the connections' which set the art-*work* in motion may be 'a task which has to be performed by the interpretative process' of this kind of criticism. But the *writing* of *The Fall*, the *work* of arriving at the final text, is not an exercise in 'discursive reasoning'; rather it consists in the difficult work of turning the 'logic' of an ideologic back upon itself, manipulating its 'chains' to produce a self-locking mechanism, a manoeuvring of contradictions into self-binding self-cancellations; the end-term is a complex *impasse* internally structured by its own dynamics and therefore with a kind of *stasis*, a 'moment' of truce, a perversely satisfactory stalemate; the 'end' of writing, the completion of the *work*, comes when any re-entry into the process of the text—by (re-)*reading* it—leads to that impasse; at that point, the text can be left alone, abandoned as self-supporting, as self-constrainted, but awaiting another reader who will set its movements in motion once more, only for them, and the reader, to arrive once more at their achieved impasse. Neither the writing nor the reading of the text can arrive at a 'resolution' of the contradictions which are displaced and condensed in the process of reading and writing and re-reading and re-writing; those operations may, eventually, allow but a temporary truce in the continual struggle with those contradictions.

The specific impasse of *The Fall* can be likened to that of a judge judging himself to be unjust according to laws which he judges to be unjust and which disqualify him from judging by them . . .—an endless vicious circle which may be the deepest in hell. But the specific operations of this text perhaps suggest a general procedure which characterises and constitutes the process of work which provides 'aesthetic' satisfaction or contentment, and gives some hint as to why some art-work is 'better', more satisfying, than other (art-)work. Think of the well-known, if apocryphal, Oxford philosophy examination paper: the candidate opens the envelope and finds a single sheet of paper, on which is written:

Is the sentence on the back of this paper a question?

He turns over the sheet of paper; the reverse side is blank. Faced with that, what does he do, what does he write? The possibilities are endless. But what guides him in his search for the 'right' response? Basically, it's the need not to 'answer' the 'question' but rather to 'block' the *problem* he confronts, to write something which will turn that 'question' back upon itself, either cancelling it out or giving back the problem to the examiner. He might write: 'If this is an answer.' If the examiner responds with 'No, it isn't', the logic of that 'if' concludes that the non-existent sentence was not a question—which is a kind of answer. What, though, would be the 'best' 'answer', the most appropriate, the most satisfying response—at least for the examinee? We would, as examinees and perhaps as examiners, 'judge' between different possible responses in terms of the degree to which they 'constrainted' the original move in this 'exchange' between examinee and examiner, between also the front and back of this sheet of paper. I think I might most happily, and securely, leave the examination-hall ('finish' the paper), if I were to turn the sheet of paper over and write on the 'other' side:

Is the sentence on the back of this paper a question?

The 'necessity' for a 'truce', the need to arrive at constraintment in writing, may arise from a more or less specific crisis or contradiction, for the writer in the first instance. In Camus's case perhaps that contradiction is legible in his pronouncements during the 1950s on Algeria:

'You must choose your side,' cry the haters. Oh I have chosen it! I have chosen my country. I have chosen the Algeria of justice in which French and Arabs will associate freely.

Quoted by O'Brien, *Camus*, p.72

I have always condemned terror. I must also condemn a terrorism which operates blindly, in the streets of Algeria for example, and which one day may strike my mother or my family. I believe in justice but I will defend my mother before justice.

Quoted, O'Brien, p.75

In January 1956, the year of the publication of *La Chute*, Camus went to Algeria to propose the one concrete idea he had: a 'truce for civilians'.

The specific contradictions of a white French Algerian in 1956–7 are an instance of that pervasive contradiction that turns support for 'justice' into acquiescence in 'injustice' when we ourselves become the targets in a 'just war' of liberation; in such a situation, faced with that problem, we would all prefer to be civilians. But though a constraintment of those contradictions may temporarily be found in the art-work—in the *work* of writing and of reading—there is no truce possible outside of that work: at most, writing or reading a work of art may allow us, for a few privileged moments, to 'work through' some of the *permutations* of those contradictions which already shape our 'damaged lives' (to use Adorno's phrase from *Minima Moralia*), may even allow us access to an 'understanding' of them, in the process of which we may arrive at the peculiar satisfaction of 'inhabiting' the world which would be constituted by their permanent, static, self-constraintment: a steady state world from which the actual movements of *history* have been expelled. There, perhaps, lies literature's subtlest attraction and temptation. In the end, however, those contradictions are, necessarily, worked through according to another logic, with quite other rules and procedures, and within that logic, the logic of history, there can be no truce at all. Always, with a shock, the dreamer has to awake—to find that the war is still continuing.

PART TWO: Thesis

Note: This section of the book began life as a Mistress of Arts dissertation, entitled 'Autobiography and Class Consciousness'. In the rush to get the book on to the market, I have not thought it worthwhile to waste time erasing the scars of its genesis, beyond removing the scholarly clutter of footnotes, references, evidence, bibliography, etc.; such detritus of a bankrupt academic-ism can be consulted by any moles so inclined in the Anderson Room of the University Library. I have, however, allowed the traces of its now-faded ideological ambience (it was completed in 1986) to remain, as a dialectical counterpoint to the other sections of this book which register the definitive advances since made in my own intellectual Odyssey.

A.A.

Part One: Introduction

There appears to be agreement on one essential: that the type of social criticism and intellectual history currently in fashion must be superseded by a composite discipline which will be a structural investigation into the relationship between theory and practice. Many literary intellectuals, while recognising the need for a new approach, are somewhat overwhelmed at the prospect of it. Lacking the philosophical training of their German colleagues and the sociological expertise of the French . . . they are simply unqualified technically for the new intellectual experience. And thus their real talent, empirical research, has tended very often to be overshadowed by their relative neglect of other fields.

TLS, 5th March 1970

The subject of this thesis is a small selection of autobiographies. The method of analysis is basically a form of 'close reading', of literary criticism. That method is used within a framework derived from a 'sociology of literature' approach, and the content of the chosen autobiographies is more familiarly met with in the context of studies in labour history. The choice of 'nineteenth-century working-class political autobiographies', broadly defined as autobiographies by people more immediately associated with a working-class background than with any other social position, and connected at some stage with some form of political event or movement, was dictated by personal preference and interest, though also to some extent by theoretical considerations.

Sociology of literature was indirectly linked, in its origins, with an interest in autobiographies. Wilhelm Dilthey placed great emphasis upon biography and autobiography as an aid to historical understanding; his pupil and editor Georg Misch provided the first major study of autobiographical writings, and another pupil, Georgy Lukacs, has been perhaps the most influential figure in the development of sociology of literature. Lukacs's early theoretical work *History and Class Consciousness* (1923) tried to establish that the emergence of the proletariat as a self-conscious class resolved in terms of *praxis* the problem of the subject-object dialectic posed by German Idealism, arguing that the class-consciousness of the proletariat was the historical or materialist equivalent of the self-knowledge of the Hegelian *Weltgeist*; but Lukacs maintained that the relevant class-consciousness was not the 'actual' consciousness of individual members of the proletariat but rather the 'imputed' consciousness of the class, i.e. that 'consciousness' which was historically appropriate to the class as a whole. This distinction has strongly influenced Lukacs's and others' subsequent studies in the sociology of literature. This study examines, therefore, a number of writings which seem peculiarly central to the problems raised by Lukacs's argument: by analysing the autobiographies of some individuals associated with the working-class movement during an important period in the formation of its political self-consciousness (from 1788 to 1886), I hope, in part, to clarify the distinction between 'actual' and 'imputed' class consciousness during that historical period.

Clearly, then, this study encroaches on the field of labour history. The development of social history and labour history has attempted to deepen and enrich previous modes of historical writing (constitutional, legal, economic etc.) by providing an insight into the experience of 'ordinary' strata of society. It was perhaps Collingwood, also greatly influenced by Dilthey, who first alerted a generation of historians to the necessity of thinking themselves back into the problems and lived experience of any period under study, and this emphasis has been strongly present in much recent work in labour history. Perhaps the most sustained attempt in the field to combine 'insight and imagination as well as discipline' (Asa Briggs's phrase) has been E. P. Thompson's *The Making of the English Working Class*, and part of the intention of that book can be seen in the introductory comment:

I am seeking to rescue the poor stockinger, the Luddite cropper, the 'obsolete' hand-loom weaver, the 'utopian' artisan, and even the deluded follower of Joanna Southcott, from the enormous condescension of posterity. . . . Their aspirations were valid in terms of their own experience; and, if they were casualties of history, they remain, condemned in their own lives, as casualties.

This thesis attempts, in its own way, to emulate that intention: by using a literary critical approach I hope to get close to the 'lives' of some participants in the long making of the 'labour movement', and by employing that approach within a sociology of literature framework I intend not to lose sight of the nature and, particularly, of some of the problems of that movement.

It is not accidental that Thompson's work overlaps with, parallels, or draws upon some currents in literary criticism. One specific parallel with the work of a literary critic can be usefully instanced here. Thompson formulates an important conclusion of his work in the comment:

By 1832 there were strongly-based and self-conscious working-class institutions, . . . working-class intellectual traditions, working-class community patterns, and a working-class structure of feeling.

The term 'structure of feeling' is apparently derived from Raymond Williams's *The Long Revolution*, where Williams writes:

The most difficult thing to get hold of, in studying any past period, is the felt sense of the quality of life at a particular time and place: a sense of the ways in which the particular activities combined into a way of thinking and feeling. . . . The term I would suggest to describe [this] is *structure of feeling*: it is as firm and definite as 'structure' suggests, yet it operates in the most delicate and least tangible parts of our activity.

Williams's work, too, crosses the boundaries between literary criticism, cultural history and history in general, yet the sensibility operating in his work is primarily that of a literary critic (a position for which Thompson has criticised him). Williams's approach, indeed, parallels a great deal of Lukacs's critical method, and one brief example from Lukacs might illustrate the grounds for expecting connections to emerge between literary criticism and labour history.

In his *The Historical Novel* Lukacs writes of the difficulty, for the novelist, of presenting a historical period not just in terms of material details but in the psychological depiction of character; he praises Walter Scott for conveying exactly 'the quality of inner life, the morality, capacity for sacrifice, steadfastness, etc., peculiar to a given age', for his 'ability to translate elements of economic and social change into human fates, into an altered psychology'. Clearly, we have here the combined interests of the historian and the literary critic: an interest both in the material 'facts' and the 'structure of feeling' of a period. The analyses in this thesis also attempt to combine both interests, but by almost reversing the procedure Lukacs sees as characteristic of Scott: I endeavour to 'translate' the 'human fate', the 'psychology', of these individuals, as expressed in their autobiographies, into 'elements of economic and social change'.

This, however, raises again the problem of method, the mode of translation. For what is common to Lukacs and most of his disciples is a curious lack of what, in England at least, has been taken to be the primary task of literary criticism: a close attention to, a detailed reading and exposition of, the actual language of the literary text. And there is perhaps a complementary failing in the use generally made of autobiographies by historians: they have tended to be taken by historians merely as personal narratives of what happened, more or less biassed or inaccurate, or as providing anecdotes of 'human interest' to enliven a dull page; but little attention has been paid to the kind of document an autobiography is, to the rather peculiar 'genre' that autobiographies constitute.

Autobiography is a form of writing which seems to slide between standard categories: it hovers between 'history' and 'creative literature', 'non-fiction' and 'fiction', if only because 'memory' is finally inextricable from 'imagination'. As such, of course, autobiography seems to offer, a priori, an area of inquiry which invites a sociology of literature approach: a form of writing which is explicitly concerned with recounting the 'life' (and, often, 'times') of an author immediately suggests itself as an area in which the connections between that life, those times and the written work itself might be closely established, or at least usefully explored. At least a 'close reading' of autobiographies might help to counterbalance some of the less closely-focussed treatments of autobiographies by historians. Indeed, the more traditional historian's approach to this body of material can safely be left to others; I have tried to concentrate upon the actual text and to relate the self-portrait in the text as a whole to wider contexts, rather than directly to the 'real' biographical details of each author's life, to the 'truth' of his account—a point I am concerned here to stress.

The method I have adopted, then, has been to rely upon what is actually said in each autobiography as a whole: to try to understand and make clear any significant pattern or unity in the work. This has involved a close analysis of any characteristic features of the writer's style and an examination of the overall structure of each autobiography. I have also suggested ways in which style and structure are related both to each other and to other aspects of the author: the political position he depicts himself as holding, the general position he occupied in the social structure, and some features of the time, and sometimes place, in which he lived. A further connection or 'homology' which emerged is the correlation between these various facets and the problems of political organisation; the significance of this last point is discussed in the Conclusion.

Part Two: Analyses

Chapter 1: Samuel Bamford: 'groping in a mental and political twilight'

(i) Aspects of the historical context

The great changes which have taken place in the nature of employment in the manufacturing districts of South Lancashire since the publication of Collier's *View of the Lancashire Dialect* have not only caused the old appearances of the country to pass away, but they have altered nearly everything appertaining to, or resulting from, the life and condition of man. At the time when Tim Bobbin was spending his jovial and facetious days at Milnrow, such a thing as a cotton or woollen factory was not in existence. . . . working hours, whether at the loom or on the farm, were, as compared with those of modern operatives and labourers, spent in leisure. There was often great irregularity in their observance of working hours, and their duration varied much, according to the wants, or habits, of individual workers, or of families.

But soon a change was destined to come over this scene of homely labour and plenteous living. In 1769, a patent was taken out for a machine to spin cotton by rollers; in 1770 the spinning-jenny was patented; in 1785 appeared improved carding, drawing, and roving frames; after which came the willow, the scutching-machine, and the lapping-frame. In 1779 the mule-jenny was invented, and in 1785 Watt had completed his steam-engine. Then came a wonderful facility of production, and a proportionate increase of employment, an increase of population, a crowding towards the great hive, of many people of all industrial classes, and from all parts of the kingdom and the world. Next, as a consequence, followed the breaking up of old associations and the formation of new ones; the abandonment of old habits; the giving up of old customs; new modes of dress became common; new modes of living were adopted; new subjects of thinking were started; new words for the expression of thought were introduced, and from that time the old dialect, with the old customs of the country and the old fashions, has been gradually receding towards oblivion.

Bamford: *Dialect of South Lancashire*, Manchester, 1850

Bamford's compressed account of the many and interconnected changes in South Lancashire at the end of the eighteenth century can be supplemented and paralleled by the comments of contemporary observers and later historians, but he makes the essential, rich, connections. Bamford was born in Middleton, near Manchester, in 1788; in 1789 there were no power-looms in Manchester and only one spinning mill driven by steam; the first power-loom was introduced into Manchester in 1790. The next few decades saw the immense expansion of the cotton industry: in 1781 5 million pounds of raw cotton was imported; by 1820 the figure was 150 million. England as a whole was still predominantly rural and agricultural, but though the new industrial developments advanced fairly slowly, Middleton was one of the areas in which, by 1812, they were concentrated. The new factories first replaced the older modes of spinning rather than weaving: in 1819 in the Manchester area there were 66 spinning mills, employing 20,000 workers (2,000 male operatives, with 18,000 female and child labourers) but also an estimated 40,000 hand-loom weavers still working in cottage-industry conditions. Individual factories were relatively small; even by 1832 the average number of employees in each was only 400, though two mills employed more than 1,000; but the size of the total population in the local towns had increased dramatically. Contemporary accounts of the combined population of Manchester and Salford give 19,839 in 1757, 27,246 in 1773, over 50,000 by 1788, between 65,000 and 74,000 by 1791—the faltering later estimates themselves indicative of the sense of uncontrollable expansion. Whatever the exact figures, an estimate that Manchester's population increased sevenfold between 1750 and 1820 would probably not be exaggerated. The total population of England was increasing by about 15% each decade in the early nineteenth century; by 1811 almost one-sixth of the entire population of England lived in the textile areas of Lancashire, Yorkshire and Cheshire, with Manchester and Liverpool the only English towns apart from London (already one million) to number 100,000 inhabitants. Those who flooded into the Manchester area during this expansion were, of course, 'strangers' to one another and to the local inhabitants. The sudden presence of numerous 'strangers' could always alarm the authorities, but the permanent immigration of so many newcomers naturally caused deep difficulties also for the local workers.

We can grasp one aspect of these difficulties by tracing briefly the history of local agitation. There had been local food-riots, for example, in 1757 and some traditional 'collective bargaining by riot', but from 1789 local clashes began to take on a more directly political character, with the formation of both a Church and King Club and the Manchester Constitutional Society. There were traditional food riots again in 1797 and some attempts at organisation in 1799, in response to the flour-shortage of 1796–1800. When the next bad harvests came, in 1808, the weavers showed further signs of self-organisation: in protest against the dropping of a minimum-wage Bill, 10,000 weavers assembled peacefully on St George's Field to demonstrate, only to be dispersed by troops. By 1811–12 there was an increasing number of local working-class meetings, to petition Parliament, to meet delegates from Ireland, even to discuss a general 'turn-out'; 'secret committees' of workers were also reported to be at work. In 1816 these groups established the first provincial Hampden Clubs, and in December 1816 a meeting of delegates at Middleton sent out 'missionaries' to other northern areas; by March 1817 there were some forty Hampden clubs in the Manchester area, with about 8,000 members, and a local radical newspaper, the *Manchester Political Register*, had been founded. That same month a mass-meeting of 12,000, prelude to the Blanketeers' March, was cleared by dragoons. In 1818 agitation concentrated on immediate economic issues: a strike of 20,000 Manchester and Stockport spinners began in July and ended with an attack on Gray's factory in Manchester on 2nd September. Late in August the weavers also struck, but despite well-attended mass meetings the weavers' strike fizzled out on 4th September when a march from Manchester to Ashton was dispersed by troops. The spinners, under their leaders Bagguley and Drummond, attempted to form a General Union, but the weavers, rejecting the 'political' Bagguley at a mass meeting, remained aloof. Only in 1819 did the weavers take up a political stance: at a mass meeting on 21st June their own leaders, Saxton and Walker, persuaded them to support the need for Parliamentary reform. The same year a delegates' meeting representing twenty-eight local workers' societies was held in June and a number of mass political meetings were organised throughout the area. By August 1819 the radical *Manchester Observer* had reached its highest circulation (4,000 copies) and had a network of northern agents. The loyalists were, naturally, also active: in 1819 they formed an Armed Association, and in July Wroe, the *Observer* editor, was charged with seditious libel. On 16th August 1819 the two forces met—at Peterloo. After Peterloo the radical movement split and declined, to revive again briefly in 1826 and then in the 1830s: in 1831, with average wages down to less than 12/– a week, the Manchester mill operatives turned again towards politics; even the hand-loom weavers, by then drastically declining in numbers, could be described as inclined towards 'revolution' rather than reform. The stage was set for Chartism in Manchester.

There are a number of points to be emphasised here. Throughout the period there is a shift from a small, relatively 'known' and homogeneous working community to a large, new kind of conurbation, in which many of the inhabitants were, in a double sense, strangers; by 1841, for example, the number of Irish in Manchester was equal to its total population in the 1770s. For any radical movement to emerge in that context there had to be a development of organisational and tactical forms: the older forms of relatively spontaneous riot and of communication by word of mouth were replaced, in a long process, by reliance on disciplined and coordinated meetings, organisational committees and newspaper circulation—one of the earliest signs of the emergence of local Chartism was the transformation in September 1830 of the *Manchester and Salford Advertiser* into a working-class radical paper. But at the same time the local authorities had to re-organise their responses to agitation; the local 'police-force' was inherited from a parish situation: in 1812, for example, Oldham had only two regular constables. Apart from the building up of a regular police, the authorities had two main resources in times of trouble: either an attempt to match numbers with numbers (in May 1812, for example, General Maitland in Lancashire commanded 79 infantry companies, 18 troops of horse, and two artillery detachments, nearly 7,000 men), or an attempt to infiltrate the radical groups with spies and informers, relying precisely on the fact that so many people in the area could no longer know the background or credentials of a stranger. And of course the loyalists, while organising their own associations, attempted to prevent the development of working-class organisations; in 1813, for example, Hay, the chairman of the district bench, proposed a Bill to regulate 'Friendly Societies'.

(ii) A representative life

That, among so many thousands in the Manchester area, Samuel Bamford should have produced the autobiography by which we know him—*Passages in the Life of a Radical* (London, 1844)—itself requires some kind of explanation. In 1814, for example, another Samuel Bamford was shot dead in a Luddite raid in Nottingham; he remains merely a name, otherwise unknown. Why autobiographies are written is never fully amenable to explanation, but at least we can partly grasp how Bamford became a point at which the general process sketched above received individual expression. For many of the currents and strands in that complex history intersected in Bamford's life. In his immediate lineage, as given in *Early Days*, we can trace a representative decline from independent farming (his paternal great-grandfather) to cottage weaving (his father), cut across at different generations by marriage with the daughters of relatively superior craftsmen (a watchmaker, a shoemaker). The family had also moved in three generations from rural Thornham to Middleton and, soon, to Manchester itself. A radical element can also be traced: Bamford claimed descent from a Cromwellian in the Civil War, and one grandfather had been arrested for High Treason in 1745, after helping the Pretender's forces. His father and Uncle Thomas were members of the 'small band' of Middleton 'Jacobins' who were, in the 1790s, 'supporters of Parliamentary Reform, as it was then advocated by the Duke of Richmond, Mr Pitt, and other distinguished characters', and the attacks on such local 'radicals' were among Bamford's earliest memories. Religious dissent was also strong in his background: his grandfather Daniel's home was, Bamford claims, 'the first that opened at Middleton for the reception of Methodist preachers, and John and Charles Wesley ... and many of the first promulgators of their doctrines, had addressed their humble and simple hearers on the floor of that ruined dwelling'. His father became a Methodist after an 'irregular youth', though he left the Methodist society during his 'Jacobin' phase. Bamford's cousins remained Methodists 'of the old primitive earnest cast'. Whatever the overall interaction between Methodism and radicalism—and the issue is notoriously complex —Bamford's Methodist background probably did, as we shall see, contribute something to his autobiographical account of his personal radicalism.

Bamford's early life continues some of the trajectories visible in his ancestry. He was born just at the start of what William Radcliffe called 'the golden age' of the weaving trade (1788 to 1803) and about 1797 he himself became a weaver. For Bamford that was, by then, a return to his origins, since around 1793 his father had been appointed manager of Strangeways Workhouse and the family lived in Manchester till, in 1795, a smallpox epidemic killed Bamford's mother, Uncle Thomas, and a younger sister and brother; after his father's subsequent re-marriage Bamford went to live with his Uncle William's family in Middleton, and 'never resided again' with his father. While in Manchester he had briefly attended Manchester Grammar School, but the return to Middleton also meant a return to the simpler forms of education he had known earlier: local Methodist schools and Sunday schools; at least Bamford's 'real old Armenian Methodists' 'thought it no desecration of the Sabbath to enable the rising generation, on that day, to write the Word of God as well as read it.' In 1803, as the 'golden age' ended, Bamford went to live with his sister in Salford and, soon after, began a succession of jobs as a warehouseman in Manchester. Living at this time in Greengate and working in Macdonald's Lane (now Lower Cannon Street) in the centre of Manchester, Bamford's recreations were still almost entirely rural: 'lonely walks in those pleasant undulating meadows', 'country strolls at eventide'. The swelling Manchester was still almost an intrusion upon a rural setting. He remained a warehouseman in Manchester till 1813—though with intervals of weaving when 'trade was going remarkably well', and one brief spell as a sailor in 1807—and kept his job even after settling with his wife, Mima, in Middleton after their marriage in 1810. Between 1813 and 1816 he was a putter-out to the Middleton weavers, and even dabbled in bookselling, but by the time he became involved in the Hampden Clubs he was settled as a weaver.

What is significant for this study, however, is not these bare bones of his life, but his own experience and expression of them, and it is useful first to analyse the elements of his experience that are given particular emphasis in his work, and to see how these relate to the general historical experience sketched earlier.

(iii) Known communities and strangers

In his *Walks in South Lancashire* (1844) Bamford includes a short, imaginary, conversation between Sir George Head, author of *A Home Tour in the Manufacturing Districts* (1840) and a Lancashire 'local'; it is entitled 'A Stranger in Lancashire' and begins with the stranger inquiring the way:

—'Pray, can you inform me which is the nearest way to Littleborough?'
—'Wot, dun yo myen past th' Chanters, at th' Lone-foote?'
—'I do not know where I should go past, sir.'
—'Oh! yo dunno' know, dun yo? but I'll goo wi' yo, an' show yo. See yo then, yo mun goo deawn th' Little-feelt, an' deawn th' Yeaw-bonk, an' streight deawn th' Wood, and yo'n soom be at th' Littleborough. Wot, aryo sum mack ov a woll-felley, or summat?'
—Stranger:– 'No sir; I am not in trade.'
—'Why, I thought yo hadn bin. Why, we'er dun yo come fro, then?'
—'I come from London.'
—'Fro Lunnon, dun yo?'
—Stranger:– 'I do.'
—'Dun yo know Peel, then?'
—Stranger:– 'Which Peel?'
—'Why, Peel at belungs to this lond.'
—'I am not aware that I do.'
—'Why, but he lives i' Lunnon!'
—'In what part of the town does he reside?
—'Th' teawn! he never lift i' Rachda' in his lyve, mon.'
—'I mean in what part of London does he live?'
—'Nay, I know nowt obeawt tat, but he lives i' Lunnon.'

In this brief exchange the contrast of dialect with 'standard' English is an index to a deeper contrast; the old farmer lives in a known community, its paths and inhabitants familiar and taken for granted; for him it is difficult to recognise that a man may be a stranger, unfamiliar with that scene, and even more difficult to grasp that 'Lunnon' is not a similarly 'known community' for its inhabitants. For the stranger, London is the focus of a quite different kind of community: England as a whole, with the capital as 'the town' and such places as Lancashire merely 'the manufacturing districts'. For the farmer, Rochdale is 'the town' and London is merely some other Rochdale. That clash of experience, separated out in this dialogue, was in Bamford's case an element in a continuing internal dialogue.

Bamford began by inhabiting a small, known community. When, for example, he lists the Middleton victims at Peterloo it is clearly as a group of people personally known to him; the local forces of law and order, and his employers, are also known individuals, not distant figures—he had once clashed with the local authorities over non-payment of a maintenance order, and his own family was intermarried with local employers; perhaps too the joint political meetings, on some issues, of masters and men had helped to widen Bamford's range of acquaintances. Perhaps the most telling indication of the nature of his local community comes in an incident after the Peterloo massacre:

I found Redford's mother bathing his wound with warm milk and water, and to please her, he said it was easier. It was a clean gash of about six inches in length and quite through the shoulder blade. She yearned, and wept afresh, when she saw the severed bone gaping in the wound. She asked who did it? and Tom mentioned a person; he said he knew him well; and she, sobbing, said she also knew him, and his father and mother before him; and she prayed God not to visit that sin upon the head of him who did it, but to change his heart and bring him to repentance. That prayer had well-nigh touched my heart also, but Tom rapped out one of another sort, to which I incontinently, as may be supposed, added my 'Amen'.

Like the farmer in *Walks*, Bamford at times seems to presume an extension of this element in his experience. For example, he attributes his own kind of personal knowledge to Henry Hunt during the large Palace Yard demonstration of 1817: 'He seemed to know almost every man of them, and his confidence in, and entire mastery over them, made him quite at ease.' He was correspondingly surprised at first to find that he, Bamford, had to identify himself to the London relief committee; it had to be explained to him 'how necessary it was, in a great place like London, to be quite certain as to the persons with whom they transacted business.' Bamford, however, had not only to learn that other places were not known communities; he had also to negotiate the breakdown of his own. He can recognise that he may be a 'stranger' to the London radical meetings, and need to be informed as to who 'two of the most influential leaders of the London operative reformers', Watson and Preston, were; but when a 'stranger' becomes locally active, 'exciting to, and carrying on, private meetings, and suspicious intrigues in our neighbourhood', then Bamford feels distinctly uneasy. In part Bamford's reaction was justified by the fear of strangers being informers, but that fear could itself only be generated in a situation where the community was ceasing to be closed. It is easy, in fact, to overlook Bamford's sheer inability to grasp others simply as strangers—a facility long since acquired by the present urbanised population. He will not speak till spoken to by strangers, even though on one occasion he realises that they are 'some of the London politicians of the working class'. The experience of London he recounts in *Early Days* remained for a long time a shaping factor in his outlook:

the men and women themselves formed an apparently unceasing current of human beings, the ever-changing hue and character of which, confused my head—wearied my attention—and made me wishful to see no more.

In later life he managed to live in London for a few years, as a minor clerk at Somerset House (1851–5); by that time he had learned to live, to some extent, as a 'stranger', and before we examine the underlying political importance of this element in Bamford, some aspects of that process of learning may be noticed.

A central feature of Bamford's experience of his known community was a reliance on 'friendship': he asserts 'friendliness' to be one of the characteristics of his own class, and his natural reaction on meeting again a co-delegate whom at first he scarcely recognises is to refer to him very soon after as his 'old friend'. But his friendships gradually soured: some 'friends' spread the rumour that he was a spy; Hunt left his co-defendants to their own resources at the trial, snubbed Bamford, and slandered Carlile; Bamford's fellow-radicals left him almost without financial assistance for his trial and the London radicals mainly forgot their imprisoned colleagues. Even in prison with Healey and Johnson, quarrels, arguments and suspicion 'at length entirely put a stop to all confidence and friendly feeling' between them and himself, and made him 'a stranger to the society' of his fellow-prisoners. He had already had the experience of being forced, briefly, to act as a 'stranger' in his own neighbourhood, in disguising himself after Peterloo; but to acknowledge that all men were basically 'strangers' to one another was a difficult process. However, his description of Manchester as a play comes close to an awareness that roles in urban society are based not on personal knowledge but on how we appear to one another, through endless mediations:

If any one wishes to see a play performed he has only to walk the streets of Manchester, or any other of our large towns, and he may behold the perfection of either tragedy or comedy enacted by performers who need neither prompter, call-boy, nor rehearsal; but all coming and going as regularly as if the piece were a play 'got up' and 'put on the stage', as the phrase is, 'put on ready for presentation'. The scenes are admirably painted—the machinery perfect in its operations, of wonderful construction, and sometimes of most awful effect. The actors might have been made for the performance of their several parts, so aptly do they go through them; whilst the dresses, decorations, and all the accessories of the piece, are sure to be wonderfully befitting. And with such a stage as this, with its ever-varying reality before our eyes, who can require sham repetition as an after-part? Not I at any rate.

He is quite explicit at one point about the need to play a role where one is a stranger: after being refused lodgings at an inn, he advises that:

A foot traveller, if he is really desirous to obtain lodgings, should never stand asking about them. He should walk into a good room—never into the common tap room—put his dusty feet under a table—ring the bell pretty smartly, and order something to eat and drink, and not speak in the humblest of tones. He will be served quickly and respectfully. . . . After his repast, he should take his pipe or cigar if he be a smoker, and whether he be or not, he should drink, chat, and make himself quite at ease until bed-time; when, all he has to do, will be to call the chamber-maid and ask her to light him to bed. That will be done as a matter of course.

Later he makes a firm distinction between the role he is prepared to play among strangers and the identity he demands within a close community; he explains why he has suddenly, while still a prisoner in transit, withdrawn his previous acquiescence to being chained:

I said it was not a sudden resolve on my part, for I never intended to enter Lincoln with the chains on. I cared but little how I appeared in London or the country through which we had passed, and where I was, as I should probably remain, a perfect stranger; but I knew the consequences of a first appearance in a seemingly degraded state, before persons with whom we must remain twelve months.

Such deliberate role-playing finally acknowledges that friendliness and direct personal relations may have to be abandoned outside the known community.

(iv) A limited politics

There is, of course, already a political 'position' implicit in some features of Bamford's allegiance to a known community and the way that allegiance crumbles, but we can make his political stance more explicit—bearing in mind that his writing is retrospective and includes a critique of his early politics. Bamford's most obvious political positions are negative: his opposition to the Blanketeers' March, to the plans for 'making a Moscow of Manchester', and in general to proposals for 'revolution'. His opposition is often linked to suspicion of planted informers, but at times this shades into a distrust of all 'professional' agitators. Yet there is a tension in Bamford's attitude on this point. He excuses his own phase of radicalism, in contrast to the Chartist phase, by arguing that:

We had not any of our own rank with whom to advise for the better—no man of other days who had gone through the ordeal of experience; and whose judgement might have directed our self-devotion.

But in fact he rejects the approach of Thomas Bacon, the septuagenarian involved in the Pentridge rising, and dismisses Watson, Preston, Hooper, Benbow and Evans as 'the blind leading the blind'. For it is not so much experienced leaders that Bamford asks for, as leaders who will give his own kind of political advice. The passage quoted above continues:

. . . and have instructed us that, before the reform we sought could be obtained and profited by, there must be another—a deeper reform—emerging from our hearts, and first blessing our households, by the production of every good we could possibly accomplish in our humble spheres.

To accept this perspective is to adopt very clearly a specific kind of 'politics'. If we look at Bamford's explicit analyses and proposals we can see their coherence with this stance, and their limits.

The second chapter of *Passages*, his autobiography, includes a fairly comprehensive statement of the political aims of Bamford's Hampden Club:

. . . resolutions were passed declaratory of the right of every male to vote, who paid taxes; that males of 18 should be eligible to vote; that parliaments should be elected annually; that no placeman or pensioner should sit in parliament; that twenty thousand of inhabitants should send a member to the house of commons; and that talent and virtue were the only qualifications necessary.

These 'moderate views' did not, as Bamford approvingly declares, include an insistence on the ballot, nor 'interfere with the house of lords; nor the bench of bishops; nor the working of factories; nor the corn laws; . . . nor a score of other matters'; for in their view, 'first obtain annual parliaments, and universal suffrage, and "Whatsoever thou wouldest shall be added thereto"'. He also maintains that 'It was not until we became infested by spies, incendiaries, and their dupes . . . that physical force was mentioned amongst us. After that our moral power waned; and what we gained by the accession of demagogues, we lost by their criminal violence, and the estrangement of real friends.' This position, typically, rests on the 'old' radical analysis in terms of 'corruption'.

Those responsible for this corruption are, in general, 'the "boroughmonger crew" ' and Bamford is careful to note how the old upper classes are true gentlemen compared with this ill-defined new group. The problem, he asserted to Lord Sidmouth, is that 'his majesty's ministers were not fully acquainted with the condition of the people' because 'the gentry, or what were called the upper classes, were too proud, or too indifferent, to examine minutely, the abodes of the poor and the distressed'. The implication here is that it is ignorance, and to some extent involuntary ignorance, of the 'higher classes' concerning the poor, that is the core of the problem.

Given that analysis, and those moderate aims, Bamford's emphasis, not surprisingly, is on non-violent, law-abiding moral pressure, to gain respect, by showing patience and even gratitude. His whole aim is attitudinal change: 'For a nation to be free, it is sufficient that she wills it', and a change in the attitude of the masses, towards reason, restraint and self-control, will effect the necessary change in the authorities towards sympathy and friendliness. In the last chapter of volume I of *Passages* Bamford offers his most extended passage of political advice:

Mildly and persuasively as a mother entreating, would reason lead us to self-examination, self-control, and self-amendment. Canst thou not control thyself, and wouldst thou govern a household? Canst thou not govern a household, and yet wouldst thou direct a nation? Come to thine own bosom and home, and there commence a reform, and let it be immediate and effectual.

One evening, he says, spent in 'rational conversation' and 'the promotion of kindly feelings', in the 'comforting of families', was 'worth more than all thou hast seen, heard or done, at Radical or Chartist meetings'. He concludes this chapter by quoting from his own translation of Béranger's *La Lyonnaise*:

It is true, the middle and upper ranks have scarcely been just towards you; they have not cultivated that friendship of which you are susceptible, and more worthy than they. Had they done so, you would not have been in the hands you now are. But you can look above this misdirected pride and pity it. The rich have been as unfortunate in their ignorance of your worth, as you have in the absence of their friendship. All ranks have been in error, as it respects their relative obligations, and prejudice has kept them strangers and apart.

Bamford's translation of *La Lyonnaise* was published as an antidote to Chartist arguments for the 'wickedly devised, and foolishly attempted "National Holiday" ' in 1839—the proposal for a general strike. Between his own phase of radicalism in 1816–19 and his autobiographical account of that phase, in 1839–41, Bamford's position has clearly moved towards an extremely 'moderate' reformism. His actual political position at the time of writing *Passages* is only made explicit in the final chapter, where his stated demands take on a laissez-faire tone ('cheap food', 'cheap labour', 'cheap rents' for cottager and farmer alike, 'cheap government' etc.); one specific change is worth noting: the only positive recommendation he makes in *Passages* as to the *means* of reform is a revision of his earlier advocacy of annual parliaments; now:

He would say, let the house of commons, be, like the house of lords, indissoluble;—members to render an account of their conduct annually; individual members be liable to be displaced by their constituents, at any time; and elected, displaced, or retained as private servants are, viz.: as they do well their duty, or otherwise. The sense of the electors to be taken annually—by ballot in districts;

all elections to be by ballot. No hustings: no nomination farce; no mob gatherings; no ruffianism; no demagogism; no canting and deception of the multitudes.

What is most significant in this change is the model of community underlying it: that the relationships between the governing and the governed are not those between groups or interests but between individuals related by personal knowledge. The belated adoption of the ballot is also indicative of this model: now Bamford is prepared to allow that all men remain 'horizontally' strangers to one another, discrete units, while their 'vertical' relations are paternalist. What disgusts him about elections is the 'mob' element, the crowd as decision-maker. This is deeply part of a development which leads him to look with loathing on a political movement or organisation based not on personal relationships but on impersonal forms of membership and solidarity. This —emerging in Chartism—Bamford dismisses as 'mob coercion'.

(v) From politics to autobiography

The limits of Bamford's political position reflect a dilemma facing the whole radical movement in the 'transitional' phase from the 1790s to the 1830s. The values that the radicals sought to maintain were often, in one sense, regressive: they looked back to a stable community, closed and face-to-face; the forms of organisation they adopted rested in part on that kind of relationship, often inherited from the small organisational forms of religious dissenters. But at the same time the need was increasingly recognised for new forms of organisation, appropriate to a national radical movement. We can grasp one of the roots of this dilemma if we look at a possible 'breakthrough' point in Bamford's own experience.

Passages, I, chapter 37, describes the mood of anger and bitterness immediately after the Peterloo massacre: 'it was reported that thousands of pikemen were on the way to Manchester, from Oldham, Middleton, and other surrounding districts'; 'all the working people were athirst for revenge, and only awaited the coming of the country folks to attempt a sweeping havock'; proposals for the 'immolation of a selected number of the guilty ones' were being discussed; in Middleton itself Bamford found that

Many of the young men had been preparing arms, and seeking out articles to convert into such. Some had been grinding scythes, others old hatchets, others screw-drivers, rusty swords, pikels, and mop-nails: anything which could be made to cut or stab was pronounced fit for service. But no plan was defined—nothing was arranged.

Bamford and half-a-dozen radicals call a meeting to organise and coordinate responses:

The day following, I attended on the hill with a trusty friend. Notices had been sent to Oldham, Rochdale, Bury, and some other places, but at the time appointed no one appeared. We waited for hours, until the afternoon waned, but no one came; and then we went down to Royton, to ascertain the disposition of the reformers of that place. Some had been severely wounded, but most of the people were carousing, and there did not appear to be any disposition to retaliate the outrage we had suffered, by force and arms. I called on William Fitton, but he gave no encouragement to such an idea. I went to John Kay, in Royley-lane, but he was as usual, imperturbably placid. He was one of the least impassioned men I ever knew.

It is clear from his persistence and from his argument with Kay that Bamford, almost alone, is still impassioned enough to continue considering seriously an armed reaction. Kay argues cogently, and mainly on tactical grounds, against retaliation, and the next day, at a delegates' meeting, Bamford himself repeats Kay's arguments. But Bamford's initial emphasis is crucial:

I told them briefly, that I would not take part in a delegate meeting to discuss the taking up of arms. That I saw not any prospect of succeeding, and if I did, they were not the men with whom I would act. I had sent for men whom I knew, but they came not; strangers came whose faces I had never seen before, and I would not act with such; neither was it to be expected that I would.

The double blockage is really one: precisely because of the refusal to work with 'strangers', to break beyond the small known community and the already established leadership, into a different form of relationship, and risk, appropriate to much larger numbers, it was impossible that any direct confrontation with the militia, still less the military, could be successful. (We ought to remember that the 12,000 troops deployed against the Luddites was a far larger army than Wellington's in the Peninsular campaign of 1808.) Without such a breakthrough, the only options left were small-scale 'guerilla' gestures or submission and defeat, or withdrawal into the a-political realm of the domestic. Chapter 38 ends, appropriately:

Some days later, I was informed of the arrest of Joseph Healey, at Lees. I began to expect something of the sort myself, and told our constable that if he got a warrant, and would let me know, I would go with him any day, or night, to Manchester, and there would be no fuss; no one would be the wiser. He said he would take that course, should he have a warrant; and I attended my business as usual.

The limits of Bamford's political analysis and practice are thus clearly related to his adherence to the experience of a known community; though that basic sense of himself did collapse, of the two options then open—into individualism or into a more organised national radical politics—Bamford basically chose the former.

That there is a consonance between the elements so far sketched and the fact of Bamford's writing an autobiography at all—the problem raised in section (ii) above —should now be fairly clear. Writing, of any kind, is, as a political act, an option for persuasion over any more active or coercive strategy; and that choice stems naturally from an analysis that bases itself on the factor of involuntary ignorance. To write about oneself is the natural response if the ignorance in question is taken to be ignorance of your kind of people and of their condition, the absence of that element of personal knowledge so important to Bamford's politics. Moreover, to write an autobiography is simultaneously an act of withdrawal into one's known base and an attempt to extend that known community, to include one's readers in it, to have a 'personal' relationship to unknown people who yet remain strangers. Writing an autobiography was almost the only way in which the tensions and dilemmas in Bamford's position could be both maintained and apparently overcome.

(vi) A passive style

But how was he actually to write it? Bamford seems to have intended his readership to include all classes, but if the purpose of the autobiography was, at one level, to persuade, the self-portrait had to attract the sympathy even of his political opponents. This involved Bamford, as we shall see, in presenting himself passively, as someone almost forced into political activity; it meant playing down any element of conscious, willed and deliberate action, of decision-taking. But the characteristically passive presentation is not simply tactical; it reflects the central feature of Bamford's actual life: the experience of living through a process of immense social change, which seemed beyond immediate and adequate human control and which he could at best only minimally influence. Moreover, the high-point, the defining centre, of Bamford's own life was the experience of imprisonment, of being caught up in a judicial process from which he could not escape and which forced him into confined inactivity: arrests, trials and imprisonment occupy the overwhelming majority of pages in *Passages*. That he should present himself passively is no accident—though to demonstrate the extent to which passive modes permeate his style would take too much space here; I can only single out some of the basic features which exemplify that passivity.

An awareness of being observed is a constant feature: Bamford 'believed ministers had eyes to see, and ears to hear, and tongues to whisper whatever recurred'. He sometimes tried to turn this into an asset: in preparing for Peterloo:

It was deemed expedient that this meeting should be as morally effective as possible, and, that it should exhibit a spectacle such as had never before been witnessed in England . . . we determined that . . . we should disarm the bitterness of our political opponents by a display of cleanliness, sobriety and decorum, such as we never before had exhibited.

But such reliance on exhibiting order and discipline could backfire. Bamford quotes a magistrate's comment, that 'the party with the blue and green banners came upon the field in beautiful order' and 'not until then did he become alarmed'. What is felt from within as an expression of responsibility is seen from without precisely as an organised threat. This difficulty arises as part of the struggle to establish an ordered opposition to an already existing order in which, to use the prosecuting counsel's revealing phrase at the trial, 'weavers and shoemakers, and other artisans, were destined to earn their bread by the labour of their hands'. That 'destined' marks an assumption of overriding, supra-human, unchangeable order, in the face of which the natural response is to submit. Bamford's position often amounted, in practice, to submission.

A single episode combines these two emphases. When Hunt visited Manchester in January 1819 Bamford 'was requested' to provide a bodyguard. Its arrival is described:

About five o'clock on the afternoon of the day appointed . . . a gang of ten rough-looking country fellows attracted some notice as they passed through several of the streets of Manchester. Their appearance was somewhat remarkable, even for countrymen. Their dress was of the readiest, fit for 'donning or doffing', their hats were mostly beyond damage by warfare, their shirt collars, clean and white, were thrown open . . . some tramped in heavy clogs, rimmed with iron, others wore strong shoes, with clinker nails grinning like a rasp of shark's teeth; all bore stout cudgels. . . . Their bearing was not less striking—they were all young men—tall, gaunt, and square-built . . . ; and as they went, tramp, tramp, along the flags, people looked, startled, and looked again; whilst the observed ones, noticing nothing, went onwards like men who knew their work, and were both able and willing to perform it. . . .

This party consisted of myself, and nine picked men of my acquaintance, from Middleton.

This description is deliberately written from an external, spectator's view-point; Bamford is merged into a strange, unknown small group, alien to the streets of the city; but they are his own group, from his own community, and they are an ordered band, marching in step, knowing their business—and armed. This is the only episode in *Passages* where Bamford presents himself as actually armed and prepared for violence; and he objectifies himself. The episode in fact ends with Hunt, drinking in a tavern, being attacked by 'a party of "gentlemen" '—but Bamford's group, drinking elsewhere, is ignorant of the attack; Bamford's concluding comment is:

Had they been taken by us in the fact, there would have been a sore and pitiable account of them in the morning. But fate ordained otherwise; they escaped.

On the only occasion when equal armed combat, on however small a scale, seems a possibility, 'fate' ordains otherwise!

Bamford's insertion into this episode is grammatically passive: 'a letter was put into my hands at Middleton, from Mr Hunt, requesting me to call upon him'; and the passive voice comes naturally to him—its effect is often to play down his own role as leader, as in his account of his own Hampden Club:

One of these clubs was established in 1816, at the small town of Middleton, near Manchester; and I, having been instrumental in its formation, a tolerable reader also, and a rather expert writer, was chosen secretary. The club prospered; the number of members increased; the funds raised by contributions of a penny a week, became more than sufficient for all out goings; and taking a bold step, we soon rented a chapel which had been given up by a society of Kilhamite Methodists. This place we threw open for the religious worship of all sects and parties. . . . The proceedings of our society . . . drew considerable share of public attention to our transactions, and obtained for the leaders some notoriety. They, like the young aspirants of the present, and all other days, whose heads are as warm as their hearts, could sing with old John Bunyan:
   Then fancies fly away,
   We fear not what men say.

The passive 'was chosen secretary' seems natural, but add to it the impersonal subjects of the following sentences, then the transition to 'we', with that final curious distancing of himself, though secretary, from 'the leaders' ('They'), and the total effect is, almost, to detach Bamford from any initiative in the whole business. It is always difficult to grasp the subject of any group-activity, to designate the 'leaders' in a democratic organisation: it is a significant feature of our language that it is awkward to express such relationships grammatically. But Bamford's way of writing reflects more than this, since his displacing of any initiatives on to undiscoverable subjects is also a feature of the way he describes actions not involving this particular difficulty.

Passages I, chapter 2, begins the narrative of the book with the following:

It is a matter of history, that whilst the laurels were yet cool on the brows of our victorious soldiers on their second occupation of Paris, the elements of convulsion were at work amongst the masses of our labouring population; and that a series of disturbances commenced with the introduction of the Corn Bill in 1815, and continued, with short intervals, until the close of the year 1816. In London and Westminster, riots ensued, and were continued for several days, whilst the bill was discussed; at Bridport, there were riots on account of the high price of bread; at Biddeford there were similar disturbances to prevent the exportation of grain; at Bury, by the unemployed, to destroy machinery; at Ely, not suppressed without bloodshed; at Newcastle-on-Tyne, by colliers and others; at Glasgow, where blood was shed, on account of soup-kitchens; at Preston, by unemployed weavers; at Nottingham, by Luddites, who destroyed thirty frames; at Merthyr Tydville, on a reduction of wages; at Birmingham, by the unemployed; and December 7th, 1816, at Dundee, where, owing to the high price of meal, upwards of one hundred shops were plundered.

In this long account, the only personal subjects of active verbs are the Luddites who, in a subordinate clause, 'destroyed thirty frames'; all other verb-constructions are passive or impersonal. This way of writing history (deeply familiar, of course, in academic writing) reifies and mystifies. In particular, active violence is elided: 'not suppressed without bloodshed'; or the subject is made ambiguous: 'where blood was shed'; or simply disappears: recounting the end of the Blanketeers' March Bamford writes:

A body of yeomanry soon afterwards followed these simple minded men, and took possession of the bridge at Stockport. Many then turned back to their homes; a body of them crossed the river below, and entered Cheshire; several received sabre wounds, and one man was shot dead on Lancashire hill.

The actual conflict is lost in the silence between the Blanketeers crossing the river and 'several received sabre cuts'. A few pages later we find:

Steadiness of conduct, and consistency of principle, were soon placed, as it were at a distance from us. Our unity of action was relaxed; new speakers sprung like mushrooms about our feet; plans were broached, quite different from any that had been recognised by the Hampden Clubs; and the people, at a loss to distinguish friends from enemies, were soon prepared for the operation of informers.

Actual human attributes are given independence, detached from specific human actions. One wishes, reading such passages, that Bamford would allow his protagonists to claim responsibility for their own reactions. Like an academic thesis-writer's, his impersonal formulations simply muffle his personal involvement.

There are in fact very few moments in *Passages* when Bamford is clearly the agent responsible for his own political engagement. The following sentence is perhaps the most decisive of any concerned with his political choices:

I determined to go forward in the cause of parliamentary reform.

—the strength of 'determined' is entirely unusual in Bamford's vocabulary. Yet even this declaration is in fact hedged almost out of existence by the surrounding sentences: the preceding page has been arguing that the absence of experienced leadership excused the excesses of the early radicals; Bamford continues:

In the absence, therefore, of such wholesome monition—in the ardour also, and levity of youth—and impelled by a sincere and disinterested wish to deserve the gratitude of my working fellow-countrymen; it is scarcely to be wondered at, that I soon forgot whatever merely prudential reflections my better sense had whispered to me whilst in durance; and that with a strong though discreetly tempered zeal, I determined to go forward in the cause of parliamentary reform.

And so, as it were, like another Crusoe, I lay with my little boat in the still water, waiting for the first breeze to carry me again to the billows.

The final metaphor cancels out the brief moment of actual decision-taking.

We can conclude this indicative analysis of Bamford's characteristically passive forms of describing political action, by noting that, in one sense, 'passivity' was almost the only means of 'control' that a working-class radical movement could have exercised at that time over the national situation. To oppose the increasingly interlocked and homogeneous nature of an emerging industrialised society required an increasingly coordinated and widespread counter-force. But once a 'Spencean' strategy of insurrection was excluded, the only viable action open to such a counter-force was, basically, a withdrawal of labour, solidarity in strike action, sustained and patient in its very inactivity. On a small scale such tactical passiveness had already appeared as a local weapon, as in the Manchester strikes of 1818; at a national level, once an extensive opposition movement had been formed in the early Chartist phase, such tactices were to be proposed as a complete strategy, in the 'National Holiday' so much disliked by Bamford. It was not so much his own innate passivity that limited Bamford's political outlook—the circumstances engendered passive response of one kind or another—but his restriction to a small-scale horizon within a known group of political allies that made it impossible for him to connect passivity with any grouping large enough, and therefore necessarily 'impersonal', to make deliberate passivity or inaction more than mere submission.

(vii) Elements of form and relationship

If we now move to an analysis of some of the structural or formal features of *Passages*, we can first link the characteristics of style examined above to one interesting element in the content of Bamford's writing. Unusually for a working-class autobiography—where wife and family, and emotional relations generally, tend to be taken for granted—Bamford's gives a notable amount of attention to the subject of women. One could suggest a specific psychological root for this relative emphasis—his loss of his mother at the age of six and his father's early remarriage. But the appropriate point seems to me different. Considerable work has been done in recent years on the connection between neighbourhood environments and modes of personal relationship; the conclusion seems to be that relationships in a 'traditional' working-class district are characteristically 'passive', the codes assumed and lived into without great personal tensions; but this means that the social skills necessary actively to create new personal relationships in a changed environment—a new housing estate, for example—can be learned only with difficulty.

If we grasp Bamford's experience of negotiating the move from known community to a world of strangers as involving similar problems of relationship then we can see that his emphasis on encounters with women is not fortuitous. Indeed, his love-life in *Early Days* is clearly polarised round two main relationships: that with Mima, his eventual wife, follows a comparatively easy and 'natural' path, with accepted codes of courting, since Mima is almost 'the girl next door', known from childhood; while that with Catherine is accidently begun, is pursued intermittently through confusions and difficulties, only to end without satisfaction, since Catherine comes from a different class, a strange world, and Bamford's responses are complex, awkward, and in the end self-defeating. His reaction to losing Catherine is to attempt to bury all emotion, 'and never more to give to woman the power of inflicting pain'. In this mood he has an encounter which clearly underlines the connection between his sense of a known community and his difficulties in reacting in such a way as to deny the patterns and modes of personal relationship engendered within such communities. A prostitute propositions him one night—his 'first time'; they find a quiet back-street; then:

Something she said about 'the sweet air of the country' [so] I questioned her as to where she came from—and did not my ears tingle, and my heart leap, when she said 'from Middleton'. 'Did I?', what was my name then? I told her, when, uttering an exclamation of joyful surprise, she would have smothered me with caresses. I next questioned her as to her name, and seemingly incredulous, she asked me if I really did not know her? I assured her I did not, and she wept to think, as she said, that she should have carried me in her arms when I was an infant, and now that we should meet here I did not know her. Who could she be? I again asked, and she mentioned a name at the hearing of which I almost sank to the earth. She had been born and brought up at the house next door to that of my parents; she was the beloved child of their early friends and associates; she married when I was but an infant, and her husband, when I could run about, used to make whip-cord, and kites, and banding to fly them with for me. I knew the man well at that time, he was still living, and it not unfrequently happened that I was in his company when I went over to Middleton. I was disgusted with myself and her. . . . My soul revolted, and I got rid of her by paying for a glass of hot liquor at 'The Dangerous Corner' public house. Dangerous indeed.

Symptomatic, too, of many of the strands of social change we have already looked at. Bamford's difficulties with women offer the same kind of difficulties as his political choices, and stem, in part at least, from the same social determinants. It is then no surprise to see him, in *Passages*, recounting the one as a comment on the other. For the writing of his autobiography also presented some of the same problems: to establish a personal relation with a reader who yet remains a stranger is difficult, and Bamford resorted, it seems to me, to indirect and oblique ways of doing so. To examine his technique of indirectness brings us close to some of the problems which are also involved in writing 'literature', in becoming a novelist.

One long sequence reveals the technique rather hesitantly at work. *Passages* II, chapters 13 to 20, are concerned with Bamford's trial at York; chapters 29 and 30 relate the final proceedings at the King's Bench, London. Between these two phases of his trial Bamford tells the story of his journey down to London, in chapters 21 to 28. These intervening chapters may seem at first 'mere' narrative, but once we recognise that this second volume is largely concerned with Bamford's politically important realisation that personal friendship is an inadequate basis for a radical movement, it may be that we can also see that these chapters help in fact to chart his confusion and progress towards disillusionment on this matter. Chapter 21 describes his departure from Middleton, and already an ominous note appears:

I should have been miserable if from any circumstances I had incurred a risk of not being in court when called, and had thereby forfeited the bail which my friends had given with me. My radical acquaintances, however, never asked me when, or how, I was going.

That slight shift, 'friends . . . acquaintances' is symptomatic, for Bamford is offered no money for his journey by the Middleton radicals. He leaves, in fact, with only his wife and little daughter to see him off:

I could not but reflect that when I went that way on the sixteenth of August, there were ten thousand with me ready to shout, sing, or do whatever I requested.

The chapter ends with Bamford's last long look back at his wife as they part outside Stockport. Chapter 22 opens with Bamford overtaking 'a young man and his wife', and the three agree to travel together; but the next day's journey begins to reveal tensions between husband and wife, John and Margaret: he a slow walker, without much conversation, she a good walker, 'sensible, well-informed' and clearly her husband's 'superior'. Soon John continues by cart, while Bamford and Margaret walk, and talk about 'matters always interesting to females, namely the history of some tender attachments'. She tells him how she had rejected an earlier lover, Robert, who then joined the army and was killed in battle, for which she sometimes accused herself. When they reach Margaret's home at Loughborough Bamford is persuaded to stay overnight and join the family reunion. Suddenly, in the middle of the welcome party, in walks Robert, the 'dead' lover; he greets Margaret's mother as 'my *other* mother' and speaks of the house as one where he left 'friends, and mayhap a little of something more than friendship?'

'Nothing beyond friendship now Robert,' said the mother, endeavouring to appear cool.
'Why, where is Margaret?' he said, 'I hope nothing has befallen her.'
'Margaret is your friend,' said the old woman, 'but she is nothing more now. Yonder sits her husband,' pointing to John.
The soldier trembled, and staggered to a seat.

Bamford soon leaves this now somewhat subdued party.

Chapter 24 deals at some length with Bamford's attempts to get overnight lodgings at various inns, and ends with the advice quoted earlier to foot-travellers to play a confident role. Chapter 25 includes his disappointment at calling at an inn once the home of an old couple who had befriended him years before, only to find a new tenant in the house. While he rests there a local constable enters with a young woman in custody for bearing an illegitimate child—and Bamford resolves to rescue her! After various complications, the young man who was supposed to have abandoned her really does rescue her, and promptly marries her—while Bamford is being charged with aiding in her escape. The chapter ends, however, with a wedding party and reconciliations. Chapters 26 to 28 bring him into London, but by now his money is nearly all spent and when he goes for help to 'the lodgings of my friend Hunt at Mr Giles's', Hunt has moved, Mr Giles is dead, and Mrs Giles does not speak 'in that friendly tone' he remembered. Arriving at Hunt's new lodgings he is received warmly enough, but Hunt makes no offer of a bed and Bamford leaves this 'friend and his family' with the thought: 'That is not the way . . . I treat my friends from a distance, when they call upon me in Lancashire.' He finally finds lodgings, but the room given him is filthy and costs him all his remaining money. On leaving the next morning he meets on the stairs 'as demure a looking piece of purity as the world ever exhibited'—she turns out to be a prostitute. Bamford wanders round London, finding no help at various 'friends' houses, till he finally remembers a 'gentleman', Mr Gibb, who had once 'behaved very kindly' to him. Bamford is received very warmly, offered breakfast, and, when he finally admits to being destitute, is persuaded to come every day for his meals and to accept some money. Chapter 38 ends:

I thanked him most sincerely. I never was more affected by an act of kindness in my life. He was in truth 'a friend in need, a friend indeed'.

It is clear that the incidents which make up this journey are all concerned with difficulties, confusions, twists, disappointments, misjudgements in relationships: friends cannot be trusted or are dead, comrades are unreliable, even marriage may be falsely founded, judgements about purity—or betrayal —may be wrong, hospitality cannot be presumed; in the world experienced in these chapters all relationships are suspect. Though love and friendship may still be vindicated—the journey begins and ends in affirmation—the context is clearly set, and set *indirectly*, for the coming disillusionment with Hunt's friendship and that of all other radicals.

Perhaps the most immediately effective instance of Bamford prompting the reader's reactions indirectly, by an apparently irrelevant anecdote, is the insertion of chapters 20 to 22 in volume I. He is in prison, awaiting examination by the Privy Council for alleged involvement in the Ardwick Bridge conspiracy. Bamford recounts a tale told by a fellow-prisoner, George Plant (sic!), also facing possible transportation or the scaffold. This story, of Plant's 'attempt to take and carry off "Saint John's Fearn seed" ' (regarded as a magic love-potion) takes up eleven pages, narrated with rich detail, vivid dialect dialogue and deliberate artifice. The suspense of a superstition-ridden expedition in the dead of night is carefully built up. The climax comes after the final spell is chanted:

They looked, and perceived by a glance, that a venerable form, in a loose robe was near them.

Darkness came down like a swoop. The fearn was shaken, the upper dish flew into pieces—the pewter one melted—the skull emitted a cry, and eyes glared in its sockets—light broke—beautiful children were seen walking in their holiday clothes—and graceful female forms sung mournful and enchanting airs.

The men stood terrified and fascinated; and Bangle gazing bade 'God bless 'em'. A crash followed, as if the whole of the timber in the kloof was being splintered and torn up—strange and horrid forms appeared from the thickets—the men ran off as if sped on the wind—they separated and lost each other. Plant ran towards the old house, and there leaping the brook, he cast a glance behind him, and saw terrific shapes, some beastly, some part human, and some hellish, gnashing their teeth, and howling and uttering the most fearful and mournful tones, as if wishful to follow him, but unable to do so.

In an agony of terror he arrived at home, not knowing how he got there. He was during several days, in a state bordering on unconsciousness; and when he recovered he learned that Chirrup was found on the White Moors, raving mad, and chasing the wild birds. As for poor Bangle, he found his way home over hedge and ditch; running with supernatural and fearful speed—the skull's eyes glaring at his back, and the nether jaw grinning and jabbering frightful and unintelligible sounds. He had preserved the seed however, and having taken it from the skull, he buried the latter at the cross roads from whence he had taken it. He then carried the spell out, and his proud love stood one night at his bed-side in tears. But he had done too much for human nature—in three months after she followed his corpse, a real mourner, to the grave.

Immediately after a brief concluding remark about Plant's fate, the next chapter opens:

It was, I think, on the 23rd April that I was taken to the Home Office with George Plant, for my fourth examination.

This sudden switch still leaves the after-image of that jabbering skull and the madness and death of the eleven-page story vividly present to the reader: the ritual examination before Lord Sidmouth that follows is coloured by the sense of terror and suspense conveyed by the ritual of the story; the reader is made to share Bamford's fear at the prospect of a death-sentence, not through any direct evocation of what it must have felt like to be awaiting judgement on a high treason charge, but by imaginative participation in the tragedy of Saint John's fern seed.

A more complex and extended example of indirect presentation of emotions is *Passages* I, chapters 10 and 11. Bamford is here expecting to be arrested after the suspension of Habeas Corpus. An atmosphere of suspicion, suspense and watchfulness has been created, with reports of numerous other local arrests, and enigmatic visits by grim-faced 'gentlemen'. Finally Bamford decides to go into hiding and with a comrade, Healey, sets off across the moors by night. Trying to find their way in pitch darkness, along unfamiliar paths, they suddenly encounter an 'owd hag' with a lantern; to their inquiries she replies that the roads lead 'to many places i' this ward . . . an' mayhap some ith'other'. She agrees to guide them. But suddenly 'lanthorn and lanthorn bearer disappeared, and the next moment there was a crash and a plash!' Healey has fallen into a ditch, and Bamford only just saves himself from following. They extricate themselves and wonder at the old woman's amazing disappearance, till suddenly they hear 'a laugh of almost unearthly tone, which came like a jeering yell upon the wind,' and see 'a light, dancing as it were, and moving at a rapid pace through the profound darkness'; then 'the laugh was renewed, but sounded fainter, and almost like a scream of pain; and the next moment the light began to descend, and suddenly disappeared as if sunk into the earth'. Shaken by these mysterious happenings, they grope on, till they spot a light, 'a human habitation which we thought must be a tavern'; the chapter ends: 'we opened the door and entered without ceremony'. By this time, however, that simple statement has acquired an aura of menace, suspense and even magic: the strange woman seems the harbinger of some deadly witchcraft. Bamford delays the dénouement by opening the next chapter with a gradual description of the interior and the people present, with growing hints of hostility and danger, till:

who should make her appearance but the same old woman who about an hour before had vanished so unaccountably. 'Excisemen!' 'Informers!' she screamed, at the top of a thrilling voice; and at that moment, each man of the company was on his feet; hands were clutching at our throats, and a prospect of certain manglement or murder, stared from those ferocious countenances.

The supposed tavern is in fact a 'hush-shop', and some of Healey's questions had roused the suspicions of the old woman, who had suddenly cloaked her lamp and turned away. But Bamford and Healey are recognised and vouched for by a poacher and they are accepted into the company. The violence they have so narrowly escaped is adequately indicated by a detailed and sickening description of a brutal fight that soon develops between the poacher and another client.

The point of this extended anecdote, so far, is to make the reader share the atmosphere of suspicion and danger that Healey and Bamford are in, by doubling that situation: they are pursued by the police, but in the eyes of the hush-shop drinkers they are the pursuers; mistrust and hostility have multiplied, to infect the whole countryside through which they move. But now the anecdote begins to take on a new significance. After the nearly fatal, and horrific, fight, Bamford and Healey leave and they arrive back at Middleton 'without further adventure'. The next paragraph reads:

And shall we part here, friend reader? On my threshold shall we part? Nay, come in from the frozen rain, and from the night wind, which is blowing the clouds into sheets, like torn sails before a gale. Now down a step or two—'Tis better to keep low in the world, than to climb only to fall. It is dark, save when the clouds break into white scud above; and silent, except the snort of the wind, and the rattling of hail, and the eaves of dropping rain. Come in!—A glimmer shows that the place is inhabited; that the nest has not been rifled while the old bird was away. Now thou shalt see what a miser a poor man can be in his heart's treasury. A second door opens, and a flash of light shews we are in a weaving room, clean and flagged, and in which are two looms with silken work of green and gold. A young woman, of short stature, fair, round, fresh as Hebe; with light brown hair escaping in ringlets from the sides of her clean cap, and with a thoughtful and meditative look, sits darning beside a good fire, which sheds warmth upon the clean swept hearth, and gives light throughout the room, or rather cell. A fine little girl, seven years of age, with a sensible and affectionate expression of countenance is reading in a low tone to her mother:

'And he opened his mouth and taught them, saying Blessed are the poor in spirit; for their's is the kingdom of heaven. Blessed are they that mourn; for they shall be comforted. Blessed are the meek; for they shall inherit the earth . . .

The Beatitudes are quoted, quietly and tellingly, in full. In a new paragraph the room is further described, and then the reunion of Bamford, wife and daughter:

. . . But my wife!
'She look'd; she redden'd like the rose
Syne, pale as ony lily.'
Ah! did they hear the throb of my heart, when they sprung to embrace me? my little child to my knees, and my wife to my bosom.

The reader has been gradually brought within Bamford's home, and finally into his feelings and sensations, even to hearing his heart throb and feeling his daughter's clasp. The contrast with the hostility and suspicion of the previous episode could not be more complete; nor could the contrast between the violence of the hush-shop fight and the atmosphere of peace given in that beautifully placed quotation of the Beatitudes.

To acknowledge these contrasts and to accept the invitation to enter Bamford's home makes it impossible for the reader to acquiesce in his possible arrest for violently threatening the peace and order of the kingdom! Yet within five pages Bamford is in fact arrested. To read the episodes which precede this arrest as mere accidental narrative, as simply an account of 'what happened', would be to do less than justice to what is written—and to how it is written. There is an artistry in the pattern of these episodes: the incidents have as much deliberate significance as those in a carefully constructed novel.

(viii) Finale and conversion

It is in the long concluding movement of the whole work that, I think, this artistry of indirect effects is brought most fully and subtly into play, and the sequence merits detailed analysis. However, in the space available, it seems best simply to pick up the analysis in the very final stages of Bamford's disillusionment with his radical 'friends'. An interlocking series of hostilities, misunderstandings and suspicions has been detailed, and Bamford's judgement on this attritional process is finally made explicit in chapter 40:

I was disgusted—I was sick and beyond the power of reasoning with the villainy which I met with at every step—I could not enter into such ungenerous warfare, nor lower myself to the rascally weapons used against me. The still, unobtrusive voice of truth, was not heard, and I was too often condemned. This was one of the most painful passages of my life. Envy, and its sure attendant —detraction, haunted me within the prison and without—I never think of that time without horror—the boroughmongers had incarcerated my body, but the refermers wounded my soul.

This paragraph ends with a prayer to God, who alone remains as a 'mighty friend'. This chapter also introduces the event that is finally to disillusion Bamford entirely with political radicalism: Hunt writes 'like a friend' to offer Bamford enough money to be able to keep Mrs Bamford with him in jail; on this occasion the money does not actually appear, but this offer is shortly to play an important role.

Chapter 41 is the final breaking point. The equation of boroughmongers and reformers is underlined in the opening paragraph: Hunt 'actually instituted an order of knighthood; the order of "Saint Henry of Ilchester'. The first knight was himself, Saxton having dubbed him, and the second knight was the said Saxton, Hunt having dubbed him in return.' The radicals are reproducing all the corruption, vanity and foolishness of the order they profess to oppose. Hunt is seen as 'deranged' and Bamford had 'now, and for ever after, done with his judgement'. Only the genuine knight, Sir Charles Wolseley, shows 'not a friendship of words only'; but the money he offers is deflected by Bamford to the imprisoned radical, John Knight—whom Bamford however immediately attacks: 'as I have found, old John would have seen me boiling the stones of the castle for dinner, sooner than he would have done me, or any one else, a like turn.' Bamford continues, 'As for my friend Hunt, no sooner had my wife become settled the second time at Lincoln, than his motive for helping her there became apparent.' That 'friend' is deeply ironic by now. For Hunt only wanted the precedent of Mrs Bamford staying with Bamford in order to demand that his own mistress join him in jail. Since Bamford has pledged himself to secrecy about this personal privilege, he refuses to acknowledge the fact publicly for Hunt. Bamford comments: 'I could not but be sensible—though Hunt's self-love, which he was constantly disclaiming, blinded him to it—of the difference between a man being indulged with the company of his own wife, and being indulged with the company of another man's wife.' On this issue they finally break. Hunt's last letter is still signed, 'I am dear Bamford your sincere friend', but Bamford only 'wrote a cool letter of acknowledgement' and they 'never corresponded afterward'. The chapter concludes:

I had seen through the veil with which devotion had covered my eyes. I would not be any longer a passive instrument of his will, and so, as I no longer suited his purpose, he had done with me, and I gained the loss of his friendship.

The paradoxical phrasing of those last words is exact. Throughout the long prison sequence, from chapter 34 onwards, the dominant theme has been the loss of political friendships. As we saw earlier, Bamford's political allegiances were based on personal relationships; an earlier sequence, on the road to

London, showed him meeting various kinds of breakdown and confusion in personal relations; now the climax has come: radical political 'friendships' cover only the same kinds of egotism, corruption and self-seeking as other, apparently opposed, forms of politics. To see through that 'veil', finally, is for Bamford a tremendous 'gain': he ceases, in his own eyes, being 'a passive instrument'—a precise description of his own self-presentation earlier. From now on the only personal relationship on which to build a life is that of married love—and Hunt's false (in Bamford's view) relationship with his mistress is firmly rejected. But pure domesticity is deeply a-political, and that realisation is a kind of conversion for Bamford.

The religious overtones of this conversion are made almost explicit in chapter 43, which recounts Bamford's release from prison and his long journey home with Mima, his wife—an idyllic tramp through an English countryside described with glowing lyricism. The high point of the journey comes when an overnight stay in Sheffield is cut short by the discovery in their bed of 'one of those noisome flat insects, so common in the beds of towns and crowded places'; this persuades them immediately to 'get out into "the green lanes"' and to 'breathe the sweet country air'. They leave Sheffield and climb over the moors till:

In the valley we had left—now as we could discover of a beautifully undulating surface, and gaily green in the sun—lay the town of Sheffield, shrouded in its furnace clouds. On our right were the wild and boundless districts I have mentioned, and before us was the wrinkled front of Mam Tor, frowning like an eld, in witch-land.

Bamford's old preference for the country, against 'towns and crowded places', emerges strongly here. But there is something more being prepared: the mysterious resonance of that last phrase, 'like an eld, in witch-land', is taken up in a passage which needs to be quoted at length:

We walked to the height of Hattersage-Grange, and there stopped to survey the vast, solitary, yet pleasing scenes. My wife was seated on a grassy knoll, whilst I stood beside her with my stick and bundle over my shoulder—my back towards the sun, whose beams were somewhat mitigated by light clouds—and my looks directed over the wold towards the Yorkshire border.
    'Well, I am convinced now,' I said, breaking a long silence, 'that Burke was not so far wide of the truth after all.'
    'What did Burke say,' she asked, 'for my part I never heard him say much of either truth or falsehood.'
    She thought I was alluding to one of the simplest of my radical comrades, whom we had nick-named 'Burke'.
    'Pho! It's Edmund Burke, the great orator and apostate that I mean.'
    'And what did he say?' she asked.
    'Say? He called the people "the swinish multitude", and I am convinced he was right; for I have discovered I am one of them.'
    'What do you mean?' she asked again, now more interested.
    'I can see the wind,' I said, 'and that's a sure sign I'm one of the swinish herd.'
    'See the wind? and what's it like?'—asked she, looking up, and laughing.
    'It's the most beautiful thing I ever saw,' I said, 'and if thou'll come here, thou shalt see it also.'
    I will suppose that the curiosity natural to her sex was excited, for she was instantly at my side. Now look over the top of the brown heath with a steady eye, and see if thou canst discern a remarkably bright substance, brighter than glass or pearly water—deeply clear, and lucid —swimming, not like a stream, but like a quick spirit, up and down, and forward, as if hurrying to be gone.

'Nonsense!' she said—'there is not anything.'

'Look again, steady, for a moment,' I said, 'I still behold it.'

'There is,' she said—'there is—I see it—Oh! what a beautiful thing.'

I gave her a kiss and said I loved her better than ever. She was the first woman who, I believed, had ever seen the vital element, the life-fraught wind.

'Is that the wind?' she asked.

'That is the wind of heaven,' I said, 'sweeping over the earth, and now visible. It is the great element of vitality—water quickened by fire—the spirit of life!'

I know not whether I was quite right in my philosophy, but we bowed our hearts, and adored the Creator; and in that, we were both right, I hope.

We stood gazing in wonder and admiration; for still, like a spirit-stream, it kept hurrying past—or as a messenger in haste; and so we left it, glittering and sweeping away—This was on the morning of the nineteenth day of May, 1821.

And reader, I dare be bound with thee, that if, having a good pair of eyes, thou wilt at the same season of the year, and on a day like ours—with a mild sun, and a quick breeze out of Yorkshire—if thou at such a season, and on such a day, climb to the top of Hathersage-Grange, and stand with thy back to the sun—Mam Tor visible on thy left hand—then also, shalt thou see the beautiful apparition—the spirit of life—which we saw. It will repay thy trouble well, I assure thee—Neither I nor mine can ever forget it, whilst memory is ours.

The passage recalls, in its function if not its quality, such passages as Wordsworth's vision of the moon on Snowdon in Book XIII of *The Prelude* (1805) or the final pages of Lawrence's *The Rainbow*. For Bamford is clearly trying to convey here an immense experience, akin to the 'new birth' experience of the Methodist convert, and the function of the passage is clearly to leave a sense of completeness, satisfaction and peace in the reader, to bring him to share a kind of conversion which is a symbolic substitute for the actual, political, conversion in question. There is a return to the known community (the mistake over 'Burke' exactly parallels the mistake in the *Walks* passage quoted earlier), and there is an acknowledgement that somehow—in a way the connection with seeing the wind does not clarify (it is that kind of symbol) —Burke was right, that such people as Bamford are 'the swinish multitude', at least on earth, and ought to keep their place. Bamford's place is now 'home', with his family around him, and the final chapter of narrative brings him home, the last paragraph completing the reunion of the family, the last words emphasising the new priority:

Our walk to Manchester the next morning was a mere pleasure trip. We scarcely stopped there, but hastening onwards, we entered Middleton in the afternoon, and were met in the street by our dear child, who came running, wild with delight, to our arms. We soon made ourselves comfortable in our own humble dwelling; the fire was lighted, the hearth was swept clean, friends came to welcome us, and we were once more at home.

'Be it ever so humble,
There's no place like home.'

There the narrative of *Passages* ends.

(ix) Conclusion

In one of his two summing-up chapters Bamford remarks that *Passages* is a work 'of novel execution'. The point of my analysis has been to indicate that *Passages* does indeed have an unusual form, that it verges on, without ever quite becoming, a work our responses to which are controlled and guided by literary techniques more often to be expected in novels and imaginative writing generally than in apparently simple narrative. Bamford, it should now be clear, is not simply writing a report of his experiences; by selection, by thematic patterning, by indirect or near-allegorical commentary and illustration, by parallels and juxtapositions, he is trying to overcome the barrier between his experience and that of readers who would not have shared that kind of experience but who might, by their response to his anecdotes and apparently irrelevant inclusions, find an echo, a resonance, a larger significance. Bamford himself recognised that *Passages* was a work which approached, or rivalled, 'literature': commenting on the encouragement he received from the serialisation of 'Pickwick, Nicholas Nickleby, Jack Sheppard', he remarks:

> Without presuming to affect an approach to the practised writers of the day, I had often thought that my romantic life, if well written, would read as well, at least, as some of the . . . trashy, unreal novels which the press sometimes deign to extol.

However, the main point to be emphasised here is that *Passages* remains a half-way house. The writing—the style and structure—is a fusion of historical documentary, personal narrative, and imaginative literature—if such category-terms can be allowed to stand. Bamford does not transmute his experience fully into fiction, into a familiar form of the nineteenth-century novel, where his relationship to his material would have required a different kind of skill or capacity: an imaginative creation of, and inwardness to, 'other' characters, a breaking beyond the bounds of his own actual life, a distancing from self. To some extent, perhaps, his meagre education set some of the limits here. But it also seems to me that there is a complex relation between his political positions and the mode of his autobiography. Just as the limits of his political stance were concerned with the difficult transformation of a close, known, personal community of relationships into extended and 'impersonal' forms of relation to unknown co-operators, to 'strangers'—a transformation Bamford eventually refused in his virtual retreat into domesticity—so the limits of his self-expression are deeply connected with his inability to enter fully into a mediated relationship with his experience and his audience.

One can put the point another way: to read a novel is to enter another community, to penetrate others' experiences, to leave the horizon of one's own 'world'; in that process, one's own experience is reflected back, refracted, prepared for judgement. To write a novel seems to require the same kinds of openness; to read an autobiography also does. But to write an autobiography does not demand openness in the same way: the horizon remains the closed circle of one's own self, even if concentric circles of self-definitions and self-identifications are traceable within that horizon. The terms used here to describe the process of reading a novel have a clear correlation with a possible description of the political mode necessary for a fully democratic participation in a social world. I tried earlier to indicate the positive reasons why to write an autobiography was a decision homologous with Bamford's limited political position (in section (v)); but to seek an elucidation of the negative limitations of his actual writing might be to arrive at a threshold of ancient literary problems—and still-present political horizons.

Chapter 2: Alexander Somerville: 'One of my faither's Simerels'

(i) Names and anonymity

The title-page includes no name: *The Autobiography of A Working Man, by* '*One who has whistled at the plough*'. The opening pages (ostensibly addressed to 'My dear boy'—the author's son) give no family surname, recounting ancestors simply in terms of 'your grandfather and grandmother, my parents', even though the second paragraph is largely taken up by a comment about names:

One of them, Lawrence, died at Perth within my recollection. I was to have been called Lawrence after him, but a change was made, and I was named after my mother's brother, a collier, living at Square, near Berwick-upon-Tweed—a worthy man, to whose name I may not have done all the honour I might have done. In my boyhood I used to regret that I had not been called Lawrence. I then thought my own name was a shabby one. Perhaps my dislike to it arose from its being so very common in Scotland.

Common or not, the reader is not told the name. He is given the name of the author's father's horse, but not his father's. An uncle's Christian name and the full name of a maternal grandfather are given, but neither of the author's parents are named. Various siblings are named, but not himself:

My brother James was born in the Cove; Peter was born a year or two after, in Thorntonloch; Janet was born next, in Wood Hall; Mary next, in Thornton Mains . . .; and, lastly, I was born at Springfield.

It is, in fact, impossible to discover the author's full name from the autobiography until its climax is reached; on page 277 a sentence of court-martial is quoted:

The Court, having found the prisoner 'guilty' of the crime laid to his charge . . . sentence him, the prisoner, Alexander Somerville, to receive two hundred lashes.

This long silence, though odd, might be explained by the convention of Somerville writing his autobiography as letters to his son, but that convention only rarely intrudes and within a few chapters effectively ceases to operate. Before an alternative explanation is suggested, the peculiar role of names in this text is worth analysing.

Other names are also omitted from the autobiography, their place taken by initials or dashes. Some of these omissions are connected with a girl referred to as 'the nameless ONE', whom he courted unsuccessfully and whose name he conceals for that reason; others concern political incidents or personal friends. The omissions might be covered by the explanation Somerville himself offers:

In consequence of this Autobiography not having been written to be published in my life-time, nor so soon as the year 1848, had I died before, I find in it several names of persons which for the present must be omitted.

Sometimes, however, it is the inclusion of a name that is notable: he gives all the names and characters of the family cows, a farm-horse and the plough-horses; on running away from home he says an individual goodbye to the corn chest, the pump, the wheelbarrow, the parritch-cart, Kidley the cow, and finally a large beech tree on which all the family had carved their names. His early world is one in which people are differentiated not by surnames but by a fusion of

Christian name and character: six casual workers all named Michael are differentiated as 'old Michael, young Michael, big Michael, wee Michael, singing Michael, and Michael the laird'. We finally learn his father's Christian name only because 'old Bonar, the orry horse' is so like 'old James, the orry man'. Somerville remembers launching a local nickname: 'In my effort to call the old woman Mary Edgly, I called her Essel, which name everybody else took up.' Mary Edgly's husband, Thomas Brown (as Somerville specifically notes, 'it is the custom for married women, in Scotland, to retain their maiden names'), used to tell him fairy tales, and 'as Thomas Brown had known the fairies personally, I had as complete a belief in their existence as I had that of the people who lived at Stobby Castle, or at Edinburgh, or anywhere else beyond Thriepland Hill and Branxton'. The very naming of people and places creates their reality, if they exist outside the child's immediate experience. As a boy Somerville shared in another old man's world, a world created by names: blind James Dawson

used to sit down and call to Sir Walter Raleigh, Essex, Burleigh, and other courtiers of Elizabeth to come to him, and when they came he sent them to fetch her majesty. He would then go into political arguments with them about Philip of Spain and the other personages and subjects of Elizabeth's reign. He would listen as if some one spoke into his ear, for their observations, and would interrupt them at times impatiently, if they did not seem to be holding a sound argument. Intermingled with such converse he would speak aside to some shepherd or farmer whom he had known in his younger days, and ask him what he thought of Burleigh's opinions. The next minute he would address me by name and ask a question as to what I thought of Queen Elizabeth's dress.

It is in this context that the author is first given any name: 'I, in the usual way, asked, "Well, James, how are ye thi' day?" he said, "Man, Sandy, I'm glad I've met ye . . . you must go this minute to the Empress, and tell her that Frank Horne must not be made a slave." ' Since the Empress is the imagined Empress of Russia, whereas Frank Horne is 'a lad from Branxton', we cannot be fully assured of the status of 'Sandy' until the name is later repeated—the only name given until the court-martial.

So far we are clearly in a world similar to Bamford's known community, where a name naturally referred only to someone within that community. However it is not only his origins in such a community that concerns us here, but also Somerville's continued interest in names outside that community. Twice we find him sitting before the gravestones of long-dead relatives and trying to conjure up their personalities simply from their graven names. In Edinburgh his 'greatest entertainment of an intellectual nature' was attending debates of the Synod of the United Secession Church, because 'many of the debaters were ministers . . . whose very names were always uttered by my father . . . with veneration'. Somerville's introduction to political discussion is through the names of politicians: when the Grey government is announced in a newspaper, he and his work-mates 'read over the list of the new ministry. Some of the names were unknown to us, and some familiar names that *we* thought should have been there were not there, the name of Hume especially.' Names are indeed for Somerville an almost effective substitute for the real person: of a friend, for example, he says: 'I hardly ever write his name, or look upon it when it is written, or listen to it when it is spoken, but the echo of that friendly counsel, and the form and image of that disastrous time, come back upon me.'

Some of the instances where names play a role in the autobiography indicate familiar social reasons for this underlying interest. For example, Somerville relates an anecdote on the disparity between apparent social importance and actual social role (a newspaper editor given priority in Canning's office), revealed only in an exchange of visiting cards—the unknown name suddenly given importance by the attached professional description. On one occasion he himself obtains a paper signed with Cobbett's name as an introduction to London contacts. Another incident shows how, in a period of social and geographical mobility, a name could often be the only element of continuity in a relationship: in 1847, as a newspaper correspondent himself, he meets some of the officers he knew fifteen years before in the army and simply by not introducing himself (or so he believed) accompanies them unrecognised. These are all minor examples of a (now) familiar experience. But Somerville's concern with names has deeper roots, which we can now trace.

His account of his first experience of class-conflict—directly in the form of a schoolroom imitation of a battle between soldiers and 'ragged radicals' in 1819—includes the comment:

Some one ran to the schoolmaster and told that I was thrashing 'Master' Somebody, for he being a gentleman's son was called 'Master', while I had to submit to a nickname, derived from the state of my clothes.

His punishment includes being demoted from the top of the class-list: the teacher 'kept slates with every pupil's name written on them', on which conduct and academic marks were totalled every Friday; on this occasion he 'watched with tremulous expectation the reading of the names'—and was placed last. In the army, too, name-lists could be manipulated to victimise:

The dinners are then cut out, each man's allowance laid upon a plate. One turns his back towards the table, and another touches a plate with a knife, and calls, 'Who shall have this?' He whose back is to the table names some one; and so on they proceed until all the plates are touched, and all the men in that room named. If Johnny Raw is to be once more vexed or victimised, a bone without meat, or almost without it, is laid upon a plate. He whose back is turned has been secretly told that this plate will be touched, we shall say, the sixth in turn. Accordingly, when the man who touches the plate with his knife says, for the sixth time, 'Who shall have this?' the reply is, 'Johnny', or 'Cruity', or whatever they call him.

The victimisation is clear; so too is the overall context of military standardisation, the reduction of every new soldier (allotted his generic nickname) to an equal facelessness, differentiated only by name and number. The experiance is, of course, traditional, but it is worth emphasising that this was precisely the context in which Somerville achieved national notice as a named individual.

As a soldier in Spain in 1835–7 Somerville had seen another aspect of military standardisation: he 'made out the returns of sick and dead men at Vittoria, every day . . . where we lost nearly four thousand men'; and since he 'kept our own company's accounts' he knew what 'every man's credit was when he died'; knowing more about the dead men than anyone else, he was 'applied to by their friends, on returning to Britain, to give information about their fate, and the debts due to them by the Spanish government'. This knowledge, and the publication of his *Narrative of the British Legion in Spain*

(1837) brought him hundreds of letters from relatives seeking advice about the recovery of pay and financial compensation; but in taking up these cases Somerville found himself in a Kafka-esque legal world in which names, signatures, lists, identifications and his own signed guarantees became so much paper for financial speculation, legal quibbling and government bureaucracy, and in which the original bearers of the names involved were soon a secondary consideration. As a youth Somerville had already, traumatically, encountered the purely legal significance of a name: he had been fined for 'coming into town with a cart which had no ticket of the owner's name and residence on it', even though the town officer knew very well whose cart it was. That early incident is already perhaps an indication of the kind of changes overtaking the known relationships of a small community, but in the affair of the Spanish certificates, where names of strangers became all-important in a network embracing the legal, communications and security systems of the country, we begin to grasp on a major scale the shape and model of a new kind of society.

(ii) 1832 and alienation

Somerville's deeper insertion into that new kind of society began, not inappropriately, with the sending of an anonymous letter to a newspaper. In May 1832, during the feverish nine days of uncertainty about the eventual reaction of the House of Lords to the Reform Bill, Somerville, then a soldier in the Scots Greys stationed in Birmingham, was one of a group of soldiers who decided to publicise the fact that the troops 'were not to be relied upon to put down public meetings, or prevent the people of Birmingham from journeying to London, to present their petitions.' This group 'caused letters to be written and sent to various parties in Birmingham and London, to that effect. Some were addressed to the Duke of Wellington, some to the War Office to Lord Hill, and some were dropped in the streets. Those letters were necessarily anonymous.' Somerville also, however, wrote a letter to a London newspaper affirming this position. Its publication led to his court-martial and flogging; a Court of Inquiry into the legality of the court-martial aroused national interest—The Times, sensationally, even replaced some columns of front-page advertisements with an account of the findings. Somerville became a local, then national celebrity, but not as a known individual, simply as a name to be used as a slogan. Again and again, he recounts experiences of this divorce between himself and his name. After release from hospital after the flogging, he is in a pub writing another letter to the press, to publicise the court-martial, when some drinkers inquire about 'that soldier that was flogged a week ago'; Somerville declines to offer information, and is then upbraided for cowardice by comparison with the writer of the original letter! In this incident there are three Somervilles: himself in the pub, the flogged soldier, and the brave letter-writer—none identified with the others.

Once his second letter is published, the public can name him 'Somerville', but Somerville himself remains unknown: 'Nobody in the crowds knew me; but many of them inquired eagerly for Somerville: "What are they doing to him?" "Why don't they allow him to come out?" They thought the gates closed to keep him in . . . none of them knew that they were talking to him.' While being escorted to the trial he meets the same unwitting inquiries about 'Somerville'. He even has beer thrown over him in a pub for refusing to 'drink to "Somerville" '! While waiting to appear at the Court of Inquiry he is enrolled, as an unknown soldier 'standing in the way', to polish the boots of the judges. During a celebration procession for the Reform Act, Somerville is on sentry duty outside the barracks:

Not one of the many thousands knew me personally, but each band ceased to play as it came near the barrack gate; each trade or section of a political union, halted in front of the gate . . . and three cheers, loud and long, were given for 'Somerville for ever'. They had not the remotest suspicion that I was the sentry, with my carbine on my arm, standing in the gateway looking at them. 'For ever!' they shouted in connection with my name.

That name soon became a profitable commercial commodity: pamphlets and broadsheets about his case were hawked around; Madame Tussaud's offered him £50 to exhibit 'Somerville the soldier'; a theatre-benefit was proposed; he was offered payment 'to lend my name to be used in a newspaper'; he was urged to invest money collected for him 'and the use of my name' in a public-house; he finally agreed to let his name be used to help launch a literary journal, but even then he was left in debt for the expenses 'incurred in my name'. The name also became a political attraction: on being recognised at a meeting, he is urged to speak: 'I was observed; some one called me loudly by name; there was shouting and clapping of hands, and a cry for me to go to the platform.' But all these 'impositions committed on the public in my name' only provoke Somerville's repugnance: he has no wish to be a celebrity and feels that his motives are misunderstood and misrepresented; he experiences a total divorce between his private existence and his public image, between Somerville and 'Somerville':

There was not, in all the metropolitan wilderness of streets and houses, and it is a wilderness to those who are alone, a more lonely being than I was, at that time. I saw my name every week on the bills of newspapers, saw and heard people reading those bills at street corners; heard my case and myself discussed in the parlours of public-houses, occasionally by persons who professed to know me intimately; none of which persons I had before seen in all my life. I felt that I was not the kind of man that everybody expected or believed me to be. They depicted to themselves a person of flashy exterior, fluent in address, able and ready to talk and speak everywhere, at any time; and so well-skilled in the ways and usages of free and easy society, as to take a hand at cards, play billiards or bagatelle, or crack jokes, crack nuts, or crack heads with equal readiness. I knew of no quality which entitled me to respect, except that I had a strong right arm and a determination not easily turned aside.

In a strict sense of the term, Somerville's name had become alienated from himself. The direct parallel to his experience of his name in its new status is his relation to the money collected for him:

There was a moral space, a chasm between me and that money, which made it different from any other money; I had not worked for it. I never loved it as my own. I never had confidence in it. . . . My brothers warned me that I was losing it; but they did not see it with my eyes, nor feel it to be an alien treasure, as I felt it.

The parallel suggests the near-contemporary analysis of Marx in the *Economic and Philosophical Manuscripts* (1844). Names, like money, were increasingly becoming an abstract, an emptied yet powerful medium of relationship; the older forms ('singing Michael' etc.) were being replaced, in Somerville's experience at least, by units on a list or rallying cries divorced from the actual, living persons who bore them. In the area of political organisation the ambiguity of this change was acute: chapter 29 recounts Somerville's involvement in an insurrectionary plot in 1834; on the strength of his reputation, he is invited to attend a secret meeting, where

I was hurried to a private room, but not before some persons had come forward to shake me by the hand as a brother unionist, and to introduce others whom I did not know. Some of these last were foreigners, who spoke English with difficulty. But they seemed to be quite familiar with my name . . . and shook me by the hand warmly; one of them advanced to embrace me as a brother democrat.

The insurrectionaries are willing to work with a man known only by name; Somerville's response recalls Bamford's: 'I expressed unwillingness to be engaged in any enterprise of that kind, with persons I did not know.' Eventually he notifies the authorities, by letter, about the plot—without revealing the names of those involved. The trust the plotters had placed in a man known only by name and reputation is betrayed.

(iii) A structure of identifications

We can move from the role of names to an examination of the structure of the autobiography as a whole by focussing on one particular episode. Among the many letters Somerville received during his celebrity phase was one from his brother Peter, with whom he had lost contact years before. They miss each other in London but hope to meet in Scotland. At Glasgow, on his way home, Somerville is met by another brother, James, who says that 'a gentleman who travelled with him from Edinburgh, had a very strong desire to see' Somerville:

We entered an apartment at the inn, where sat a personage with a weather-beaten face, whiskered, respectably dressed—something like the mate or master of a ship that had been on a long voyage. We bade each other good morning, and made several observations about weather, politics, country news, and so forth, and still it did not occur to me that this bearded, weather-beaten, naval-like personage was more than a fellow-traveller with James from Edinburgh.

James, at last, said to me, 'I suppose you do not know who this is?' I looked at the stranger, and said, 'No.' 'Did you never know,' James continued, 'any one in the east country of the name of Peter Simerel?' 'Peter Simerel,' I replied, 'there were no Simerels but ourselves in the east country, that I know of; I do not remember of a Peter, but,'—I was going to say—'our Peter.' I did not get it out. It was our Peter. When he found me trying to recollect him, and could not, the tears rolled out of his eyes, over his weather-worn face, and he cried 'Sandy! don't you know me?' I, like him, hardly able to make myself intelligible, cried 'Pate, I did not know you.'

That recognition-scene is, it seems to me, almost a micro-model for the structure of the autobiography. In Appendix III Somerville writes:

Here, then, is the cause of publishing my Autobiography, as hinted in the seventh chapter. The time for confessing why I had consented to publish it, had not then come. My hope was, to raise as much money by the first volume, as would enable me to introduce an account of the Spanish expedition, and my concerns with the Spanish government and the certificates; and end by saying, 'I have paid all; I am free, and shall now work for myself and my family.'

Somerville had been extensively maligned for allegedly speculating in the Spanish certificates by obtaining payments due to war-casualties by buying up their claims. His autobiography was originally to be a prelude to clearing his name. But we have already noted that his name does not appear in the autobiography until the crisis-point of the court-martial. The effect of this silence is to delay identification by the reader of the unknown but (in intention) sympathetically portrayed individual of the earlier passages with the once well-known political martyr of the 1832 period; once that identification or recognition has been made, and it has then been further insisted that in 1834, 1839 and 1848 Somerville 'saved' the country from revolutionary plots, a further identification could be made: of that Somerville with the Somerville unfairly accused in the case of the Spanish certificates. At the point where his narrative actually moves to a self-justification of his dealings in the certificates, Somerville prints a letter which begins, significantly:

Sir—And is it really possible, that you are the same Sergeant Somerville who was pay-sergeant of the Grenadier company of the 8th Scots, when we lay in 'Auld Bartholomew Convent', just out of Saint Sebastian? Oh, sir, if it was not for the one thing more than another, I would come this very minute to see you. If you be the person that I mean, you must be a tall, full-faced man, stout made.

The autobiography was, it seems to me, constructed to provoke the same kind of reaction by the reader. But the bones of that underlying structure are only visible beneath what might seem a considerable muddle. Appendix I tells us:

It is now necessary to state, that the Autobiography up to this point, including the note appended to the last chapter, was published in weekly fragments in the *Manchester Examiner* the last chapter having appeared in that paper on . . . 15th February 1848. It was intended that the note appended to that chapter should form the end of this volume; and that, if the public evinced any desire, or sign of a desire, to have a second volume of the Autobiography; a second, containing an account of my two years of military service in the civil wars in Spain, and other matters occurring since, would be published.

But the 1848 revolution in France, and the possibility of its being imitated in England, intervened and Somerville added to the published autobiography the appendices on 'The Political Revolutions of 1848' and 'The British Revolution', plus two 'extra chapters from the autobiography', presumably intended for the 'second volume', the appendices on 'Military Experiences in Spain' and 'the Spanish Certificates'. Clearly the 1848 edition was opportunist and incomplete. But the actual effect of publishing his 'continuous narrative' only up to 1834, with appendices then covering 1839 and 1848, was not simply to make the narrative incomplete: it very neatly avoided precisely that period in Somerville's life, during the mid-1840s, when he was secretly employed by the Anti-Corn Law League. By omitting that period entirely, he avoids the possibility of his reader making yet another, and perhaps unwelcome iden-tification. Somerville does identify himself (on the title-page) as the 'One who has whistled at the plough', one of the pseudonyms under which he wrote disguised ACLL propaganda, but the fact that he was an ACLL employee is never revealed. In a later work, *Conservative Science* (1860), Somerville quotes from an M.P.'s letter in 1843 which plainly shows that at that time even the identification of Somerville as 'The Whistler' was to be avoided: 'I am frequently asked in the House of Commons who the writer, calling himself "One who has whistled at the plough", is. Of course, I preserve your incognito.' Norman McCord puts this matter in its context:

The Leaguers, on Cobden's recommendation, engaged a writer especially suited to this work —Alexander Somerville, the 'Whistler at the Plough', as his articles were signed, and 'Reuben' as he appears in the correspondence of the League leaders. Somerville's connection with the League was kept secret—hence the use of the code-name Reuben for him in the correspondence, and in his writings he posed as a disinterested observer of the rural scene. In this capacity he did a good deal of useful work for the League, writing under several different names.

(iv) The Anti-Corn Law League

Clearly, the interest shown in names in the autobiography itself is part of a wider problem for Somerville, which is partly reflected in the structure, perhaps incomplete and muddled, of the whole work. But the importance of names and of fusing different public and private identities is a reflection of something wider still. One could, for example, easily compare the latent structure of the autobiography with a familiar device in Victorian novels: the early appearance of a 'stranger' who is eventually identified, in the dénouement, as the mysterious wealthy patron or long-lost relative. Or one could note Thackeray's use of various pseudonyms to avoid being identified by the public as the single author of widely disparate works, published in periodicals of varying prestige. It is, however, the significance of Somerville's connection with the ACLL that I now want to develop.

That the League was a new political phenomenon has often been emphasised. *The Quarterly Review* even regarded it as an unconstitutional conspiracy. What worried contemporaries and has fascinated later historians was the League's superb efficiency and organisation. It was this that gave it the edge over its opposition. What has not, however, been sufficiently stressed is that the strength of the League came from its operating, organisationally and tactically, in a world of *names*. Its early reliance on travelling propaganda lecturers was a failure. Only when the League concentrated its energies in a new direction did it become a powerful pressure group. The germ of that shift is seen in an announcement in the ACLL *Circular* for 24th September 1840:

The Council of the National Anti-Corn Law League wait only for the completion of the year's registries [of electors] at the hands of the revising barristers, to carry into operation the plan which has long occupied their attention—of appealing directly and personally to the constituencies of the kingdom.

Three years later this germ had grown. In a speech in October 1843 Cobden proclaimed: 'we propose to provide a copy of every registration list for every borough and county in the United Kingdom. . . . We intend to bring these registers to a central office in London;' that was to be the new kind of base; from that central office, the League planned to correspond once a week with 300,000 of the 800,000 electors in the country. Somerville's own account of the League's offices in Manchester makes the essential point:

From this office letters to the amount of several thousands a day go forth to all parts of the kingdom. While here, I saw letters addressed to all the foreign ambassadors, and all the mayors and provosts of corporate towns of the United Kingdom, inviting them to a great banquet which is to be given in the last week of this month. The amount of postage for letters going out during the week ending 7th January was £18-2-6; but the amount of postage was frequently as much as this in one day—for a single day it had been as high as £38. In this office copies of all the parliamentary registers of the kingdom are kept, so that any elector's name and residence is at once found, and, if necessary, such elector is communicated with by letter or parcel of tracts, irrespective of the committees in his own district.

Whistler at the Plough, 1852

Somerville goes on to describe the sending out, by post, of 3½ tons of tracts each week, twelve different tracts for each elector and tenant farmer in the country. We can add to these activities the later tactics of the League in persuading its supporters to register as voters and in having opponents struck off the register, often by dubious methods: quibbling over the exact description of an elector in the register, having one elector challenge as many as 2,000 names on the local lists, swamping the Post Office with last-minute objections to forestall appeals. The League also urged supporters to 'qualify' for voting by buying land *en bloc* and parcelling it out under separate names. The League also used, as the Chartists spectacularly did, the tactic of petitions—and objected strongly when its opponents allegedly used coercion to swell counter-petitions.

All these facets of the League's organisation and activity rested on the deliberate exploitation of an increasingly available way of grasping, and manipulating, the society as a whole: precisely as a network of names and addresses. Older modes of political relationship and pressure—patronage, local 'influence', kinship alliances, family connections—were being partly superseded by a form of national association of mutual strangers, organised as names on lists, petitions, subscriptions, registers, mailing accounts. It was perhaps a transitional phase: the 1832 Reform Act had enfranchised only an extra 217,000 electors; with the later Reform Acts the electorate became too large to be appealed to 'directly and personally'—psephology based on numerical statistics replaced petitions of individual names, mass newspapers took over from mass correspondence as the dominant national means of political communication and influence. Our own period is familiar with national registers of names and addresses—we all use telephone directories —but in the 1840s they constituted the ground for an important shift in political organisation and consciousness, and perhaps also in the definition of democracy and of party-political priorities.

(v) Aspects of the historical context

The political exploitation of names and addresses by the ACLL can be placed in a wider context of social and administrative changes in the 1830s and 1840s. The Registration Act of 1836, requiring the systematic recording of births, deaths and marriages under secular auspices, provoked the complaint in Parliament that by divorcing the naming of a child from its baptism the religious rite would be forced into disuse and oblivion. By 1851 even the religious practices of the population had become the subject of centralised statistics, under the extended scope of the 1851 Census. In 1835 the Merchant Seamen's Act established the first national register of labour, and by 1842 the names, addresses and characters of 258,000 seamen were listed at the Admiralty. In 1839 the Penny Postage Act set a seal on the development of a national network of postal correspondence. In 1837 another method of sending a message to a distant name and address was patented: the electric telegraph; by 1852 4,000 miles of telegraph cable linked not only every major town in Britain but stretched across the Channel too. The development of the telegraph system was closely tied in the initial stages to the expansion of the

273

railways: by 1848 1,800 miles of railway had telegraphic equipment, and in 1849 the first land-sea telegram was sent under the direction of the South Eastern Railways' electrician.

The social and commercial effects of railway expansion, reaching its peak in the mid-1840s, have been extensively studied and here we need only recall the basic figures: in 1834 about 200 miles of line were open, by 1850 the figure was 6,500; between 1845 and 1847 8,592 miles of railway track were sanctioned by Parliament. In Samuel Smiles's view, in 1849, the railways had so shrunk the effective size of the country and so eroded the distinction between town and country that 'by their means has Great Britain become as one great city, the streets of which are the iron roads which now stretch across it in all directions'; when in 1844 *The Quarterly Review* rather similarly compares the rail-network with the system of Roman roads and 'streets', we are however struck by an interesting point: instead of such labels as 'Watling Street' the rail network is composed of such units as 'The York, Newcastle and Berwick', 'The Manchester, Sheffield and Lincolnshire', 'The London and Birmingham', 'The Leicester and Swannington', 'The Bristol and Gloucester'. For most of the 1840s these well-publicised railway companies ensured that the very geography of England could be summarised in a list of companies' names, and, conversely, that the regions and towns of England became the names of familiar commercial institutions.

Names played a minor, but again interesting, role in the other great process of amalgamation occurring in the 1840s, in the commercial and financial sectors. The Bank Charter Act of 1844 centralised nearly all note issue, making the signature of the chief cashier of the Bank of England almost the sole formal guarantee of national currency. Yet the effect of this restriction was reduced by the further development of the private cheque system in the late 1840s—one's own signature playing an increasing role as a form of currency. Also in 1844 the Joint Stock Companies Registration and Regulation Act required companies to file 'particulars of name and objects, with the names, addresses and descriptions of the promoters' with the Registrar of Companies; previous Chartered Companies Acts of 1834 and 1837 had required the naming of only two officers for liability purposes. The practice of merely 'lending' one's name as a 'sleeping partner' helped, of course, to raise acutely the problem of limited liability in this period, particularly after the commercial crisis of 1847. During the crisis itself part of the credit imbalance arose from the continued willingness of discount houses to take over semi-fictitious bills 'simply because they were guaranteed by the joint-stock bank's signature'. No wonder that in Dickens's novel of commercial crisis and collapse, *Dombey and Son* (1846–8), almost every character has a curiously ambivalent relation to his own name! No wonder too that *Who's Who* began publication in 1849.

These specific features of the legal, administrative, financial and commercial developments in the 1840s all indicate ways in which a new kind of society was emerging, characterised by an increased sense of the unity and uniformity of the country effected through more elaborated systems of communication and transport. Both people and places were being connected in new ways, and personal knowledge of both was in many ways being extended and changed.

The status of personal names was, in that context, undergoing a curious shift which it is difficult to recapture as an experience. It is difficult enough to delineate accurately the extent to which broader administrative developments during the period effected, or were meant to effect, an increased uniformity or centralisation of government control, as recent debate about the Victorian 'revolution in government' indicates. In *Little Dorrit* (1855–7, ch. X) Dickens of course created a parody of government centralisation in the Circumlocution Office; but we can perhaps see an earlier and actual symbol of the 'revolution in government' in the extensions to Somerset House in 1835 and 1856, to enable that versatile Government building to house the centralised statistical knowledge of the society. Perhaps the insurrectionaries of 1816 were perversely prophetic when, as Somerville notes, they singled out Somerset House as an appropriate revolutionary headquarters. Ironically, the rebel of 1819, Samuel Bamford, became in 1851 a minor clerk in Somerset House.

Somerville's insertion into that new form of society can be traced not only in his receiving numerous letters from strangers because of the publicity given to his name, or in his work for the ACLL, but also in his explicit interest in questions of banking and national finance: he wanted to integrate the Bank of England, taxation, the National Debt, minting, insurance and savings-banks into 'one national institution'. Such concerns are of a radically different kind from those of the closed and local community of the Lothian family into which he was born. In the new social world he could no longer simply identify himself, as he once did, as 'one of my faither's Simerels'; in this new world his name had a public existence, to be protected, written to, registered, exploited, sold and alienated. It is that experience—the subjective dimension of the social developments exemplified in the ACLL methods and the processes sketched above—that is given shape in the content and structure of his *Autobiography*.

(vi) Conclusion

We can, in conclusion, both locate some of Somerville's other work briefly in relation to this same strand in his writing and return finally to his autobiographical efforts. His collected newspaper articles of the 1840s and his 'Letters from Ireland', published as *The Whistler at the Plough* in 1852, his *Free Trade and the League: A Biographic History* (1853), and such short pieces as the superb *A Cry from Ireland* (1843) are all characterised by an emphasis on the specific case, on the living people involved. The strength of the 'Whistler' articles comes from the embedding of Somerville's economic analyses in particular conditions, specified farms, named landowners. The history of the League is constructed as a series of vignettes and mini-biographies of 'the pioneers of freedom of opinion, commercial enterprise, and civilisation'. *A Cry from Ireland* is an individual cry, the detailed and moving case of one particular tenant persecuted by his landlord. And, in similar vein, Somerville finally offered his own life as an individual example.

The 1860 Canadian edition of his autobiography has the unexpected title: *Conservative Science of Nations (Preliminary instalment), Being the first complete narrative of Somerville's Diligent Life in the Service of Public Safety in Britain*. It was intended in part to clear his name of various accusations by a journalist and to 'introduce' the author to a Canadian public after his emigration. But it was also part of a wider propaganda for what Somerville called 'Conservative Science', the main tenet of which asserted that 'the human being is the prime constituent of public wealth; and that the guardianship of human happiness is the true function of any Political Economy, worthy of being called a Conservative Science'. The purpose of the 'Diligent Life' was to 'retrieve Political Economy from a chaos of crudities, in its austere materialism . . . to demand that as guardian of public wealth, it obey the absolute logic of its position, and take cognisance of the prime element of wealth, the human being.' This view of political economy Somerville dates from 1848; he quotes a letter from John Bright about Somerville's proposal for a series of tracts, and comments:

In the forgoing, Mr Bright said: 'If you succeed in convincing them (the workers) that non-interference by law with *labour* and with prices, whether of *labour* or of other commodities &c'. In these words he confounded two very different things as one. He meant by *labour* the *person*—the personal health, life, and limb of the factory worker, as well as the skill which brought forth the products of the spindle and loom at which the worker was employed. I separated the *person* of the worker from *work* and *skill*.

In this 'economic heresy', as Somerville calls it, he is close, in feeling at least, to Dickens, to Ruskin, and even to the young Marx, who analysed both the alienation of the worker from his own work and skill and the unique nature of labour as a market-commodity. And though Somerville was, for example, drastically confused about the nature of capital and its specific forms, using the same term to cover very different phenomena, his emphasis at this point is a necessary one in political economy. In a society increasingly grasped in abstract terms, where money dominated the modes of economic exchange and people were coming to be connected merely as a network of names and addresses to be exploited for bureaucratic political and commercial purposes, it was important to re-assert the value of the specific, whole, living human being. It was precisely that point which the concentration on the individual case in his newspaper writings was designed to make as vividly as possible, and it was that concern which Somerville singled out when, in *Conservative Science*, he summarised his life:

As for Radicals, Whigs, Tories, and any such party alliances, I never was of them. Mine has not been a life of small politics. Much of my literary life has been spent and my brain worn to incapacity for literary labour, in rescuing the science of Political Economy from the soulless materialism which had made it, in the mouths of Whigs and Radicals, odious to the People.

Perhaps we can conclude that just as Wordsworth and Coleridge, at the beginning of the century, finally found the most amenable and appropriate form for their projected 'philosophical poem' and 'Organum vere Organum' to be an autobiographical one, in *The Prelude* and the *Biographia Literaria* respectively, so Somerville, unable to engender an adequate work on Political Economy in terms compatible with mid-century theory and practice, could only finally offer the lesson of his own life instead—as someone who had not only whistled at the plough but had also experienced in an acute fashion the alienating distance between public role and private person increasingly possible in a new form of social world. As Somerville himself once remarked: 'Strange are the results sometimes of a search after facts and names.'

Chapter 3: James Dawson Burn: 'wandering to leave time behind'

(i) Mobility and class locations

J. D. Burn's life seems, from his *Autobiography of a Beggar Boy* (1855) to have been one of constant movement, first with his mother and stepfather, as a travelling beggar and itinerant trader, then, after breaking with his parents, as a wanderer in search of work: 54 miles in one day, 62 miles another day, 1,400 miles for a new job. Even after his marriage he travels for the Oddfellows Society or for trade jounals. In his sixties he uproots his family and spends three years in America; in his seventies he finds stable employment for ten years, the longest continuous job of his life—but, almost symbolically, as a clerk with the Great Eastern Railway Company. So constant is the impression of movement in the autobiography that the reader is surprised at Burn's claim to have lived in and around Glasgow for nearly twenty years.

His travels were not only territorial. He also moved through one occupation after another: in rapid succession, for example, tinker, miner, farm-labourer, smuggler, harvester, shearer, office-boy. When he finally served the apprenticeship he longed for it was always looked back to as 'the grand turning point', but though he became a time-served hatter that trade soon underwent basic changes which restricted his chances of employment and again he turned to a variety of jobs, for example dock-labouring and freelance lecturing within the same week, meanwhile selling copies of his own *History of Odd Fellowship* (Glasgow, 1846) to meet immediate needs.

The social disparity between the personae he adopted on that last occasion highlights the tension he constantly tried to overcome: his repeated aim was to find a 'resting place' and 'become a recognisable member of society'. One can trace the roots of this urge in part to his early experience of isolation even within his own family: he describes himself as a 'stranger' in that family, or rather families, for he was, he says ironically, 'blessed with three fathers and two mothers'; his mother and stepfather transferred him to his real father and the latter's new wife in Ireland, and on meeting his mother again he finds her with a third 'husband'. He remembers his mother and stepfather casually transferring him to a strange family for three months, and his sense of being 'cast adrift upon the world'. His own break with his (Irish) family is equally casual: sent out to gather turf, he finds himself on the main road to Belfast and, 'after standing reflecting for a few minutes', 'turned my face towards Belfast and my back to a friendless house', from that time 'tearing two syllables from my name' to 'sever the only remaining link that bound me to my family' (he never discloses what that name had been).

Burn's sense of not having an inherited 'place' is not simply a matter of having no regular family or secure trade; it also includes a shifting sense of which social group he belongs to. In 1858 he presented himself as both a working man and an employer; in 1865 he described himself as 'one of their own order' when speaking of 'the working classes'; in *A Glimpse*, published after 1867 but not otherwise dated, he claims that he has been discussing issues 'from a working man's stand-point of view'; in 1882 he saw himself as neither working-class nor with the financial means to be above that class. Yet in the

278

1855 autobiography he is lucidly aware that there are class differences which permeate most aspects of life, and that those from one class can rarely penetrate the sense of life felt by those from another:

Like a large number of my own class, I was born in poverty, nursed in sorrow, and reared in difficulties, hardships and privations. It is only such as have passed through the various substrata of civilised society who can justly appreciate the feelings and sufferings of the thousands who continually live as it were by chance. . . . The man who can dine is very differently situated to the poor wretch who, after he has had one meal of victuals, has no idea where or when he may be blessed with another! Those members of society who are blessed with a regular supply of food and raiment may be said to be antipodes to the accidental feeders, and their modes of thinking, in every sense of the word, as opposite as are their ways of living!

Fortunately, according to Burn at one point, one quality is, ultimately, common to all classes: 'Although I have had to fight my way through a busy world, where all classes of society were continually engaged in looking after their own affairs, I am happy to bear my humble testimony to the general diffusion of that god-like feeling which so closely allies man to his Creator' —sympathetic charitableness. In *A Glimpse*, however, he comments that the working classes are 'not one whit more selfish than the people who formed the upper strata' and that he has 'found very little difference in the conduct of men, whatever class they belonged to, when their real or supposed vested interests were interfered with'; for Burn, at that period, 'There is a no difference in feelings of selfishness between the employers and the employed'. These analyses, in terms of basic goodness or selfishness, clearly imply a political as well as 'moral' outlook; but Burn's political stance is made more explicit and specific in the *Autobiography*.

(ii) Political trajectories

Burn himself sketches very clearly the stages of his involvement in politics. He was elected in 1831 as hatters' delegate to the Trades Committee of Western Scotland, then to the Radicals' 'Central Committee'; 'seized with a wild enthusiasm, and for a time politically mad', he took 'an active part in all the proceedings of both the Whig and the Radical parties in Glasgow for several years', with 'rarely a single night in the week . . . not occupied, either in sub-committees, or in the general committee'. After six months he was elected 'a member of the standing committee of the Reform Association', composed of 'the resident gentry, merchants and manufacturers of the Whig party'. During the agitation for the Reform Bill in 1832 he 'had the marshalling of the whole of the out-door displays in Glasgow', including one demonstration involving '200,000 people'. The way Burn envisages his role at this period is interesting: he speaks of the Trades Committee as 'an excellent school for young beginners in the science of oratory and public debating' and of the demonstrations as 'a display of self-possessed determination', marked with 'solemn import' rather than 'boisterous mirth'. On the largest meeting he comments: 'I was somewhat afraid that the leaders had raised a power they could not subdue'. In other words the mode of politics he at heart accepts is that of the debating chamber and the committee and sub-committee, with occasional emphasis given to a position by massive numerical support, that support, however, hopefully under the control of 'leaders' who, though initially 'elected', are finally seen as those who have 'raised' the masses in support and ought to be able to 'subdue' them.

Given this version of politics, it is no surprise that Burn later objected to a mode of political agitation that threatened to go beyond debating-chamber forms, the Chartist movement. Of that period he remarks: 'While I was in Greenock I had in some measure identified myself with the Charter movement, but up to that time the agitation had been conducted upon something like rational principles'; when, however, he goes on to describe the 'People's Parliament' and its plan for a 'sacred month' (a general strike) his language becomes virulently hostile: 'satanic', 'hellish suggestion', 'infamy', 'infatuation'. He summarises his speech from the chair of a meeting in Greenock, in which he proclaimed that 'one of the immediate consequences . . . would be to let loose the whole vagabondage of the country, who would rob, plunder, and murder the innocent and defenceless members of society'; yet, magnanimously, he does not blame the 'working classes', only the 'mercenary horde' and 'set of hungry knaves' who were the 'majority' of the National Convention. In sharp contrast to his praise for the debating workmen of the 1832 Trades Committee, the leaders of the Chartist movement are nearly all dismissed with the comment: 'if these men were honest, they must have been mad, and if not mad, no conduct could have been more infamous'; only John Collins—whom Burn knew—William Lovett and Henry Vincent escape censure—and Collins is, noticeably, described as 'respectable'.

It is that 'respectable' that gives the familiar clue. Burn was, on his own account, no minor figure in local working-class politics: his tavern in Glasgow seems to have been a Radicals' gathering-place; in 1837 he can 'call a meeting of the Liberal party for the following evening' which 5,000 people attend; he was active also in Trade Union circles, first at local level, then as Glasgow delegate to various national meetings of the Journeymen Hatters' union. He can not only claim to have known the leaders of the great Glasgow cotton spinners' strike of 1837 but to be 'personally acquainted with many of the men whose names figured in these exciting times', including the national Charter leaders. Yet by 1855 he was explicitly on the side of the 'middle classes'; the fifth chapter (or 'Letter') of the autobiography, concerned in part with Peterloo, ends with a eulogy on 'the extraordinary energy and directing power' of the 'middle class element' which 'during the last thirty years . . . have attained for it a moral force unprecedented in the history of the country', so that 'whatever social advantages we now enjoy over those of the preceding age, are in great measure due to the well-timed exertions of this now powerful class'. It is, then, no surprise to find, in the penultimate, reflective Letter, that Burn erects a defence of hereditary property and argues that more equitable distribution of wealth would be detrimental to society. The haziness of his notion of class at this point is clear when he remarks that 'it matters very little whether the riches be held by one class or another, inasmuch as there will always be a select few who will possess great wealth'. One's real consolation, he urges, is to be found in 'friendship' and 'the human family'.

This support for middle-class efforts and values has to be seen partly in the light of the particular configuration of Glasgow Chartism during these years.

As in other Chartist centres, but perhaps more acutely, there was a two-fold struggle within Glasgow Chartism, over the issue of moral force versus physical force and over the role of the middle class as allies. These issues tended to become confused, but with no simple demarcation of pro-middle class Chartists supporting only moral force policies; only rarely, however, as in the great demonstration of 21st May 1838, was there a simple fusion of all the tendencies. Burn's particular hostility to Feargus O'Connor and his horror at violence, even industrial 'violence', would seem to place him firmly on the side of the conciliatory middle-class groups who opposed O'Connor, and his approach to Roebuck in 1837 and membership of John Bright's Parliamentary Election Committee in 1852 would reinforce this assessment. So too, indirectly, would his concentration, from 1839 onwards, on the Oddfellows Society rather than on political activity; preoccupation with 'social' efforts and friendly societies was in any case characteristic of one strong strand in Glasgow Chartism, a strand that Burn certainly regarded as perfectly 'respectable'.

(iii) Respectability and deception

The context for this pro-middle class attitude is also, of course, personal. As was noted above, Burn's autobiography reveals a constant urge for a respectable 'place' in society. A direct connection between this personal urge and his political activities interestingly affects the final section of his autobiography. He writes:

I am now about introducing you to the last scene in the shifting drama of my truly chequered life, up to the present time. In the month of May, 1853, I was offered employment from a gentleman to whom I had been recommended by a mutual friend. The conditions of the engagement offered were more liberal than I had been accustomed to for some time; I was therefore not slow in accepting the offer. The character of the business was perfectly new to me; but I had every confidence of being equal to it, and have since justified my own expectations, and the expectations of my employer.

In the last paragraph of the book he again alludes to the 'present business': 'For the last two years, I have held a situation of considerable responsibility, during that time I have come into contact with many of the first class commercial men in the United Kingdom.' What is interesting is that the nature of this 'business' is never disclosed. The 1882 edition of the autobiography adds, however, the name of his employer: a 'Mr Hill'; later it is mentioned that Mr Hill was once editor of the *Northern Star*. The supplementary survey of various social changes in that edition deals at one point with 'trade protection' societies and businesses, and mentions that from 1838 a weekly *'Black List'* was compiled by 'Mr William Hill', who in 1853 (the date of Burn's employment by 'Mr Hill') 'added the English lists of weekly mercantile defalcations to his Scottish publication'; this 'new *Mercantile Gazette* was charged two guineas a year, and when the debt-collecting was added the charge was three guineas'; this whole 'system of espionage' was eventually sold to a Mr Stubbs in 1860. With this further information one suspects Burn's motive for not revealing the nature of his 'business' in 1855. In the final pages of the 1855 edition Burn is claiming to have achieved his goal of respectability: he emphasises that 'my great struggle in the battle of life was to find my proper position in society' and concludes: 'you have now before you an honest history of my life up to the present time', from which the reader can learn 'what energy and determination . . . are able to accomplish'.

This sounds impressive. But one wonders how many of his contemporary readers would have accepted an agent of a 'system of espionage' and 'debt-collecting' as 'respectably' employed. Moreover, his employer had not only, as the Rev. William Hill, once edited the *Northern Star*, the Chartist newspaper, but had in 1842 been arrested for 'uttering seditious language', and on his release in 1843 had been fêted as a hero at numerous Chartist banquets throughout the country. As late as 1847 Hill was editing the *North British Weekly Express*, 'The Only Democratic Newspaper Published in Scotland', which became the property of the leading Edinburgh Chartists in late 1847. To have identified Hill as his employer, even in 1855, would have made his 'history' slightly more 'honest' but would surely have raised further doubts as to Burn's achieved 'respectability'.

(iv) Hovering between styles

Burn's political opinions and his lack of a secure social position are now adequately clear and we have seen one instance where both play a part in affecting the autobiography. A detailed examination of the general characteristics of his style would also reveal a reflection of his social and political ambivalence. Only a few examples can be offered here.

One notable feature of his style is a frequent ambiguity of tone. For example, when he writes of his stepfather that his 'health and constitution had been sacrificed before the altar of patriotism and glory in the Peninsular war' the tone hovers between sarcasm and piety. A similar hesitancy is provoked in the reader when Burn, himself a 'beggar boy', describes those beggars proficient in heart-tugging stories and personae as 'artistes' who were 'no mean ornaments to their honourable profession'. The exact tone of this is indecipherable, but it is similar to other descriptions of begging, the intention of which is slightly less implicit: 'The begging trade, with its gross deceptions . . . I believe was somewhat repugnant to the feelings of my parents; whether they left the business from conscientious scruples, or from a feeling of independence, I really do not know, but . . . we became transformed into respectable travelling merchants, or pedlars'. Or, of an overnight stay in Ely, 'while I was there I had a very flattering invitation to join two genteel young men in their regular *cadging* trade, both of whom had successfully passed their probation in the profession . . . they fully initiated me into the mysteries of their business.' The choice of middle-class terms for what are decidedly not middle-class 'businesses' simultaneously hints a question-mark as to the difference between 'respectable' and disreputable ways of earning a living, and yet suggests sufficient irony to allow the middle-class reader his instinctively defensive dismissal of such a thought. In some instances, however, Burn very clearly uses middle-class phrasing to expose and challenge middle-class assumptions: 'When I retired from business, it was into the private life of poverty'; or, very neatly, 'My new employer very unfortunately laboured under the sin of poverty'.

This juxtaposition of two vocabularies, two sets of value-assumptions, two worlds, to challenge one of the elements involved, can also operate on a larger scale. A good example is the poker-faced paragraph:

About this time there were two little circumstances occurred, which were matters of gossip for the time being. The one was the coronation of William the Fourth, and the other was the death of Sandy McKay, in a prize-fight between him and Simon Byrne. Just twelve months after this, Byrne was repaid in the same coin by being killed in a pugilistic encounter with Deaf Burke.

An equally brief passage shows Burn deliberately mingling inflated and colloquial language with serious and critical effect:

Your professional pickpocket looks down with contempt upon a knight of the *scranbag*, and the *highflyer* turns up his genteel proboscis at the common cadger. A lady who may have shared bed, board, and affections of an aristocratic letter-writer, would feel herself as much humbled in allying herself with a plebeian *charity irritator*, as my Lord Noodle's some time affection receiver would have in espousing one of his lordship's ploughmen.

This comment, illustrating that 'nearly every class of people in the kingdom have a moral code of their own, and every body of men its own standard of perfection', is more complex than it perhaps appears. The juxtaposition of street slang and outrageously elegant terminology is obvious; but 'proboscis' not only deflates the highflyer by its pretension; it also parodies a linguistic fastidiousness that in certain circles refuses to acknowledge the common human condition (in the matter of noses, at least) that the structure of the two sentences asserts. For the effect of the sentences, read together, is to elide the class barriers: 'knight' is obviously metaphorical, and the highflyer is clearly a great deal removed socially from my Lord Noodle; but the mind is tempted to complete the phrase 'my Lord Noodle—and his Lady': the 'lady' who opens the second sentence tends to insinuate herself into his lordship's arms, but a second thought recalls that she is allied to 'an aristocratic letter-writer', whose status is highly ambiguous: does 'aristocratic' refer to accepted social scales, conjuring up some Byronic figure indulging himself with a low-class prostitute, or is the reference to the hierarchy of the street, the lady being the respectable spouse of a literate artisan, or is the 'letter-writer' merely some sophisticated variant of a 'charity irritator'? And why the odd phrase 'some time affection receiver' for my Lord Noodle's companion; is she perhaps not his lady at all? As the figures evoked in these two sentences mingle themselves promiscuously in the imagination, the way is prepared for Burn's quiet revision of his opening dictum, and the real point is made: whatever the moral code, 'in comparing men's actions and motives, I have found that the difference is very frequently only in the degree'—the beggar and the nobleman, as he concludes, will both barter their wives away, given a profitable occasion.

As in this passage to some extent, Burn often expresses himself in ways that are tinged with artificiality; he has an autodidact's self-consciousness about writing, a sense that there are 'better' ways of putting what he has to say than the straightforward, almost oral, style that seems latently natural to him. At times one is reminded of certain moments in Hardy's novels, with their somehow apologetic mingling of literary manners. Burn frequently prefers slightly unexpected alternatives to everyday statements: 'Castlereagh had quietly given himself a passport to the other world', 'hydropathic immersion', 'I gave a hostage to the state' (for 'my son was born'!). His grammatical constructions are often slightly deflected from correct forms and at times his self-consciousness about language takes the form of a weak pun (a pair of clogs as 'these wooden understandings'). His writing, as a result of these familiar but extensively deployed stylistic devices, is constantly interesting and occasionally even impressive: the phrase 'a young lady, who was then verging into that equivocal age where love lingers between hope and despair' gains much from the grammatically dubious 'verging into', while the terse description of Malvern as 'one of those delightful places where the dilapidated in health can be washed, dried and mangled at pleasure, and returned to their friends regenerated members of society' is both just and memorable.

Sometimes, however, his linguistic unease betrays a deeper unsureness, as in his comment on the Dublin beggars, who, 'in their unmitigated rags, are a unique specimen of the *genus homo*; and amid their mountains of motly rags there is a world of *devil-ma-care*, light-hearted fun and humour, and their ready wit sparkles with exuberance from the fountains of originality'. The distance between the clichés of these last phrases (it is difficult to read them as **parody**) and his earlier description, sharp and precise, of handbarrow beggars **as** 'these dilapidated and crumpled-up fragments of the *genus homo*' tempts one to see Burn as paternalistically distancing himself from his own past in the former passage: the language parallels the hypocritically unfeeling acknowledgement of a carelessly dropped coin from the now respectable commercial traveller.

In this last example the tone and vocabulary of one world are uncritically adopted to the detriment of any felt engagement with the scene described: it is held at length and jocularly pitied. But his writing seems more often to straddle two worlds, employing distinct styles, uneasily fusing two linguistic registers. Burn's refusal or incapacity to write in one consistent style is perhaps the linguistic equivalent of his reconciliatory politics, a sense that both sets of implied values can be used on particular occasions; it is certainly a reflection of his continuing inability to become a securely placed and 'respectable member of society'.

(v) Form and accidents

The overall structure of the autobiography directly communicates one central feature of his life, which, in Burn's view, he shared with his whole class:

There are a number of circumstances connected with the life of a working man, which people in an independent sphere cannot feel—the smallest accident in the machinery of a family dependent upon labour, is frequently sufficient to turn the current of life from one of comparative happiness to irredeemable misery.

This comment recalls and expands that striking phrase, quoted earlier, 'accidental feeders'. The accidental character of life pervades the autobiography: Burn is constantly entering upon 'new phases' in his existence, taking new turnings, being unexpectedly involved in this or that, falling ill, losing jobs. He describes himself as having 25/– 'to begin the world again with', speaks of minor events as 'preludes to change in fortune', refers to his leaving one job as 'the second grand crisis of my life'; he remarks of one attempt at establishing his own business that 'this little step once more altered the future tenor of my life, and plunged me into a train of circumstances as varied as it is almost possible to imagine'; he speaks of his 'rapid changes in condition of life and strange transformations in . . . social position'. The sense of life as a 'journey' is at times used to reconcile the frequency of 'changes' with the attainment of an 'end': 'I dare say you are getting tired in following me through the mazes of my wayward fate. I think you will agree with me, that my journey thus far has been sufficiently varied, even for the most hungry lover of change. You have, however, still a few more milestones to pass with me, ere I can bring you up to my present position.' The metaphor of milestones implies a destination, but even 'my present position' remains precarious, for the passage continues: 'Whether I shall now be allowed to finish my journey on the downhill of life free from the toils and vicissitudes of my past career, is a mystery time alone can solve.' We can see Burn here trying to achieve a simultaneous sense of chaos and coherence in his life and in the autobiography; it is this attempt in the structure of the work as a whole that we can now analyse.

In the Preface Burn insists that his life has a clear outline, falling into three parts: the first part 'will introduce the Author in the character of a wandering vagrant', the second part 'will show the reader the misdirected energies of an uneducated man', while

the third epoch of the Author's life may be said to have been ruled by a series of conflicting circumstances, over which he appeared to have had little or no control; however, the reader will not fail to observe that the same laudable determination of character which saved him from moral shipwreck in early life, still enabled him to weather the storms of adversity in more advanced years.

Despite this sketched outline, however, the pattern of the *Autobiography* itself does not seem to fall in any way into a three-part structure, though Burn throughout the work continues to imply that some pattern will clearly emerge. In particular, the highlighting of his apprenticeship as the 'grand turning point' attempts to give it a significance that the rest of the autobiography does not support. Immediately before recounting his apprenticeship, almost exactly half way through the work, Burn provides a personal resumé, emphasising that 'up to this period I had been the slave of circumstance' and that 'my life was frequently upon the turning point, when the merest accident would have made me a vagabond without redemption'. It is true that he is never again a beggar, but the crucial factor is more his becoming an adult: both before and after this point he works as a labourer and in other casual employment and is still very much (as the Preface states) subject to chance circumstance. Moreover, his life during the apprenticeship itself turned out to be 'just as unvaried and monotonous as that of any ploughman'. His final summary of his life rests, in fact, partly upon the reader suspending his recollection of the fortuitous shifts of the second half of the autobiography and partly upon his believing Burn's dubious claim to have finally achieved respectability—a claim the concealed facts barely sustain (cf. section (iii)). The various summaries Burns offers and his highlighting techniques do help to convey some sense of control over the chaos, but the main device for achieving both reactions from the reader has so far been mentioned only in passing: the casting of the whole autobiography into an epistolary form.

The *Autobiography* is made up of thirteen chapters headed 'Letter I' to

'Letter XIII'. Letter I is datelined 'Aberdeen, September 20th, 1854'; Letter VI has 'Alloa, November', X is headed 'Edinburgh', and XII and XIII respectively 'London, August 24th, 1855' and 'London, September, 1855'. The other Letters have no place or date attached. Each Letter opens with 'My dear Thomas', and a vocative style is frequently used, but there is no final salutation or signature to any Letter. The various effects of this epistolary structure are important. For example, it allows Burn regular opportunities, in the opening paragraphs of Letters, for reflective comments, even miniature essays, which help to impose some sense of coherence (e.g. IV, VI, IX, XI). That the Letters are written to his son has its own side-effects: the realisation that 'Thomas' is Burn's own child is delayed until over half way through the work (the absence of final salutations helps to ensure this) and then comes casually, immediately after Burn's account of how he 'hated' his own father 'as if he had been my most deadly enemy'—and that account is thereby given an unexpected resonance. With his son as recipient Burn can also avoid one central problem for autobiographers: rather than end the work with presentiments of approaching death, or offer explanations for concluding at a particular stage in life, Burn is justified in taking the story only up to the point where his now adult son needs no further information, knowing whatever remains or is to come as someone personally acquainted with Burn.

But the letter-form has a further and much more important effect on the autobiography, and particularly its opening and ending. In opening the *Autobiography* and reading the first dateline, the reader is immediately located at a specific time and place, 'Aberdeen, September 20th, 1854'. The effect of this is curious: we read the account of early beggar-life and wanderings as if from a static position; we are at rest and so too, as the notion of writing the letter in 1854 implies, is the author. Both reader and author are deliberately distanced from involvement in the content by the form; we read and he writes from a clearly stable and retrospective standpoint. The absence of datelines on Letters II to V inclusive and VII to IX inclusive has a more latent effect: the sense of stability is initially carried over, but in the heading to Letter VI ('Alloa, November') it is indicated, casually, that these Letters too are written on a journey—a journey in both time and space, from Aberdeen in September to Edinburgh (Letter X) via Alloa in November; that journey is to be completed in London in exactly one year (I: September 1854, XIII: September 1855). The time-scale of the form is leisurely (a year for 500 miles or so), contrasting both with the rapidity, frequency and length of the journeys recounted in the content and with the time-span of the work, a whole lifetime. How far this interaction between two time-scales is deliberately intended is perhaps difficult to decide (though the erratic presence of datelines requires some explanation), but one further effect of the epistolary structure does seem deliberately arranged.

In Letter XI we read: 'In September 1854 I travelled from Newton-stewart to Dumfries. This was within a few months of forty years after my runaway exploit'—in the same area. We suddenly realise that the journey mentioned here (one undertaken for his finally 'respectable' job) is presumably the first part of that very journey on which Letter I was written, itself recounting Burn's early life in that very same area. This recognition leaves the reader with a sudden sense of strands finally gathered up: the past and the present are not merely compared but curiously fused; the superimposition of the two journeys encloses the end of the 'journey' of Burn's life in its beginning and the beginning in its ostensible end, insinuating a sense of completeness, of closure. The struggle to exact order from accidental chaos is, almost, achieved and the structure of the autobiography, as it finally falls into place, parallels and enacts the achievement of that central aim of Burn's life, the attainment of a 'resting place', of stability within movement.

(vi) Aspects of the historical context

The attempt to so arrange his life-story that it insinuates a simultaneously static and changing pattern suggests a wider context in which we might read the 1855 *Autobiography*. Burn's own repeated emphasis on his apprenticeship as a hatter provides a starting point. The title of 'Journeyman Hatter' has a double resonance, of both time and distance, for the hatters were among the first groups of workers for whom we have evidence of a 'tramping system'. As early as the 1730s the hatters had tramping 'houses of call', though they did not adopt the 'blank' or chit system of relief till 1798, and they even designed their Union emblem to portray tramping. The purpose of the tramping system was, clearly, to provide a form of unemployment benefit: a journeyman on the road, looking for work, would in effect receive unemployment benefit from his colleagues in each area he passed through. Such an organised circuit of 'houses of call' for accredited 'strangers' rested upon an organised union or 'combination' of workers, while conversely the system itself helped to found union branches; the hatters were, again, among the first groups of workers to form a trade union. We might note that Burn's travels in search of work were no more extensive than those of a tramping artisan, that the tavern he owned for a time in the late 1830s was called 'The Hatter's Arms' (as were most of the public houses used as houses of call by tramping hatters), and that he served as a hatters' delegate to Trade Union meetings and on radical committees.

By the time Burn wrote the *Autobiography*, however, 'tramping' was undergoing a general and significant change. The unemployment of the 1830s and particularly the 1840s was, for some trades, a national rather than a local phenomenon, and tramping was therefore an inappropriate protection. Increasingly, static out-of-work pay began to be introduced instead; the Steam-Engine Makers and the Ironfounders both introduced national 'donative payments' in 1851 and other trades gradually followed suit during the 1860s and early 1870s. By 1878 George Howell could describe the tramping system as totally obsolescent. The historical and economic reasons for this decline in tramping are complex, but there was also a latent structural fragility in the system: a balance had to be maintained within a Union between those members 'on tramp' and static branch members; clearly, not all members could be simultaneously 'on tramp', though a national depression could logically demand such a situation if no alternative relief was available—indeed, in the depression of the early 1870s some trades regularly issued tramp-cards to 10% or even 25% of their members every year. From the 1850s the problem of unemployment relief began to be met in other ways, partly by static relief and partly by the traditional but now, in some unions, officially encouraged and subsidised solution of emigration, an international 'tramp'.

Encouragement of emigration is often regarded as a mark of 'New Model Unionism', and certainly static relief was practised by the classic 'New Model', the Amalgamated Society of Engineers, from its foundation in 1851. The notion of a widespread 'New Model Unionism', from 1850 onward, has of course been strongly challenged and the traditional picture has been modified by recent research, but many of the elements of the traditional version of 'New Model Unionism' are explicitly present in Burn's own case. In *A Glimpse* (c. 1867) he argues for emigration, aided by Trades Unions, in preference to strikes and supports Councils of Conciliation in trade disputes; like Applegarth before the Royal Commission, he emphasises the overlap between Trades Unions and Friendly Societies and castigates the 'Sheffield Outrages'; he also quotes that model of the New Model, the *Handbook* of the Amalgamated Society of Engineers. Burn's position on the Nine Hours Bill marks him as a 'non-militant' even in Trades Union affairs: he opposed the Bill on the grounds that increased leisure would lead to drink and that shorter hours would involve a reduction in wages. This consonance between Burn's views and those of the 'New Model' section of Trade Unionism (whatever the historical size or importance of that section) is based, I would suggest, upon shared premisses or problems, a common problematic which can be briefly traced.

The *Operative Bricklayers' Society's Trade Circular*, under the control of Coulson, a member of the 'Junta', argued on 1st December 1861 that 'the machinery of trade-unions . . . might be turned to raise millions of men in social position and thereby lay for centuries of years the foundation of national freedom and power', and that the vote had to be sought 'purely as a measure for the advancement of the respectable working classes in their social position, and as a guarantee for their industrial rights and privileges'. This emphasis is echoed by a Reform League pamphlet, *To the Trades Unionists of the United Kingdom*, issued in 1865: 'Let us once be able to maintain by the force of intellect and truth our rights as workmen in that House, and depend upon it we shall rise in the social scale.' In 1867 Ludlow and Lloyd Jones, the Christian Socialist allies of the Junta, saw Co-operative Societies as already having the same effect, raising nearly 150,000 of the working classes

collectively, if not individually, by this means alone, into the position hitherto occupied by the shopkeeping class. . . . Thousands of working men in these various establishments [co-operative production units] are learning to enter into the position and to share the interests of the employer class.

These various formulations share a basic premise: that millions of people, the 'respectable' working class or even the whole working class, can be 'raised' in the social order and yet that the social order will somehow remain, in a curious way, intact. Though the explicit hope is reserved for a more or less elastic group of 'respectable' workers, the logical assumption behind such a hope, or strategy, is that everybody could eventually become a shopkeeper, an employer, a ruler. The hope implicit here is structurally similar to the hope that everybody in a Union could be simultaneously 'on tramp' and yet receiving benefit from the 'other' members, the non-existent static branch members. Put more theoretically, the metaphor of 'raising' implies a model of society as simultaneously static and moving; this is, of course, possible in absolute economic terms (a general raising of the standard of living from which all groups equally benefit), but for everyone to be raised socially vis-à-vis other groups is logically impossible, nor is it possible for a whole class (as distinct from an individual) to be 'raised' relative to the class 'above' it without a considerable change in the structure of the whole society. It was, as we have seen, in the form or structure of his autobiography that Burn faced a similar problem and, by sleight of form, by a technical device and by deception, 'solved' it, presenting his own life as simultaneously static and moving; but in terms of a whole society no such solution is possible, though the hope of a similar 'solution' seems to have been what united the Junta and their allies from the 1850s to 1870s.

We can, briefly, note other related aspects of the political, social and economic problems of those decades. The cooperation of Christian Socialists with the Junta highlights one development in the period: a renewed attempt at an alliance between middle-class and working-class reformers. In the early 1850s, after the 'collapse' of Chartism, Hume, Sturge, O'Connor, O'Brien, Lloyd Jones, Bright and others were involved in various attempts at class collaboration, in the 'Little Charter', the revived 'Complete Suffrage Movement' group, the National Reform League, the Parliamentary and Financial Reform League, etc. In the late 1850s and throughout the 1860s strong links were formed between some middle-class reformers and some working-class groups in the campaigns leading up to the 1867 Reform Act. The alliance tended to be with 'the labour aristocracy' (the term will have to serve here) while the Parliamentary debates and drafting committee manoeuvres during the 1866 and 1867 sessions often revolved round the problem of drawing lines between the 'labour aristocracy' or 'respectable' working class and the somewhat less respectable workers, in terms of franchise qualifications. One crucial issue in these debates over the Reform Bills was the 'lodger franchise', which was so continually controversial because it involved not only questions of technical definition but also that deep prejudice against people without a permanent home and address which in part underlies the characteristic conservative equation between political responsibility and personal property. It connects at this level with another problem which was emerging to middle-class consciousness from the 1860s on: the presence of 'casual labour' (which increasingly included Burn's own trade of hat-making) in London and elsewhere. For by an ignorance of the structural determinants of casual labour and by a sliding equation of 'casual' with 'poor' and 'poor' with 'dangerous', the middle class tried to 'solve' the 'problem' of casual labour in London partly by an emphasis on re-housing: to give the working class permanent homes was somehow seen as encouraging them to have permanent jobs. Once again, we can see Burn's own equation being made, between 'respectability' or 'responsibility' and having a fixed location, a home address.

(vii) Literary echoes

Burn's work can be placed not only within a specific historical context but also in relation to certain literary strands in the period. The *Autobiography* can, for example, be seen as a contribution to the 'biography of success' genre typified by the works of Samuel Smiles. As J. F. C. Harrison points out, 'Potted biography was the staple of the greater part of the literature of success . . . [and] a useful quarry was found in the autobiographies of working-class leaders such as Samuel Bamford, Alexander Somerville, and Thomas Cooper.' Burn's general attitudes and recommendations parallel those of Smiles in his emphasis, for example, on 'character' in 1855 and his attacks on 'selfishness' in the 1860s; the metaphor of 'resting place' and the search for a 'home' is also, of course, shared with Smiles (see, for example, the chapter on 'Healthy Homes' in *Thrift*, 1875). Burn's aim is most often expressed as the desire to become 'respectable' through the 'energy and determination of his character'—a truly Smilesian formulation—but in later works he expressed some unease at this notion of the self-made men; in *Three Years in America*, for example, he comments that the 'worst class of manufacturers we know of are some of those who have immediately risen out of the labour ranks'; moreover:

The want of consideration for men's feelings and sentiments is one of the leading traits in the American character. This I look upon as a consequence arising out of the system of equality which reduces every man to the level of every other man.

However, even in 1855 Burn emphasised, in a way Smiles always refused to do, the elements of regular failure in his own life—even though he finally claimed 'success' for himself.

In 1855, the same year as Burn's *Autobiography*, Dickens began *Little Dorrit* (1855–7), in which he takes as his hero a middle-aged failure, Arthur Clenham, and presents in the inventor Daniel Doyce an 'honest, self-helpful, indefatigable old man who has worked his way all through his life'. Clenham introduces himself with the comment: 'I am such a waif and stray everywhere, that I am liable to be drifted where any current may set . . . I have no will'—which recalls not only Burn's self-description as a 'wandering vagrant' and his semi-orphan status but also his constant use of water imagery of a similar kind, for example:

Whatever we may think of our free-will, there can be no doubt, but we are often impelled forward in our careers by a directing power over which we have no control, and such seems to have been my case in this instance. I was therefore carried headlong into a stream of contending circumstances, and like a chip of wood amid the boisterous waves of a stormy sea, I was dashed hither and thither without any controlling power of my own.

Dickens's emphasis on passivity in *Little Dorrit*, even in the case of Doyce, is one indication of a change in his values which the novel as a whole reinforces. Earlier novels, for example *Oliver Twist* (1837–8) and *Nicholas Nickleby* (1838–9), had employed a plot in which a 'genteel' hero (whether by birth or character) first descended into the social or economic depths and finally re-emerged as a truly restored or revealed 'gentleman'. After *Little Dorrit*, an apparently similar plot in *Great Expectations* (1860–1) in fact undermines the convention, for Pip has no initial gentility and deliberately sets out to acquire that status, only to find in the end that his social position as 'gentleman' rests on the generosity of a convict. The complexity of Dickens's treatment of the themes of 'self-help' and the status and nature of 'a gentleman' cannot be traced here, but the change sketched above indicates that neither notion was for him unproblematical. Nor indeed was the slogan of 'Self-Help' entirely clear for Smiles himself, as his later self-defence against critics and his insistence that it meant more than material advancement shows; that he originally conceived the notion in the context of working-class communal, rather than individual, self-help efforts in Leeds radical circles may have contributed to this ambiguity. Burn's uneasiness about his actual 'respectability' in 1855 and his later criticisms of some self-made men perhaps shows a similar awareness of the problematic nature of self-help, even as a personal strategy. However, his use of the interaction between epistolary datelines and the chronology of his career parallels Dickens's earlier and more confident use of circular plot: whereas Nickleby and Twist both begin as 'gentlemen' yet only have their true status ratified at the end of the novel, Burn, as the 'letter-writer' of 'September 20th 1854', 'begins' as the 'respectable' traveller which the end of the autobiography asserts him to be; the content of the rest of his life intervenes only as a descent into the depths from which he has, all the time, already emerged. It was perhaps not entirely inappropriate that the first edition of the *Autobiography* should have been dedicated to Charles Dickens.

(viii) Conclusion

A concluding note can be added. In 1882 Burn published a revised version of his autobiography. It is basically the 1855 version plus a continuation, of approximately the same length, dealing with further fortuitous changes in his later life: his period in America, followed by clerical work, publishing, some journalism, etc. The emphasis on trying to achieve respectability, on what he now calls the 'dream' of 'acceptance', is even more marked than in 1855—and he did, indeed, finally receive a grant from the Royal Literary Fund and become a 'member of the Gentleman's Club'. But there is, sadly, very little trace in the 1882 edition of the interesting features of the 1855 version, perhaps because Burn no longer felt so acutely the ambivalence of his position. He is, as we have seen, quite open about the identity of William Hill; the style of the added chapters lacks almost entirely the earlier juxtaposition of disparate vocabularies and is only rarely marked by a striking phrase; there is very little organisation in this latter half and it seems to have been written not at one time but in sections during the last forty years of his life. Most importantly, the epistolary structure is entirely abandoned and the division into Letters and the vocative form are erased from the whole work, including the sections retained from the 1855 version. This is, one presumes, partly because his son, Thomas, the supposed recipient of the 1855 letters, had died in the meanwhile —there is a moving chapter (XXVI) recounting the deaths of this son and of Burn's paralysed, mentally ill wife, and recalling the earlier losses of a dozen children. But other children were still alive, and the main reason for the absence of the 1855 structure is, surely, that its effect in 1855 was no longer needed, or desired, by 1882: the context had changed too much, the age of fragile equipoise had finally gone.

One new feature of the 1882 volume is, however, of some interest. The work includes a long 'Supplement' entitled 'Glimpses of English social, commercial and political history during the eighty years, 1802–1882'. This is almost entirely composed of detailed histories of an enormous range of mundane objects—buttons, needles, envelopes, bicycles, tinned food, etc., etc. In this nearly ludicrous yet oddly engrossing fascination with the world about him and the detailed knowledge of its every aspect that Burn seems concerned to demonstrate, we can perhaps see emerging in a new form the old urge: to find a secure, a 'known' place in a society in which he could, at last, feel at home. Yet the very peculiarity of the attempt, the collapse into an almost unorganised compendium of raw data, of miscellaneous 'information', of random empirical knowledge, simultaneously reveals the extent to which he had still not, quite, succeeded. Though he 'never lost caste' Burn remained 'one of the outside links in the chain of civilised society'; somehow he seems to have been always, like many of his class, 'a stranger in what should have been a home'.

Chapter 4: Thomas Frost: 'talking by turns of politics and poetry'

(i) A Chartist and something more

Thomas Frost begins the second chapter of his *Forty Years Recollections* (1880) with the statement:

Forty years ago the minds of vast numbers of the thinking portion of the working classes throughout the most highly-civilized countries of the world were filled with ideas of the perfectibility of human nature and the reconstruction of society upon the basis of universal liberty, equality and fraternity.

Frost himself, filled with such ideas, was attracted first to the 'Owenian Socialist movement' when he was sixteen. At first, he comments, 'the scheme of the philosopher' of New Lanark 'interested me chiefly in its metaphysical aspect', but as he became 'impressed with the connexion between the influence of circumstances in the formation of character and the new organisation which Owen desired to give society', he began to realise that 'Socialism, as expounded by Owen, seemed to present a perfectly practicable solution of a problem which had been for some time working in my mind, namely, how the progress of the physical sciences and mechanical arts could be made most conducive to the happiness and well-being of the people'. But 'in those days no small amount of moral courage was required in the man who avowed himself a Socialist', for 'if a Chartist was suspected of designs tending to the wholesale infraction of the eighth commandment, a Socialist was held in horror as certainly capable of violating the entire decalogue'. Put in more positive terms, Owenism was recognised as offering a far more total perspective than Chartism, proposing not just 'the Six Points' but, indeed, 'ideas of the reconstruction of society and the perfectionation of human nature'. Frost recognises quite explicitly that he was then 'a Chartist and something more', 'as the advanced reformers of that day were wont to describe themselves', in the sense that 'as yet I, with many more, occupied towards Chartism the position which the professors of that political creed held towards the Corn Law repealers. We believed the demand for the Charter to be a just one, but the goal of our aspirations was far beyond it, and we were unwilling to waste our strength in agitating for anything less than the reconstruction of the entire fabric of society.' With this perspective, he 'did not at that time connect myself with the Chartist organisation'.

Frost is here speaking of 1839, but by 1847, after various intervening experiments, he became convinced 'that social amelioration of every kind must make slow progress until the masses acquired political power', and when a branch of the National Land Company was founded in Croydon, followed by the 're-formation of a branch of the Charter Association', Frost not only joined both but also became a member of 'the Association of Fraternal Democrats, meeting monthly at a dingy public-house in Drury Lane'. The Fraternal Democrats have been recognised by historians of Chartism as the extreme wing of Chartism at this period. Their 'Principles and Rules' announced that members 'renounce, repudiate and condemn all political hereditary inequalities and distinctions of "caste" ', and declared that 'Governments elected by and responsible to the entire people is our political creed', that 'the earth with all its natural productions is the common property of all' and that the society's 'moral creed is to receive our fellow men, without regard to country, as members of one family, the human race; and citizens of one great commonwealth: the world'. Frost's membership of the Fraternal Democrats indicates that his perspectives at this stage were still broad, international, total, indeed Utopian. And though in terms of practical politics he, like many, broke with the 'extreme wing' in 1848 and reconciled himself to a more 'reformist' position, it is this initial and repeated urge towards a 'total' position that seems to give the clue to the significance of his wide-ranging activities and writings of later years.

(ii) Communes and poetry
This urge to totality is already apparent in the way Frost recounts the source of his interest in Owenism:

I had just been reading Coleridge's 'Religious Musings', and the brief address in which the philosopher of New Lanark had set forth the principles of his new constitution of society sent me to the poem again. The scheme of the philosopher seems to be the due response to the aspirations of the poet.

It is this pattern, of moving from literature to politics and back 'to the poem again' that is reproduced both within the *Recollections* and in Frost's actual life. The third chapter of *Recollections* describes how Frost first met the local Chartists, in the figure of Jem Blackaby, who 'might have been the prototype of Alton Locke, for he was a poet as well as a politician'. The chapter opens with an account of the clash between Cobden and Blackaby at Croydon, in which Blackaby demonstrated how Chartism included and went beyond the demands of the Anti-Corn Law League; then follows a description of Blackaby as both debater on Owenism and as poet, and then a summary of Chartist activity in 1839–42; the chapter ends with the conclusion: 'The poetry of Coleridge and Shelley was stirring within me, making me "a Chartist and something more" '. Thus the chapter itself moves in turns between 'poetry' and 'politics'.

The next chapter is concerned with Frost's practical attempts to go beyond the perspective of Chartism itself, first in seeking membership of the 'Utopian' Alcott House Concordium, then in trying to establish his own semi-Owenite commune. Chapter V relates how Frost then tried to found a journal which should serve all the various 'schools and sects of social reformers . . . without being the special organ of any one of them'; this project (somewhat Utopian in itself!) to provide a single forum replacing 'the *New Age* of the Concordists, the *Communist Chronicle* of the Communist Church, the *Model Republic* of the Charter-Socialists, the *Rising Sun* of the Etzlerites, and the *Progress of the Truth as it is in Jesus* of the White Friends' finally involved Frost simply in financing the profitless extension of James Goodwyn Barmby's *Communist Chronicle*, until Barmby and Frost separated on the two issues of religious allegiance and paternalism, each continuing a journal briefly, Frost the *Communist Journal* and Barmby the *Communist Chronicle*. In its short life the joint *Chronicle* had included a series of 'studies of Saint-Simon, Fourier and Owen' and a 'romance' by Barmby entitled *The Book of Platonopolis*; this fiction was summarised by Frost as:

a vision of the future, a dream of the rehabilitation of the earth and of humanity; of Communisteries built of marble and porphyry, in which the commoners dine off gold and silver plate, in banqueting-halls furnished with luxurious couches, adorned with the most exquisite productions of the painter and sculptor, and enlivened with music; where steam-cars convey them from one place to another as often as they desire a change of residence or, if they wish to vary the mode of travelling, balloons and aerial ships are ready to transport them through the air; where, in short, all that has been imagined by Plato, More, Bacon, and Campanella, is reproduced, and combined with all that modern science has effected or essayed for lessening human toil or promoting human enjoyment.

Such an extreme vision was bound to fade. This chapter concludes on a sobering note: 'Communism died out in England very rapidly.' Frost explains:

The Co-operative movement . . . drew into it all the more practical and less imaginative of the thousands over whose minds Communism had for a time exercised a potent charm. The comparative prosperity resulting from the development of free trade converted those whom Communism attracted only by the glowing prospect of material amelioration which it offered, and who formed the residuum of the movement.

On the other hand:

The fewer thinkers and dreamers retained their faith in Utopia perhaps, but they abandoned the distinctive characteristics of their respective sects and schools, ceased to expect the realisation of their day-dreams of the future in the present century, and directed their powers to the accomplishment of more practicable, and therefore more immediately useful reforms, if less lofty in aim, than the regeneration of humanity and the reconstruction of the social fabric.

This seems like an acknowledgement of Frost's own lowered sights. But the next words—which open chapter VI—are 'Popular literature forty years ago', and the chapter is concerned with the history of literature for 'the masses', including Frost's own first attempts at serial fiction. By the juxtaposition of these two chapters Frost is, in effect, implying that he is to be numbered rather among the 'thinkers and dreamers', the more rather than less 'imaginative', those still seeking the Utopia; but, as the juxtaposition also underlines, if the practical realisation of Utopia is to be acknowledged as extremely distant, then recourse can be had back 'to the poem again', to literature. It is this pattern, evident in the arrangement of chapters III to VI, that, transposed in various ways, we can now examine in Frost's life and writings as a whole.

(iii) The entire fabric of society
It is the emphasis on 'entire' that is the starting point. Just as the Chartists went beyond the single-issue campaign of the Anti-Corn Law League, so Frost's positions as Owenite, Concordist, and Fraternal Democrat, attempt to include not just a single issue or the 'Six Points' but every aspect of 'the social fabric'. To an impressive extent Frost's own life reflects this urge: his interests, concerns, involvements, connections, seem at some point, in some way, to have touched almost every significant aspect of his age. A mere listing, by reducing and abstracting, is unsatisfactory but at least demonstrates the range of Frost's antennae.

Already we have briefly mentioned his contact with the now obscure London scene, in the 1830s, of radical communes—of 'physical puritans', of 'Swedenborgians, Millenarians, Southcottians, White Quakers, and the like', his connection with the Chartist movement and the National Land Company, and the beginnings of his popular writing. Additions can be made in each area—politics and literature—and in new areas. At the age of eighteen he sent a 'treatise on the Thirty-Nine Articles of the Episcopal Church, bristling with arguments, deistical and necessitarian, against every point of the Church's belief' to Henry Hetherington, ex-editor of the *Poor Man's Guardian*; the treatise was declined on the grounds that 'nobody cares anything about the 39 Articles'; in February of the following year, of course, John Henry Newman published Tract XC, *Remarks on Certain Passages of the 39 Articles*. Frost flirted more than once with religious questions of the day: his first appearance in print was a short article in the *Freethinkers' Information for the People*, which 'anticipated the hypotheses which subsequently produced so much sensation in the anonymously-published *Vestiges of the Natural History of Creation*'. In the early 1850s Frost occupied his 'leisure hours in amateur mission work among the wretched inhabitants of squalid and poverty-stricken Bethnal Green, and assisting the curate of St. Phillip's in teaching the ragged urchins who attended his Sunday-school'; he quotes the suspicious hostility of one minister at his attempts here to fuse socialism and Christianity; again Frost is paddling in an important current in Victorian religious history; about the same year, in 1853, F. D. Maurice was deprived of his Professorship at King's College for publishing his *Theological Essays* and in 1854 Maurice helped to found the London Working Men's College, perhaps the most enduring product of Christian Socialism. By the 1870s we find Frost producing a number of stories for the Religious Tract Society, though this connection was short-lived.

It was his 'own observations on the development of the most simple forms of vegetable and animal life' that prompted his 'anticipation' of Chambers's *Vestiges*, and the habit of observation of nature seems to have been constant with Frost. About 1876 he moved to Southborough, about two miles north of Tunbridge Wells, where he quickly 'made considerable additions to a series of descriptive sketches, interspersed with notices of bird and insect life, which I had commenced in Surrey', and soon published them as three volumes in a series of *Half-Holiday Handbooks*. Again, he is touching upon some important elements in the later Victorian age: the beginnings of a 'problem of leisure' for a majority, added to a variant on the amateur naturalist craze. By this time—the 1870s—Frost had a great deal of experience in the field of popular writing. He had begun his working life as an apprentice in a printing office and had quickly suggested to his employer, Cornelius Chapman, the publication of a local magazine, the first number of which appeared, as *Chapman's Miscellany*, in 1843. Frost graduated from this to work as a printer for William Dugdale, a bookseller who sold Sue, Voltaire, Carlile, and other 'comparatively unobjectionable' works, but also 'guinea books of erotic engravings, imported from Paris'—another important, if buried, facet of Victorian taste. After only a fortnight at Dugdale's, Frost returned to Croydon and set up his own press, first publishing a couple of his own pamphlets (on cosmogony and on Owenism) and then a local *Penny Punch* under his own editorship—again, he was moving quickly on to a new fad. About the same time he made his first appearance as a newspaper correspondent, in the columns of *Lloyd's London*

Newspaper. His subsequent activities in journalism and popular literature were numerous. He began with anonymous 'penny number' serial fiction modelled on Sue, then made some early attempts at writing drama (which were eventually rewarded indirectly when his first story for *Boys of England* was dramatised) and then, more successfully, at 'converting popular dramas into short stories for Purkess's Library of Romance'. After writing penny number fiction for a time (including another story which was dramatised, 'The Mysteries of Old Father Thames'), Frost concluded that 'this class of literature was being superseded by the *London Journal* and *Reynold's Miscellany*', so tried for work as a hack periodical writer; a successful serial story for the *National Instructor* led to enrolment on the staff of *Chambers's Papers for the People* in 1850. His experience on the *Instructor* and *Chambers's* soon left him confident enough to 'run four stories at the same time, three in numbers, and one in a periodical', and he began to sell most of his serial stories before writing more than a dozen episodes; he even turned down an exclusive contract with Edward Lloyd. Much of his writing was clearly hack-work, but a more disinterested motive lay behind some of his fiction: he claims that

when a man is able to express his views on politics, and on political and social economy, in a manner which obtains him thousands of admiring readers—as I had done in fiction—the confession of his political opponents that they consider him dangerous is the highest compliment they can pay him.

In fact Frost even completed, at Macgowan's request, a half-written novel by the best exponent of this tactic among the radical Chartists: Ernest Jones's *The Lass and the Lady*, published in 1855.

Jones himself formulated other links between politics and writing which Frost exemplified. In 1852 Jones wrote:

It is clear . . . that if education is to be safe, the people must become their own educators—and we therefore draw the attention of our readers to the important requisite: *a literature for the young*. Our democratic literature is all written for the adult—we must have a literature written expressly for the child of the working man. And since the class-books of the rich are the exponents of class-government, ours must be the exponents of popular sovereignty.

It is doubtful whether Frost grasped the point that clearly, but he certainly figured fairly prominently in the production of 'a literature for the young'. His first story for *Boys of England* was in 1869, and by 1871 he had written 'about a dozen serial stories' for that and other publications owned by Brett (Brett's *Boys of England*, begun in 1866, was the most successful of the mid-century 'new brand' of boys' periodicals). Frost was soon recognised as sufficiently successful in this field to be asked to edit *The Gentleman's Journal*, an attempt to enter the battle between Brett and his main rival W. L. Emmett. Frost's boys' stories for the Religious Tract Society, in which care had to be taken 'to combine the incidents with a healthy moral tone, and to make them subservient to the teaching of the Gospel', would probably have horrified Ernest Jones, but the RTS were pleased enough to recall Frost as a contributor to their new, and outstandingly successful, *Boys Own Paper* in 1879: one of Frost's stories, 'Wrecked on a Floe', appeared in the first number; but the editor, J. M. Macaulay, declined further stories from Frost. Whatever Macaulay's objection, Frost could certainly by that time claim to be numbered among the 'masculine purveyors of imaginative reading to the millions', along with such names as Stagg, Stevens, Suter, Percy and Vane St John.

Frost had known Percy St John some fifteen years earlier, during his first full editorship, of Cassell's *Magazine of Art*. Another member of Cassell's staff at that time, E. B. Neill, provided Frost with his next line of work: Neill was then London correspondent of *The Birmingham Journal* and *The Liverpool Albion*; he asked Frost for a hack-article on emigration to Canada, and the result was Frost's engagement 'to write the leaders of the *Birmingham Journal*, and to report Select Committees and Royal Commissions, and furnish résumés of Parliamentary papers, both for the *Birmingham Daily Post* and the *Liverpool Daily Post*'. Frost wrote for the *Birmingham Journal* till about 1859, then began to write leaders for the *Liverpool Albion* on foreign politics and social questions. The *Albion* was, however, less liberal than the *Journal* and Frost found his radicalism being muted. While writing for the *Albion* he also began writing 'the leaders and leaderettes' for the *Shrewsbury Chronicle* and continued to do so till 1872, when the increasing costs of paper and compositors' wages forced general economies in the newspaper world. The same year the *Albion* changed hands, and Frost found both the new political line and the new terms of his contract objectionable. The *Gentleman's Journal*, which Frost was also then editing, also closed that year. He resolved, he says, never to write another line for a newspaper. But when in 1875 his mother died he returned to his native Croydon and soon contributed a series of 'Recollections of an Old Croydonian' to the local *Croydon Chronicle*. Then between 1876 and 1880 he wrote 'several serial stories for a Sheffield newspaper', probably the *Sheffield Evening Post*, founded in 1873. In 1881 Frost was offered the sub-editorship of the Sheffield paper; in January 1882 he moved to the sub-editorship of the *Barnsley Times*; in October 1882 he moved again, to the sub-editorship of the *Liverpool Evening Albion*. In Sheffield and Barnsley he had found himself in conflict with Conservative proprietors over editorial policy, and in Liverpool a merger between the *Albion* and the *Liverpool Telephone* soon brought that editorship to an end; he thereupon returned to Barnsley as editor of the *Barnsley Independent*, the *Barnsley Times* under a new name. Despite the avowed non-partisan character of the 'new' paper, after the 1885 General Election it reverted to its old Conservative bias and Frost again found himself an unemployed journalist.

To conclude this survey of Frost's concerns and interests some further points at which he touched important Victorian themes can be briefly mentioned. He once planned a book 'on the origin of man and the migrations of the race in prehistoric times' in which he proposed 'to reconcile the existence of several distinct varieties of the genus *homo* with the hypothesis of a common origin by means of a theory of development'. He planned another book on the Italian revolution and wrote a two-volume study called *The Secret Societies of the European Revolution*. He wrote articles in the *Albion* on military strategy, on the disadvantages of fortresses in modern warfare, engaged in a debate with Admiral Sir Howard Douglas on the use of rockets, and wrote a lengthy article for the *United Services Magazine* which paralleled von Moltke's innovations in strategy. An article by Frost in *Et Cetera* propounded the theory, later verified by Stanley's explorations, that the Lualaba was not the Nile but the Congo river. Eighteen thousand copies of his *Half-Hours with the Early Explorers* were sold, catering to the vogue for naval exploits, as did many of his stories. The Indian Mutiny prompted Frost immediately to edit a *Complete Narrative of the Indian Mutiny* in 1857. He was an early contributor to the Dickensian industry with his *In Kent with Charles Dickens* (1880) and was among the first historians of 'popular culture', with his *Circus Life and Circus Celebrities* (1875), *The Old Showmen and the Old London Fairs* (1874) and *The Lives of the Conjurors* (1876). As late as 1896 five of his essays appeared in a collection entitled *The Lawyer in history, literature and humour.*

The sources Frost traces for these various works are impressively varied and even esoteric, yet the resulting books, like his life, seem as much a miscellaneous jumble as an ordered whole. In fact, the significant point about this intriguing range of interests, involvements and activities, is not that they are internally coherent, linked as a group of connected preoccupations by any immediate association, but that they are connected together only insofar as the history and society of the period itself through which Frost lived was a 'totality'. It is, in fact, peculiarly appropriate that Frost should have become by the end of his life primarily a newspaper editor, since the task of an editor is, daily, to assemble large amounts of miscellaneous news and information concerning every aspect of the contemporary world, and yet present the result as in some sense a cohesive whole. Frost himself comments on the miscellaneous nature of his knowledge, precisely as an asset to his journalistic career:

One qualification of no little importance in reporting which I possessed at this early period of my journalistic career was the great amount of miscellaneous knowledge which I had gathered in the course of my varied reading and occupations, and which an excellent memory had enabled me to retain. I soon found that, whatever might be the subject before any Parliamentary committee which I had to report, I knew enough about it to discriminate readily between what was important in the evidence and that which was trivial or irrelevant.

But the move from assimilation of material to discrimination of relevance always involves options, which may well be disputed: Frost's squabbles over political and editorial policy with Conservative newspaper proprietors under-lined this point for him. For the society he was reporting could not, after all, be grasped as a coherent totality: newspapers necessarily offered divergent interpretations. An attempt to make completely consistent sense of every aspect of the social and political world was bound to fail.

So too was Frost's attempt in his own life. In a split society only a split life is possible. An attempt to live a totally embracing life can then only be seen as a series of fragmented lives. Frost frequently recognised this of his own life:

the literary labours of his later years have differed so widely in character as to evoke from the critics some amusing speculations as to his position and pursuits. While one has conjectured that the writer must have been in the habit, throughout his life, of travelling from one fair to another, associating with clowns and acrobats, another has surmised that he is a veteran revolutionist who has kept himself dark, and that his associates in the past have been the foreign refugees who haunt the cafes around Leicester Square.

Again:

Here was one of their own townsmen, whose name had become known in the literary world, and whose work had been criticised in the reviews and the newspapers, living in their midst, and they knew it not, never thought of associating with the authorship of books which bore his name on the title-page the man with whose form and face they had been familiar on public platforms, and in the business life of the town thirty years before.

Frost, one feels, could only have achieved his complete and rounded self in a quite different society, one that he pictured to himself in his youth, reconstructed 'upon the basis of universal liberty, equality and fraternity', and which he tried at first to realise on a small scale in his projected commune. But, in the real world of nineteenth-century England, such a project was defeated, unfinished, necessarily anti-climactic. Here it is important not simply that the project failed, but that the precise way in which, for Frost, the political project crumbled and the utopian dream receded deeply shapes his autobiographical self-presentation.

(iv) 1848 as anti-climax

Two chapters in *Recollections*, VIII and IX, tell the crucial tale and their construction is symptomatic. Chapter VIII opens, literally, with 'The revival of the Chartist movement in Croydon', and Frost's first personal involvement. The narrative is then suddenly interrupted, in what seems a curious digression but actually parallels the earlier oscillation in chapter III between 'poetry and politics', by a three-page reminiscence of Jem Blackaby: memories of an evening in 1844 when, in idyllic surroundings, he had met Blackaby again after a gap of a year, and a brief account of Blackaby's poetry, including a poem on 'the night-flowering cereus', a 'strange and beautiful cactus . . . the flowers of which unfold their petals at night, and perish before sunrise'. The original thread is then picked up again in a paragraph which links the Chartist agitation to the contemporary movement in France led by Odillon-Barrot and describes how the Republican secret societies are preparing 'to take advantage of the expected collision with the Government'. Frost remarks that he had prophesied the French Revolution of 1848 'before the close of 1847', and then recounts his membership of the Fraternal Democrats and the FD meeting at which 'suddenly the news of the events in Paris was brought in. The effect was electrical'. From that meeting, and the wild street demonstrations that followed, Frost hurried back to Croydon, 'the first person to announce the event' there. The Croydon branch organised a meeting to further the Petition and the next few pages present Frost in the role of negotiator with the town authorities. A digression concerning forged signatures to the immense Petition then leads up to the Kennington Common demonstration of 10th April 1848—with Frost beforehand refuting grim predictions of an armed battle to come. The tension of the account heightens till the supposed 'arrest' of Feargus O'Connor turns out to be a meeting for a compromise arrangement between the Chartist leader and the police. Frost himself 'breathed more freely' when the compromise was announced. But then the tension in the narrative slowly builds up again, as police reinforcements and the immense crowd jostle at Blackfriars Bridge:

Blackfriars Road . . . was thronged with people, so densely packed that they could scarcely move, owing to the refusal of the police to allow more than two or three at a time to pass through their ranks. Altercations and fights ensued, ending with the more irascible of the crowd being removed in custody, and were followed by rushes at the police, who beat back the crowd with their truncheons. The exasperation increased as time wore on, and as the crowd became more dense, the pressure upon those in front produced a forward movement which the police were unable to resist. They began to yield ground; the crowd pressed onward, the ranks of the police became broken, and, with a tremendous shout, the dense mass surged over the bridge, sweeping the police before it.

My way lay in the opposite direction . . .

The anti-climax of this final sentence leads smoothly into the almost symbolic encounter:

Threading my way through the scattered and scattering groups I entered the White Swan, on the southern side of the common, to refresh myself with a glass of ale. There, at the crowded bar, stood Blackaby.

That quiet evening in the pub in 1844 being thus recalled, Frost again reminisces about half-hours later spent in the shoemaker-poet's garret, and the chapter ends, with apparent inconsequence, with Frost's memory of a 'sensational incident' during one of his visits to Blackaby. He offers the incident as 'a ghastly illustration of the "juxtaposition"—to use a word which Blackaby much affected—of life and death'. On a visit to Blackaby's lodgings, Frost suddenly found himself 'brought up sharp by a black coffin, standing upon the second-floor landing, at right angles to the dirty, uncarpeted stairs'; the final sentence of this chapter which traces the rise and fall of Chartism as a mass movement is then:

To reach Blackaby's room, I had to step over the coffin, which contained the corpse of a lodger, who had wound up a fortnight's debauch by going home in the still hours of the night and hanging himself.

This seems much more than just a fortuitous 'juxtaposition'. One's suspicion that Frost's arrangement here is more complex than that of mere historical narrative and reminiscence grows as the account continues.

The next chapter, IX, concentrates on the immediate aftermath of 10th April. It was only then, 'when the futility of moral force seemed to be shown', that 'an appeal to arms was thought of'. Frost details the 'new organisation', comparing it with 'the system introduced by the secret insurrectionary committee of 1839, which was borrowed from that of the United Irishmen'. These 'ominous' changes resulted in the quiet, disciplined march of an estimated 80,000 men through London on the night of 29th May, without public notification being necessary. The atmosphere then gradually darkens as the chapter proceeds, with details of the stockpiling of small-arms, the secret committee's meetings, delegates from the Young Ireland movement, attempts at infiltration by police agents, till Frost recounts his calling at the London 'office' of the 'Executive Committee' on 9th June. As he left, a stranger

informed me, without the least hesitation, that the preparations for insurrection were completed —arms and ammunition provided, missiles collected on roofs of houses for assailing the military and police while passing through the street, and openings made in party-walls to enable the insurgents to pass from house to house. Whit Monday had been fixed for the rising, which was to be prepared for by the massing of the metropolitan branches at Blackheath and Bishop Bonner's Fields.

With 'only three days before the blow would be struck', Frost thought deeply 'as the train bore me to Croydon that evening': 'But what should I do? That question occurred to my mind again and again.' Eventually, 'Clear to my mind as the sun at noon to my material vision was the rightfulness of the meditated revolt.' But this decision meant that, in effect, Frost did nothing: a local Croydon meeting had already been arranged to coincide with the planned demonstration, to draw off potential police reinforcements from the main London meeting. Frost did not divulge the further news, to 'avoid compromising' his colleagues 'in the existing doubtful situation', resolving that 'it would be time enough to move when a promising movement had been made in London'. Then, on the evening of the 11th, the stranger arrived at Frost's home, to await there the result of the following day's insurrection, since, as 'a member of the revolutionary secret committee', a warrant had been issued for his arrest.

The following pages again present Frost as the negotiator with the local authorities, arguing the case for the legality of the proposed Croydon meeting; the constitutional arguments move rapidly to a threat of force by the Town Council, as 500 special constables and 150 troops move to occupy the site of the planned meeting. Frost returns to the Chartist committee, who condemn the magistrates' action as 'arbitrary and unconstitutional'. Then as the time of the meeting, and the London insurrection, approaches, small groups of Chartists begin to encounter the eighty police placed as the first line of the Town Council's forces. The heavy rain descends in torrents. The tension mounts.

The courage of my colleagues was now put to the test. On my rising and asking them what they intended to do, there was a dead silence for a few moments, and then a resolution to abandon the meeting, on the ground of the unfavourable weather and the measures adopted by the authorities was proposed, and was carried by a majority of, I think, five to two.

For Frost this moment was the beginning of his own move away from Chartism towards the Parliamentary Reform Association, and the incident must have recalled his earlier choice-point between Chartist and middle-class groupings: that meeting of Cobden's Anti-Corn Law League interrupted by Blackaby six years before:

The Leaguers had just ascended the waggon which had been drawn up against a corn warehouse to serve as a platform, when the dark clouds which had lowered ominously since noon began to discharge their aqueous contents, and umbrellas went up like a sudden growth of gigantic mushrooms, as well on the waggon as over the heads of the crowd below. A consultation seemed to be held by the Leaguers as to the course to be pursued under these adverse conditions; but there were no symptoms of retreat on the part of the crowd, and the indecision was ended by General Thompson stepping forward, and saying, as he extended one hand towards the throng below, 'If it doesn't rain there, it doesn't rain here.' Loud applause greeted the remark, and the proceedings were commenced.

But the bathetic rain in the later incident marked the end, not the beginning, though a few scenes were left to play. That evening Frost and the 'stranger' (Rose) waited for news from London. At 10 pm Frost

stepped into the sloppy street; and, leaving the town behind me, ascended an eminence, and looked northward as anxiously as the watchers by the Vistula did on a certain night, half a century ago, when the signal was to be given for the rising in Warsaw. But not one of the conflagrations which Ritchie's corps of 'luminaries' were to have kindled reached the sky.

The false sunrise never came, and the rest of the chapter explains the failure of both the attempts at insurrection in that year, on 12th June and 15th August, ending in the trial of the secret committee and the eventual fate of Mullins, the Home Office spy who had betrayed the revolutionaries.

But the chapter does not quite close there. The final paragraph returns to Blackaby:

Blackaby did not live to see the greater part of his political creed made part and parcel of the Constitution on the proposition of a Conservative minister. Failing health induced him to seek the purer air of Northampton, and I never saw him again. Whether he continued to court the Muses, or had all the poetry crushed out of his nature by the severer labour rendered necessary by an inferior description of work, I know not. If he left any manuscripts they have probably been used to light fires, or are stowed away, dusty and cobwebby, in some obscure corner of the house in which he died. His strength diminished as his health failed, and with it the means of supporting life unaided; and he succumbed at last to sickness and poverty, and removed to the house of his brother, in the village of Hunsdon, near Ware, to die.

There is a quiet nobility in this passage; we feel through it the sadness of Frost, but also more than that, for Blackaby has figured since chapter III almost as a symbol of a fusion between poetry and politics and of a hope for the working classes that can no longer, after 1848, be sustained. Frost records, as his feelings during the night of 12th June, 'anxiety and a degree of disappointment', a disappointment that turned to a kind of disillusion, for 'when the crisis had passed, I was so strongly impressed with the conviction that a revolutionary movement was hopeless', that it is this sense of loss, a final loss of utopian perspectives, as well as the loss of his friend, that we feel as the chapter closes. The 'night-flowering cereus, the flowers of which unfold their petals at night, and perish before sunrise' and the false sunrise of Ritchie's luminaries hover between the lines of that last paragraph, as it records Blackaby's death before the passing of the Second Reform Act, a reform which could only give a faint light in the shadow of previous, lost hopes. By then even the poems have probably gone up in smoke.

This chapter is the breaking point. Revolution, 'the reconstruction of the entire fabric of society', 'the perfectibility of human nature', never again seemed practicable to Frost. A coda, chapter X, dealing severely with Feargus O'Connor, Harney and Ernest Jones, brings the movement finally to a close, ending, appropriately, with Jones's death. The final words of these three chapters are, respectively, 'hanging himself', 'to die' and 'his death'. They seem deliberately apposite. The second movement of the book, slow and sober, opens with *Papers for the People*, Parliamentary reform, and mission work in Bethnal Green (chs. XI, XII, XIII). The following chapters then orchestrate these themes, alternating literature (Cassell's, ch. XIV; provincial journalism, ch. XV; popular literature, ch. XX), parliamentary politics (Palmerston, ch. XVII; the Reform Act, ch. XVIII; Gladstone, ch. XXXI) and popular semi-political agitation (the 1855 Hyde Park riots, ch. XVI; the Hyde Park railings incident of 1867, ch. XIX). But the themes are now dis-connected from each other, each chapter a separate unit: both the tension and the cohesion of the earlier half are lessened. There is a sense of anti-climax, of unfinished business, of lines pursued but never completed, in this second half of *Recollections*.

(v) Inconclusions and rationality

The sense of a premature ending is perhaps inevitable in any autobiography, but the emphasis above on anti-climax, lack of conclusion, bathos almost, is given curious support by a puzzling feature of Frost's writings. He frequently inserts anecdotes and stories into his works, and the majority of these actually have unsatisfactory, inconclusive endings. A simple example is from his *Reminiscences of a Country Journalist* (1886):

A fortnight after the adventure just related, I visited that village again, and found, on getting into the road, that I had a mile and a half, or more, to walk. It was already dark, and the road was not much lighter where, at a little distance beyond Darton, I saw a red flame casting a flickering glare upon the mud, and on reaching it found that it proceeded from a coal fire in an iron basket, where a colliery tramway crossed the road on the level. A sound as of an approaching train reached my ears, and, on looking in the direction whence it proceeded, I discerned a distant red light. I paused for a moment, but the train seemed to be moving slowly, and I ventured to cross.

Fortuitously, the last words quoted come at the foot of the page; the reader turns the page, expecting to read of a serious accident or at least a narrow escape—to find a new paragraph beginning: 'I did not go that way again, however.' No accident, no escape, not even a further comment—except another anecdote about an awkward short-cut. Other anecdotes in the same work have similarly inconclusive endings: an extended reminiscence about a cousin who suddenly left home, and whom Frost unexpectedly met again, finally ends, after four pages, with the cousin's return to his wife and the deadpan comment: 'But I never discovered the cause of his mysterious disappearance.' Three other tales of 'missing persons' end with a similar lameness; in recounting one, for example, Frost devotes almost six pages to a quite false lead he followed up, to the wrong missing girl! A variant on this device is the opening of chapter XIII of *Reminiscences*:

A dark shadow had been cast upon the pathway of my life, and I could not escape from it. It clung to me relentlessly as the Old Man of the Sea to the shoulders of Sinbad, and I had no power to shake it off. It paralyzed all my efforts for material advancement, and reduced me to the position of a horse in a mill. In some respects the horse had the advantage.

Seven years passed, with the grip of my devilish burden constantly tightening. Desperation at length gave me strength to cast it from me, but the shadow still pursued me, and came at unexpected turns across my path, poisoning my life with the consciousness that we were still breathing the same air.

But this is a riddle, the interpretation of which would not greatly interest my readers, even if I were disposed to open the closet in which my domestic skeleton of those years was concealed.

I doubt if many readers are 'not greatly' interested after this cryptic statement, but Frost is content to leave it there.

The closest analogue to this odd strand of inconclusiveness in Frost is the detective novel, but one that is sometimes content to offer no solution. A clear example of this is Frost's analysis of the evidence for the location of 'Dingley Dell', in *In Kent with Charles Dickens*, where, after five pages of close topographical argument, he cleverly narrows down the choices—and simply leaves the problem there. A similar example is his attempt to check the historical accuracy of 'the strange adventures of Ambrose Gwinett', contained in *The Life and Strange Adventures and Voyages of Ambrose Gwinett*, an 'autobiography' which 'in the catalogue of the British Museum Library bears the conjectural date of 1731' and is attributed to 'Isaac Bickerstaff'; after nine pages of inquiry Frost's account ends inconclusively with 'I gave it up'. What is odd in the inclusion of such anecdotes and inquiries is that the reader seems to be expected to feel an interest in the process, the trail, for its own sake, and not for the sake of any conclusion; in these various stories anti-climax seems to be a virtue.

The parallel with a variant on the detective genre is not entirely fortuitous perhaps; it was in the year after Frost's *Reminiscences* that Sherlock Holmes made his first appearance; the boys' stories and the Sue-type well-made thriller had prepared the way; so too, further back, had Godwin and Poe. Poe died in 1849; by 1924 D. H. Lawrence, in *Studies in Classic American Literature*, could remark impatiently: 'These terribly conscious birds, like Poe and his Ligeia, deny the very life that is in them; they want to turn it all into talk, into knowing. And so life, which will *not* be known, leaves them.' The detective novel is an extreme exercise in rationality, in knowing; it implies a belief in an ordered world, where cause and effect cohere, clues and solutions are cleanly connected, and life can in the end, whatever the mystery, be made sense of. But against that confidence, a different version of life and the world was being increasingly advanced in the closing decades of the century, whereby the world and the ego itself are questionable, perhaps fragmentary, bundles of experience and aperçus. Frost, in the early 1880s, shows clear signs of being caught between these two versions: his unfinished anecdotes and lines of inquiry, and his vast quantities of miscellaneous knowledge barely held together and incoherently organised, are deeply part of the same structure of feeling which, after 1850, experienced society, anti-climactically, as unable to be transformed as a whole. It is in this context perhaps that one can make sense of the fact that he wrote two autobiographies within six years: it is in his *Recollections* and *Reminiscences* that he tries to make (his) 'life' into something that can be 'known', but no single work can 'hold' his life. He wrote, anti-climactically, *two* autobiographies.

(vi) Newspapers and known communities

Though there is a considerable overlap in the contents of *Recollections* and of *Reminiscences*, what is most striking is the extent to which they are mutually exclusive. A great deal of *Recollections* is concerned with Frost's various political involvements, yet in *Reminiscences* politics are scarcely mentioned. Only in the context of his difficulties in finding a sufficiently 'liberal' newspaper to work for does Frost give any extended treatment of his continuing political options, but in relation to his earlier commitments he merely remarks:

I am not aware that my political antecedents had any influence whatever on my career as a journalist, as I believe they were completely unknown, so small had been the part I had played in the arena of politics, until the publication of the *Recollections*.

This claim certainly narrows the notion of 'influence'. For if we examine, from a new angle, the 'small part' he did play in politics, an important connection emerges which helps not only to account for the apparently apolitical emphasis of *Reminiscences* but also to illuminate a substantial element in the social history of the period covered by Frost's life.

Some facets of Frost's early opinions and activities can here be linked together. Following Owen he 'contended that the character of each individual is formed by the circumstances by which he is surrounded', and one reason why Frost did not become a member of the Alcott House community was that:

Greaves and his disciples maintained, in diametrical opposition to Owen's views, that the existing generation could not be perfected, or even appreciably improved, since no amount of education or moral training, or any other external condition, could repair the defects of birth.

A related issue finally separated him from Barmby:

He advocated the paternal system of government, I the democratic. 'Neither democracy nor aristocracy,' he wrote, 'have anything to do with Communism. They are party terms of the present. In the future, governmental politics will be succeeded by industrial administration.' In the present, however, it was not clear to me that men, even in small bodies, would submit to autocratic rule, however sugar-coated with a paternal aspect.

Frost here touches two of the most deeply significant issues of his age: the debate on the role of external factors on character formation, and the choice between paternalism and democracy. An option for paternalism goes naturally with a reliance on external influence on the less gifted 'masses', while belief in the somehow innate goodness of the 'people' tends to act as a premiss for a commitment to 'democracy'. Frost at first tried to combine an adherence to democracy with an Owenite emphasis on external condition; the attempted practical fusion was the small-scale commune deliberately creating an alternative environment with a feed-back effect on personal relations and 'character'. But once he left this commune (or Commun-ist) phase behind, he veered between various combinations of emphases. The National Land Company perhaps represented for him the commune ideal on a larger scale. While being involved in the 'mass' activities of the National Charter Association he nevertheless admitted that 'The men who openly and actively take part in any political movement are always a few compared with those who hold the same views, but do not declare themselves,' and this quasi-'vanguard' position underlies his membership of the Fraternal Democrats and his contacts with the 'secret' insurrectionary committees. His later membership of the Parliamentary Reform Association implies an acceptance of both a paternalist and a pressure-group perspective. The theoretical problem underlying Frost's shifting options has been neatly formulated by Marx:

The materialist doctrine concerning the changing of circumstances and education forgets that circumstances are changed by men and that the educator must himself be educated. This doctrine has therefore to divide society into two parts, one of which is superior to society.

Since Frost's fundamental perspective was opposed to any such division of society, his way of facing the implications of this problem brought him, superficially, close to Robert Lowe's solution ('We must educate our masters'), but with a crucial difference. Frost's concern with information and education for the masses, with popular literature and journalism, goes beyond Lowe's acquiescence in the long tradition of 'sharing culture downwards'; Frost's position embodies more than that: a recognition of the inherent value of the already existing culture of the masses. In writing his various volumes on 'popular culture', on circuses, fairs, showmen, Frost was extending and deepening that interest in popular ballads, tales, legends and customs which had already played a part in widening the whole notion of culture during the nineteenth century. What is at the root of his interest, however, is a grasp of the close interaction between social and cultural life and between personal contributions and communal experience. That grasp is presented in the opening pages of *Reminiscences* not as an intellectual position but as deeply part of the way he experienced his own life and existence. The memories recounted in the first chapter are very clearly communal memories, as a few passages will show:

This house was many years ago in the occupation of a linendraper named Stapleton, one of whose daughters informed a cousin of my own that there was a closet in the house, the door of which had been nailed up by some former tenant, perhaps a century before, and had never been opened since.

If my memory does not deceive me as to these traditions, this was the house in which lived a singular old woman, who was long remembered by the name of Mother Hotwater, and of whom many strange stories used to be told when I was a boy.

I well remember her sitting on the doorstep, with her basket of fish by her side, relating to my grandmother and one of my mother's sisters, in a very graphic manner, the incidents of Ned's great fight with White-headed Bob.

The late Dr Gardiner used to tell a story, illustrative of gipsy life and character under conditions which have long ceased to exist, which, if only for that reason, is worth telling again.

This participation in local rather than individual memories rested, for Frost, on social conditions which were almost ceasing to exist as he wrote, the conditions of a known and almost rural community. The replacement of that Croydon, known intimately as a boy, by the London suburb it had since become is one of Frost's major preoccupations in the opening chapters of his *Reminiscences* and he draws on longer memories than his own, including his parents', to establish its solid identity:

My mother remembered Norwood when the hamlet consisted of about a score of farm-houses and cottages scattered at considerable intervals along the lanes which intersected the woods, and the only means of communication with the metropolis was the carrier's tilted cart. From the parish churches of Lambeth and Camberwell to that of Croydon there was not a single place of worship, so sparse was the population, the former places, now so populous, being then but villages, and the latter, now a suburb of London, a quiet country town.

The close topographical details of the opening pages rest firmly on a sense of both continuity and discontinuity: for Frost the locality is still 'Croydon' even though the changes in parts of the area and town have been so great that the returning native loses his way. But the 'Croydon' which exists for Frost has, therefore, a rather curious ontological status: it exists precisely as a created world, composed not just of physical reality alone or in memory alone, but as a human 'world', one that Frost experiences not with the eyes of a Baedeker tourist but with a perception saturated by consciousness of its history and its inhabitants, including its dead, a consciousness which is not just of the individual but of the whole local community. In that kind of experience, of being 'at home' in a specific place, the Owenite distinction between 'external' conditions and 'internal' consciousness finally breaks down.

That sense of being 'at home', of having interiorised a whole community's way of life, is, of course, an intensely 'local' one; it cannot, in the same form, be extended to a whole society—if only because the very notion of 'community' is an intensely selective one. But if we seek an analogue to this breakdown of the distinction between the influence of external conditions and the growth of consciousness, operating at the level of a whole society, then at least one area offers itself. It is precisely in the realm of communications that a similar lack of distinction can operate: the complex network of newspaper publishing and educational apparatuses may in one sense be part of the 'external conditions', but the actual experience of reading or learning is one where external-internal barriers crumble. Education is a process of internalisation, the contents and approach of a particular newspaper become the shared memory of its regular readers, creating in its own way a known map of the whole society. Frost's option for journalism and his efforts in popular literature, then, can be seen from this angle as in continuity with the problems of his early positions, just as it can in terms of his urge to span and totalise the whole society.

The second of those early problems—that of paternalism versus democracy —is clearly related to some of the problems of the newspaper world. The creation of a common political consciousness through a newspaper can be a peculiarly élitist activity; the notions of 'reporter' and 'editor' are inherently paternalist. The practice of the *Northern Star* in printing unedited reports about their own activities from the secretaries of Chartist 'localities', as opposed to relying on 'reporters', was an early attempt to overcome this dilemma; even the *Star* however was dominated by the editorial directions of O'Connor. By the late decades of the century the relative independence of professional journalists was being clearly eroded and the final pages of *Reminiscences* deal with precisely this problem: Frost recounts how he joined the first National Association of Journalists soon after its formation in 1884; but its aims were strictly limited to Trade Union demands of better pay and working conditions. One could locate that particular response within a wider political and economic analysis of the period, but the immediately relevant point is that the broader problems of the press at that time hark back to a specific dilemma already apparent in Frost's earlier work on popular entertainments. His *Circus Life* had ended with an endorsement of Dickens's Sleary, in *Hard Times*, that 'people muth be amuthed. They can't be alwayth a-learning, nor they can't alwayth be a-working'. This embodies a fundamentally different perspective from Frost's emphasis in early life on 'how the progress of the phy..ical sciences and mechanical arts could be made most conducive to the happiness and well-being of the people', and on the need for widespread knowledge to apply those means. The option being firmly followed by the mass newspapers towards the close of the century must have seemed to be one of offering amusement as the *only* alternative to working, with the process of 'a-learning', at least in the sense of political education, being almost totally abandoned, by comparison with the unstamped papers of the earlier part of the century, the 'underground' world that produced the *Communist Chronicle*, or the decades of the *Northern Star*. It was in that context that new directions opened in art, either towards 'art for art's sake' or towards the provision of knowledge, relevant to political understanding, in semi-fictional semi-documentary form.

(vii) Conclusion

Frost's two autobiographies are best seen in terms of this complex set of problems. The broad distinction between their respective contents parallels that between politics and culture, which itself is related to the division between 'knowledge' and 'amusement', while both divisions are aspects of that sense of a fragmented society which, after the anti-climax of 1848, replaced the utopian hope of a totalised society in which every aspect could be held in coherent connection. The fact that Frost wrote two autobiographies is itself an aspect or symptom, at the personal level, of this fragmentation. Yet at the same time an autobiography, in straddling the divisions between imagination and documentation, is an assertion against that fragmentation. And in particular one feature of Frost's autobiographies indicates opposition to another, related, fragmentation: that in which individual life and social history are seen as divorced from each other. For Frost's life-stories contain surprisingly little of what can be regarded, now, as 'purely personal' history; both works present Frost's life precisely as part of a common history. In the same way, his histories of popular entertainment merge gradually into reminiscences of his own acquaintance with and memories of the field he is investigating.

In reading Frost's various works, taken together, we can enter from a fresh angle into what in some respects constitutes, far more than many more 'literary' works (though in a way akin to them) the communal memory of this period we have inherited, and in doing so we can perhaps recognise—beyond the particular echoes of a strangely familiar world of communes and mass demonstrations, of insurrectionary agitations and popular culture, of 'poetry and politics'—a deep and even disturbing continuity.

Part Three: Conclusions

'What are you working on?' Mr K. was asked.
'I'm having a lot of trouble: I'm busy preparing my next mistake,' answered Mr K.

(i) Relationships and form

This thesis began without a thesis. It set out not so much to prove any specific propositions as to see whether a particular method of critical analysis could be usefully applied to a certain kind of writing. The individual chapters of analysis have tried to respect—and even to some extent to reproduce—the specific patterns and structures of each work, but it is also possible to read these autobiographies in terms of what is revealed as common to them, rather than what characterises each individually; it is by considering them from this angle that we can now begin to suggest some tentative conclusions.

All four studies revealed, in different ways, a concern with relationships, personal and social. The tension between belonging to a known community and learning to be a 'stranger' to and with others was central to Bamford; in particular his relations with women offered an index of wider social problems. Somerville, like Bamford, was born into an intimately known world, but learned, in a distressing way, to live as a person simultaneously known and unknown in a larger and different kind of social world, in which even his own name became alienated from him. Burn, on the other hand, marked his chosen break with his family origins by deliberately erasing two syllables from his name, and those origins were, like Bamford's, characterised by a loss of parental love; Burn seems to have spent the rest of his life seeking a role and a home, and his autobiography is actually offered as an expression of his parental relation to his son. Frost, by contrast with all three others, is ostensibly undisturbed by a sense of his occupying many roles and personae, and easily accepts that, as a writer and journalist, he is both known and unknown to society; yet, like Bamford, he places friendship—the particular friendship with Blackaby—at the centre of his *Recollections* and can also be seen as trying in a new way to rediscover the experience of a known community. Frost's community was not, however, a local one, as Bamford's was: as an editor, Frost was related to a wider society in two ways, both as trying to organise the daily news of a whole society and as a spokesman for many different local communities.

That Frost found little difficulty in writing numerous novels, whereas Bamford mainly hovered on the brink of the novel-form, is perhaps related to that difference in mode of relation to their communities. For to write is to enter into a relationship with a community of readers, and various forms of writing involve and imply various forms of relationship (as, indeed, different modes of distribution imply different modalities of 'community' among readers). Bamford, as we saw, attempts to persuade his reader to enter into a sympathetic, sometimes intimate and sometimes even inward relationship with himself: he invites the reader to participate, not directly but obliquely, in his own deepest emotions and experiences, using poetry, parallels and juxtapositions with considerable effect, yet leaving the main imaginative effort and impact somewhat subliminal or latent. Somerville's relation with his reader is also latent, in a different way: that the writer is 'Somerville' and various finally identical 'Somervilles' is left to be discovered gradually, as the reader makes the identifications step by step; it is an odd form of relationship, but directly reflects Somerville's actual experience of being recognised and mis-recognised. Burn deliberately appropriates an epistolary form—thereby harking back to the prehistory of the novel-form itself—and in presenting a direct relationship with his son (one of paternal advice) indirectly brings his reader into a collaborative relationship with himself and his ambitions: by reading the autobiography as if from Burn's own achieved position of relative stability, the reader endorses and validates his claims. Burn's relation to his reader is both one of advice—he offers a 'biography of success'—and of tantalisation, suggesting constantly a coherence that only eventually, and somewhat spuriously, emerges. Frost's textual tactics are equally tantalising: whereas Burn insists on alleged turning-points, Frost nonchalantly presents casual anti-climaxes; but Frost also offers an impressive over-view of a whole society, outpacing Burn's more inchoate attempt to do so in his 1882 *Supplement*.

To write, to communicate at all, is to enter into a relationship; to write a work of a conventionally classifiable kind—a novel, a drama, a letter, a television script, an academic article, a thesis—is to participate in (and thereby help to perpetuate) an existing set of social relationships, ranging from the established relations of production (the relations between author and publisher, script-writer and television company, academic and editor, examinee and examiner, etc.) to what might be termed the relations of expectation: the reader expects, and the author implicitly agrees to provide, a particular kind of enjoyment, satisfaction, information or illumination. Those relations of expectation are embodied not just in the structures of production and distribution of a complex industry of communications, but in the conventions of writing itself: they are indicated in what is normally thought of as 'genre'. Insofar as a work is clearly written within a particular genre, it rests upon, recreates, and endorses a more or less specific set of social relations.

But in what sense is 'autobiography' a 'genre'? It is notoriously difficult, for example, for a librarian to classify an autobiography: does Collingwood's *Autobiography* go into the 'History' section, is Freud's *An Autobiographical Study* to be shelved with 'Psychoanalysis', can *Thomae Hobbes Malmesburiae Vita carmine expressa* really be regarded as a philosophical, still less poetical, work? A traditional category of writing, a familiar genre, embodies an established convention, a way of writing that operates within a certain set of purposes and problems and utilises a known and cumulative set of solutions: how to maintain suspense, how to depict a character, how to present information clearly, etc. But an autobiography is concerned with rather less specifiable problems ('life'?) and the notion of inherited, cumulative solutions seems peculiarly inappropriate, since the ostensible subject of any autobiography is, on one definition, 'unique'. In writing an autobiography, above all, it seems that

> every attempt
> Is a wholly new start, and a different kind of failure.

Certainly in the case of these four texts it seems difficult to categorise them as other than individual attempts and different kinds of failure.

(ii) Organisation and class

Yet part of what this thesis set out to test was whether a more general connection could be traced between 'working-class' autobiographies and the shared class of their authors—the implicit claim of much 'sociology of literature'. So far, however, in each analysis only particular connections between the individual work and its historical context have been suggested. But another passage from *Four Quartets* can perhaps lead us towards a more general set of connections:

> We had the experience but missed the meaning,
> And approach to the meaning restores the experience
> In a different form . . .
> . . . I have said before
> That the past experience revived in the meaning
> Is not the experience of one life only
> But of many generations

When Samuel Bamford complains that

We had not any of our own rank with whom to advise for the the better—no man of other days who had gone through the ordeal of experience; and whose judgement might have directed our self-devotion

the reader is offered a broad hint: Bamford is presenting himself as a 'man of experience', whose judgement we should accept, just as Burn later offers his own experience as a model for his son. But there are other ways of learning from, and even inheriting, the 'experience' of an earlier generation: as an author inherits a genre, so it is possible to inherit—to enter into—an organisation, an institutionalised form of social relations which embodies a cumulative response to certain kinds of problem. An organisation, like a genre, is a structure of relations—and so too is what we call 'class'. Class is a relational term in two ways: to 'belong to' a class, to be 'classed', is simultaneously to be identified with, in some respects, other 'members' of that class, and to be both differentiated from and in an active relation to another 'class'. Crucial to the practical definition of those inter- and intra-class relations is the role of class organisations, and if we now reconsider these four works in terms of the problems of class organisation we might recover other facets of their 'form' and 'meaning'.

In the analyses of all four, many organisations have been mentioned: the Manchester Constitutional Society of 1798, the Hampden Clubs of 1816, the secret committees of 1811–12, the Armed Association of Manchester Loyalists, Henry Hunt's 'Order of Knights', the Anti-Corn Law League, the National Charter Association, the Glasgow Trades Committee, the Journeymen Hatters' Union, the Oddfellows' Society, the Amalgamated Society of Engineers, the Fraternal Democrats, the National Land Company, the National Association of Journalists, and even 'the Secret Societies of the European Revolution'. The history of the nineteenth century, and particularly of the working class from 1780 to 1880, is permeated with organisations. But such organisations, it was implied above, are, like genres, solutions to problems. It is the problems rather than the particular solutions that are finally legible in these autobiographies.

Bamford's central problem was that he was unable, finally, to break out of his known community, to operate in a world of strangers. But the 'making of a class' involves, precisely, the achievement of an acknowledged relationship between people who are, in personal terms, strangers to one another. It involves both an ability to recognise an affinity, an economic and political identity of interests, with strangers whom one may never even meet, and a willingness to acknowledge and work with strangers from the same class whom one does meet. Bamford's experience of having to identify himself to radicals in London is one aspect of how that recognition can be made; his unwillingness to introduce himself to other radicals, casually met with, is perhaps one mark of his limits in this respect. But for Bamford, in general, any organisation that tried to bring together and coordinate the efforts of a class, rather than a local community, could only be seen, ultimately, as a form of coercion. Yet unless that breakthrough, both in perception and in practical activity, was made, only an impotently passive response at the local level was possible, and the result would tend to be the breakdown of existing local groupings and a retreat into a guarded and ultimately defenceless domesticity by each individual. The analysis of Bamford seems to exemplify this underlying pattern in that phase from the 1790s to the 1830s which Thompson has labelled 'the making of the English working class'.

But even if that recognition of the need to ally with 'strangers' was achieved, another problem could emerge: one might accept that individuals from different areas had to become connected, or organised, in new ways, but if the modes of relationship available were themselves inadequate, if the attempt to connect reduced the relationship of those connected to a merely abstract and empty knowledge of each other, then the implicit model of the society to be built upon the basis of that mode of organisation could still be felt as deeply unsatisfactory as a counter-response to the society whose alienating effects had been the motor for opposition in the first place. It is precisely that mode of relationship which can result from merely subscribing to or 'joining' a 'national' body which then treats its 'members' primarily as numerical units. The Anti-Corn Law League seems to exemplify this model, as did Chartism to some extent: with the increased use of massive petitions and demonstrations as the main form of agitation, the ordinary Chartist could become merely a signature and a figure in a newspaper estimate. At the same time, however, the Chartist land scheme attempted to offer a return to an earlier form of local, face-to-face and non-bureaucratised community where personal dignity and sense of 'identity' could be maintained. The two implicit models of society in this mixture of tactics and programme were perhaps ultimately incompatible. Somerville's work is focussed on the period which included the beginnings, apex and final decline of Chartism (1832–60), and his writings as a whole seem to show him as caught in precisely this problem—the incompatibility of two different social definitions of identity. Some of his particular experiences, however, indicate the extent to which earlier problems had been solved: for example, his name can now act as sufficient recommendation for other radicals, though strangers to him, to accept and work with him.

By the 1850s the problem of authenticating the credentials of a stranger had long been solved within the Trades Unions, through the 'blank' system. But in that decade a new form of an old dilemma perhaps appeared. For even when an organised relationship between members of the same class has been achieved, as in Trades Unionism, a problem remains: for if 'class' is also a relation between classes and if the existing relation is not seen, or is no longer seen, as modifiable in a radical way, then one response is to seek a more satisfying integration within the existing structure of social relations. For an individual to do so is a relatively unproblematic option, requiring simply a sustained effort at personal advancement and some self-deception; but for a class as a whole to 'advance' without modifying the overall social structure is self-contradictory. Such a strategy implies either that while major transformation of the society has been suspended, nevertheless a major change has somehow occurred within the society (a paradoxical model of society as simultaneously static and moving) or that the society as a whole is 'advancing' (perhaps in economic terms), thereby enabling each sector or stratum to 'improve' its (e.g. economic) position while remaining fixed in relative terms—and such an operation is extremely fragile, implying that no fundamental dislocation of relative status and strength will occur while the possibility of such dislocation is constantly and inherently present in the process. Both these paradoxes are legible in the form of Burn's self-presentation: simultaneously static and moving, accidental and coherent, patterned as constant but abortive 'turning-points' and yet seen as moving smoothly to a declared goal. The structural parallel between this pattern and the policies and perspectives of 'New Model Unionism' is fairly clear: an attempt to profit from the increased prosperity of an imperialist society without dangerously challenging those exploitative structures of the society which were, in one sense, the basis of the prosperity available to be shared. In that perspective, class-collaboration and an uneasy fusion of styles of organisation is the predictable outcome.

A different response to the problem of finding or forging a mode of organisation (and, implicitly, a model of the new society) could be to achieve a small-scale personal community and then extend the ethos of that community gradually to the whole society; this was Frost's 'Owenite' or 'Commune-ist' solution. But to achieve the transition from a shared way of life on a small scale to an equivalent way of life on a national scale would require something at the national level akin to those elements of personal knowledge, shared 'culture', shared interpretation of social reality, shared values and the possibility of mutually communicating ideas, experiences and reasons for decision which are necessary to sustain an unexploitative community at the face-to-face level. A national newspaper is a medium in which and through which some of those elements can be created, while the rediscovery and reactivation of a tradition of 'popular culture' is another means of trying to provide a common basis for a unified and non-divisive society; both newspapers and 'popular culture' were, as we saw, important for Frost. But the creation of those elements alone would clearly be inadequate if directly economic and political structures remained unchanged, and, correspondingly, a combination of new economic and political modes of organisation without the dimension of concern with 'cultural' aspects of living could still result in a bureaucratised and 'alienated' society; both elements would be necessary for any hegemonic or totalised opposition to and replacement of the existing society, for the society to be re-made not simply in the past image of any particular class but in terms of an entirely new form of social relations. The sense that one or other of these elements was in some sense available but not both simultaneously or not both in a unified manner could result in a feeling of tantalising anti-climax; one thinks of the various trajectories of those movements of the period from 1880 to 1900 and beyond—Fabianism, the Independent Labour Party, the 'New Unions', the Social Democratic Federation. For Frost, writing in the early 1880s, that anti-climax had already occurred some thirty years before—yet the pattern of his *Recollections* still suggests a continued attempt, even so, to fuse 'politics' and 'poetry'; in his later searches for missing persons one sometimes has the odd feeling that what he is still looking for and hoping to meet is the dead Chartist and poet, Jem Blackaby.

(iii) Form and organisation

One can, then, suggest that the pattern of homologies revealed in the analysis of each autobiography can be related to a *logical sequence* of *problems* of *organisation* facing the working class as a whole in the nineteenth century. But—it may be objected—to talk about the problems of the working class 'as a whole' being present somehow in the autobiographical writings of four individuals is to imply a rather curious claim: that, at least, these four are in some way 'representative', though in any obvious sense they are clearly not. We can now, however, recall some points made briefly in the Introduction. It was there pointed out that Lukacs distinguished between 'actual' and 'imputed' class consciousness; clearly, the 'actual' consciousness of these individuals has to be analysed in terms of their specific lives and problems, and the individual analyses have tried to respect that specificity. But to suggest that some aspects of the content and, particularly, the form of these writings can be related to more general problems is to indicate that the notion of 'imputed class consciousness' may be to some extent intelligible not in terms of solutions to particular problems arrived at by individuals or groups but in terms of a general

315

framework of problems which precisely because they remain as unsolved problems provide the context in which specific solutions are offered. Insofar as the personal problems of relationship experienced by these authors were directly dependent upon wider problems of relationship—of organisation, of class relations, of 'identity' itself—these texts can be read in two ways.

Thus, Bamford's inability or reluctance to work politically with strangers could have been overcome (if at all) had there been available to him a political organisation which he could trust, of which he was a member, and which could have provided adequate credentials to each of its members as a way of 'identifying' them to each other. Somerville's sense of an alienating divorce between himself and his name could perhaps have been overcome in the context of an organisation in which each member was personally known to every other member, or at least in which the temptation to use people in a purely instrumental fashion was not present. Obviously Burn's dilemma of how to achieve a satisfactory position in the social structure while not endangering that structure would not have arisen had the possibility been available of successfully transforming the whole social structure in such a way that beggars need not have existed, that 'respectable' was not an epithet restricted to only certain functions and people in the society, and that different ways of living and even speaking did not carry with them overtones of social status and worth. Frost's attempt in his life to encompass and connect every aspect of a society would remain abortive unless a society could be created which was genuinely coherent, in which the connections between the various actions of individuals and groups and the various products of the multiple interacting processes in the society were at least transparently visible and at best intentionally coordinated.

This is not to say that such political organisations or forms of society were historically possible in 1819, 1832, 1855 or 1880 (or even possible in principle), but that a *need* for such organisations and modes of society is implicit in the personal and political problems of Bamford and Somerville, Burn and Frost. And, of course, implicit in the need for such organisations is the need for a different kind of society, of which the political organisation is to be the creator and perhaps the prototype, just as the need for a new kind of society implies the need for an appropriate means of achieving it. The *desire* for a new kind of society is indeed explicit in Bamford, Somerville and Frost (and even at times in Burn), though they remain relatively—and perhaps inescapably —inarticulate about the precise shape of that society, while the *demand* for a resolution of their particular problems as individuals is fully explicit. The analyses I have offered perhaps indicate that the need to solve certain organisational problems is neither fully conscious nor simply 'unconscious' but, to use Goldmann's term, 'non-conscious'. One can therefore read these texts both as narratives of certain personal concerns and problems, and as articulations of social problems of which their authors are perhaps not even explicitly conscious. Moreover, the problems involved in writing at the narrative-level can be seen as a *displaced* response to the problems of organising at the social or political level; if the problems of relationship cannot be solved in practice, by the creation of an appropriate organisation, they can be 'solved' in a literally formal sense by writing an autobiography: Bamford can make his stranger-readers into 'friends', Somerville can validate and fuse his own complex self-identifications, Burn can achieve a steady respectability, Frost can embrace the whole society and even partly fuse 'poetry' and 'politics'—but all only in the sphere of *writing*, in the literary relations their texts construct. The way in which these authors are 'aware' of the problems of changing their relations to others is as a problem of literary form.

Aspects of this argument are indirectly echoed in the final essay in Lukac's *History and Class Consciousness*, for example: 'the self-knowledge of the proletariat is a knowledge of its objective situation at a given stage of historical development', yet 'for each individual worker, because his own consciousness is reified, the road to achieving the objectively possible class consciousness . . . must pass through the process of comprehending his own immediate experience only after he has experienced it', since 'a problem always makes its appearance first as an abstract possibility and only afterwards is it realised in concrete terms'.

That final essay is entitled 'Towards a methodology of the problem of organisation', and Lukacs finally sees the concrete form of the objectively possible class consciousness as embodied in the particular form of an organisation, a political party, since:

Organisation is the form of mediation between theory and practice. And, as in every dialectical relationship, the terms of the relation only acquire concreteness and reality in and by virtue of this mediation. The ability of organisation to mediate between theory and practice is seen most clearly by the way in which it manifests a much greater, finer and more confident sensitivity towards divergent trends than any other sector of political thought and action. On the level of pure theory the most disparate views and tendencies are able to co-exist peacefully, antagonisms are only expressed in the form of discussions which can be contained within the framework of one and the same organisation without disrupting it. But no sooner are these same questions given organisational form than they turn out to be sharply opposed and even incompatible.

In reading these passages from Lukacs, one is tempted to note again the parallel between literary form and political organisation: it is in the *form* of their autobiographies that these writers both revealed, made comprehensible, and reconciled, in a displaced mode, the antagonisms and incompatibilities in their actual situations. In reading their autobiographies, therefore, we can perhaps grasp not only those actual situations, those 'actual' consciousnesses, but also the fundamental desires, the organisational needs and the political demands which deeply structure them.

It is this emphasis that may help to clarify another question raised in the Introduction: the nature of the 'labour movement'. For insofar as the four individuals examined were related to the 'labour movement', as in some sense they all clearly were, I would suggest that it was partly by being involved in the *problems* of what comprises a 'movement' and *how* it is constituted; an appropriate way of 'reading', or writing, 'labour history' might therefore be not only in terms of 'solutions' (actual organisations, actual events, influences, achievements, crises, etc.) but also in terms of those deeper problems to which more or less satisfactory solutions were proposed, theoretically and practically. The continuity and shape of a movement may indeed lie most basically at the level of a continuity and inheritance of still unresolved problems, and the study of these autobiographies may help us, in a new way, to comprehend some of those problems more clearly, and perhaps to recognise in our own problems of organisation—legible in the complex histories of parties, sects and groupings of the last few decades—a definite continuity of need.

SUITE-TALK

Reader's Report on:

ANNE ARTHUR, *READING LITERARY RELATIONS*

Summary
On attached sheet.

Comments

The MS is very long indeed, perhaps 200,000 words. It needs to be cut pretty severely if it is to be published. There's an initial difficulty about suggesting cuts however, since the MS I received is a bit peculiar in that either the title-page has been inserted at the wrong point (it occurs at page 97 of the MS—a somewhat Shandyan procedure!), *or*, as I suspect, Ms Arthur has submitted a whole book (pp.97–884) *plus* some extra bits and pieces for *possible* inclusion. One other possibility occurred to me: that she is offering us a kind of 'cut-up' work of criticism (like a cut-up novel); she says in her preface that the sections 'can be read in any order'. I presume this isn't really on; *no* publisher could risk such a book and even *hope* to sell it!

However, there's an even more tricky problem about suggesting cuts. I'm not sure just what *kind* of book I'd be trying to cut. The sub-title says it's a 'dialectical text-book'. 'Dialectical' suggests the dialectical procedures of Plato, a *dialogue form* of argument, and indeed part of the MS *is* in a kind of dialogue form (and Plato is mentioned frequently). But apart from this section, the only way in which the MS recalls the Socratic dialogues for *me* is in the systematic elusiveness of the author herself; she seems to be both present and absent in her own text—but that's hardly enough to justify the description 'dialectical'. So I suspect that 'dialectical' is meant to be taken in the sense suggested by David Caute in his notion (in *The Illusion*) of a 'dialectical novel'. For the MS does seem to offer itself as a rather peculiar kind of fiction; I was reminded of a recent comment by Terry Eagleton (who, incidentally, comes in for a fair amount of comradely criticism in the MS—it seems like a private battle at times! Is Arthur a friend of Terry's or something??):

aesthetic theory has outstripped artistic practice to the point where theoretical texts seem sometimes to offer themselves as their own artefacts simply for the lack of others.

If Arthur *is* doing this, she's attempting a pretty ambitiously 'modernist' work (at least in the sense advanced by Gabriel Josipovici in his *Lessons of Modernism* or in that famous interview in *Orbit*)—one in which the text operates by a kind of 'dialectical *intra*-action', every element in it 'in dialogue with' every other element. At least in this case, I suppose, each separate element is reasonably lucid by itself, which is *something*! This intra-action seems to happen on the large-scale as well as in local effects, and it's probably worth spelling the point out to clarify the problems of cutting I'm bothered about.

If we take the text as a work of critical *theory*, then according to the gist of its main argument (roughly, as far as I can see it, that 'literary' texts are transpositions of particular 'apparatus' practices), the work *is itself* a 'literary' work (since it pretty clearly 'transposes' the practices of the educational apparatus); but if we are therefore to take it *as* a work of *literature* (a kind of modernist *fiction*), then presumably we don't have to take its main argument *seriously* (that argument too is just part of the *fiction*); but then if we don't take the argument seriously, there seems no reason to treat the thing as itself 'literature'; but then if it *isn't* 'literature', its main argument is presumably *wrong* (but how can a *fictional* 'argument' be 'wrong' anyway??). In other words, the whole text seems to put the reader into a double-bind (a procedure the bloody thing actually discusses itself!). It reminds me, actually, of Lukacs's *History and Class Consciousness* in that respect—if poor old GL was right he was wrong.

This device of the 'double-bind' seems to operate 'locally' as well. For example, there's a poem simply inserted at one point called *Coy Supervision*. No author is given, so presumably it's by Anne Arthur herself. But it's clearly a male chauvinist poem (it's about a teacher leering at a girl-student during a class). But if *Anne* Arthur wrote it, surely it must be a *parody* of a male-chauvinist poem? It is, in any case, already a parody of Marvell's (male-chauvinist) *To His Coy Mistress*. But *surely* 'Anne Arthur' is a *nom de plume*—and a bad pun at that. If so, the *real* 'author' may not be a woman at all (and there's no way of telling, except by the style). So the reader has to decide whether the poem *is* a parody of sexist attitudes or not. Given that it looks to me like a bad poem anyway, this may not be worth deciding—though I suppose one could argue that the 'complexity' or 'ambiguity' of *this* 'poem' is located not in what's there on the page but rather in the questions it raises about its author, and therefore about itself (is this an eighth type of Ambiguity??). It may even be a parody not of *a* poem (Marvell's) but of (a) 'poem'! If so, how do we judge it to be good *or* bad *as* a 'poem'??

The same problem of knowing how to 'judge' occurs at the level of the *whole* text as well. One of the 'extra' bits speaks of the possibility of a *self-destructive* work of criticism (self-destruct painting and all that). Well, that means that if this text *does* 'destroy' itself as 'criticism', if it's actually a terrible book of criticism, by that criterion it's really a success! In fact, one of the speakers in the dialogue section quotes Wordsworth's Preface about the author not fulfilling the expectations of the reader, not meeting the terms of an implicit 'contract' (did we *commission* this thing, by the way??); the same section suggests the possibility of a 'new' twist in literature: a 'performative utterance' that doesn't actually perform what it utters (or the other way round, or something like that!). Again, the suggestion seems to be that *this* text is that kind of 'literature' (the only example given is playing chess against yourself . . .). But since it's not

322

clear that it *is*, we seem to be stuck with something that falls between two stools: is it 'criticism' or 'literature'? Or neither? Or both? Since it's pretty clear that the author could have come up with some pretty familiar kind of (marxist) criticism, and so resolved the ambiguity if she'd wanted (she's at least *competent*, I'm sure), presumably the ambiguity is deliberate. (Though maybe 'deliberate' *is* the wrong word—she might be some kind of nut: there's a disturbing amount in the MS about madness of one kind or another, and aren't double-binds something to do with schizophrenia??) *If* the 'ambiguity' *is* deliberate, then the work's 'failure' to *clearly* become 'literature' may be a deliberate failure as well—that failure may be a way of *suggesting* the 'Book' that *might* have been written but which Anne Arthur simply disdains to write (just as she doesn't bother to answer all the questions in the law section). The text may then be meant as a kind of *shadow* of another 'BOOK' (a peculiarly Platonic notion again) or as an invitation to the reader to *write* that Book (a rather Adrian Stokes notion of art!). Or the whole thing may be a dismissive *parody* of the (Mallarméan?) *ambition* to write such a 'work of art' these days, to write the 'Book to end all books' (as a rather sub-Benjamin passage somewhere in the thing puts it).

So I'm rather puzzled! The various sections of the book don't help much either, even if (or particularly if) they each have a 'dialectical' relation to the whole. For example, the long section on 'law' suggests to me that the whole book may be itself an example of 'lawlessness'—implying a kind of *anarchist aesthetics* (cf. the discussion of anarchist science)—or an example of 'breaking the laws of aesthetics' (because that's the *right* thing to do now—cf. the curious discussion of Chandler and Camus). Again, the whole detective fiction sequence implies that this too may be a kind of 'detective fiction', in which we have to *find out* what the 'mystery' is in the first place, or who the author is, or what her character is, or even 'who killed the Book?' And the fairly short (thank God!) section on 'literary conversions' actually seems to *justify* all these 'ambiguities', 'double-binds' and so on as *common* features or strategies of fiction, from Richardson through Coleridge to Joyce and Eliot: once we've embarked on a text, the text will eventually 'trap' us and make us 'change our mind' about it by forcing us into a double-bind, so that we can only go on reading it if we make sense of it in terms we resist because they're logically contradictory. The same section actually has the cheek to hint that certain texts force us to become 'paranoid' about them, registering *every* element (or whatever) in them as deliberate and part of a complex, multiply cross-referencing pattern of motifs, themes, images, phrases, memories and thoughts; there's some evidence that this text is demanding the same manic attention—even the dedication is incorporated into its pattern since it's lifted from Herbert's 'Dedication' which is later discussed *as nauseam*; I suppose even the title is part of this sick joke, since I personally immediately thought of the problem of *ordering* it in a shop (I have a lisp, and trying to say 'Reading Literary Relations' is bad enough even without one! I suppose it goes better in French anyway: *Lire Relations Litteraires?*).

I'm beginning to think this report's becoming paranoid! I'm therefore going to take my revenge on the text and suggest some pretty savage cuts!

1. Omissions

(a) The 'lecture notes' on Lukacs and Trotsky can go. They're redundant both in content and form: we don't need the variations on the 'lecture' theme by having a lecture, then a student's notes on another lecture, then a lecturer's notes for yet another lecture. And though the *argument* on Trotsky is interesting and it probably is useful to be reminded that at the height of the struggle over Lenin's succession he went off to write, of all things, *Literature and Revolution*, I nevertheless don't feel that the *explanation* of *why* he did it is very compelling.

(b) The sections directly on the 'transpositions' of the Educational Apparatus and the Family Apparatus can go. Some of the discussions of love-poems is interesting, but too detailed, too much like ordinary practical criticism. And the educational section seems redundant since the work is itself an example of what it discusses here. It's a *bit* of a shame to lose the stuff on Borges and on Philip Rieff, and maybe the bit on Clive James, but better to drop them.

(c) The section entitled 'Fromage' had better go completely. It *might* be drastically cut, but to insert a whole PhD thesis at this point seems extreme (the kind of extremism Ms Arthur seems to enjoy!). In any case, I can't see what the discussion of working-class autobiographies has to *add* to the case already established (they're pretty inferior pieces of writing anyway, and who's going to read through them just to read this section in the first place?). And including a *research* thesis seems to dent the otherwise quite neat pattern of playing around with *teaching* practices.

(d) Most of the 'extra bits' seem to me not really worth including, though I quite like some of them. But since I'm not even sure if they *are* part of the MS, or perhaps just a mistake by the office in sending out the parcel (are they parts of some *other* book maybe?), I'll not comment further.

2. Possible additions?

The section on 'law' *might* be expanded. There are a *lot* more examples that might be discussed, and some of the 'unanswered questions' might actually be written from those 'rough' notes. I'd be particularly interested to see something fuller on Williams's *Volunteers*—though I presume we don't want the 'Brecht and Law' bit fleshed out: there's too much on Brecht around anyway. Anyway, given the problem of over-length anyway, I don't suppose any additions are feasible.

3. Local suggestions

(i) I think the argument in the 'lecture' goes badly wrong at one point, even in its own terms. Basically, it's not the case that a particular 'apparatus ideology' is 'further transposed' as an 'aesthetic ideology', but rather that an 'aesthetic ideology', which is necessarily relatively autonomous from *any* apparatus (since it partly shapes our reactions to them *all*—some people find policemen wonderful), *governs* the process of transposition of apparatus relations into textual relations. I suggest that Ms Arthur be advised to revise her argument on this point—though she may realise that the implications are pretty radical for her whole case.

(ii) She might think this one through by considering the 'aesthetic ideology' which is indicated in her own section *titles*. These clearly refer to a *gastronomic* ideology of 'culture' (her discussion of 'taste' and 'consumerism' ought, incidentally, to acknowledge this). I found these titles a bit irritating; she might consider changing them, to deploy perhaps another set of terms which would be equally plausible (e.g. musical terms, like Flourish, Voluntary, Overture, Sonata, Minuet, Fugue, Cadenza, etc.—she discusses music at various points in any case, and even quotes stuff about music criticism and about Schoenberg's *First String Quartet*; Bartok gets in somewhere as well if I remember rightly). If she *does* keep to the 'meal' notion, she might quote at some point Fielding's famous description of his own novel in terms of a menu (it's in *Tom Jones* somewhere).

(iii) Another quotation she might consider for inclusion, perhaps even as a key-note passage, is Adorno's comment on 'immanent criticism' in *Cultural Criticism and Society* (in *Prisms*, p.32). This could well go with a quote from Benjamin that could be salvaged from an 'extra' bit: the one about Brecht's poems having a paedogogical effect before a poetic one.

I have a great many other local suggestions, comments and criticisms to make, but I'm in some danger of rewriting the whole text in this report. I'll conclude by offering a perhaps outrageous recommendation, which I'd better briefly justify after everything I've said.

Recommendation

Someone once remarked that in enjoying a work of art one should enjoy the work of *art* not enjoy oneself. Well, I'm not sure if this is a work of art, but I actually rather enjoyed myself reading the MS. That was primarily because I found myself *enjoying working*. The text does demand that the reader *work* (it even turns into a do-it-yourself kit at some points). The real work that's invited is to *improve* the text, while trying to maintain its rather peculiar character (e.g. trying to find other terms than the culinary ones while maintaining the puns on educational practices). I can imagine a reader finding that work rather fun—after all, it's part of *my work* to write this report, but I've even enjoyed suggesting cuts! They might even find it quite *funny* to do. For example, when I'd finished reading the whole thing, I went back and reread the lecture bit (to check the point I made earlier)—and found the whole thing quite absurdly lunatic the second time around: the incredible solemnity and pedantry of the exercise struck me as idiotic (particularly after the discussion of Poe! . . . it made it all 'poe-faced': Sorry!), and I found myself then comparing the lecture with the seminar; I'd found the seminar slightly insane the first time, but now I realised that if these students really were taught by *that* lecturer they *would* end up a bit the same way (the mirror-image effect). But then I realised that they are actually *more intelligent* (except one!) than the lecturer—so maybe there's hope for them! It seems to me that this experience of re-reading, and of working out the 'characters' of each section, *confirmed* my suspicion that the whole thing isn't really a work of critical theory or practice at all. Should it be

325

published then? I *recommend* that it *should*, suitably doctored—but as part of the *fiction list*! We might then even be able to point to a 'novel' which has partly steered past the problems posed by Perry in his famous footnote! And, more to the point, at least *that* way we wouldn't have to do an index, or provide notes—both of which would take up *pages*, and be pretty expensive, and it's already too *long* anyway, whether it's fiction or notherwise!

J.G.

Review Section — Dialectic of Unenlightenment

B. Sharratt, *Reading Relations: a dialectical text/book*, Harvester Press, 1979.

This absurd book should never have been published. It probably shouldn't be reviewed either. In fact, it would be kinder not to do so. But since the book seems to me typical of a general tendency which I find deeply disturbing and politically dangerous, it is good to have such a symptomatic target. For a start, the book is very clearly a first effort. I have no idea who B. Sharratt is, but I have no doubt that he has committed the classic mistake of the neophyte author: attempting an over-ambitious first work, which stretches his area(s) of competence so thin that his deep ignorance becomes immediately transparent. The sub-title already betrays him. To characterise a piece of work as 'dialectical' is to gesture towards a complex and exacting tradition of inquiry. One ought to know what one is talking about when one uses that term. Sharratt clearly has no conception of either the classic *materialist* sense of 'dialectical' within the tradition of Marx-Engels-Lenin, or the technically philosophical sense of the term in Hegel, still less in recent developments in the philosophy of logic. For example, he seems to have no awareness of the ways in which recent Soviet and Brazilian work has developed dialectical logics in the direction of inconsistency-tolerant logics; a fleeting reference to Gödel indicates the limits of his competence here. I would advise him to buy and study, for example, Jürg Hänggi, *Formale und dialektische Logik in der Sowjetphilosophie* (Winterthur, 1971), or A. Sarlemijn, *Hegel's Dialectic* (Dordrecht, 1975); he might then obtain and read Newton C. A. da Costa's crucial and influential 1963 doctoral dissertation at the Federal University of Parana, *Sistemas formais inconsistentes*. *Then* let him use 'dialectical' of his own work, if he dare.

The main title too indicates his own arrogantly incompetent appropriation of a technical term. The echo of Althusser in '*Reading*' is irresistible, but he then proceeds to deploy '*Relations*' in a way utterly inconsistent with Althusserian theory and terminology. Has he simply forgotten, or not understood, that crucial passage in *Lire le Capital* (Petite collection maspero, pocket edition, 1969, t. i, pp.178–9; ET, p.139ff.):

C'est l'union de l'humanisme et de l'historicisme qui représente, il faut bien le dire, la plus sérieuse tentation, car elle procure les plus grands avantages théoriques, du moins en apparence. Dans la réduction de toute connaissance aux rapports sociaux historiques, on peut introduire en

327

sous-main une seconde réduction, qui traite les *rapports de production* comme de simples *rapports humains*. Cette seconde réduction repose sur une 'évidence': l'histoire n'est-elle pas de part en part un phénomene 'humain', et Marx, citant Vico, ne déclare-t-il pas que les hommes peuvent la connaître puisqu'ils l'ont *'faite'* tout entière? Cette 'évidence' repose pourtant sur un singulier présupposé: que les 'acteurs' de l'histoire sont les auteurs de son texte, les sujets de sa production. Mais ce présupposé a lui aussi toute la force d'une 'évidence', puisque, contrairement à ce que nous suggère le théâtre, les hommes concrets sont, dans l'histoire, les acteurs des rôles dont ils sont les auteurs. Il suffit d'escamoter le *metteur en scéne*, pour que l'acteur-auteur ressemble comme un frère au vieux rêve d'Aristote: le médecin-qui-se-soigne-lui-même; et que les *rapports de production*, qui sont pourtant proprement les metteurs en scène de l'histoire, se réduisent à des simples *rapports humains*.

? I will perhaps come back to the *metaphors* Althusser has unerringly chosen, *en avance*, for puncturing this discreditable *mélange* of 'dialectical' dramaturgy and pseudo-'psychoanalytical' posturings. At present, it is hardly worth saying that *Reading Relations* includes a number of crass and laboured, and intellectually contemptible, 'criticisms' of Althusser, particularly of his *Eléments d'Autocritique*. They are beneath further consideration.

The actual *'literary* criticism' the text offers, with an ostensibly disdainful but practically feeble and pathetic pretence of distancing itself from 'criticism', immediately comes under the decisive *guillotine* of the sharp critique of (literary) criticism erected and operated by the practitioners of the only genuine *criticism* in England today: the *Screen* circle. A recent formulation in *Screen Education* (Number 27, Summer 1978, p.36, reviewing *Screen Reader I*, ed. John Ellis) makes the point succinctly:

> *Screen Reader* claims to offer a discourse not as *alternative* to others but one which has gone *beyond* others, and which can therefore 'know' them in a way they cannot know themselves. The crucial break here is with 'practical criticism' (particularly in its variation as the *auteur* theory) which presupposes an autonomous reader 'experiencing' an equally autonomous text (hence the typically adjectival terminology qualifying the reader/text relationship—'provocative', 'stimulating', 'intriguing', etc.). So the discourse is limited to an endlessly 'pluralist' re-creation of the text only as it shows itself. But this 'experience' of the text is possible only because of codes and structures transcending both text and reader and enacted across them. It is towards an understanding of these that *Screen* has addressed itself, a project of analysis not wilfully but *necessarily* theoretical, and necessarily situated on terrain beyond the traditional discipline of 'criticism': linguistic structuralism, historical materialism with its account of social and ideological structures, psychoanalysis as an attempt to theorise a human science of the subject.
>
> ... The *Screen Reader* assumes authority on the basis of a coherence in its theoretical foundation. This claim is implied in the presentation of the anthology. Stylistically, practical criticism works through a competing proliferation of 'personal' re-interpretations; it is therefore fundamentally a discourse of individual polemic (masked by that urbanity we all know so well from the *Times Literary Supplement*). As itself a structuring element the (asserted) coherence of *Screen* is enacted in a discourse which is/sets itself to be collective and impersonal: not a *struggle* for knowledge but a struggle for *knowledge*. The texts selected for the *Screen* anthology are editorially mediated only through a brief introduction by John Ellis. This presentation assumes that they are otherwise properly mediated by the informing coherence of the discourse, each individual contribution taking a position which is itself placed by a knowable continuity. An actual heterogeneity within will appear on the outside as an enforced homogeneity ('the *Screen* position' i.e. 'dogmatism' etc.). But such heterogeneity is—or should be—recognisable not merely as genuine diversity of position within the overriding continuity but as an increase in understanding made possible by the foundation, that is, as changes which are an *advance*. This is the claim asserted by John Ellis when he writes:

'Whilst it may be that the authors represented here do not now agree with some of the statements made in their names, this is so only because their subsequent work has advanced on the bases established in these texts.'

The *Screem Reader*, then, can and should be read as a review of past work which clarifies a 'line of march' in order to indicate directions for future development.

Sharratt's own 'dogmatism' takes the form of an enforced *hetero*geneity in his own discourse, an informing *in*coherence, which, far from clarifying any 'line of march', results in a constant zig-zagging, a wild threshing of methodologies which it would be over-polite to characterise as: 'two steps backward, one step to the side, about turn, and eyes crossed'. At its worst (and it is mostly at its worst), the 'criticism' generated by this methodological anarchism and eclecticism is rankly juxtapositionist, a mere random—indeed exultingly random—yoking together of heterogeneous 'facts', quotations, gobbets, *aperçus*, asides, and parentheses. No possible *pattern* of thought, no *procedure* for *thinking*, is even preliminarily or provisionally established by this exercise in intellectual delinquency that it would be a misguided compliment to call derivatively Dadaist. One might, grudgingly, concede that what we now have is the first exemplar of *Punk* criticism.

Part of the folly of this futile flourishing of incompatible and imcomparable fatuities derives from the unprincipled appropriation of *fragments* of procedure, method, and conclusion from an entire medley of methodologically and politically diverse 'authorities'. The resulting discords make only for mental cacophony. Sharrat veers like an unbalanced weather-vane between the fashionable winds that buffet him from every corner of the 'intellectual' 's compass: from Aristotle to Zen, from Blum to Yseglias, from Colletti to Xenophon, from Derrida to Wilden, from Eliot to Voloshinov, etc., etc. At the centre of this 'totalising' turbulence is a predictable major mentor. Though some of the more deeply debilitating passions Sharratt has indulged are perversely *concealed* by the text—the implicit commentary on Colletti's chapter, 'The Concept of the "Social Relations of Production" ', in Part II of *Il Marxismo e Hegel* is a case in point, the obscenely nudging relationship with Nietzsche another—that arch-exemplar of 'l'union de l'humanisme et de l'historicisme', the ex-neo-Kantian Stalinist Lukacs, is finally paraded before us in all his tattered robes as the ringmaster of this triple circus travelling in all directions simultaneously.

The long and insufferably boring chapter on 'Autobiography and Class Consciousness', with its titular debt to Lukacs blazoned upon it, was the only act in this farcical *mélodrame* which raised even a grim smile from this reviewer. It is, I have no doubt, the key to the whole mechanism of Sharratt's bemused mind. In it he traces, with a certain empiricist competence, the dilemmas of political allegiance legible in the deep structure of a tiny selection of British working-class autobiographies of the nineteenth century. There is a striking continuity and consistency between the facets of the four-fold 'problematic' he exposes and the structuring principles of his own work. As Bamford seeks to establish a 'personal relationship' with *his* readers, so Sharratt attempts to read all texts, including his own, as encounters between *personae*, variations of a 'personal' (or even erotic) 'relation' constituted by the

329

interpenetration of writing and reading selves. As Somerville constructs an elaborate textual hide-and-seek, with his own name as the elusive 'It', so Sharrett disperses his alienated identities through a variety of cunning passages, half-closed doors and ambiguous thresholds; I shall return later to the *name*. As Burn orchestrates his alleged 'journeys' into a spiral of superimposed trajectories, pointing beyond their surface stability to an insecurity of fundamental location, so Sharrott builds himself a *mise-en-abyme* in which to counterfeit, and hide, himself as controller of his own drifting fate in the whirlpool of historical circumstance and textual chances. And as Frost splits his published self into two divergent and scarcely overlapping self-portraits, so Sharatt offers us two books in one, introduces two authors nestling within the same covers but barely touching at their extremities. As we read the accounts of these autobiographies a chain of literary devices imposes itself—from 'dear reader' to quasi-schizophrenic semi-pseudonymity—which seems to have entangled the author of those analyses himself.

Which gives us the clue to the 'mystery' posed by one of his multiple *personae*: the work is not, as the rather silly *Reader's Report* (the double half-puns are execrable) 'tentatively' hints, a detective-story with a new twist (who is the *detective*?), but manifestly and disastrously an 'experiment in autobiography'. What we have is *A Portrait of the Academic as a Young Radical* cross-fertilised with a rewriting of André Gorz's *Le Traitre*. The whole *structure* of the book (if one ignores such surface and superficial organisational pointers as the pre-packaged food parcelling or the ludicrously mathematical sectioning of lengths and (reading) times) is clearly given by the *ad*-ventures of an academic in search of a sinecure. The book traces a clear line from note-taking through being taken note of (invitations to deliver the papers, etc.), to the eventual accolade of being commissioned as a subaltern, or a *lieutenant*, in the pen-pushing army of Academia. Hence the enclosure of the Thesis itself: it *precedes* the book (the First Book) in which it appears, it establishes the essential 'Qualification' for the 'job' *already* 'performed' in Part I: Lecturing. And, equally, though subordinately, we can follow the fate of the *student* through the apparatus (and its concurrent traumas, ranging from adolescent self-discovery to failing an exam). The elaborated layers on this typically academic exercise of advertising one's own career are too jejune to peel off any further.

But what is of mild interest is that this structure of the book undermines the case presented by (parts of) the text. The *general* political direction the text adopts is that 'Western Marxism', and particularly what it barbarously calls Lacanian–Althusserianism, is the theoretical elaboration of an *impasse* confronting the European working class—an *impasse* the Thesis clearly locates as far back as 1880. But what actually emerges from this 'analysis' is not a *general impasse*, but a very specific and localised *impasse*: that of the 'radical academic' and, particularly, I suspect, the ex-'radical student' of the late 1960s, whose 'long march through the institutions', whose own extended political *rite de passage*, has turned into a slow revolve of university corridors and committees in the 1970s, a game of professorial chairs in which the music gets more and more funereal and the strains of *The Red Flag* get ever fainter as the title gets ever more appropriate. This book expresses and exposes *that* impasse in a peculiarly cruel way. But the book's *political* importance is *nil*; the impotence of that position has been clear since June 1968.

What the book *then* does to itself is to take the obvious next step: into self-destruction. The despair of the 'radical academic', faced with not only the unruffled calm of the ageing Senior Common Room which has survived yet again its annual agonising over the latest tiny backward 'reform' but also the present intake of quiescent and indifferent students, turns into an attempt not to *take* power but to *refuse* it, to destroy the only power left in its hands: its own. The Teacher (and with him the Intellectual and the Writer) plays the Fool. That may even be a good way of teaching, but what this book also comes close to en-acting out is the breakdown that often results (yet another 'stage' the average academic 'passes through' anyway). But what is worrying is that beyond a *deliberate* breakdown there is only suicide, the final voluntary relinquishment of all power. *Or*: an *actual break* with the whole field of the academic double-bind—the next plane to Latin America, or wherever, with which the book itself opens. Hovering, in latent panic and rage, between these two 'worlds', the 'radical academic' may even turn (again) into the reactionary, by taking his blind revenge upon his students—by making them *all* look like fools in one of his seminars.

This lurking presence of breakdown (rather than what is *really* needed, the thaumaturgical touch of an 'epistemological break' with the last remnants of humanism and historicism) brings me to my final conclusions.

There are a number of determinate absences in this text, silences that speak loudly. One is 'class'. Despite the regular skirmishings, class remains fundamentally unspoken. I don't myself know what class-origins Sherratt may have (or even national and racial origins, come to that). But one effect of this finally rather *sad* text is to make me reaffirm my own. As Franco Fortini says (or, rather, *reads*, from his own book, *I Cani del Sinai*), in the Straub-Huillet film, *Fortini-Cani*:

The complexity of the real, the reading of it at an infinite number of levels, does not free anyone from an objective simplification, from the inscription of every life in an order of behaviours which are class behaviours; subjective simplification, expressed in ideological terms, which I use, like everybody else, never pretends to be an instrument of scientific statement but its provocation, a reagent which leads others to state their own class identity.

This text/book *might*, I suppose, be *read* as a provocation, a reagent which leads others to state their own class identity, itself a threshold or *rite de passage*. But the advice of this review is not to read it at all (you shouldn't need to by now, surely?), still less to buy it (it's horrendously expensive—the text, of course, is simply blind to the conditions of its own production as a book). In the end, it is a futile exercise, a self-indulgence, an Aristotelian *reve*. The only place for it to be read properly is in a corner—as a long-running entry in *Private Eye*'s Pseud's Corner, if it was big enough. But if it is to be read at all, if you really want to read it after reading my comments, it might best be read as a typical instance of the self-conscious fiction of post-modernism. It can't do any *harm* if you read it like that, but there are at least two criticisms to be made of it even at that level.

First, and *very* briefly, though it clearly deploys various pseudo-psycho-analytical terms (and devices: at times reading it is like being on a psycho-analyst's couch), its grasp of Lacan, despite his intermittent guest-appearances, is minimal. Which is one reason why it remains a deeply *sexist* work: at its heart, its base-line strategy is to foist upon *a woman* the whole pathetic performance. *That* speaks volumes! Related to this, one has to say that it is a text haunted by an illusory spectre, not the ghost of Hamlet's father, but the spectre of its own death, its own dis-appearance. *That* is sick.

Second, like many modernist fictions, it betrays its real drives, in its language. And that language is both blissfully paranoid and, like so much modernist writing, peculiarly inflected by an implicit 'theology' of the 'word'. So that once you become caught within the sub-Joycean play of its linguistic motifs, running puns, verbal chimings, overtonal echoes, not even a single letter is safe from the insistently attentive gaze it commands. I began this review by attacking the political misappropriations of the title. A further facet of that title then struck me: *Reading Relations* implies that what we are *reading* is a structure of *relations*, the relations, primarily, of that eternal triangle drawn by the Oedipal trio. But who *occupies* the pre-established positions in those relations? Who *are* these hidden 'relations'? Who is the *real* author? Who, damn it, is 'B. Sharratt'? Even the initial is enigmatic. Male or female? Benedict or Beatrice? I then realised that since the title alludes to its French heritage (*Lire Relations Litteraires* as the *Reuter's Rapport* kindly points out), so might the name. And in French 'Sharratt' *(la charrette)* means 'hand-cart'—and a Derridean pun erupts: the author is simply playing his or her first card even before the *hors-d'oeuvre*. (The Ducs de la Charrette were, I believe, French crusaders.) The question that seems to be posed, ultimately, to the reader (via a *bad* classroom pun) is whether he/she wants to join in, whether he/she wants, in reading *Reading Relations*, finally 2B or not 2B Sharrat .

S.P.

A reader's para-reading of Reading (Literary) Relations

We wrote $R(L)R$ but we write here as a reader of it. One reader, its first. Being the writer endows our reading with no privilege except perhaps that of intimacy with the text, of very close reading; the writer may be wrong, and no reader, of course, is 'right'. There are no answers at the back of *this* text-book, though, admittedly, *Suite-Stalk* already contains two perfectly credible readings. This brief para-critical analysis therefore supplements, does not replace; neither does it repeat, for example, points of agreement with the paranoid *Reader's Report* or the hostile *Review*; it will be compressed, not comprehensive, indicative not demonstrative.

Thinking above the flow

Perhaps the simplest way to demonstrate some of the structuring principles at work in the book is to provide a diagram (which can then serve as an analytical index and reference-guide)—see figure.

The diagram mainly speaks for itself. We could add refinements; for example, mathematical (the third 'R'): there are various ways of totalling the units in/of A, Bi, Bii, C, so that they come to permutations of the magic number 14 ($6+8$, $5+6+3$, $5+3+3+3$, etc.), with a certain 'balance' or fulcrum operating at the 'break' between *RLR* Part One and Part Two, between the Antitheses and the Thesis (or which, alternatively, counterpoise ABiiC to Bi, e.g.). This in itself already indicates one important 'dialogue' at work in the book, that 'between' a Leavis-influenced anti-Althusserian 'thinking' (Blum 'theorising') and a Lukacs-inspired 'labour history' (working-class-practice) equally hostile to Althusser; yet, of course, it is Althusser's own work that provides one major, if not immediately visible, principle of overall organisation: the arrangement of sections according to the various 'Ideological Apparatuses'—a strategy signalled in the 'tough meat' (overdone steak) part of the rigorously pedantic *Lecture* (that title being itself a clue to the location of the 'key' to the text). Even less visible, more suppressed, is the more fundamental exploitation of the 'Family' Apparatus; without spelling it out in full, it should be clear that the whole text is pro-created by a pattern of inter-penetrations—the climactic moments of inter-course being marked by, e.g., the deliriously punning commentary on (be-coming) Charlotte Brontë (preceding the emergence of Anne Arthur) and by the sexist seduction poem

Coy Supervision (just before the Law, in the shape of *Tom Jones*, steps in); again, refinements could be pointed out: the intermittent appearances of parents and children (and one abortion), the gender ambiguity of the first few names in *Seminar* (before the alphabetical sequence brings George Herbert back), the intermittent plunges into Oedipal analysis, etc. What is most deeply repressed, however, is the racial(ist) theme which haunts the text as its guilt (those forgotten memories of Latin America, Barbados, Algeria, etc.). Enough said on overall structure.

No.	Educational/ Publishing Apparatus	Menu	I.S.A.s	Family Apparatus —creation of Subject	Dates	Additional Notes
A		HORS D'OEUVRE		(dedication)		PRE-BOOK
1	Quotes	Aperitifs			1968, 1974	
2	Notes	Crudités	'Entering into' Academic			(Latin America)
3	Conference paper	Potage	Apparatus as Academic	love-poem		
4	Review	Poisson	Author of			
5	N & Q article	Entrée	Book	penetration	1801, 1901	(Trotsky quote)
B i		ANOMOLETTUS: Part One: Anti-theses				BOOK BEGINS
1	Pt I Lecture	Main Course (meat: tough overdone steak)	'Science/ Theory'		1859	1 hour
2	Pt II Seminar	Extras: Vegs.	Religious Apparatus		1630–33?	2 hours
	1—Chris	(carrots)				
	2—Dai	(dressing)		ambiguous genders		
	3—LN	(egg-plant)				
	4—Phil	(fennel)			1647	
	5—George	(gravy)				
	6—Bert	(potatoes)			1948–68	(Eurocentrism)
	7—I	(sauce)		love-poem	1748	(Barbados)
3	Finals Exams	Dessert	Legal Apparatus	The Law		3 days
	1—Fielding				1748	
	2—Poe				1842	
	3—Chesterton				1911	
	4—Chandler				1939	(nationalism)
	5—Kafka				1914f	
	6—Camus			self-judgement	1956	(Algeria)

No.	Educational/ Publishing Apparatus	Menu	I.S.A.s	Family Apparatus —creation of Subject	Dates	Additional Notes
B ii	ANOMOLETTUS: Part Two: Thesis					
1	*Introduction*	Cheese-board	Political Apparatus	auto-biography		Lifetime(s)
2	*Analyses*					
	1—*Bamford*			'strangers'	1819–41	
	2—*Somerville*			'the name'	1848–60	
	3—*Burn*			'identity'	1855–82	
	4—*Frost*			'totality'	1880–86	
3	*Conclusions*					BOOK ENDS
C	SUITE-TALK					POST-BOOK
1	*Reader's Report*	Sweet/ Fruit	Academic politics & Publishing gambles	Paranoia		
2	*Review*	(no tea)		Repudiation		(Latin America)
3	*Paracritus*	(the bill)		The names		
					written (1976–79)	

Thinking within the flow

The self-reflexivity of the text, its dialectical 'play' within the play, is clearly visible in every section—examples range from its discussion of its own origins (the contract in *Lecture*) to its struggle for a terminology for its own termination (in *Camus*), from its instructions for reading (e.g. 'mimicking') to its various commentaries on its own dramatic/narrative and written/oral character (e.g. the declared debts to Derrida). Part of the performance of *Bert* is perhaps worth a brief comment, as a working example.

Once Bert starts quoting Eagleton (when the layers of speaking/writing 'subject' become a whirlpool) he becomes caught in the very chains of the unconscious he is denying; he is led by his own 'dia-logic' into switching sides in his own argument (a moment of 'conversion' to neophyte semiotics) and in refusing, repressing, that conversion he is drawn (predictably) into the racism he explicitly combats; from there he spirals into paranoia (a two-term logic is characteristic of Bert's mental style) and finally even into speaking his own 'name of the Father'; out of that identity-crisis comes, however, a certain 'truth': the suggestion that the most apposite 'constraintment' (he, of course, 'lacks' *that* concept) of the *impasse* he (incorrectly) diagnoses, would be a 'novel'. The whole text does, indeed, offer itself, intermittently, as a novel—while raising explicitly (throughout the *Seminar*) the question of what is involved in 'reading' a text 'as literature'. The *Thesis* also raises this question, in the form: 'one can criticise an autobiography as if it were fiction?' (The *Thesis*, incidentally, has more functions than *Review* notices: in part, it 'answers' *Bert*'s problem about the Anderson thesis, it 'stands in for' those

335

drearily familiar treatments of nineteenth-century novels in most English marxist criticism—this text is its own 'baggy monster'—and it re-introduces 'history' after *Camus* has 'expelled' it, etc.). But the text doesn't actually *call* itself a 'novel', though it demands to be 'read' *like* a novel—as the next section indicates.[1]

Reading across the text

Finally, as one example of the 'novel' features of the text, we will briefly pursue one strand of connections across the text; the 'alert' reader will pick up many more. The relation between *Bert* and *Fielding* provides a point of entry. The date 1748 (*Tom Jones* and *L'Esprit des lois*) links them, as does the resumed duel between Althusser and E. P. Thompson, which takes us back to 1956 (and therefore forward to *Camus*, which again quotes *Tom Jones*, thereby effecting a 'closure' on *Examinations*) and also forward to *Thesis* (which opens with EPT and 'answers' Anderson); Thompson's phrase 'the law's own logic, rules and procedure' underpins the treatment of 'logic' in *Poe* (which brings in chess, echoing *Dai*'s use of Beckett and Lenin's sacrifice of chess in *Chesterton*), which culminates in *Camus's* account (via Adorno's phrases, 'inherent form' and 'immutable questions and antagonisms of the individual compositional structure') of the *art-work*'s own 'logic, rules and procedure' (the Schoenberg quote 'echoes' the structure of *Reading Relations* itself, of course), and then leads into the 'logic of history' in *Thesis*; that recurring problem of 'logic' also recalls *Seminar*'s discussion of Plato/Aristotle and the question 'can I class myself?' (a question the autobiographies partly answer and which the text also asks: 'can it class itself as a novel?'), while the notion of art-*work* (cf. dream-*work*) links back both to the diagrammatisation of 'work' and to the discussion of Benjamin's 'Author as Producer' in *Lecture*. But if the author *is* a 'producer', the text might correspondingly be seen as an object of *consumption*, as indeed the 'menu' headings suggest—and that running menu (with its English and French order-variants) again takes us back to *Tom Jones* (cf. the opening words of that novel); but Fielding there makes explicit the connection between meal and money, cash and consumption, use-value and exchange-value, in a way that *RR* finally doesn't (*its* meal ends only with (a) missing T——wot, no char?—and no black coffee even in sight). Various sub-chains could be traced from each of these interlinked moments in the text (the 'threshold' dates, e.g.), but our skeletal para-reading is intended merely as

---

[1]The nearest the text gets to self-baptism is in the portmanteau word ANOMOLETTUS—the embedded puns can be unpacked into a rather pleasant para-poem:

> a man o' letters
> > un homme, 'e let us/
> anomolous,
> > anonymous,
> > > anomie-letters/
> an omolette and lettuce/
> an homme-let(te)/a novelett(us)/
> —a nomel ate us

Our favourite pun-chain, however, is the one that can be traced from the currants, dates and dry raisins of *Entrée*.

a few tips for readers, as a preliminary (or posthumous) prompt to your own response.

One problem remains, however. We have declared ourselves as the writer (though, obviously, and precisely as *writers*, we do not necessarily agree with what is *written*). But one tactic of the text is our anonymity, the plays upon our very pseudonyms. So how do we sign ourselves off? We considered a further set of allusive personae (the favoured candidate was 'Gilberte Budgeon'), but eventually opted, simply, for our own *first* names. So we finally end, with love and peace, as

Yours truly,
Marie & Bill

A serious afterword on the social relations of literary production

Chronology and acknowledgements
This book 'originated' as a conference paper written during and delivered to a conference on 'The Interdisciplinary Study of Literature and Society', held as a farewell tribute to Asa Briggs, at the University of Sussex, 7th to 10th July, 1976.

Contract signed: 29th October 1976, at University of West Indies, Barbados.
Deadline for manuscript: 30th June 1978.
Drafts of various sections delivered as papers to:
University of East Anglia: Interdisciplinary Course
University of Kent: Staff Research Group, Humanities
University of Sussex: Postgraduate Seminar
University of Keele: Literary Society
University of Wales: Literary Criticism Weekend
University of Sussex: Philosophy Weekend
British Sociological Association Conference on 'Culture', Brighton, Easter 1978.
    I am grateful for the helpful criticisms offered on these occasions. I am also grateful to the following, who made specific suggestions in response to early drafts of particular sections: Gabriel Josipovici, Terry Eagleton, Dave Punter, Alan Wall, Marion O'Connor, Jim Bradley, Arthur Sale. I am also indebted to the general experience, during this time, of teaching a course on film with Ben Brewster and John Ellis. The section on working-class autobiographies is adapted from a PhD thesis supervised by Arthur Sale and examined by Raymond Williams and E. P. Thompson. I am very grateful for their help and interest.
Writing commenced: 1st June 1978. Typing finished: 29th October 1978.
    I am very grateful indeed to various friends who helped during this writing period, either by keeping distractions, including themselves, away from me, especially Marion, and/or for putting me up/putting up with me, especially Terry and Gabriel. I would also like to record a considerable debt to Spike Milligan and the Goon Show recordings for sustenance during this period.
    None of the people mentioned so far are in any way responsible for the final product.
    Manuscript sent to publisher: 5th November 1978. I am grateful to Janet Clarke for secretarial help at this stage.
    Manuscript revised and considerably cut, July 1979. I am most grateful to

John Mepham for editorial suggestions at this stage, and to Sue Roe for subsequent editorial advice.

Final manuscript sent for typesetting: 16th July 1981. I am grateful to Beth Humphries for her work at this stage.

Proofs received and corrected: 16th October 1981.

Book published: February 1982.

I am particularly indebted to John Spiers, Managing Director of Harvester Press Ltd., for commissioning and publishing the text.

I will not try to list all the published books and articles to which I am indebted. But I am also in debt to the following publishers who have given permission to quote copyright material:

George Allen & Unwin Ltd. and Basic Books for a passage from Sigmund Freud, *The Interpretation of Dreams*, [translated under the general editorship of James Strachey] in vol. V of *The Standard Edition of the Complete Psychological Works of Sigmund Freud*; Basil Blackwell Publisher Ltd. for a passage from Rodney Needham, *Belief, Language and Experience*; Calder & Boyars Ltd. for a passage from Samuel Beckett, *Murphy*, and for a passage from Samuel Beckett, *Still*; Cassell Ltd. for passages from G. K. Chesterton, 'The Blue Cross', in *The Complete Father Brown Stories*; Chatto & Windus Ltd. and the author's literary estate for a passage from F. R. Leavis, *Education and the University*; Eyre Methuen Ltd. for passages from *Brecht on Theatre*, edited and translated by John Willett; Faber & Faber Ltd. and Harcourt Brace Jovanovich Inc. for passages from T. S. Eliot, 'Tradition and the Individual Talent' and 'Dante' in *Selected Essays*; Faber & Faber Ltd. and Viking Penguin Inc. for a passage from Charles Rosen, *The Classical Style*; Hamish Hamilton Ltd. for passages from Albert Camus, *The Fall*, translated by Justin O'Brien, for passages from Raymond Chandler, *The Big Sleep*, and for passages from *Raymond Chandler Speaking*, edited by D. Gardiner and K. S. Walker; Heinemann Educational Books Ltd. and Beacon Press Inc. for passages from Jürgen Habermas, *Legitimate Crisis*, translated by Thomas McCarthy; Lawrence & Wishart Ltd. for a passage from V. I. Lenin, 'Left-Wing Communism—An Infantile Disorder'; Macmillan Press Ltd. and Barnes & Noble Books for passages from Terry Eagleton, *Myths of Power*; Merlin Press Ltd. for passages from Georg Lukacs, *History and Class Consciousness*, translated by Rodney Livingstone, and for a passage from E. P. Thompson, *The Poverty of Theory and other essays*; Oxford University Press Ltd. for a passage from F. M. Cornford's notes to his translation of Plato, *The Republic*, and for passages from Raymond Williams, *Marxism and Literature*; Oxford University Press Inc., New York, for a passage from *From Max Weber*, edited and translated by H. H. Gerth and C. W. Mills; Penguin Books Ltd. for passages from E. P. Thompson, *Whigs and Hunters*; Pluto Press Ltd. for a passage from Caryl Churchill, *Light Shining in*

Buckinghamshire; Rapp & Whiting Ltd. for the poem 'Definition' from Erich Fried, *On Pain of Seeing*, translated by George Rapp; Martin Secker & Warburg Ltd. and Schocken Books Inc. for passages from Franz Kafka, *The Trial*, translated by Willa and Edwin Muir; Sheed & Ward Ltd. and The Continuum Publishing Corporation for a passage from Theodor Adorno, *Philosophy of Modern Music*, translated by Anne G. Mitchell and Wesley V. Bloomster; Tavistock Publications Ltd. and W. W. Norton Inc. for a passage from Jacques Lacan, *Ecrits: a selection*, translated by Alan Sheridan; E. P. Thompson for passages from *Albion's Fatal Tree* by Douglas Hay, Peter Linebaugh, John G. Rule, E. P. Thompson and Cal Winslow; Verso Editions & New Left Books Ltd. and Harcourt Brace Jovanovich Inc. for passages from Walter Benjamin, *Understanding Brecht*, translated by Anna Bostock, and from Walter Benjamin, *Charles Baudelaire*, translated by Harry Zohn; Verso Editions & New Left Books Ltd. and Monthly Review Inc. for passages from Louis Althuser *Lenin and Philosophy*, translated by Ben Brewster; Verso Editions & New Left Books Ltd. for passages from Louis Althusser, *Politics and History*, translated by Ben Brewster, from Louis Althusser, *Essays in Self Criticism*, translated by Ben Brewster, from Terry Eagleton, *Criticism and Ideology*, from Paul Feyerabend, *Against Method*, and from Lucien Goldmann, *Immanuel Kant*, translated by Robert Black; George Weidenfeld & Nicolson Ltd. and Writers and Readers Publishing Cooperative for a passage from John Berger, *G a novel*.

The author sincerely apologises to any holder of copyright material used in this book for which permission has inadvertently not been sought or obtained.